HEMINGWAY
The Final Years

MICHAEL REYNOLDS

W. W. NORTON & COMPANY
New York · London

Excerpt from "Sailing to Byzantium" by W. B. Yeats courtesy of A. P. Watt Ltd. on behalf of
Michael B. Yeats. Also reprinted with the permission of Simon & Schuster from *The Poems of
W. B. Yeats: A New Edition*, edited by Richard J. Finneran. Copyright © 1928 by Macmillan
Publishing Company, renewed 1956 by George Yeats.

For information about permission to reproduce selections from this book, write to Permissions,
W. W. Norton & Company, Inc., 500 Fifth Avenue, New York, NY 10110

The text of this book is composed in Walbaum
with the display set in Mona Lisa Recut and Glamour Medium.
Composition by Platinum Manuscript Services
Manufacturing by the Maple-Vail Book Manufacturing Group
Book design by Charlotte Staub

Library of Congress Cataloging-in-Publication Data

Reynolds, Michael S., 1937–
    Hemingway : the final years / Michael Reynolds.
        p. cm.
    Includes bibliographical references and index.
    ISBN 0-393-04748-2
    1. Hemingway, Ernest, 1899–1961—Last years. 2. Authors, American—
20th century—Biography. 3. Journalists—United States—Biography. I. Title.
    PS3515.E37Z75469 1999
    813'.52—dc21
    [B]   99-17141
                                      CIP

ISBN 0-393-32047-2 pbk.

W. W. Norton & Company, Inc., 500 Fifth Avenue, New York, N.Y. 10110
www.wwnorton.com

W. W. Norton & Company Ltd., 10 Coptic Street, London WC1A 1PU

1 2 3 4 5 6 7 8 9 0

Further praise for *Hemingway: The Final Years*

"Reynolds chronicles [these years] masterfully, and every page pulsates with Hemingway's anger and paranoia. For decades Carlos Baker was heavyweight champ of Hemingway biographers . . . but now he must pass the crown to Reynolds, who with this final volume proves unequivocally that he is the true Hemingway scholar. A powerhouse of a biography as big as Hemingway himself." —*Library Journal*

"[A] compassionate portrait." —*USA Today*

"Masterful. . . . Makes what may well prove to be a significant contribution toward breaking the cultural logjam surrounding Hemingway and his place in American fiction." —*Oregonian*

"Extensively researched and vividly evocative." —*Christian Science Monitor*

"Definitive . . . a model of biographical judgment. Its report is accurate, its prose appropriately spare, and its comprehension sympathetic, but not fooled, not beguiled." —*Buffalo News*

"Stunning . . . completes [Reynolds'] sensitive and perceptive portrait." —[Raleigh] *News and Observer*

"Reynolds' biography is fluid and informative and the events he brings to light show a Hemingway very different in his later years than the figure previously available for public consumption." —*Boston Book Review*

"Reynolds has come as close to crawling inside Hemingway's head as anybody. . . . Reynolds is comprehensive in his research, yet his books feel anything but academic; in fact they're page-turners." —*Book*

"An artful biography of a true artist. . . . Despite his unflinching portrayal of the flaws and weaknesses in Hemingway's character, Reynolds leaves no question as to his achievement as an artist." —*Richmond Times-Dispatch*

"Reynolds' rapt readers will retain the haunting image of Hemingway trapped within his once hale, then battered and drug- and alcohol-poisoned body as the awesome firepower of his unique, epoch-defining mind slowly diminishes." —*Booklist* [starred review]

"Superbly written and eminently readable . . . seamlessly places every detail and encounter into its wider context." —*Providence Sunday Journal*

"With each new meticulous and beautifully written volume in this masterful biography, Reynolds has added to his preeminence as Hemingway scholar; this work has proven to be at the cutting-edge of research. Penetrating, compelling, exemplary in its critical apparatus." —*Choice*

This book belongs to my wife, Ann,
who shared the research on all five volumes,
    who came across the pass at Roncevaux,
    who remembered the names,
    who read between the lines,
    who made the difference.

            ye ben verrayly
The maistresse of my wit, and nothing I.
My word, my werk, is knit so in your bonde,
That, as an harpe obeyeth to the honde
And maketh hit soune after his fingeringe,
Right so mowe ye out of myn herte bringe
Swich vois, right as yow list, to laughte or pleyne.
Be ye my gyde and lady sovereyne;
As to myn erthly god, to yow I calle,
Bothe in this werke and in my sorwes alle.

                        GEOFFREY CHAUCER

. . . all stories, if continued far enough, end in death, and he is no true-story teller who would keep that from you. . . . There is no lonelier man in death, except the suicide, than that man who has lived many years with a good wife and then outlived her.

ERNEST HEMINGWAY, *Death in the Afternoon*

The symbolic killing off of the old hero must always be an incomplete act, for even in death and discard the hero retains a dangerous amount of negative mantra.

FREDERICK TURNER

Contents

Maps

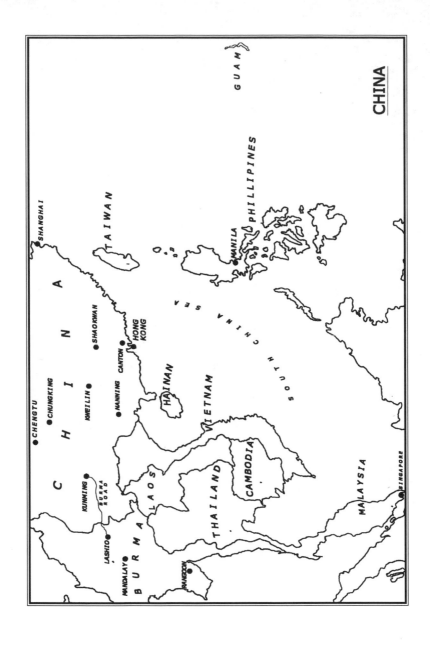

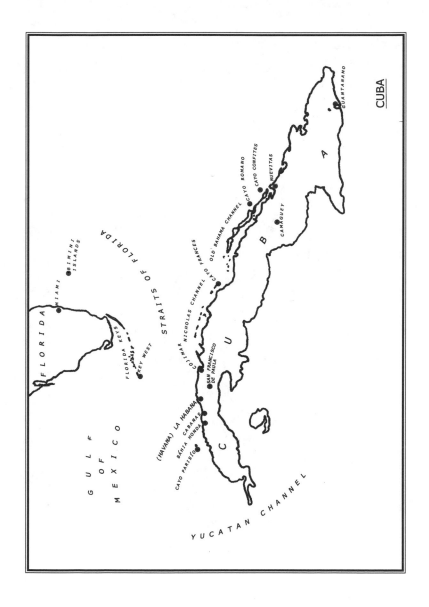

CUBA

GULF OF MEXICO

FLORIDA

STRAITS OF FLORIDA

MIAMI

BIMINI ISLANDS

FLORIDA KEYS

KEY WEST

NICHOLAS CHANNEL

COJIMAR

(HAVANA) LA HABANA

SAN FRANCISCO DE PAULA

CABAÑAS

BAHIA HONDA

CAYO PARISÍ

CAYO FRANCES

OLD BAHAMA CHANNEL

CAYO ROMANO

CAYO CONFITES

NUEVITAS

CAMAGUEY

GUANTANAMO

A

B

C

U

YUCATAN CHANNEL

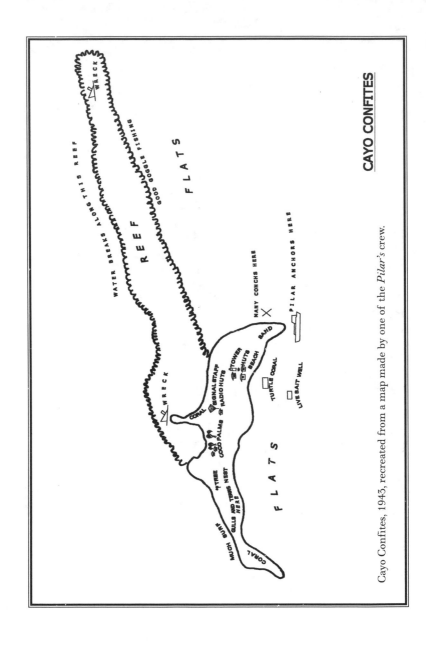

Cayo Confites, 1943, recreated from a map made by one of the *Pilar's* crew.

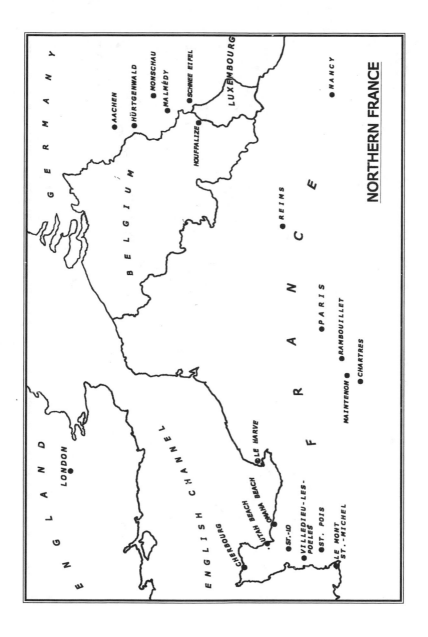

NORTHERN FRANCE

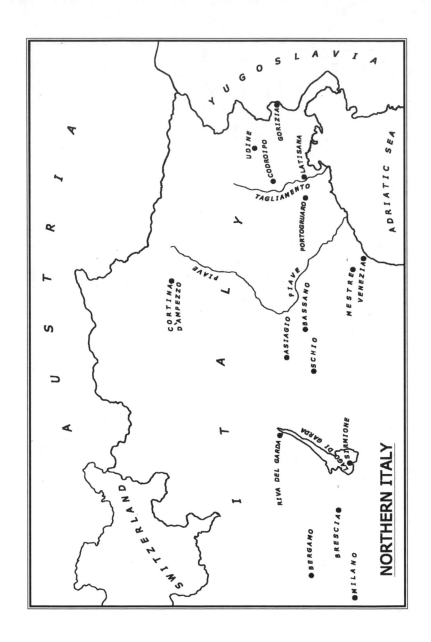

NORTHERN ITALY

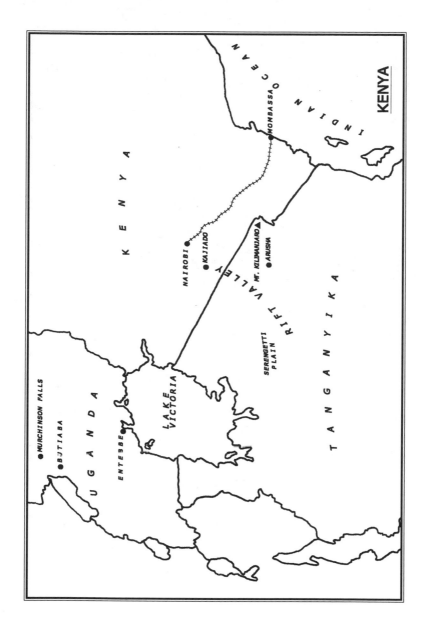

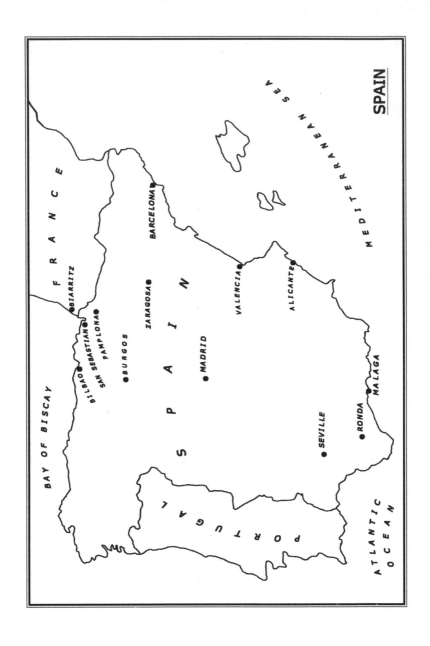

The Fortunes of War

JULY 1940 TO NOVEMBER 1944

And while I am talking to you mothers and fathers, I give you one more assurance. I have said this before, but I shall say it again and again and again: Your boys are not going to be sent into any foreign wars.

Franklin Delano Roosevelt, October 30, 1940

I think it better that in times like these
A poet's mouth be silent, for in truth
We have no gift to set a statesman right . . .

William Butler Yeats
"On Being Asked for a War Poem"

CHAPTER 1

Ringing the Changes

July to Early Winter 1940

With thigh bone snapped by his falling horse and pain now beading his face in sweat, Robert Jordan lay as quietly as possible, calling on all his reserves for one last effort. It was not a question of would he survive or not. As soon as the bone splintered, his death was certain. The only question was whether he could hold off the pain long enough to do one last thing well. His small flask of absinthe was lost in the fall, and no matter how he tried, he could not think past the pain. He could not think about the girl, nor his father dead by his own hand, nor even his Civil War grandfather. At that last moment when he felt himself slipping into unconsciousness, the Nationalist cavalry officer came into view below him. Positioning his extra clips close at hand, Jordan sighted quite calmly down the barrel of his submachine gun at the moving target. "He was waiting until the officer reached the sunlit place where the first trees of the pine forest joined the green slope of the meadow. He could feel his heart against the pine needle floor of the forest."[1] Having come full circle, he was back where he started three days earlier, before he had received the incredible gift of the girl, Maria, before El Sordo's death on that other lonely hilltop, before Pablo stole the dynamite plunger but came back with the extra horses, before the bridge was blown.

On paper, only three days had passed between the typescript's opening page and its last one, but it had cost seventeen months of Ernest Hemingway's life and the end of his second marriage to create those three days. In March 1939, when he started the story of the dynamiter and the band of Loyalist partisans, the Spanish Civil War was all but over. The elected government's effort to defeat Franco's fascist revolution was doomed when America, England, and France refused to support a leftist government being helped by the Russians. No matter that Hitler's Nazi Condor Legion was bombing Guernica; no matter that Mussolini's Italian troops were in the Spanish trenches; no matter that sound journalists warned, time and again: if the world did not fight fascism in Spain, it would have to fight it across Europe later. Now in steamy late July 1940, as Hemingway read through his typescript one last time in his New York hotel room, the European war was edging ever closer to American participation, despite President Roosevelt's campaign promises to the contrary. The Nazi blitzkrieg, having rolled over Poland, Norway, Belgium, Holland, and most of France, was now poised to invade England itself. Meanwhile, as if the mounting war with fascism were not the issue, the ever vigilant congressional investigating committee of Martin Dies continued to worry the nation about the communist threat to American values. Stories spread that Reds operating the radios on U.S. ships, and other communists, were slipping into the United States through Cuba.[2]

Five years earlier, as a lover of military history and a hater of war, Hemingway laid it out as bluntly as possible, telling his *Esquire* readers that a European war was brewing in which America should play no part. "Never again," he wrote, "should this country be put into a European war through mistaken idealism, through propaganda, through the desire to back our creditors."[3] That was the disillusioned Hemingway speaking, the young man sucked in by propaganda during World War I. Spain changed his point of view. After ten years of following Spanish politics more closely than what was happening in the United States, Hemingway believed in the Spanish earth, its working class, and its rituals, without ever embracing the politics of socialism or its radical left, the Communist Party. Seventeen years after idealism died in the muddy trenches of the Somme, Passchendaele, and Verdun, it resurrected in the Spanish conflict only to die a different death when fascism triumphed while democracies refused to help.

Now, with German troops marching down the Champs-Elysées, German U-boats once again shutting down the British island, and the Luftwaffe bombing London, Hemingway's warning to America seemed far away and long ago. If the war came to him, he would fight to save his homeland and his people, but never to save the politicians who started the war. Soon, he knew, there would be no choice, but on this day, his mind was completely absorbed in the story of Robert Jordan's last few hours on earth. As he told his editor, Max Perkins, after living with Jordan for seventeen months, he hated like hell to kill him off.[4] With Jordan's death, of course, Hemingway killed off, once more, a piece of himself. That's how he felt about his writing: each book a little death, another story he could never again write. All that was left him to do were tedious revisions of the galley and page proofs, arguments with his editor over certain words, and then the reviews that his clipping agent collected for him, reviews he always read and never liked.

Alone in the Hotel Barclay, it was easier for Hemingway to lose himself in his book than to think about his personal life, which had become incredibly complicated. His first wife, Hadley, and their son, Jack, were in Chicago, where she was remarried to Paul Mowrer, her income supplemented by Ernest's parting gift of all royalties from *The Sun Also Rises*. His second wife, Pauline Pfeiffer, and their two sons, Patrick and Gregory, were in the Key West house waiting for her divorce from Ernest on grounds of desertion to become final. For the last year and a half, he had been living in Cuba with Martha Gellhorn while still married to Pauline, whose strong Catholic conscience resisted the idea of divorce. Mixing more debris into already muddy waters, Ernest enlisted Pauline's uncle, wealthy Augustus Pfeiffer, to ask Pauline for a reasonable divorce settlement, for she had more than enough money of her own. Fooling no one but keeping up a facade, Hemingway posted and received his mail at the Hotel Ambos Mundos but lived with Martha first in the Hotel Biltmore Sevilla and later in a run-down, rented farmhouse, La Finca Vigia, on the outskirts of Havana. While Ernest labored over his typescript, Martha was working on a *Collier's* magazine exposé on German fifth columnists in Havana.[5]

Having worked all morning on his typescript, Hemingway gathered a roomful of friends, for he hated to be alone when he was not writing. Outside in the streets the temperature hung at 88 degrees with humidity to match; inside the Barclay, it was not much better. When Robert Van Gelder from the *New York Times* arrived, he found the room crowded with a lawyer, a Spanish Civil War veteran, and others unidentified, circled around a bucket of ice, soda water, and a fifth of Scotch. Van Gelder, taking it all in, caught the scene in a thumbnail sketch:

> Hemingway looked elephant-big, enormously healthy. His talk is unevenly paced, a quick spate and then a slow search for a word. His chair keeps hitching across the floor toward the other chairs, and then as he reaches a point, a conclusion, he shoves the chair back to the edge of the group again.[6]

Gustavo Durán, an old friend and admired combatant in the Spanish war, was sitting on one of the beds, listening to the conversation as it easily shifted from English to Spanish to French. Four months earlier, Hemingway told Durán in a letter that he was finally writing the really good book that he once thought he might write in his old age, which he imagined would not be quite old because Hemingways usually shot themselves or someone did it for them.[7] When talk turned to the lost war in Spain, Durán said, "The world now is very confusing. It is amazing how sure we once were, Ernest, that our ideas were right." Hemingway replied, "The fight in Spain will have to be fought again." Durán said nothing.

Those conspicuous by their absence at the Barclay were faces once mainstays in the entourage Hemingway customarily gathered about himself. Poet and old friend Archibald MacLeish, who once flew through winter storms to be with Hemingway when he was hospitalized in Montana, was no longer part of the inner circle. After accepting President Roosevelt's nomination to be Librarian of Congress, MacLeish said publicly that the postwar writers, like Hemingway, in their disillusionment with the "war to end all wars" had "educated a generation to believe that all declarations, all beliefs are fraudulent, that all statements of conviction are salestalk, that nothing men can put into words is worth fighting for . . . those writers must face the fact that the books they wrote in the years just after the war have done more to disarm democracy in the face of fascism than any other single influence."[8] Two weeks later, in response to *Life* magazine's request for authors' rebuttals, Hemingway accused MacLeish of having a bad conscience while Ernest had fought fascism every way he knew how and had no remorse, "neither literary nor political. . . . If the Germans have learned how to fight a war and the Allies have not learned, MacLeish can hardly put the blame on our books."[9]

Even more conspicuously absent were Gerald and Sara Murphy, owners of the Mark Cross department store and two of Hemingway's earliest and most ardent supporters. When Ernest was distraught with the agony of leaving his first wife, Hadley, for Pauline Pfeiffer, it was Gerald and Sara who gave him comfort. Gerald told him, "We love you, we believe in you in all your parts, we believe in what you're doing, in the way you're doing it. Anything we've got is yours." During his separation from Hadley, Ernest lived in Gerald's cold-water Paris studio. When Gerald feared Ernest was living without funds, he put $400 in his Morgan Guaranty bank account without being asked.[10] The day after Van Gelder observed Hemingway and friends, a letter from Sara at the Murphy summer place in East Hampton arrived at the Barclay: "Dear Ernest—I hear you are in N.Y.—& it would give us such pleasure if you would come down here to spend a few days . . . it's very peaceful, & cool seabathing."[11] For five months, Ernest was unable to answer the Murphys' letter, unable to face them when he was separated from Pauline and living with a much younger Martha.[12] Always looking for others to blame for his problems and quandaries, Ernest usually found a woman to be the responsible party: his mother deprived him of his college education, threw him out of the house, and drove his father to suicide; Pauline separated him from Hadley as if he were a sack of potatoes; Jinny Pfeiffer, by telling Pauline of his affair with Martha, had ruined his second marriage.

During the days following the Van Gelder interview, the heat wave that was killing hundreds across the Midwest continued to stultify New York. There in the Barclay hotel room with the window open, Ernest was sweating heavily, his wire-rimmed glasses cutting into the bridge of his nose, his eyes blurring from the marathon reading. The electric fan on the coffee table waved its head, moving warm air from one part of the room to another. As sections were finished, they were rushed to the printer, who was hurrying them into galleys for an October publication. Hard-pressed to stay ahead of the typesetters, Hemingway stuck to his task. Wednesday, July 31, Hemingway's editor, Maxwell Perkins, told him that they had only enough copy for one more day's work. That morning the *New York Times* reported that 3.6 million aliens in the United States were being registered and fingerprinted by the FBI, and the book page noted:

> Ernest Hemingway up from Cuba where he has been round-ing out his new novel "For Whom the Bell Tolls," has been in New York the last few days. The new novel which Scribner's will bring out in October, is a love story with the Spanish Civil War for a setting. Mr. Hemingway will return to Cuba in a few days.[13]

On top of his dresser was the signed contract, dated July 15, call-ing for Hemingway's royalties to be 15 percent on the first 25,000 copies sold; thereafter they rose to 20 percent, higher rates than most authors received, but Ernest Hemingway in 1940 was not most authors. He may not have published a best-selling novel dur-ing the entire 1930s, but through his nonfiction, his *Esquire* arti-cles, his Spanish Civil War journalism, and his personal exploits hunting in East Africa and marlin fishing in the Gulf Stream, he had become the most widely read male author in America. On Thursday, Max asked for another two hundred pages if it were at all possible.[14] Anything was possible, of course, if Ernest worked hard enough, long enough.

No matter what else happened in his life—sick children, angry wives, broken arms, bad weather, petulant friends—the one thing which he never scanted was his writing. If he was a less than atten-tive father, an uneven friend, a faithful or unfaithful husband, the one standard of self-measure that remained constant was the qual-ity of his writing. So long as his writing ethos remained inviolate, he was true to himself: whatever outrageous fortune might assail him, that certainty was his shield. Seldom leaving the hotel room, he finished the typescript revisions for the printer, who set the galleys in record time; this book would go from typescript to the public readers in only three months. As soon as the galleys were packed, Hemingway was on the train to Miami, where he boarded a Pan-American clipper for the quick flight to Havana. Martha and her mother, Edna, met him at the boarding dock.

Her coiled blond hair now grayed at sixty, her blue eyes still brilliant, Edna Gellhorn was standing on the dock beside her daughter, the two of them startlingly alike, both beautiful and both equally independent. Edna may have deferred more to the dominant males of her era than Martha ever did, but the older woman was also more adept at getting her way. To Hemingway, who was vulnerable to older motherly women, Edna was more like the mother he wished his had been. Ernest "loved my mother," Martha said later. "Both of my husbands loved my mother, always . . . they loved her more than me . . . and they were absolutely right."[15] The feeling was guardedly mutual. Edna appreciated Ernest and was tolerant of his casual lifestyle. Although she caught Ernest on an emotional high, his book finished and galleys arriving, Edna nevertheless saw something beneath his surface that made her feel sorry for him, something that eluded Martha at the time. Whatever she saw led her to advise her daughter not to marry the famous author; advice Martha did not easily ignore.

As a younger woman in St. Louis, Edna Gellhorn marched with suffragists seeking the vote, and three months before the Nineteenth Amendment was ratified, she organized the St. Louis League of Women Voters.[16] With her, quite frequently, was her small daughter, Martha. During the 1916 Democratic Convention in St. Louis, Edna was on the planning committee that lined the streets leading to the Coliseum convention center with seven thousand women; at a strategic corner, a tableau was arranged of women draped in white, gray, and black representing states with full suffrage, partial suffrage, or no suffrage for women. "At the top was . . . Miss Liberty. Down in the front . . . were two little girls . . . who represented future voters."[17] One of those little girls was Martha Gellhorn.

Having grown up at the side of her politically progressive mother, Martha was herself an activist but not a joiner. "A self-willed, opinionated loner . . . never a team player," was how she later characterized herself.[18] Rather than organize the voters, Martha's goal was to prick their consciences through her journalism and her novels. It was Martha's personal friendship with Eleanor Roosevelt that allowed her to arrange for a White House showing of *The Spanish Earth*, the Joris Ivens film supporting Loyalist Spain, with Hemingway reading his own narrative. In November 1938, Martha was in Prague when the Czech government capitulated to Hitler's claim on the Sudetenland. Among the journalists on the last free flight out of Prague, Martha carried with her testimony of the Nazi terrorist tactics. In December 1939, she left Hemingway at the Sun Valley Lodge in Idaho to take a *Collier's* assignment in Finland, arriving there as the first Russian bombs were falling on Helsinki. Ernest may have commanded more money for his journalism, which he often viewed as a means of support while gathering experience for his fiction, but Martha was the more dedicated journalist. Almost to a fault, she was passionate about the downtrodden, the war-torn, and the victimized. That May of 1940, she wrote a friend, "It is extremely pretentious to take the world's troubles as your own, but I must say they concern me more gravely than anything else."[19] In Ernest Hemingway she thought she had found a man of the same ilk. She could not have been more wrong.

No sooner had Hemingway returned to Cuba than galleys arrived from Scribner's, keeping him happily busy while Martha planned their trip to Sun Valley for the fall season. At the same time Hemingway received his proofs, Scribner's sent a set for consideration to The Book-of-the-Month Club (BOMC) along with Perkins's addendum: "Two short chapters, amounting to 1,500 words in all, will bring the book to a conclusion." These chapters, which Hemingway had outlined, were meant to tie up loose ends. Max assured the BOMC that "These chapters are written, but not yet to the complete satisfaction of the author. He wished to wait until after reading the proof up to this point before perfecting the end."[20] Perkins also marked up another set of galleys which he sent to Hemingway on August 14, suggesting a number of changes, some typographical, some substantive, none so onerous as revisions Hemingway was forced to make a decade earlier.[21] This time Ernest, in anticipation of censorship, avoided the problem up front by either not translating Spanish obscenities or by creative use of English. In *The Sun Also Rises* (1926), Mike Campbell wanted to say, "Tell him the bulls have no balls," but in the reactionary climate of 1926 America, Perkins told Hemingway "balls" was not a word Charles Scribner would print. Instead, the bulls were said to have no horns.[22] In *For Whom the Bell Tolls*, when Robert Jordan is asked by a needling Pablo what a Scot wears under his skirt, Jordan tells him, "*Los cojones*" (206). When Jordan says that the girl, Maria, was put in his care, one of the partisan replies, "And thy care is to *joder* with her all night?" (290). Max Perkins, who himself was never known to say "fuck" in anyone's company, either did not understand or did not object to the word in Spanish. Nor did he protest when Hemingway used abstractions in such a way that only the purest of mind could not translate them:

> "Thy duty," said Augustin mockingly. "I besmirch the milk of thy duty." Then turning to the woman, "Where the un-nameable is this vileness that I am to guard?"
>
> "In the cave," Pilar said. "In two sacks. And I am tired of thy obscenity."
>
> "I obscenity in the milk of thy tiredness," Augustin said.
>
> "Then go and befoul thyself," Pilar said to him without heat.
> (92)

On August 26, while Perkins was writing to say how pleased Scribner's was that the Book-of-the-Month Club had taken *For Whom the Bell Tolls* as its November selection, Ernest was packaging the first 123 pages of galleys for air-mail shipment to New York, keeping the last 18 for more work. All the requested corrections and revisions, he said, were made or answered, grammar improved, and references to masturbation toned down. But he remained uncertain about the book's conclusion. He had additional scenes after Jordan sighted down the submachine-gun barrel, but they seemed like talking about the boxing match after it was over, or like his several failed endings to *A Farewell to Arms* where he tried to tell what happened to the survivors after the war. That tendency to tidy up loose bits, he said, was always a problem for him; but the book "really stops where Jordan is feeling his heart beating against the pine needle floor of the forest." Two days later, Max's telegram confirmed that they should leave off the epilogue.[23]

While submerged in final corrections, Ernest's emotional center took a heavy hit when Martha began questioning the wisdom of their marrying. At four in the morning Ernest wrote her a note, saying her news busted his heart and left him with a first-class headache. He knew that for the last eighteen months he had been "no gift to live with," as she put it, but she must remember how he helped her with her book—*The Heart of Another*. But if she was not going to marry him, she should tell him before he took the *Pilar* alone to Key West giving himself too much time to think: another veiled threat of suicide. He closed his in-house note telling her that Mr. Scrooby (his penis) now referred to himself as "us."[24] In these and other private letters, Hemingway's ardor and frustration reached levels similar to his courtship of his first two wives. Martha was his "Mookie," his "Chickie"; he was her "Bongie," or her "Bug." Words did not always move another writer like Martha so easily, but she did reaffirm her intention to marry Ernest.

The problem was not that Martha loved him too little but he loved her too much. To Rodrigo Diaz, his pigeon-shooting companion and sometime doctor, Ernest was always at risk in his relationship with Martha. Easily hurt, he was tremendously vulnerable beneath the tough exterior with which he faced the world. Diaz thought Hemingway was born either too soon or too late, a man who would have been more comfortable in another era. A practicing psychiatrist, Dr. Franz Stetmayer, was an interested observer of Ernest's behavior with Martha. His conclusion was that she was the less committed of the two and that Ernest was terribly afraid of losing her.[25] Separately, the two left Cuba—she to St. Louis to see her mother; Ernest to Key West—to rendezvous at Sun Valley.

As soon as galleys were in the mail, Ernest motored his fishing boat, *Pilar*, ninety miles across the Gulf of Mexico to Key West for winter safety and repairs. The Hemingway house on Whitehead Street was empty. Pauline was in New York; their sons, Patrick and Gregory, were already in Sun Valley, Idaho, with their stepbrother Jack (Bumby), awaiting Ernest's arrival. With little delay, Ernest picked up a new Buick convertible from the Key West dealer and spent a day selecting half the books out of his Key West library for eventual shipment to Cuba.[26] Leaving Key West with old friend and factotum Toby Bruce at the wheel of the Buick, the two men made good time driving the almost three thousand miles to Union Pacific's resort at Sun Valley, arriving as the fall hunting season opened. At the same time, Martha took the train to St. Louis to tell her mother that she and Ernest would marry as soon as his divorce was final, although she also told Clara Spiegel, a Ketchum friend, that she felt somewhat trapped by the idea of marriage.[27]

The Sun Valley Lodge, which the wealthy railroad financier and now diplomat Averell Harriman opened in 1936, was one of the first multi-use western resorts catering to the moderately wealthy, the famous, and those on the rise. When guests stepped off the Union Pacific train at Shoshone, they were met by the Lodge station wagon to be driven up the valley past smooth brown hills, through the old mining town of Hailey, past Club Rio and the Alpine where sheepherders, miners, and Sun Valley dudes could gamble and drink. Turning right at Jack Lane's Mercantile store, they did not stop because Jack was not fond of outsiders. "Hell, he wouldn't even get up to wait on 'em," Bud Purdy recalled. A mile east of Lane's was the well-modulated western world of Sun Valley. There eastern dudes found hunting and fishing guides at the ready, a skating rink with instructors and visiting stars like Sonja Henie, a ski basin with chairlifts, live music in the evenings, a comfortable bar, airy rooms, sleigh rides in winter, a rodeo in summer, cookouts in the fall, a movie theater, a first-class dining room, Basque cooks, an in-house photographer, and a public relations staff. In Silver Creek, trophy trout lurked in the eel grass; in the fall fields, pheasant were abundant, and on the irrigation canals ducks were plentiful. Antelope and elk hunts were available in season. In the main dining room on almost any fall evening, one might see a Hollywood movie star, a famous musician, or even a best-selling author like Ernest Hemingway. In an effective publicity effort, Sun Valley offered well-known personalities like Hemingway free use of the facilities providing they allowed their names and pictures to be used to promote the resort.

That fall of 1940, when Paris was occupied by German troops

and London was burning, Ernest and others arrived at Sun Valley for what many thought would be the last Christmas before America was involved in another war. On the dance floors of the country, fools rushed in to find their love on Blueberry Hill, while Glenn Miller's swing band took the young through Tuxedo Junction on moonlit serenades. Two former vaudevillians—Bob Hope and Bing Crosby—took their movie fans on the humorous road to Singapore, which by February 1942 would be occupied by invading Japanese. On the front page of American newspapers, there were plenty of signs: the U.S. Navy was building two hundred new ships; the first peacetime draft in the nation's history became law; the defense budget received a second $5.25 billion supplement. Before the year was out, Ernest would be suggesting that seventeen-year-old Jack ought to delay college to spend a year fishing and working, because war was coming: "A man might as well catch a steelhead [trout] in this life if there's only one life."[28]

Whatever the future held, Ernest was more concerned with his novel, the last eighteen galleys of which he air-mailed to Max Perkins on September 10, along with its dedication: "This book is for Martha Gellhorn." Scribner's and The Book-of-the-Month Club were advertising the book heavily in trade publications and on newspaper book pages. When the novel was published to rave reviews on October 21, Ernest and his publisher knew they had a best-seller. The *New York Times* called it "the best book Ernest Hemingway has written, the fullest, the deepest, the truest." *The Nation* said the novel "sets a new standard for Hemingway in characterization, dialogue, suspense, and compassion." *The New Yorker* found it touching "a deeper level than any sounded in the author's other books." *Saturday Review of Literature* thought it to be "one of the finest and richest novels of the last decade." Even Edmund Wilson, once his early champion but afterward disappointed with the 1930s Hemingway, was able to say, "Hemingway the artist is with us again; and it is like having an old friend back."[29]

Ten days later, BOMC increased its initial order to an astounding 200,000 copies, and the book was already in its third Scribner's printing for a total of 360,000 copies. In the following six months, 491,000 copies of the novel were sold.[30] Full of himself, expansive, joking, surrounded by all his sons and his wife-to-be, Ernest was riding an emotional high further fueled by Paramount Pictures paying $110,000 for the film rights to his book. In such a mood, he was already fabricating stories of the novel's inception. To Gustavo Durán, he claimed that the novel rested on his experience commanding a company with Kemal in the Greco-Turkish War, and on his participation in various Cuban revolutionary movements, as well as being a descendant of Major Colquhoun Grant, who fought with Wellington in Spain during the Napoleonic Wars.[31] None of which was true in the sense of having taken place; all of which was true in the sense that each claim was what Hemingway wished had happened.

As a *Toronto Daily Star* reporter, Ernest was not present when Kemal and his Turks ravaged Smyrna, but he once wrote about it as if he were a witness. Nor had he yet been directly involved with any of the numerous Cuban revolutionary movements, although he watched them develop with great interest, writing about them in discarded portions of *To Have and Have Not* (1937). From his youthful admiration for Teddy Roosevelt, Hemingway developed his need for both the active and the contemplative life, neither satisfying without the other. But reality was never quite able to match his expectations. When the trench mortar shell ruined his right knee and killed men standing next to him in World War I, Hemingway was decorated by the Italian government as a war hero. Ashamed afterward to have been only a Red Cross ambulance man and not an active combatant, Ernest made up fantastic stories of being an Italian officer with the Arditi troops. In Spain during the 1920s, he followed the bullfights with religious fervor, but knowing bullfighters and watching from the *barrera* was not enough; he had to create the impression that he himself had been in the bull ring. Intrigued with revolutions, spies, and clandestine operations through reading, watching, and talking with Charles Sweeny, a professional soldier of fortune, Ernest always wanted to be a revolutionist. During the Spanish Civil War, he reported accurately from the very edge of battle, but with his deep reading in military history and tactics, he yearned to be a field commander, preferably one operating beyond the reach of higher authority.

When not writing, he was happiest outdoors with some novice whom he could instruct, for in any situation, Hemingway was the teacher of others. As friends would testify, Hemingway placed novices in the best position for the first shot, or in the chair for the first marlin strike. Hemingway was always organizing small groups of friends to participate in some outdoor activity. That fall, after hearing farmer Frees's complaints about the abundance of rabbits, Ernest organized the great rabbit hunt. Gathering together some fifteen shooters—Greg and Patrick, movie stars Gary Cooper and Merle Oberon, rancher Bud Purdy, Sun Valley employees Don Anderson and Taylor Williams, among others—he positioned them in a semicircle, herding the rabbits through brush toward an irrigation canal. As Bud Purdy remembered it, "we lined up there and pushed all those rabbits back toward the canal and when they couldn't cross the canal, they'd come back. I'll bet we shot five hundred rabbits that day. . . . Cooper and I kinda got out of the way after a little bit. I was scared of too many people shooting. . . . Hemingway was a great guy to organize, you know, where you'd be sneaking up on a duck, he'd always tell us where to stand and what to do, you know. He was the general."

No one who met Hemingway ever forgot him. He was the strange attractor around whose light all manner of men and women circled: movie stars, millionaires, cooks, crooks, bartenders, writers, soldiers. Forty-one years old and at his physical peak, he was not the most handsome man in the room, but he was the most magnetic, a sometimes shy man who listened intently, enjoyed good stories, and spoke carefully. Bud Purdy's wife, Ruth, remembered him as a man who "had a kind voice, was always nice to people, and made you feel important."[32] He studied terrain the way some men study the stock market; his reading in history, military tactics, and biography was considerable. In early October, while awaiting publication of *For Whom the Bell Tolls*, Hemingway ordered from New York a typical spectrum of bedside books: *The Ox-Bow Incident*; a Margery Allingham murder mystery; Van Wyck Brooks's new literary history, *New England, Indian Summer*; Edmund Wilson's *To the Finland Station; Audubon's America*; Raymond Chandler's *Farewell My Lovely*; and *How to Play and Win at Poker*.[33]

With ducks thick in neighboring creeks and canals, and out on Tom Gooding's ranch pheasants fat with grain, Hemingway could not have been happier. Hunting frequently with Gary Cooper, who was more a Montana cowboy than a Hollywood movie star, Ernest posed for countless pictures, holding the day's bag. Cooper, he found, was a better rifle shot; Ernest was best wing-shooting with his over-and-under shotgun. Both men had come of age in an America so abundant with game that bag limits seemed onerous, and predators were to be eliminated. On his 1933–34 African safari, Hemingway had amused himself shooting hyenas; Cooper did the same with hawks on telephone poles and coyotes in the field.[34] The two were both artists and outdoorsmen, fitting comfortably together in the field and at supper. Hemingway complained that Martha was so impressed with Cooper that she wanted Ernest to dress better, but nothing, he said, was going to make his face any better.[35] Both men knew and admired each other's work: Cooper had portrayed Frederic Henry in the 1932 film version of *A Farewell to Arms*. Already there was talk between them that Cooper might become Robert Jordan for the movie version of *For Whom the Bell Tolls*.

In November, *Life* magazine sent Hemingway's friend from the Spanish Civil War, Robert Capa, to Sun Valley to photograph Ernest as part of a feature on the filming of the movie. In the photo-shoot, he was to include Martha, news of whose pending marriage to Ernest was in the wind, Walter Winchell having said so to "Mr. and Mrs. America and all the ships at sea" on his syndicated radio show. The volatile Hungarian photographer, whose specialty was war coverage, covered the pheasant shoot as if it were a battleground. When Hemingway's divorce from Pauline became final on November 4, and Edna Gellhorn arrived at Sun Valley for a pre-wedding party, Capa was standing on a bar stool, blasting away at Hemingway and company, spent flashbulbs popping off the camera like empty shells.

On November 21, in the Union Pacific dining room in Cheyenne, Wyoming, Ernest and Martha were married by a justice of the peace.[36] The next day from Key West, Pauline wrote, thanking him for pheasants he sent to her when Patrick and Gregory returned home, thanking him also for the mounted warthog head from their safari, and wishing him happiness with "Mart," whom she no longer called "Miss Einhorn."[37] Two days later the newlyweds stopped briefly in Kansas City's Hotel Muehlbach to visit Luis Quintanilla, artist in residence at the University of Kansas City. Hemingway had supported Quintanilla's artwork in New York and his counterespionage work in Madrid during the Spanish Civil War. In the hotel room a local reporter caught up with Ernest as he mused about what he might write next: "one a story of the Gulf Stream. That would be factual like *Death in the Afternoon*. And I would like to write a book for my boys." Martha, who was on her way to New York to accept an assignment from *Collier's* for feature stories on the Japanese war with China, closed off the interview, saying, "Right now I'm the war correspondent in the family."[38]

On December 21, 1940, while Hemingway was on his way back to Cuba for Christmas, Scott Fitzgerald died in Sheila Graham's Hollywood living room, a simple failure of the heart. On his book-shelf was a copy of *For Whom the Bell Tolls*, signed: "To Scott with affection and esteem, Ernest." In response Fitzgerald had praised the book, telling Ernest it was "better than anybody else writing could do. . . . I envy you like hell and there is no irony in this." In his notebook, he thought otherwise: "It is so to speak Ernest's 'Tale of Two Cities' though the comparison isn't apt. I mean it is a thor-oughly superficial book which has all the profundity of *Rebecca*."[39] Within three months, three of the men most influential to Hemingway's early career were dead: Scott Fitzgerald, James Joyce, and Sherwood Anderson. Modernism, whatever that word meant, had become a historical period, and what would follow was not yet written.

CHAPTER 2

To Mandalay and Back

January to September 1941

On the last day of January 1941, Martha with her *Collier's* assignment, Ernest with his *PM* journalist's credentials boarded the *Matsona*, bound for Hawaii. Eager to see the Asia of her reading—Manila, Hong Kong, Chungking, Singapore—Martha was ill prepared for the months that followed. Hong Kong appeared to her "as if nailed together hurriedly from odd lots of old wood and sounded like a chronic Chinese New Year." Encircled on three sides by invading Japanese and teeming with refugees, the Crown Colony was throbbing at an hysteric pitch. Martha was appalled by the poverty, the hopelessness, and the lack of sanitation. "The sheer numbers, the density of bodies," horrified her. "There was no space to breathe." She could not believe the ease with which Ernest picked up enough local patois to make himself understood by waiters, rickshaw coolies, and street vendors. He loved the Chinese food that made Martha's stomach queasy; he was like a small boy lighting firecrackers in their hotel room until she made him stop. But she could not stop the reality of the Hong Kong streets: "Why do they have to spit so much? . . . You can't put your foot down without stepping on a big slimy glob! And everything stinks of sweat and good old night soil."[1]

In Hong Kong, the China News Agency reported the couple were collecting materials for a new novel.[2] In fact, Ernest and Martha were going into China not only to report on the Sino-Japanese War, but also to collect intelligence for the U.S. government. Through Martha's connections with the White House, they were asked to observe closely the politics of the China war. In Hong Kong, they were briefed by Lauchlin Currie, whom Roosevelt had sent to study the China situation where a quasi-democratic Chiang Kai-shek was or was not using U.S. military aid to suppress the communist left for his own purposes while also fighting the Japanese. Carl Blum, the general manager of the Rubber Company of the Far East, also briefed them on the strategic importance of the Orient.[3]

A month later, from the inland vantage point of Shaokwan, where her hotel bed was a plank and the latrine a "stand-up hole-in-the-floor toilet down the corridor," Hong Kong looked much better to Martha. Desperate to keep somewhat clean, she was depressed when Ernest told her she was a fool to touch the water and never to use it to brush her teeth. Later, when her hands developed "China Rot," a highly contagious fungus, Martha was forced to wear awkward gloves over a "malodorous unguent." "Honest to God, Martha," Ernest said, "you brought this on yourself. I told you not to wash." On their way from Shaokwan to the front lines of the Chinese war, the Hemingways traveled by motorized sampan and then small ponies through mud and rain, arriving finally at the Seventh War Zone:

> Headquarters were sometimes a new wood house, sometimes a house made of lashed mats on stilts above the duck pond. The pond water was rotting garbage and mud . . . pigs rooted in the muck, flies swarmed, and over all villages hung the smell of China: night soil. We passed through slatternly villages, each adorned with a triumphal arch for us and a duck pond with malaria for them.[4]

Day after sodden day filled with such squalor left Martha despondent. There in a cold stone house, bedded on the stone floor, mosquitoes and flies circling overhead in the dark, Martha said, "I wish to die." "Too late," answered Ernest. "Who wanted to come to China?" Finally, having seen their fill of Chiang Kai-shek's army in the field and having toasted themselves to the point of oblivion, the conspicuous couple began the trip back down the river.

Forty-three hours later, they arrived back in Shaokwan, road-weary and almost resigned to whatever came next. The evening of April 3, they bedded down on the train to Kweilin in what was advertised as a first-class compartment. What Martha found was dirt, cigarette butts, orange peels, and cinders. There was no dining car, no food. They ate oranges and hard-boiled eggs washed down with boiled water. Twenty-five hours and four hundred miles down the track, they got off in Kweilin, where their expected military flight to Chungking was not awaiting them. Someone had not sent the message. They checked into the Palace Hotel, where bedbugs reigned and the down-corridor toilet was overflowing. "The sight was more appalling than the stench," Martha said later, "though the stench was superlative."[5] By late the next afternoon, Ernest's explosive tirade (his first on the trip) produced the Douglas DC-3 that flew them to Chungking, the working capital of Free China.

The next morning they were greeted by the finance minister of China, H. H. Kung, with whom they ate breakfast, lunch, and supper. Kung was an old friend of Ernest's uncle, Dr. Willoughby Hemingway, a medical missionary who died in China in 1932, and who was responsible for Kung attending Oberlin College. While a student, Kung was several times a guest at the Hemingway family home in Oak Park. Now he was able to open doors for Ernest and Martha that would otherwise have been closed. He asked them to stay at his house, but Ernest begged off; instead, they stayed at the unoccupied house of Kung's brother-in-law who was in Washington, D.C.[6] With the Kung connection, road life was somewhat easier for the Hemingways in Chungking, and Ernest continued to gather intelligence, including a somewhat clandestine interview with the communist political figure, Chou En-lai. A major difference between Ernest and Martha was by now quite apparent. Ernest was able to accept whatever the local social conditions were as a given, while Martha was almost always angered and appalled by the same conditions:

> grey, shapeless, muddy, a collection of drab cement buildings
> and poverty shacks, the best feature a lively market. . . . Crowds

of thin cotton-clad expressionless people swarmed in the streets. Lepers abounded. They were beggars and forgivably spiteful; you hurried to find money in your purse; if not quick enough, they touched your shrinking skin.

Ernest thrived in Chungking, developing contacts, gathering information, and making the most of his opportunities. As Martha later admitted, "He did not value cleanliness far above godliness like me, and wasn't reduced to despair by all the manifestations of disease."[7] Soon he was alone on a flight to "Chengtu in north Szechwan Province where the caravans come down from Tibet and you walk past yellow and red lamas in the dust-deep streets of the old high-walled city." There he saw and obtained photographs of the 100,000 workers who, without machinery, were building an airstrip over a mile long, one hundred and fifty yards wide, and five feet deep, capable of landing an American B-17 Super Fortress, building it from scratch in three months time. "China," he learned, "can do anything China wants to do."[8]

On the evening of April 14, a Chungking farewell party for the Hemingways was hosted by various organizations—the Chinese Journalist Association and the Sino-American Cultural Interflow Association among others. At the Chialing Hostel, more than three hundred people were gathered when

> Dr. H. H. Kung led Mr. and Mrs. Hemingway into the hall. . . . Ernest Hemingway has a rosy face with brown mustache. Colossal and muscular, he is apparently much taller than Dr. Kung, the Vice Premier. He shakes hands, politely and elegantly, with his greeters. Oh, each finger of his seems thicker than the stalk of a pen which produces panic when grabbed. . . . With golden hair and a water-melon seed shaped face, Mrs. Hemingway looks like a blonde, but without blue eyes. Of light color, she is beautiful, wearing an exquisite wrist watch and ring of jade. Moreover she is graceful and charming as Jeanette MacDonald, the famous movie star. . . . [The guests were] served peanuts, cakes, steamed dumplings, spring rolls, and goblets brimming with wine whose color resembles that of Mrs. Hemingway's golden hair. [9]

From the capital, Martha went south to Java and Singapore; Ernest flew south, following the vulnerable Burma Road, which supplied the Chinese Army, to its source at Lashio. From there, first by car and then by slow train, finally arriving in Rangoon, Hemingway filed four stories for *PM* newspaper, by which time Martha was in Batavia on her *Collier's* assignment. Ernest's return flight went back up to Kunming, where a storm had most of the passengers vomiting, and from there to Hong Kong, which was socked in with a two hundred-foot ceiling. Three times the pilot tried to land before finding a way down to the tiny landing strip across the bay.[10] Five days later Ernest was in Manila awaiting passage on one of the transpacific flying boats. While there he reported to the Army Intelligence team for debriefing. On May 13, he had gotten as far as Guam, where the plane landed to refuel and rest the pilots. The next day they took off for Wake Island, but four hours later at the point of no return, they turned back because headwinds were too strong: they did not have enough fuel to reach Wake. On May 16, they launched once more for Wake, refueled, and rested long enough for Ernest to get sunburned on that tiny wishbone before continuing on to Midway, where rough weather almost grounded them. Finally they reached Hawaii, where there was another two-day break before flying on to San Francisco. By the time he set foot on American soil, Hemingway had spent twelve days crossing six thousand miles of the Pacific.[11]

In June 1941, when Hemingway's stories were featured in *PM*, a majority of his American readers were unconcerned with the war in China and deeply opposed to sending U.S. troops, planes, or ships to the European War.[12] Charles Lindbergh told an America First rally in Chicago that Britain had already lost the war; on university campuses college students were holding "peace" rallies and strikes against participation in a foreign war. The American Youth Congress heralded the demonstrations as evidence of student opposition to Roosevelt's plan for convoying ships to rescue England and Russia. The Youth Committee Against War said, "Mr. President, we hold you to your pledge against involvement. Convoys mean a shooting war. We oppose war."[13]

Isolationist or aggressive, the nation's eyes were focused on

England, not China. Hemingway's analysis of the four-year Sino-Japanese War did not turn many heads, but it was extremely accurate. He said that an American war in the Pacific would begin when Japan attacked the Philippines, or the Dutch East Indies, or Malaysia. "But the real reason for fighting Japan will be that if she moves south in the Pacific, she will be attacking the control of the world supply of rubber." No rubber, no tires; no tires, no trucks or airplanes. But there were other needs that would drive the Japanese south: Philippine iron ore and Dutch oil fields. At present, Japan's oil and iron were supplied by England and America. "Japan has not enough iron to manufacture armament and munitions. She has not enough oil to refine gasoline for her planes or to fuel her battleships. . . . If the U.S.A. and Great Britain shut off her gasoline and oil she would be forced to move south toward oil at once."[14] His analysis of Chiang Kai-shek's army was equally astute: with two million troops well armed and trained to fight defensively in the mountains where Japanese artillery and tanks were ineffective, the Chinese would fight as long as America supplied resources and money. But without a competent air force or an influx of serious artillery, Chiang would not be able to mount an offensive. Having seen the Chinese pilots fail miserably against the superior Japanese Air Force, Hemingway said, "Any real American aid . . . would have to include pilots."[15] When Hemingway's story ran in *PM*, General Claire Chennault was conducting closed and confidential briefings with the best military pilots in America, explaining his venture for a volunteer force to fly P-40 Tomahawks against the Japanese along the Burma Road. His band of adventurers, who would not fly their first missions until December 1941, became the legendary "Flying Tigers."[16]

In late May, Ernest and Martha were together once more in Washington, D.C., to be debriefed at the Office of Naval Intelligence (ONI) and to report to Secretary of the Treasury Henry Morgenthau. Hemingway emphasized the strategic importance of support to Chiang Kai-shek: a long ground war in China would engage a majority of the Japanese Army, delaying their drive into Southeast Asia and the Philippines. By building two less battleships and using the money to support the Chinese, America could buy a year's grace in the Pacific, enough time to build up the two-ocean navy so crucial to its national defense. Such a navy "can destroy any Eastern enemy . . . a powerful enough navy imposes its will without having to fight."[17]

At the time, he did not dwell on the issue of the communist presence in the war, but a month later, he wrote Morgenthau a six-page, single-spaced, typed letter detailing the conflict between the Kuomintang wing (Chiang Kai-shek) and the communists (Mao Tse-tung and Chou En-lai)—a conflict which he prophesied was going to produce a civil war unless a defensible geographic division of the huge country gave each side its own territory. The communists would continue fighting the Japanese, but they were also extending their sphere of influence, just as Chiang was doing. Chou En-lai, Hemingway reported, was brilliant, charming, and intelligent—the only communist with direct access to Chiang. In Chungking, "window-dressing" communists were allowed to move about freely; elsewhere they were hunted down and imprisoned, as were any liberals critical of Chiang's government. While Chiang said he wanted the communists to become part of a unified China, he also kept a large reserve army out of the front lines to contain the communists should they start a civil war.[18]

En route to Havana, Ernest and Martha stopped in Key West long enough for them to pick up the *Pilar* and Ernest's sons, Patrick and Gregory, for their summer vacation at the Finca. On June 6, Ernest was sitting on a familiar bar stool at Sloppy Joe's while the owner and close friend, Josie Russell, put his place in order before taking a fishing vacation with Hemingway in Cuba. Since their first trip to Havana in 1932, the two hard-drinking compatriots fished together for marlin every summer it was possible. Joe Russell, onetime rumrunner and now revered Key Wester, was immortalized by Hemingway in *To Have and Have Not* (1937). The local reporter caught Hemingway holding forth, but could not get him to talk about his China trip. "You see how it is, kid," Hemingway explained. "I'd like to give you this China story and let you write it, but it's coming out in *PM* Monday, and they'd call me a louse if I gave it away now." He and Josie planned to fish hard for six weeks, stopping only for a quick trip to New York to see the Joe

Louis–Billy Conn heavyweight championship fight. "Louis may knock him out in a round and you're robbed," Ernest explained, "or it may turn into a battle you'll want to tell the kids about." What was he going to write next? "Well I can't say. No, it isn't about China, just about some of everything." Before sundown, Josie and Ernest were on the water for the night passage to Havana; Martha was in Miami with his sons catching the Pan-Am flight to meet the fishermen there the next morning.[19]

Josie and Ernest never made it to Madison Square Garden for the Joe Louis–Billy Conn fight, missing one of the "Brown Bomber's" most exciting title defenses. On June 21 in the *Pilar*'s irregular log book, Hemingway wrote, "Mr. Josie died." The *Key West Citizen* gave more details:

> Joe Russell . . . died at 3 o'clock yesterday afternoon in a Havana hospital. Ernest Hemingway . . . telephoned Joe Russell, Jr. here last night to tell him of his father's death. The elder Russell had gone into the hospital for a minor operation and was said to be recovering only a few hours before death came, apparently from a stroke.[20]

Another death close to the bone, another reason not to look back. "Losing Mr. Josie was no fun for Mr. Josie," he told Pauline. "And I was riding with him somewhere in it all only should have protected him better and truly. Though he always had so much sense and judgment and so I didn't worry."[21] After assisting Russell's son with the paperwork involved in moving a dead body from Cuba to Key West, Hemingway kept his hurt to himself. The loss was an irreplaceable one. Josie Russell at fifty-one was the older brother Ernest never had, the drinking and fishing companion he needed, the salty, red-faced bootlegger who was the real thing.

Back at Finca Vigia, which Ernest had purchased outright with $12,500 of his money from Paramount Pictures before leaving for China, Martha and he faced the usual problems created by lengthy absences: a leaky roof here, a malfunctioning pump there—the housekeeping problems that neither relished. Yet there was plenty of ready money to pay for repairs, to loan to relatives, and to pay for a new Lincoln Continental convertible in August.[22] By the first of

April, the Book-of-the-Month Club paid Scribner's for 252,000 copies of the novel, and Scribner's had sold another 239,000 copies. Although Ernest, as always, said he was disappointed his publisher had not pushed the book harder, his complaint was halfhearted.[23] The Hemingways' only financial worry was their joint income tax for 1941. Under the progressive tax rates, Ernest and Martha might owe 60–70 percent of their net income. He said his children, when asked what their father did in "Mr. Roosevelt's war," could say that he had paid for it.[24]

Another pressing problem was the mountain of unanswered mail that piled up during their trip. Martha hired a young woman, Patricia Cahill, two afternoons a week to take Ernest's dictation and type it up, but she proved to be very slow. One of her first letters was dictated to Ernest's younger brother, Leicester, for whom Ernest was a role model and hero. For Ernest, his twenty-six-year-old brother was a source of worry. A year earlier, Leicester and a British friend, Tony Jenkins, had sailed a leaky boat through the Caribbean in search of clandestine Nazi activity. The results of their amateur espionage, published in the *Baltimore Sun*, reported suspicious caches of diesel fuel which might one day be used for Nazi U-boats, furtive men who sounded a lot like fascists, and letters arriving in out-of-the-way places with German postmarks.[25] That diesel fuel was used by most of the small freighters in the Caribbean did not keep the two spies from assuming it was destined for German U-boats. Sailing their schooner *Blue Stream* further into the maze of small islets, they heard waterfront gossip that in 1938 Germans scouted the uninhabited Miskito Keys, a perfect site for fuel dumps and anchorage for seaplanes, but the two "snoopers" found no hard evidence. Further down the coast, they thought they were propositioned to run fuel oil to a Nazi submarine. The offer came to naught, but for the two adventurers it "confirmed the fact that the Nazis have honeycombed the waterways and cays off the wildest and most remote part of the Central America and can use their preparations at will in a Blitzkrieg of the Caribbean."[26] In a Puerto Rico post office, they discovered ahead of them in line two men speaking German. "One received mail with the postmark Berlin, the other Dusseldorf."[27]

Ernest was less than impressed with the feature stories, realizing how thin the evidence and how inexperienced Leicester was as reporter or spy. Trying to find his brother some employment, Ernest set up an interview for him with the Office of Naval Intelligence in Washington, where Leicester worked in radio intelligence for the next two years. Worried that he might not understand the difference between newspaper journalism and intelligence work, Ernest advised him to control his imagination, stick to verifiable facts, and not try to interpret them until he was fully trained.[28]

In late July, when it was obvious that Ernest's stenographer was far too slow, Martha wrote her friend in Havana, Jane Armstrong, at the American Consulate, who found a replacement; but at the end of August the new secretary, Miss Sherbine, was forced to return to the States.[29] One of the last letters she typed was Hemingway's angry response to his Scribner royalty statement where he found that he was bearing the entire legal cost of a spurious plagiarism suit, a deduction Hemingway felt should be shared by his publisher. He closed the letter questioning Edmund Wilson's *The Wound and the Bow* analysis of his fiction, saying he could not tell what his purported wound actually was, but he had a helluva bow, and when he wrote his memoirs, Wilson would get its full effect.[30] Eight years earlier, smarting from Gertrude Stein's portrait of him in *The Autobiography of Alice B. Toklas*, Hemingway had threatened to set the record straight with his own memoirs "when I can't write anything else."[31]

That summer of 1941, Hemingway was a writer without a book to write, for he had used up most of his material from the 1930s— Key West, Africa, Spain—and he did not know enough about China to use it as a setting for anything beyond journalism. Four days earlier, Martha told Jane Armstrong that Ernest was on the edge of writing his memoirs, but the word—memoirs—put him off. Too pretentious. Martha suggested calling it something else and get on with it, but evidently the time was not right. She was certain the book would eventually be written.[32] Using his own experiences, a writer gets his first two or three books free before his writing catches up to the present moment. After that, he has to create his fiction based on the lives of others and his own imagination. Hemingway's readers and critics thought that his fiction came straight from his own life, which was only true for large parts of *The Sun Also Rises*, less of *A Farewell to Arms* and some of his early stories. His 1930s fiction was set in places he knew well, but the characters were never himself, and the plots were all invented. Never having been a bootlegger, never having killed anyone, never having been gut-shot, he was not the one-armed tough guy, Harry Morgan, in *To Have and Have Not*. Never having been a counterespionage agent in Madrid, he was not Philip Rawlings in *The Fifth Column*, nor was he ever Robert Jordan in *For Whom the Bell Tolls*. Since finishing the manuscript for the *Bell*, a year had passed in which he had written nothing but the feature stories for *PM*. Now, in the August heat of the tropics, he was sweltering in that purgatory reserved for writers with no idea of what to write next.

When Ernest was irritable, nothing went right in his near vicinity, particularly his relationship with Martha. At some point in the summer, he left her an in-house note quoting Rilke: "'Love consists in this, that two solitudes protect and touch and greet each other.'" He suggested that they begin again to be the friends they knew they could be.[33] Through the humid Cuban summer, while Martha put finishing touches to her collection of stories, *The Heart of Another*, Ernest's predictions about the coming of a Pacific war appeared less theoretical as America's neutrality became more fictional each week. The public might want to avoid war, but their president and Congress, using massive deficit appropriations, were arming the nation as quickly as possible. The Selective Service program for a peacetime draft was in place for all men between twenty-one and twenty-eight, and the Army Air Force was recruiting pilots to man its newly acquired planes. While the East Coast worried about German air raids should war erupt, and the FBI made headlines arresting German spies, the potential war in the Pacific edged closer. On July 24, President Roosevelt suggested that the United States might stop selling oil to Japan. By August 1, the new Gallup Poll said 51 percent of Americans favored checking Japanese expansion in the Pacific even if it meant war. In midsummer, Pan-American pilots began ferrying American-built bombers to England, and Roosevelt froze all Japanese assets in the United

States, warning Japan, whose army now occupied Saigon, to stop its expansion in Southeast Asia. Surreptitiously and apparently without the president's knowledge, Assistant Secretary of State Dean Acheson imposed a de facto embargo on oil being sold to Japan. What followed was now inevitable.[34]

With his usual emotional mood swing toward moroseness following a book's publication, Hemingway was more angry with his publisher than his president. Despite the enthusiastic reviews of *For Whom the Bell Tolls*, Hemingway focused on the handful of critical responses. When the Pulitzer Prize Committee announced there would be no award in fiction for 1940, Hemingway acted as if it did not matter to him: "If I'd won that prize," he said, "I'd think I was slipping. I've been writing for twenty years and never have won a prize. I've gotten along all right."[35] But beneath the nonchalance he presented to the world was an ego as fragile as any writer's: the prize did matter, but not in public.

In case Max Perkins and Charlie Scribner had missed his point earlier about his anger over the legal costs of the false plagiarism suit, on the last day of August, Ernest repeated it in a lengthy night telegram, ending it:

TELL CHARLIE IF HE NEEDS ANY MONEY WILL BE GLAD TO LOAN IT TO HIM RATHER THAN HAVE HIM STEAL IT FROM ME AND IN THE END WE WOULD BE BETTER FRIENDS AND HE WOULD HAVE MORE MONEY.

The next morning, he sent another telegram asking Max and Charlie to disregard what he said.[36] The issue was past, but not forgotten; it would continue to flare up in Hemingway letters for the next three months. Within days of sending the telegrams, Ernest and Martha headed north for Sun Valley, where Toby Bruce was waiting for them with Ernest's newly purchased "paradise green" Lincoln convertible.

Like the migratory birds he loved to hunt, Hemingway, when unimpeded by events beyond his control, moved with the seasons: spring through late summer there was marlin fishing in the Gulf Stream; in the fall, bird hunts in the West; then warm winters at the Finca. By the time Ernest and Martha reached Sun Valley that September, the coming of war hung like a shroud across the country. In his Labor Day radio broadcast to the nation, President Roosevelt pledged that "we shall do everything in our power to crush Hitler and his Nazi forces." Three days later, a German U-boat fired two torpedoes at the U.S. destroyer *Greer*. On September 11, Roosevelt ordered the Navy to destroy on sight any hostile submarines or surface raiders found "in the waters which we deem necessary for our defense." Those waters now extended in the Atlantic as far as Iceland, and in the Pacific all the way to the Philippines.

CHAPTER 3

Voyagers

September 1941 to Christmas 1942

All that fall, Ernest and Martha lived at Sun Valley, once again nonpaying guests of the resort, along with several Hollywood faces. Robert Montgomery and his wife, Barbara Stanwyck, were something of a disappointment to Ernest. Montgomery was too tiny to be taken seriously, Hemingway said, and Stanwyck, his "tough mick" wife, was ugly, but nice and intelligent.[1] Gary and Rocky Cooper, director Howard Hawks and his stunning wife, Slim, were there at Ernest's request so that Hawks and Cooper might discuss the possibility of Hawks directing Cooper in the filming of *For Whom the Bell Tolls*. Cooper was as "aw shucks" plain as ever, a good man in the field and around the table afterward. Slim Hawks was something else: young, beautiful, and attracted to Ernest in what she thought of as a nonsexual way. "I had never known anyone so intelligent," she explained. "His mind was like a light . . . illuminating corners in your own head that you didn't even know were there. He had a tremendous influence on my thinking, my literary taste, my enjoyment of things simple and open, my recognition of and distaste for pomposity." She found the physical side of Ernest less attractive. Wearing the same clothes for days in a row, Ernest never seemed quite clean to her, a chronic female complaint since his high school days when potential dates complained that his fingernails were never clean and his hair unkempt.[2]

Other guests included Robert Capa, whose camera seemed to follow Hemingway; Leland Hayward, a prominent Hollywood agent;

and his wife, the actress Margaret Sullavan. There were dances and parties at Trail Creek Cabin, gambling at the rough tables in Ketchum, and bountiful hunts of whatever was in season—antelope in the Pahsimeroi Mountains, ducks on Silver Creek, pheasant at Dietrich. Hemingway's three visiting sons were pampered by Martha, went hunting with Ernest, and returned to their respective mothers. Elsewhere, the world was moving inexorably toward the war Ernest told his hunting companions would begin in the Pacific. "We'll probably get it for a Christmas present," he said. "Or maybe wake up New Year's morning with an unshakable hangover."[3] On October 30, the U.S. destroyer *Reuben James*, on convoy duty off Iceland, was sunk by German torpedoes, killing a hundred American sailors. On November 1, without revealing their secret December 1 deadline, the Japanese warned that if the United States did not halt its economic blockade, Japan would seek vital resources farther south.

On October 27, Martha's book *The Heart of Another* was published by Scribner's under her own name—not as Martha Hemingway, as Ernest asked, although it was copyrighted by Martha Gellhorn Hemingway.[4] Ernest worried over the book like an expectant father, advising their mutual editor, Max Perkins, on the contract, design, and marketing, taking the dust jacket photo of Martha himself. Reviewers, who generally liked the collection of stories, were all too quick to see the Hemingway influence, which Martha seemed to accept as fair response. Early in their relationship, Martha, who was no novice, was open to Hemingway's paternal instruction; later she deeply resented his saying that she was now the writer in the family and he her manager.

Between hunts and children, Hemingway took time to read Scott Fitzgerald's posthumously published *The Last Tycoon*, edited in its unfinished condition by Edmund Wilson, and published with as much fanfare as Scribner's could muster. Stephen Vincent Benét's review advised, "You can take off your hats now, gentlemen, I think perhaps you had better. This is not a legend, this is a reputation—and, seen in perspective, it may well be one of the most secure reputations of our time."[5] Hemingway, however, could find little good to say about the almost novel or the short stories that Wilson included in the volume. He told Perkins that Scott "still had the technique and the romance of doing anything, but all the dust was off the butterfly's wing for a long time even though the wing would still move until the butterfly was dead."[6]

Hemingway was somewhat rankled that Fitzgerald, once his close friend, was entering the literary pantheon to the beat of such memorial drums. The *New Republic*'s "In Memory of Scott Fitzgerald"—a collection of authors' anecdotes—was extended over two issues, featuring John Dos Passos, Budd Schulberg, John O'Hara, and Glenway Wescott, among others, remembering poignant Fitzgeraldean moments. Wescott's rather long and self-promoting essay repaid Hemingway for his satirical portrait of Wescott in *The Sun Also Rises*. Recalling the early days in Paris, Wescott described a conversation with Fitzgerald when Scott was urging Hemingway on all his acquaintances:

> Hemingway had published some short stories in the dinky deluxe way in Paris; and I along with all the literary set had discovered him, which was fun; and when we returned to New York we preached the new style and peculiar feeling of his fiction as if it were evangel. Still, that was too slow a start of a great career to suit Fitzgerald. Obviously Ernest was the one true genius of our decade, he said. . . . What could I do to help launch Hemingway . . . my enthusiasm was not on a par with his; and looking back now, I am glad for my sake that it was not.[7]

By the time Wescott wrote this piece, he was no longer a promising young writer, and Hemingway's own reputation had taken on a life of its own. In 1941, eight anthologies reprinted eight different Hemingway stories, several with apparatus for study. In November, Robert Penn Warren requested reprint permission for "The Killers" which, along with a stunning interpretation, would be part of an influential college text, *Understanding Fiction* (1943).[8] In his mid-November letter to Max Perkins, Hemingway offhandedly said he could not come to New York for the Limited Editions Club award to him of their Gold Medal for fiction. On the same day he apologized at some length to Sinclair Lewis for not being able to attend the ceremony where Lewis would make the presentation, but promised that Scribner's would provide a stenographer to record the event. Never having had any awards for his writing, he said this one made him feel "damn good," especially when a writer whom he admired, like Lewis, was one of the judges.[9]

But he did not tell Lewis that it was almost as difficult for him to accept public adulation as it was to bear critical attacks. In Oak Park, where Ernest grew up, they said that "praise to the face was open disgrace." Yet when Max Perkins failed to have the requested stenographer at the award ceremony, Ernest was furious and hurt, saying he wanted never to see the medal. Instead it should go to Scribner's to remind the firm how carelessly and callously they had treated him. It would have been useful to have reprinted Lewis's speech as a pamphlet, but now that would never happen. He would never read the speech. His children would never see it. Nothing his publisher might now do would mollify him.[10]

By the time he wrote those letters, the December 7 Japanese carrier attack on Pearl Harbor had sent the heart of the United States Pacific Fleet to the bottom of the bay. The USS *Arizona* along with seven other battleships and ten other naval vessels were sunk or badly damaged. Hickam Field and its aircraft were bombed out, and bloody Scofield Barracks was filled with wounded Marines. As the smoke cleared, two hundred American planes were smoldering and three thousand men were dead or wounded. The war that had been blowing in the wind since November 1919, the war consuming most of Europe and half of the Pacific Rim, that war was now sitting down to breakfast all across America. Whatever plans people had for next year were as useless as the *Arizona*. Young men, whose president once promised they would never die on foreign soil, were about to leave home, many for the first and last time. Their sweethearts would receive letters from Army Post Offices; their parents, telegrams beginning: "We regret to inform you." Americans would learn a new vocabulary, a new set of values; new icons would become part of their collective memory. New graveyards would be arranged in exotic places; new songs would echo forever in the heads of the survivors, along with images too hard to bear. The intensity of the next four years would reduce the two decades between wars to vague memories and faded photographs. The generation who came of age with the Great European War (1914–18) was leading its children into another one, a war that would once more change the surface of American society.

In time for Christmas, Ernest and Martha returned to Finca Vigia, which Martha continued to resuscitate from its fallen state, and where both writers, as soon as their joint tax returns were finished, began new work.[11] Centered on a young Caribbean girl, Liana, whose beauty was both her power and her misfortune, Martha characterized her work as "a simple unambitious novel, just a story about some people on a small Caribbean island. It has nothing to do with the war or with current events."[12] Ernest was working on two long short stories, which he interrupted to write an introduction for a Crown Publishers collection of fiction and nonfiction to be called *Men at War*. What started as a simple task became more complicated when he disagreed with many of the selections, insisting that some be dropped, others added. In New York, Max Perkins began making suggestions, and Hemingway's military friends—Colonel Charles Sweeny and Marine Colonel John Thomason at the Office of Naval Intelligence—also became involved. Before the book was completed, Ernest was grousing that Scribner's should have published the book so they could have made some money on it; instead, the collection was his first contribution to the war effort, a "weapon" that might "do some good."[13] Without referencing Archie MacLeish's charge that his fiction had undermined the values of his 1920s readers, Ernest was putting his shoulder to the war wheel as best he could.

Using quotations from Karl von Clausewitz's *On War* for his thematic divisions of the anthology, Hemingway's finished selection would open with Julius Caesar's invasion of Britain and close with the Battle of Midway (June 1942). In between there were over a thousand pages of fiction, history, and firsthand accounts of what war can do to the warrior. Several of the selections were double-edged, not only telling about man's experience in battle but also telling Hemingway's readers something about his own writing. Having written crucial parts of *A Farewell to Arms* from secondary sources, Hemingway included all of Stephen Crane's *Red Badge of Courage*, his precursor for creating believable fiction out of research. Juxtaposed with Livy's classic account of "Horatio at the Bridge" he placed his own account of El Sordo's last stand in *For Whom the Bell Tolls*. In a left-handed acknowledgment of sources, Hemingway reprinted T. E. Lawrence's description of blowing up a train in *Seven Pillars of Wisdom*, a book that echoes throughout the *Bell*. After calling attention to Fabrizio's experience at Waterloo in Stendhal's *Charterhouse of Parma*, he placed Victor Hugo's "Waterloo" up against Frederic Henry's retreat from Caporetto in *A Farewell to Arms*.[14] These selections and their placement were not accidental. By juxtaposing his work with that of Tolstoy, Stendhal, Lawrence, and Crane, Hemingway set the terms of the competition, asking to be judged against the best of the best.

Still seething from the so-called Allies' refusal to help Loyalist Spain in its heartbreaking fight against the fascist rebels, Hemingway made his political position as clear as possible:

> The editor of this anthology, who took part and was wounded in the last war to end war, hates war and hates all the politicians whose mismanagement, gullibility, cupidity, selfishness and ambition brought on the present war and made it inevitable. But once we have a war there is only one thing to do. It must be won.[15]

As much about the responsibility of the writer as about the effects of war, Hemingway's introduction was personal and blunt:

> The last war . . . was the most colossal, murderous, misman- aged butchery that has ever taken place on earth. Any writer who said otherwise lied . . . writers who were established before the war had nearly all sold out to write propaganda during it . . . a writer should be of as great probity and honesty as a priest of God. He is either honest or not . . . after one piece of dishonest writing . . . which he knows in his inner self is not true, for no matter what patriotic motives, then he is finished. . . . And he will never be at peace with himself because he has deserted his one complete obligation.[16]

Reviewers found Hemingway's personal commentary and lecturing discursive and badly put together, but they were unaware of its subtext. Already Hemingway was being asked why he was not involved with the war effort. In a defensive response to a *Time* magazine journalist who wanted to know what he was doing to help America win the war, Hemingway said only his children had the right to ask such a question.[17] It was to those three sons—John, Patrick, and Gregory—that *Men at War* was dedicated.

All across America, men and women were asking the same question of themselves. Men, draftees or volunteers, were being trained in sometimes tedious routines and physical drills, preparing them for the invasion of beaches months away. As the government took more and more control of Americans' daily lives through rationing, blackouts, air-raid drills, and volunteer programs, housewives began saving bacon fat in coffee cans for the nitrates that would eventually become part of war-bound ammunition; their husbands, by day, subscribed to war bond drives, pledging part of their monthly salaries; at night they worked as air-raid wardens; their children collected tinfoil and scrap iron. Then the whole family helped dig up the side yard for the "Victory Garden," trading fresh corn with the neighbor who was raising pullets.

All through the summer of 1942, while Ernest was rearranging the contents and writing the introduction for *Men at War*, the war was close at hand, but he had no way to get to it. Too old for the draft, too controversial for the government, and too far from Key West, his options were limited. In April, the U.S. Marines at Bataan surrendered to the Japanese Army, the worst U.S. military humiliation since the Sioux destroyed Custer. In May, the German plan of Admiral Doenitz, Operation Drumbeat, began its attack on the American pipeline of war material flowing to England and Russia. Knowing how crucial oil, gasoline, and aviation fuel were to fighting a war, the German U-boat commanders focused on three refining centers: Aruba in the Caribbean; and New Orleans and Houston in the Gulf of Mexico. Knowing that without bauxite there was no aluminum, without aluminum no airplanes, the German raiders also centered on the British and Dutch Guianas, which then produced most of the ore in the western hemisphere.

On the evening of February 16, at the entrance to Lake Maracaibo, where Venezuelan crude oil came across the bar in shallow draft tankers to be refined at Aruba, it was a calm, warm night. At the Lago refinery on Aruba, the graveyard shift came to work with the night lights fully lit and flare gas burning. Each month this refinery, the world's largest, was producing 7.1 million barrels of gasoline, aviation fuel, and lubricants, most of which was going to support the British war effort. At 1:30 a.m. in a coordinated attack German U-boats turned seven tankers into burning hulks, shelled the refinery with surface guns, and left without a scratch on their gray hulls. Observing the smoking ruins the next morning, the Chinese crews refused to sail without protection, forcing the refinery to shut down and Lake Maracaibo oil production to stop, having no more storage space. Nineteen ships went down that month in the Caribbean; nineteen more the next month; eleven in April; thirty-eight in May. Between February and November 1942, almost twice as many ships were sunk in this confined area as were sunk on the North Atlantic convoy routes. By the end of November 1942, 263 ships were on the bottom of the Caribbean Sea.[18]

To enter the Gulf of Mexico, the U-boats had only three routes, all of them narrow and thus dangerous: the Straits of Florida, the Old Bahama Channel at the northeast end of Cuba, and the Yucatan Channel at the southwest end of the island (see Map C). Once safely into the hunting ground, the German subs found little effective opposition. The U.S. Navy's Gulf Sea Frontier Command had only recently implemented a convoy system between Key West and Norfolk, Virginia, for which it had minimal protection. American antisubmarine warfare (ASW) was on-the-job training.[19] Because of news censorship, the general population never knew the extent of the losses at their peak, nor when the losses slackened.

By May 1, the submarine threat was so intense in the Gulf of Mexico that all shipping was stopped along the north coast of Cuba until convoys could be established.[20] Seventeen days later, a further order came down from the Naval Commander of the Gulf Sea Frontier: "Movements are stopped between Gulf or Caribbean ports and U.S. Atlantic Coast . . . and from Gulf and Caribbean ports to east coast of South America."[21] In those first eight months of 1942, when attack ships and planes were few and their crews inex-

perienced with new electronic gear, U-boat commanders were earning Iron Crosses on every trip west. Although Havana and other
Cuban ports did not contribute to the tanker traffic, the island,
which barricaded a major section of the Gulf, had primary shipping lanes on all sides. In June and July 1942, over thirty ships were
torpedoed within easy reach of the Cuban coast. No longer an
American protectorate, the coming of war put Cuba's neutrality in
a precarious position, which it swiftly resolved in its own best interests by declaring war against the Axis powers and cooperating with
the U.S. antisubmarine efforts. Quickly, small tent outposts were
established on remote islands and keys off the north coast to support U. S. Navy seaplanes and to act as supply bases when antisubmarine cutters were in the area. By mid-April, Army Air Force
planes using bases in Cuba were patrolling the Yucatan and Old
Bahama Channels by day and later by night.

Initially undermanned and outplanned, the United States did
what Americans have always done best: it improvised solutions with
whatever materials were at hand. Less than a month into the war,
the Coast Guard began organizing East Coast yachtsmen and small
boat owners into auxiliary units. Larger private sail- and motor-dri-
ven ships were "rented" at a dollar a year for submarine patrols in
coastal waters.[22] In late June, with ships being sunk at unsustainable rates, the Navy took desperate measures:

> Washington, June 27 (AP)—In a move to put a great fleet of
> small boats into the war against submarines off the Atlantic and
> Gulf coasts, the navy called today for all owners of seagoing craft
> to volunteer the services of themselves and their vessels. . . .
> Approximately 1,200 small boats are in such service now . . .
> [and] it is hoped that upward of 1,000 additional small boats for
> offshore navigation may be added to the auxiliary. . . . Boats
> found to be qualified will be equipped with radio, armament and
> suitable anti-submarine devices as rapidly as possible.[23]

Soon the recruitment for the auxiliary patrol was intensified.
Secretary of the Navy Frank Knox issued a call for "patriotic
yachtsmen and small-boat owners" to come to the aid of their
country, offering them

the opportunity which they have been so earnestly seeking: to serve their country and combat its enemies in the sea-going manner for which their experience fits them. . . . These boats are needed right now—not only for . . . Harbor Patrol duties but for actual offensive operations against enemy submarines.[24]

By the time Secretary Knox issued his plea, Ernest Hemingway's private war against the U-boats was well underway.

From his reading about World War I Q-ships, Ernest saw immediately the possibilities for an armed auxiliary boat the size of the *Pilar* patrolling as a fishing craft. If such a secretly armed ship could lure a German submarine to the surface, it might be able to get in the first shot, crippling the raider.[25] Early in the war, German submarines operating in the Caribbean and the Gulf of Mexico were, in fact, liable to attack on the surface, using their deck guns to conserve torpedoes. The long-range Type-XI U-boat common in the Gulf was formidably armed for surface combat: a primary 105mm deck gun, a 37mm auxiliary gun, and two 20mm machine guns.[26] On May 2, Ernest read in the local paper of a running battle between a lightly armed tanker and a U-boat off the north coast of Cuba. Attacking on the surface with its deck gun, the submarine sank the tanker after a two-hour exchange of fire.[27]

The only impediment to Hemingway's joining the auxiliary was his location, Cuba, where no such opportunity existed. The island-nation was at war with the Axis powers—Germany, Japan, and Italy—and the Fulgencio Batista government cooperated with the United States, barring Axis nationals from entering Cuba and interning aliens on the Isle of Pines. The Cuban Navy and Air Force, using obsolete American ships and aircraft, were patrolling Cuban territorial waters, but that did not mean that an American national, not even Ernest Hemingway, could form his own auxiliary under the Cuban flag. Nor, of course, had Hemingway any intention of going to war under the Cuban flag. Instead, he worked through the American Embassy, where First Secretary Robert Joyce was helpful in putting Ernest and his fishing boat *Pilar* into the war effort; but it took several months for the idea to become reality.

About this same time, the new American ambassador to Cuba, Spruille Braden, became worried about the loyalties of the 300,000 Spanish residents of Cuba, as many as 10 percent of whom were thought to be dedicated Falangists and therefore potential sources of aid to the Nazi cause. Until the FBI could find the right men for the Havana station, Braden recruited Hemingway to organize a makeshift intelligence service, which Ernest set to enthusiastically. As Braden remembered it, Hemingway "enlisted a bizarre combination of Spaniards: some bar tenders; a few wharf rats; some down-at-heel pelota players and former bullfighters; two Basque priests; assorted exiled counts and dukes; several Loyalists and Francistas. He built up an excellent organization and did an A-One job."[28]

Although Martha and others thought the "Crook Factory" something of a joke, the new Ambassador Braden thought Ernest's reports on the activities of Spanish Falangists in Cuba significant enough to include them almost verbatim in several long reports to the State Department.[29] The crucial diplomatic question was, what would Cuba do if Franco's Spain joined the Axis in the war?—a very real possibility given the German-Italian support of Franco's successful rebellion. In October 1942, Spruille Braden's cogent review of the Cuban situation documented the Spanish Embassy's clandestine support of the Falange, which was generating Axis rumors and propaganda. There was also the strong possibility that the Falangists were gathering information on military installations, communicating with and refueling German U-boats, and planning and executing "attempts at sabotage." Despite being outlawed by the Cuban government, the pro-Nazi Falange was both active and dangerous to American interests.[30]

Ernest's long-standing fascination with spies and counterspies was, for this brief period, completely in synch with prevalent American war fears. America was a nation on edge, expecting the worst. When crude sound detection gear picked up what seemed to be two flights of unidentified aircraft, the entire San Francisco Bay area was blacked out all the way to Sacramento for almost an hour. When Jacob Steinberg's lights failed on the Williamsburg Bridge, he made the mistake of stopping his truck. Unable to fix them, he continued on toward his Brooklyn home, never hearing the warning whistle from the soldier on guard duty at the bridge. Jacob did hear the five warning shots, however, one of which flattened a tire, another almost hitting him. In Indiana, the Civilian Defense Headquarters was asked by a county official, "Would it be possible to have a bomb dropped in our county to have the people realize this country is at war?" He was told, "We're saving all bombs for Tokyo."[31] On June 13, the fears became a reality when a Nazi U-boat landed four saboteurs on the south shore of Long Island. Four days later, another group of German agents was put ashore close to Jacksonville, Florida. On June 27, J. Edgar Hoover, head of the FBI, called a late evening news conference to announce all eight agents were under arrest, their caches of explosives recovered, and the safety of the nation for the moment assured. Their objectives, he said, were the bridges leading into Manhattan, three major aluminum plants, the New York City water supply, the hydroelectric plant at Niagara Falls, and key rail centers. Shortly after noon on August 7, six of the eight German agents were executed in a portable electric chair installed at the District of Columbia jail.[32] By the time the saboteurs were dead, 250 enemy aliens, many of them naturalized American citizens, were in jail, charged with various subversive goals, most particularly blowing up the Pennsylvania Railroad's horseshoe curve outside Altoona.[33] And the British-Honduran businessman suspected of refueling German U-boats in the Caribbean and smuggling spies into the Panama Canal Zone was arrested by the U.S. Navy at sea.[34]

With its large international population, its critical location, and its long history of revolutionary activity, Cuba was not immune to the war fears on the mainland. In April, the *Havana Post* reported that "almost fifty Germans, Italians and Japanese were rounded up and arrested in a swift and simultaneous action by agents of the Enemy Activities Section of the Cuban Bureau of Investigation. . . . [charged with] espionage and other illicit activities on behalf of the Axis powers . . . most of those arrested are on the U.S. blacklist." Among those arrested were several associated with the German spy ring at Nuevitas, "from which port several freighters have departed during recent weeks and been later sunk by enemy subs off the

Cuban coast."[35] On July 14, as Hemingway's "Crook Factory" was being formed, the FBI sent Raymond Leddy to the Havana embassy as an attaché to replace the FBI agent who could not "tell fact from rumor."[36]

On June 26, all three of Hemingway's sons—Jack (eighteen), Patrick (thirteen), and Gregory (eleven)—arrived on the Pan-Am flight in time for Patrick's fourteenth birthday two days later. Martha at thirty-three—blond, lithesome, and lovely—was more like an older sister than a stepmother. For Jack, still called "Bumby" or "Bum" by his father, Martha was his second stepmother, replacing Pauline Pfeiffer, the mother of his two stepbrothers. Having hunted with her at Sun Valley the previous fall, all three sons seemed at ease around this lovely woman who treated them with unaffected kindness and amazed them with her ability to say "fuck" in a way so ordinary as to be inoffensive. They were also impressed with the renovations she had made at the Finca. When she found the farm in 1939, it was overgrown with weeds and badly in need of repairs. After Ernest bought the house and property, Martha had refurbished the six large and airy rooms into a tropical haven.[37] Ceiling fans moved the humid air, cool in the morning, warm by noon. Slowly, Martha came to accept the constant battle with the insect life. Through open windows came the *comejen*, a flying white ant with a termite's taste for wood. The *traza*, small and wormlike, preferred books, silks, and linens, while out of the bread box trailed a company of small, mahogany-colored ants. In an effort to disrupt if not control the ant problem, small cans of kerosene were placed under the legs of stoves and cupboards. Compounded by mosquitoes in several sizes, scorpions, tarantulas, and centipedes, the insect war was never won, nor was it ever finished.[38]

As Jack remembered that summer, the Finca's swimming pool was filled and functioning; next to it was the crushed coral tennis court, and at the front of the house, "an enormously old ceiba tree . . . with its large, high-reaching roots extending from the bulbous trunk like sinuous flying buttresses of smooth, gray bark. Many orchid plants live on its trunk and among its broad branches." Greg remembered the view from the hilltop, the lights of Havana seen in the night, and the lush greenery and tropical flowers where hummingbirds made their nests.[39] With a cook taking care of meals, a driver for the three cars (Plymouth, Buick, and Lincoln), tennis matches, live pigeon shoots, and deep-sea fishing on the *Pilar*, summertime life at the Finca was a boy's dream.

For Martha, that summer at the Finca may have been a dream, but not a completely pleasant one. On the tennis court with her stepsons or at the Floridita for supper, she was perfectly delightful, but beneath the surface her impatience with the war, with the slow Cuban life, and with her stalled novel festered. As she told Eleanor Roosevelt, the president's wife and her close friend, she needed to understand the characters better. She also needed to get away from the Finca, where she was the designated housekeeper, a role that held no joy for her. As she said later, "During that terrible year, 1942, I lived in the sun, safe and comfortable and hating it."[40]

Martha was an incurable traveler who preferred road life to home life, not unlike Ernest. If she had to be at home, she wanted more solitude than the Finca provided that summer. Hemingway's three sons crowded the six-room house; his coterie of Basque jai alai players were constant visitors; the butler, the cook, and the gardener needed continuous attention in a language she could not speak well; and the Crook Factory, with its overly dramatic secrecy and its operatives arriving at the Finca at all hours, was an impediment to her writing.[41] What she had not understood about Ernest during their four-year affair was his need to assemble groups to participate in the activity du jour: fishing in Michigan; skiing in Austria; bullfights in Spain; marlin fishing in the Gulf Stream; hunting in Wyoming—whatever his seasonal interest, it required a loyal group of fellow travelers, preferably one or two of whom required mentoring. That summer he was teaching his sons the finer points of wing-shooting live pigeons, the rituals of the cockfights, and the intricacies of betting on the jai alai matches.

What Ernest did not understand, or appreciate, about Martha was her need sometimes to be alone, sometimes to follow her instinctive impulse to be at the heart of the action elsewhere. In 1938, leaving Ernest in Paris, she had struck out to cover the Nazi takeover of Czechoslovakia, barely making the last flight out of Prague with her story. During Christmas 1939, she left Ernest at

Sun Valley to cover the war in Finland. As biographer Bernice Kert has written:

> When she was away she longed for him. When she was home she found it difficult to put up with his exasperating habits. At the same time she scolded him for not bathing, or for drinking too much, or for telling some silly lie about his exploits, she would make an impressive effort with his sons, his cats, his parties, his guests. When nothing changed she boiled up with frustration and knew only one way out, to get away for a while.[42]

Soon after the arrival of the Hemingway sons, Martha, needing respite from being Mrs. Hemingway, reverted to Martha Gellhorn journalist at large, traveling albeit on Mrs. Hemingway's passport.

She convinced her *Collier's* editor to pay her expenses in the Caribbean for a series of articles on the effects of the submarine war. By July 20, she was writing Ernest a birthday greeting from Port-au-Prince, Haiti. For the next three months, she traveled the Caribbean by plane, motorboat, and sailing sloop during the heart of hurricane season; she fought off mosquitoes, rescued a cat, slept on plank floors, survived dengue fever, fractured her wrist, flew on a submarine patrol, was disappointed with a bauxite mine, and traveled by dugout canoe up a jungle river until she fell off the map.[43] She talked her way into and out of restricted areas, visited a French penal colony where the convicts, "dead-eyed skeletons in red and white striped pajamas, cut wood in the jungle until they died of exhaustion and disease." But Martha never saw a submarine, never realized due to censorship how many ships were going down around her. For her three-month adventure, *Collier's* paid her expenses and bought two feature stories: one that detailed the poverty and squalor of Puerto Rico's poor; the other describing the boredom of American troops guarding an equally boring bauxite mine in Surinam.[44]

While she was gone, Ernest was the good father and even better companion to his sons, but he was also enlarging his counterintelligence activities to include sub patrols with the *Pilar*. On July 28, Ernest took young Patrick and Gregory with him as part of his crew to investigate alleged German sympathizers resupplying submarines out of nearby Matanzas. Part of the assignment included investigating a coastal cave reported to be a supply drop point. When the cave narrowed to the point that Winston Guest could not squeeze through, he sent Patrick and Gregory crawling back into the space where they found nothing at all—a false lead. But Ernest wrote Martha that they came close to intercepting a "tin fish."[45] Into August, while Martha continued on her Caribbean fact-finding trip, Ernest and his *Pilar* crew carried out short patrols within easy reach of Havana while they waited for clearance from Navy Intelligence to patrol around Cape San Antonio, the southern tip of Cuba. All through September and into October, they waited for orders that never came.

Finally in early October, with Martha not yet returned, Ernest and his crew began working with hand grenades, machine guns, and satchel charges on practice targets out in the Gulf Stream.[46] His first mate, Winston Guest, whom Ernest met on his 1933 African safari, had checked into the Hotel Nacional in early September, ostensibly to tend to his mining interests in Santa Clara.[47] At six foot five, "Wolfie" was an easygoing man, a ten-goal polo player, an excellent athlete, and a Columbia University law graduate. Like Hemingway's counterparts on the east coast of the United States, Ernest's objectives were basic: keeping track of coastal traffic, particularly small ships that might be refueling U-boats; investigating floating debris; and if possible locating U-boats on the surface. U-boats, however, rarely surfaced during the day, preferring the cover of darkness for their attacks and for the necessary recharging of batteries.

While accepting all of the objectives assigned to the coastal patrol, Hemingway was also dedicated to a risky plan of actually disabling a U-boat at sea. Without radar, sonar, or MAD gear, the *Pilar* could not patrol at night, nor could it locate a submerged submarine. The slight wooden structure of the fishing boat would not support the twin 50mm machine guns Ernest hoped to install, leaving him with only light machine guns for his crew and a bazooka incapable of penetrating a U-boat's conning tower. Undeterred, he hoped to arouse the curiosity of a German commander to the point he would surface to inspect the *Pilar*. If they could get close enough to the submarine, they would attack with grenades and light machine guns to clear the deck, and a satchel charge encased in a fire extinguisher would be tossed onto the conning tower and with luck down the open hatch, where its explosion would prevent the U-boat from submerging. Then by radio the *Pilar* would call in U.S. Navy cutters to finish the job. Highly risky, perhaps even suicidal, the plan was grounded in the reality that U-boats did sometimes stop small boats at sea to relieve them of fresh fruit and fish.

Ambassador Braden was sufficiently impressed with Ernest's counterintelligence efforts and his enthusiasm for the sub patrols that he "scrapped the regulations, got him what he wanted, and sent him on his way." Hemingway's uncanny ability to outdrink the ambassador and his guests also impressed Braden:

> [Hemingway] could consume an astonishing amount of liquor—any kind of liquor—without appearing to feel it. . . . I don't know how many cocktails we had before dinner; but Ernest didn't take cocktails, he took absinthe drip. During the dinner we had white and red wine, followed by champagne. When [the wives] . . . left the table, he ordered another bottle of champagne, just for the two of us. . . . [Afterward] I had highballs, but Ernest went back to his absinthe drip. And he remained cold sober.[48]

Or so it seemed to the ambassador, who was trying to hold his own.

FBI Agent Leddy reported to Washington that Hemingway convinced Ambassador Braden to finance "certain coastal patrol and investigative work on the south coast of Cuba." Braden had "acceded to HEMINGWAY'S request for authority to patrol certain areas where submarine activity has been reported. . . . [censored] . . . he has secured from the Ambassador a promise that his crew members will be recognized as war casualties for the purposes of indemnification in the event any loss of life results from this operation."[49] Wary of Hemingway's clandestine activities, but not yet worried about them, Agent Leddy's main concern was keeping the bureau informed. Hemingway, as Leddy noted, had an abiding distrust of the FBI, dating back to early 1940 when the FBI charged several Americans with participating on the Loyalist side of the Spanish Civil War. In an August letter to his old friend and sometime poet,

Evan Shipman, Ernest said he did not write "personal things because we are at war and anybody who thinks indiscreetly or criticizes in time of war adds to whatever dossiers or photostatted letters he has assimilated."[50] As his FBI dossier would one day reveal, Ernest did well to keep this advice in mind.

After a Washington, D.C., briefing with new American Ambassador Spruille Braden, Martha, back from her dangerous excursion, flew on to New York on October 11 for a medical check-up, a hair session at Elizabeth Arden's, lunch with Charlie Scribner, and a little shopping before returning to Washington to visit at the White House as Mrs. Roosevelt's guest. About this same time, Agent Leddy at the Havana embassy was writing a follow-up letter to Director Hoover about Ernest's counterintelligence activities:

> Of further interest in this matter is a visit of Mrs. ERNEST HEMINGWAY (the former MARTHA GELLHORN), to Washington . . . to be the personal guest of Mrs. ROOSEVELT . . . the Ambassador [Braden] outlined to her certain aspects of the intelligence situation in Cuba in order that she might convey the same, in personal conversation, to the President and Mrs. ROOSEVELT. This has specific reference to the Embassy's request for approval of financing by the American Government of internment and investigative programs brought out by the Cuban authorities.[51]

When Martha returned to the Finca at the end of October, she reported to Ernest the kinds of military gossip rampant in Washington and in Miami: wives and girlfriends who knew exactly when convoys were leaving, troops arriving, and airlifts to West Africa departing. Out of her conversations came a report to Spruille Braden detailing the lax security on the mainland. One friend gave her "the date that 150 U.S. bombing planes, loaded with U.S. troops, took off from Brazil to West Africa, and I believe he told me it was a daily occurrence."[52]

Each morning in November, Martha and Ernest ate breakfast with Gustavo Durán and his wife, Bonte, who were houseguests at the Finca. Durán, a former Loyalist officer and friend of both Hemingways, had been called in to take over the Crook Factory operation, leaving Ernest free to concentrate on changing the *Pilar* from a fishing boat into a Q-boat. All of which was immediately reported by Agent Leddy directly to J. Edgar Hoover.[53] Each morning at 6:30 a.m., planes took off from mainland bases and San Julien (Cuba), to begin their daily patrols of a body of water littered with the flotsam and jetsam from sunken ships, bombings, and convoy traffic. Up and down the trafficked channels, oil leaked from the bowels of old and new wrecks. The sea itself was littered with lost oars, fragments of cargo, loose mines, tattered life jackets, and empty life rafts with no story to tell.[54]

In newspapers and on the radio, the war on all fronts appeared desperate, its outcome in doubt. In fact, the war in Europe and the Pacific had, without full fanfare, reached turning points. Deep in Russia, the German Army was bleeding itself to death at the gates of Stalingrad. In the Pacific, the Japanese Navy was devastated at the Battle of Midway. In the Solomon Islands, U.S. Marines, despite heavy casualties, were taking the island of Guadalcanal away from Japanese defenders. On both fronts, counterintelligence was quietly changing the odds in favor of the Allies. At home, American codecrackers broke the Japanese Purple Code; in England, their counterparts solved the German Enigma Code that directed its U-boat wolf packs. In the last four months of 1942, Germany lost almost fifty U-boats to Allied attack. Over the next five months, over one hundred U-boats were destroyed, and the Battle of the North Atlantic was all but finished.[55] In September, the trial of two German spies began in Havana. For both men, the death penalty was being asked. "One was making drawings of the new air base being built outside Havana. The other was arrested with a radio transmitter and secret codes." Both were found guilty, and one sentenced to die.[56]

While Ernest turned over his Crook Factory operation to Gustavo Durán, he was busy in Havana arranging for the voyage of the *Pilar*. Beginning his late morning in Havana at the Hotel Ambos Mundos to check his mail drop, he then walked a few doors up to the American Consulate, later lunching at El Floridita with consulate friends, and perhaps finishing his rounds with a browse in the International Bookshop—all situated on Obispo Street. These conveniently grouped locales were his base of operations in those days of 1942, establishments where he was known on sight and where he trusted the proprietors. For drink and fresh seafood, Ernest most favored the golden-friezed Floridita, its metal shutters up, its eleven doors open to the busy street life. Inside the café overhead fans were turning, and the great mirrors behind the bar kept the room under observation from Hemingway's habitual seat at the left-hand corner of the bar where Constantino mixed the daiquiris. In those days before air conditioning, the only refrigerated part of the Floridita was the seafood display case, where one could choose fresh shrimp, crawfish, or stone crabs served with slices of tart lime and a small bowl of mayonnaise. The Floridita was a safe place to leave or pick up a message, use the phone, or listen to the waiter's report of curious Americans speaking fluent German.[57]

On November 2, Hemingway reported to Colonel Hayne Boyden at the U.S. Embassy that he and his crew were prepared to leave for a shakedown cruise no later than November 11, providing all the "materials" required arrived in time. Though her pirate black hull and newly painted dark green deck were out of the water for antifouling paint and a new stern bearing, the *Pilar* in four days would be ready for outfitting. It was vital, Hemingway said, that the training exercises with guns, grenades, and satchel charges be conducted in an area to the west of Havana if their first armed patrol was going to be along the northeast coast.[58] Four days later, with the *Pilar* still out of the water, a late tropical storm of near-hurricane strength came out of the Gulf, hitting Cuba broadside and delaying the final outfitting of his Q-boat at the Casablanca shipworks. Finally, on November 20, Hemingway; Winston Guest; Gregorio Fuentes, the cook and most experienced sailor; Pachi, the Basque jai alai player; and two other Cubans passed under the battlements guarding Havana Harbor, moved out into the Gulf Stream, and turned westward.

Nineteen days later, while anchored for lunch inside the Colorado Reef, the crew spotted a large, white-hulled ship moving rapidly eastward toward Havana, thick smoke pouring from her stacks. Identified as the Spanish ship *Marques de Comillas*, the freighter appeared in the Zeiss field glasses to have a smaller boat in tow. Keeping the ship under observation for forty-five minutes,

Hemingway became suspicious as the *Comillas* appeared to slow down. At a trolling speed of seven knots, the *Pilar* moved into deeper water on a NNW course to close with the ship when she turned due east. At a distance of three miles, the smaller gray ship in tow seemed to be a submarine, which turned away from the *Comillas*, picked up speed, and quickly left the *Pilar* behind. Immediately their observation was reported via shortwave radio in code to the American Embassy in Havana.[59] From there it went to the Commander of the Gulf Sea Frontier, who requested Havana authorities to keep track of a possible spy arriving on the SS *Marques de Comillas* that afternoon, adding:

> Lt. Dr. Duffy, Aide to the Naval Attaché Havana, advised that reliable parties reported to have observed the Marques de Comillas slow down and stop while a smaller vessel, suspected of being a U-boat, went alongside. At 22-53/83-25 in a cove on the east side of Punta Alacranes near the village of La Mulata. Occurred on Dec. 9. The observers, two reliable Americans and four Cubans, state they were within five thousand yards of the boat in question when the incident occurred.[60]

When the *Comillas* docked in Havana, Agent Leddy, with the "cooperation" of the Cuban police, interviewed the forty crew members of the Spanish ship and

> some fifty passengers . . . most of the latter known as anti-fascists repatriated from Spain. None of the persons interviewed would admit sighting a submarine. . . . The negative results of this inquiry were reported. Thereupon Hemingway submitted a memorandum stating that it would be a tragedy if the submarine were carrying saboteurs . . . and that the Legal Attaché discounted Hemingway's report because it had not come from an FBI agent.[61]

Careful to report any information that might undermine Hemingway's counterintelligence work or his coastal patrols, Agent Leddy had never forgiven Hemingway for introducing Leddy at a jai alai match as a member of the Gestapo.

Soon after Hemingway's memorandum suggesting that the FBI

bungled the *Pilar* report on the *Comillas*, a flurry of FBI documents were generated out of Agent Leddy's office and at the
bureau. In Washington, Agent D. M. Ladd, to whom Leddy reported, compiled a four-page report for Director Hoover, reminding
him first that Hemingway was on the side of the Spanish Republic
in the Spanish Civil War, and that he had been accused of being a
communist. He explained that Hemingway's Crook Factory was, in
Leddy's opinion, getting out of hand. Expanding from an investigation of the Falange to include the "involvement of Cuban officials in local graft and corruption," Leddy feared that Hemingway's
activities "were going to be very embarrassing unless something is
done to put a stop to him." If the Cuban press ever figured out that
Hemingway, with the embassy's blessing, was investigating
General Benitez, the head of the Cuban police, "serious trouble
may result." Ladd ended his report with Leddy's assurance that he
could "handle this situation with the Ambassador so that
Hemingway's services as an informant will be completely discon-
tinued."[62] That same day, in response to Ladd's memorandum,
Hoover wrote Leddy suggesting that he "discuss diplomatically"
his misgivings about Hemingway's intelligence operation, adding:
"Any information which you may have relating to the unreliability
of Ernest Hemingway as an informant may be discreetly brought
to the attention of Ambassador Braden. In this respect it will be
recalled that recently Hemingway gave information concerning the
refueling of submarines in Caribbean waters which has proved
unreliable."[63]

Two days later, Hoover sent an interoffice memorandum to
Agents Ladd and Tamm, warning them to put distance between the
agency and Hemingway. Anything critical that the FBI might
report to Ambassador Braden would be repeated immediately to
Hemingway. "Hemingway has no particular love of the FBI,"
Hoover wrote, "and would no doubt embark upon a campaign of
vilification." As for Hemingway's value as a counterspy, Hoover
said Ernest was "the last man, in my estimation, to be used in any
such capacity. His judgment is not of the best, and if his sobriety is
the same as it was some years ago, that is certainly questionable."[64]

With his crew dispersed for Christmas, Hemingway returned to the Finca to await the December 26 arrival of Patrick and Gregory. As soon as the boys moved in, Martha packed her unfinished novel and flew to St. Louis to visit her mother. The tension between husband and wife over the Crook Factory and the sub patrols was temporarily deflated but not forgotten. On the last day of 1942, she typed Ernest a sweet, melancholy letter, made the sadder from reading Dostoyevsky's letters to his wife. She hoped that his next patrol, scheduled to begin on January 12, would be successful.[65] As the year closed out, it was becoming obvious the tides of war were turning: the Russians were slowly and at great cost pushing the Germans out of the Caucasus; the Japanese thrust in the Pacific had been stopped; in North Africa, the British were holding their own against Rommel. When Naval Intelligence said there were no U-boats operating in the Gulf of Mexico, the usual night patrols of the sealanes out of Miami were canceled for Christmas Eve. In Japan, Prime Minister Tojo told the Japanese Diet that the real war was just beginning. Much the same might have been said about the married couple living in Finca Vigia.

CHAPTER 4

American Patrol

January to July 1943

Trapped in Chicago by foul weather, Martha explained to Ernest by letter that she could not be back at the Finca before he left on his January 12 patrol. Given that circumstance, she would spend a few more days with her mother, whom she realized was more important to her than even her stalled novel. "The story is safe inside," she said. "All that is necessary now is the discipline to finish it and I know I will do it." The letter was full of love for Ernest, which seemed to burn in Martha more fiercely when they were separated than when together. With miles between them, not knowing when she would see him next, Martha admitted their last year had been less than perfect, but there was a cathedral candle burning to protect him and the boys.[1]

The *Pilar*'s departure was also delayed until January 20. Fully outfitted with small arms, grenades, a high-frequency direction finder (Huff Duff), submarine recognition guides, code books, and a sophisticated radio complete with a Marine sergeant to operate it,[2] Ernest and his crew—Winston Guest, Gregorio Fuentes, Pachi, and Sergeant Don Saxon—put out from Cojimar in winter weather to patrol the north coast west of Bahia Honda. One of their specific charges was to relay information of the *Marques de Comillas*, which the U.S. Navy, despite Agent Leddy's assurance that the *Comillas* was not in contact with U-boats, wanted to keep under surveillance.[3] For three months now, there had been no ships sunk in the Gulf of Mexico, but "a new school of Eyeless fish," as the cautious embassy letter called the submarines, "was expected in these waters."[4]

The *Pilar* and her crew, only a tiny blip in the larger defense picture, conducted themselves as if the war depended upon their vigilance. Reports are filed on the time tables assigned; codes used; watches kept during the night hours. A running evening poker game eased the boredom of men living in cramped space and without the amenities of home. Periodically who owes whom how much is totaled up in the log book as faithfully as the expenditures of gasoline and the barometer readings.[5] Gregorio, part-time steersman and full-time cook, can with equal dexterity read water depths without reference to charts and prepare a dinner of mutton fish sautéed in lime juice, onions, and garlic. To maintain their cover story of being on a scientific expedition, the outriggers are always mounted, baited or not, as they patrol outside the coral reefs at trolling speed. Not fast enough to close on a surfaced U-boat heading away from her, the *Pilar* relied on their opponent's curiosity or his need for supplies to bring the sub to them: they were the bait. Three days after they left Cojimar, word of two possible U-boat contacts came down the intelligence chain—one on the eastern edge of the Frontier; one in the Old Bahama Channel, close enough to the *Pilar* to raise the crew's adrenaline level.[6]

Their first patrol was in bits and pieces, returning to Cojimar periodically for fuel and supplies and a few days ashore. Ernest dropped in and out of the Finca, where Martha's story of the mulatto girl's loveless marriage to the island patron was filling out. Ernest kept up with her work in progress, and also found time to reopen old wounds at the embassy. On the evening of February 8, while he and Martha were eating supper in the Floridita, they were joined by some embassy people, including the newly arrived assistant legal attaché, Ed Knoblaugh, whom Ernest and Martha once knew as a fellow journalist during the Spanish Civil War. Hemingway also knew Knoblaugh from reading his book *Correspondent in Spain*, which he felt supported Franco's revolution. Because Knoblaugh worked under the legal attaché, Agent Leddy, Ernest knew without being told that he was also a special agent for the FBI. After polite dinner conversation, Hemingway spent the next two days preparing a lengthy typed indictment of Knoblaugh, which he sent directly to Ambassador Braden.

By giving Knoblaugh oversight on Falangist activities in Cuba, the ambassador was, Ernest thought, assigning a sympathizer to report on fascist subversives. Without questioning Knoblaugh's patriotism, Hemingway cited numerous passages from *Correspondent in Spain* quoted by pro-fascist writers. He concluded that the new assistant legal attaché was "unsuited for any operations which might involve his having to investigate any Falangist or Spanish Fascist activity."[7]

Hemingway's demands that Knoblaugh be transferred were countered by Agent Leddy's defense of Knoblaugh, after which the ambassador decided that the issue was not as critical as Hemingway insisted. As Leddy informed the bureau, "It is known that Hemingway and his assistant, Gustavo Durán, have a . . . personal hostility to the FBI on an ideological basis, especially Hemingway, as he considers the FBI anti-Liberal, pro-Fascist and dangerous as developing into an American Gestapo."[8] The Civil War in Spain, supposedly finished in 1939, was still being fought in less violent ways among its several constituents. Hemingway backed off from this confrontation, returning to sea for another six weeks.

The remainder of February and all through March 1943, the *Pilar*'s crew kept uneventful watch of the bays, cays, and surface traffic in their assigned area. For almost five months now there had been no U-boat activity in the Gulf, but no sooner did they return to home port for replenishment and repairs than the German *U-155* at the end of its Caribbean patrol came through the Yucatan Channel and up the north coast of Cuba. On April 1, almost within sight of Hemingway's favorite port of Cabañas, the *U-155* torpedoed and sank the Norwegian freighter *Lysefjord*. A day longer on station would have put the *Pilar* in the rescue operation that saved eleven of the freighter's crew. Two days later the American tanker *Gulfstate* was sent to the bottom of the Florida Straits by the same U-boat. While Hemingway caught up with correspondence and his crew enjoyed shore leave, the Gulf Frontier Command made every effort to trap and destroy the German raider. Armed blimps and aircraft flew day and night over the three escape routes out of the

Gulf. The Cuban Navy sent three newly acquired cutters to patrol the Old Bahama Channel. After a week of false leads and no hard contacts, it was assumed the U-boat had slipped through the net and was on its way back to Germany.[9] During the six weeks the *Pilar* was re-outfitted for an extended patrol, two merchantmen were torpedoed in the Old Bahama Channel, triggering an intense response from the Commander of the Gulf Sea Frontier. On May 15, five miles behind a passing convoy, a positive sub contact was made in the heart of the Nicholas Channel, redoubling the search, which yielded no further results but cost four planes that went down in the Gulf during the operation.

Hemingway used the down time to write his old friend, Archibald MacLeish, now heading President Roosevelt's Office of Facts and Figures, about their mutual friend and longtime expatriate, Ezra Pound. Since January 1941, Pound had been making regular radio broadcasts from Rome, spewing vitriolic anti-Semitism and supporting the Fascist government of Mussolini while belittling the British and American war efforts. MacLeish himself was targeted by Pound, who characterized Archie's new appointment as "a gangster's brief and he has been entrusted with the defense of a gang of criminals and he is a-doing his damnedest."[10] In April, Hemingway asked MacLeish for the timetable and wavelength of Pound's broadcasts, thinking to listen in on the *Pilar*'s sophisticated shortwave receiver. Certain that Ezra would eventually face an American court, Hemingway wanted to be informed, for he and Archie, as old friends of Ezra from their Paris days, might have to testify.[11] On May 5, writing from the Finca, Ernest thanked MacLeish for the Pound information and asked for photostats of Ezra's broadcasts. "If Ezra had any sense," he said, "he would shoot himself."[12] After Pound was indicted for treason by a federal grand jury, Hemingway wrote Allen Tate that those whom Ezra once helped must do all they could to prevent his postwar hanging even if it meant climbing up on the gallows with him.[13]

On May 20, the daily intelligence report from the Gulf Frontier Command alerted its several components that the Hemingway crew was back on the water:

COMGULF advised that . . . Havana had reported that the American 38 foot motor boat PILAR, black hull and green deck, was operating from Havana eastward along the north coast of Cuba on a scientific mission and identifies herself on aircraft approach by an American flag during the day and flashing "V" at night.[14]

Passing quickly through the Nicholas Channel to the hunting grounds of the Old Bahama Channel, the *Pilar* ran inside the reefs, checking the bays and inlets; somewhere along the north coast of Cuba, Gulf Command said a U-boat was lurking.[15] On May 29, Hemingway and crew set up rough camp on Confites, a flat disk of sand with a few palm trees, a wooden shack with a radio antenna, and the Cuban colors flying from a flagpole. A bored Cuban officer and two enlisted men who manned the isolated station were an unenthusiastic welcoming party. The next morning Hemingway sent Winston Guest in their auxiliary boat into Nuevitas, where there was an American consul and a U.S. Navy liaison office which would be their supply depot for the next two months. Two days later, Wolfie returned with twelve live chickens, two turkeys, one small pig, soda water, and eggs. On Confites, the crew established their menagerie, fattened the pig on corn and garbage, and conserved water, for it would be almost two weeks before they could be resupplied.[16]

Each morning they were up and out on the channel before nine, running at trolling speed and noting down any passing traffic for their evening radio report. Each evening they came into Confites with the light failing, measured their port and starboard fuel tanks, and cleaned up the *Pilar* for the next day's patrol.[17] While Gregorio prepared supper, Don Saxon made his coded radio report of the day's observations and took down instructions for patrol duty. Almost every evening Ernest wrote Martha back at the Finca, even though the letters might wait for days before being sent ashore. After supper, the evening poker game by lamplight commenced. If the sea breeze died, mosquitoes would end the game early. When the once-a-week mailboat came by, a new chapter of Martha's novel in progress would arrive for Ernest's critique: Liana, the native wife

of a rich, white patron who treated her as a possession, was deeply
in love with a French tutor hired by her husband to civilize her.
Caught between two worlds—a dirty shack in the hills where her
mother lived in poverty and the white world of her husband—
Liana was no longer happy in either. Winston Guest remembered
Hemingway sitting "up late with an oil lamp reading and correcting" the manuscript.[18] On most nights, the captain and crew were
asleep before ten and up with morning sunrise.

Later, some acquaintances would say that it was all a lark, a way
to get rationed gasoline for the *Pilar*, but none of those people were
on Confites that June of 1943 when the U-boat war resumed, and
Ernest never told them about it. After months of comparative quiet,
during which the Gulf Command in no way relaxed its vigilance,
intelligence reports indicated that the Germans were sending subs
back into the Gulf. All that June at Cayo Frances, the twelve Navy
officers and seventy-eight enlisted men were on constant alert,
their seaplanes on daily patrol. The *Pilar* was sent into isolated cays
to search for transmitters alerting U-boats of convoys passing
through the Old Bahama Channel. June 8–10, Operation
Friendless, as Ernest had named the operation after one of his
Finca cats, went ashore on Cayo Chico and Cayo Megano Grande,
assuring the Gulf Command there were no *fugaze* (fugitives) on
those islets.[19] On June 8, ASW Group 5 at Cayo Frances was ordered
to intensify its search for a U-boat entering the Old Bahama
Channel at the edge of the *Pilar*'s patrol area. On June 14, while the
Pilar was on patrol for sixteen hours, the planes of ASW-5 dropped
"mouse traps" and depth charges on a U-boat in 400 fathoms of
water off nearby Cayo Fragoso, producing an oil slick five miles
long with enough flotsam to call it a "likely sinking."[20]

After the early June flurry of action, silence descended on the
channel: no German voices broadcasting late at night; no U-boats
reported in the close vicinity. The convoy system and heavy patrols
had accomplished their mission. On June 16, Hemingway's two
vacationing sons, Patrick and Gregory, in the tow of Winston Guest,
joined their father on Confites. During eleven days with no children to bother her, Martha was able to finish the novel, which was
called *Liana* for lack of a better title.[21] Liana's tutor and lover,

Pierre, after promising to take her away with him to Martinique, gives in to her husband, Marc Royer, who convinces Pierre that he could never take a Negro wife back to France, nor does he have any way to support her in Martinique. Consoled with Marc's promise that he would not send Liana back to live in a shack, Pierre slips away from the island in Marc's motorboat. Liana, seeing herself as merchandise at the mercy of white men, uses Marc's last razor blade to slit her wrist.[22] On one of his return trips to Finca Vigía, Hemingway referred to Martha's fiction and their own lives, saying that she had him mixed up with Marc Royer. There was no need for Martha to destroy the love they shared to take a foreign correspondent's job, although he thought she was foolish to pursue her irrecoverable youth.[23]

On Confites, his young sons sometimes went out on the daily patrols, but most often were left ashore with Gregorio as guardian.[24] With his new telescope Patrick bird-watched by day, star-watched by night. Greg collected shells, swam inside the reef, fished, and watched the palms blow. The high point of any week was the arrival of the supply boat, the *Margarita*, carrying blesséd ice, fresh bottles of water, canned fruit, sometimes a bottle of McCallum's Perfection Scotch Whiskey, sometimes even Coca-Colas. Each day Winston Guest diligently took their live pig out for a swim, so diligently in fact that one day Gregory, out goggle-fishing, looked up to see the pig swimming out to sea, finally disappearing over the horizon. At night, as often as not, Ernest could be seen beneath his kerosene lamp rereading *War and Peace*. Back at the Finca, Martha was threatening to have two of the male cats castrated in order to control their violent night fights. Ernest hated the idea, saying he would rather have the vet kill them or that he would kill them himself when he returned. He promised Martha that as soon as he got his submarine, he would help her get wherever on the war front she wanted to go.[25]

After forty days at sea, working in cramped quarters, the *Pilar*'s captain and crew were beginning to get on each other's nerves. No matter how tasty, Gregorio's cooking was now boring. They never had enough ice, beer, or gin. On July 4 their permit to operate from Confites expired, but they had no message from Naval Intelligence to return to Havana. Bored and on edge, Hemingway wrote Martha a seven-page, lonely letter asking her not to give up on him and reminding her how easily and deeply she was able to hurt him with threats of leaving the Finca, whose exterior was now pink over faded yellow. Maybe he was as ugly as she said he was, and maybe he could not dance because she said he could not, but inside he felt as if he was still in his twenties. And Mr. Scrooby, his faithful penis, was eager to return to her. Two nights before, he dreamed that he had made love to a lovely, silver-colored bear, which was a sure sign it was time for him to come home.[26] Finally, on the morning of July 9, Don Saxon copied out the coded orders telling Hemingway that his patrol was over, his permit to return to Havana arriving on the supply boat along with future plans for Operation Friendless.[27]

After months of heavy duty, the *Pilar*'s engine was in bad shape, intake and exhaust valves loose, piston rings badly worn, gaskets corroded, prop damaged, and her drive shaft out of alignment.[28] The next day she began her slow trip back to Havana, the crew weary but ready for shore leave, and equally ready to be set free from the malodorous feet of Don Saxon, festering with jungle rot, which had not responded to Ernest's treatment of sulfa drugs. On July 18, the *Pilar* limped into Cojimar harbor, Ernest fully bearded and his two sons much browner than when they left. The day after they returned, a Navy blimp while attacking a U-boat in the Florida Straits was shot down by the sub's 20mm guns. Nine of the blimp's crew survived; one man was eaten by sharks.[29]

A year later, *Saturday Evening Post* would publish "The Battle of Florida," making public, in a small way, the story of the Gulf Frontier Command's war with the U-boats. Explaining how initially ill prepared the United States was for battling the raiders and how the magnitude of the sinkings was kept secret in 1942–43, the article gave examples of civilian yachtsmen performing heroically against the U-boats. The quickly formed Coast Guard Auxiliary had men like Willard Lewis who encountered a U-boat on the surface and was nearly successful in his effort to ram it with his forty-five-foot fishing boat. When asked what he expected to accomplish by ramming a steel submarine with a small wooden boat, Lewis replied, "I aimed at her conning tower, and I might have messed up something. That sub was trying to get men ashore. I thought so then, and I was sure of it when it turned out that saboteurs had been landed later on that night farther up the coast." Actions by civilian volunteers, operating mostly at their own expense, were kept secret by the government in order to make the effort effective and for fear of turning every small fishing boat into a Nazi target. "The minutemen in motorboats did not greatly affect the formidable course of the struggle itself," the *Post* story said. "They were a mere stop gap—the 'something' that was better than nothing."[30]

Upon returning to Havana, the first thing Hemingway did was order a new marine engine for the *Pilar*.[31] The first thing Don Saxon did was get roaring drunk, arrested, and bailed out by the naval attaché. Patrick and Gregory helped Martha and the embassy crowd plan Ernest's forty-fourth birthday and welcome-back-from-the-sub-wars party. It began at the Club Cazadores del Cerro where the best wing shots in Cuba gathered to test each other against the flight of *tira pichon* (live pigeons) with sizable bets riding on the side. For the party, "the most unorthodox collection of targets were set before shotguns . . . pigeons . . . a covey of quail . . . six [Mexican] tree ducks . . . a half bushel of Cuban oysters with mangrove steamers . . . a dead guinea pig, seven clawless lobsters, and four small tuna. Constantino, the bar tender at the Floridita, contributed an immense . . . moro crab . . . [which] would be saved for Ernest's last shot."[32]

After considerable drinking at the club, shooters and shouters regrouped at the Finca beneath the enormous ceiba tree for a pig roast that started with a priest's blessing, at the end of which one of the Basque jai alai players beaned another Basque with a hard roll. Ernest rose to his feet, and from his patriarchal beard came the judgment: "That was wrong. On my birthday you can't throw rolls until dessert. *No hast'el postre.*"[33]

CHAPTER 5

Intermezzo

August 1943 to May 1944

They had been a couple now for seven years, the first four clandestine, the next three married. Their affair, begun in war-torn Spain, was cathartic for both; their exhausting trip to China, a bonding experience. But their life at the Finca became a Jekyll and Hyde marriage that neither Martha nor Ernest nor anyone else understood very well. Apart, they wrote each other loving letters. Together for longer than a week, they embarrassed their friends with loud arguments. Living in comparative luxury in a peaceful setting while the wider world was burning pricked Martha to her very core. She was too comfortable, too safe, too domesticated. In one of her last letters to arrive at Confites, written in that bittersweet sadness of having finished her novel, she tried to explain her condition:

> I wish we could stop it all now, the prestige, the possessions, the position, the knowledge, the victory. . . . You have been married so much and so long, that I do not believe it [marriage] can touch you where you live and that is your strength. It would be terrible if it did because you are so much more important than the women you happen to be married to. . . . I would like to be young and poor and in Milan and with you and not married to you. I think I always wanted to feel in some way like a woman, and if I ever did, it was the first winter in Madrid. There was a sort of blindness and fervor and recklessness about that sort of feeling which one must always want. I hate being so wise and so careful, so reliable, so denatured, so able to get on.[1]

She was certain he would not understand her letter, which he did not. They could not go back: the past was irretrievable except with words on paper.

No sooner was Ernest back from Confites than he was talking about the *Pilar*'s next extended cruise. At the same time, *Collier's* asked Martha to go to England as their correspondent. After having spent six months as lady of the Finca with its attendant responsibilities, Martha felt as if she were becoming someone she never wanted to be: a housewife. More and more their arguments centered on Ernest's failure to commit to the war as a journalist, which was the only role that Martha could envision. Ernest could not or did not want to understand his wife's need to reaffirm her identity as Martha Gellhorn. Martha never understood his morbid loneliness when left alone, particularly at night. All that late summer and early fall of 1943, they sniped at each other in vicious ways that usually worsened the more Ernest drank. Gregory, who remembered his father as a heavy drinker in Key West but seldom drunk, was surprised to see Ernest drunk at the Finca, where he also allowed both Greg and Patrick to drink. Ernest's theory was that the boys would learn their limits and remain within them. "Papa would be just drunk out of his mind, but able to do it because Juan (the chauffeur) would drive the car home. So he could get as drunk as he wanted. . . . He'd have all these drinks at the Floridita . . . just unbelievable drinking." Or so it seemed to a twelve-year-old Greg.[2]

There was no easy answer to his father's drinking, nor to his irrational arguments with Martha, but Greg had seen it all before in the Key West house when his father's second marriage was coming apart because of Martha. This time there was no other woman. There was only the war to which Martha longed to go, and about which Ernest had mixed feelings. Because neither Ernest nor Martha felt connected to the war in the Pacific, their eyes turned only toward Europe. Ernest had been to a European war in 1918 when he believed that the world could be made safe for democracy; he still had shrapnel in his legs and a rebuilt right kneecap to remind him of that war and the death he almost bought there. Taking serious risks with little apparent fear or forethought,

Martha never seemed to consider her own mortality; Ernest lived with his like an old friend.

For a year now he had been fighting this war as best he could—counterintelligence and submarine patrols—living largely in a male world with occasional spots of domesticity. It was a world cut off from Martha except for the rowdy shore leave drinking at the Finca between cruises. During that year, the global war had changed. Rommel and his Panzer forces were run out of North Africa; Allied troops had invaded Sicily; from forward bases, bombers were systematically destroying Nazi ports, factories, rail centers, and airfields. In the mid- and North Atlantic, the German U-boats were so decimated during the first six months of 1943—151 U-boats destroyed—that the Gulf of Mexico was no longer threatened. Martha, who put little credence in her husband's tales of the north Cuban coast, urged him to give up the submarine patrols and come to England with her, for in his absence, she had accepted the *Collier's* ETO (European Theater of Operations) assignment. As Ernest admitted in letters, they needed the income *Collier's* offered, for he was living on savings and advance loans from Scribner's, and Martha insisted on paying for her share of their household expenses. For Martha, the assignment was more than a paycheck: if she could get Ernest to England, together again with the "chaps," they might recapture the excitement of Madrid when life was a day-to-day proposition and artillery shells rattled their hotel.

Martha misunderstood Ernest's lack of interest in going to another war as a journalist, but then she misunderstood the *Pilar* patrols also. Having spent six weeks as a Red Cross man in World War I (1918), and having covered the Greco-Turkish War (1922) as a reporter for the *Toronto Daily Star* and the Spanish Civil War (1937–39) as a journalist for NANA (North American News Alliance), Ernest was loath to repeat the frustrations of watching the action without being able to participate, and not since his brief experience as a reporter in Toronto (1923–24) had he written news stories. He was a feature story writer whose personal perspective was always a key ingredient in the story. Already there were hundreds of competent journalists supporting the U.S. war effort, younger men without bum legs who, when the time came, would go ashore with troops, leap out of airplanes with the paratroopers, and give America's newspapers the stories the censors wanted them to read. That was their job, but it was not Hemingway's job. Having grown up as a boy with a grandfather who commanded troops in the Civil War, having observed the deployment of troops at close range in Spain, and having studied battlefield tactics in books from the time of Napoleon forward, Ernest wanted to command troops in battle, but with the freedom that independent ven tures like the *Pilar* patrols allowed. His story of the dynamiter and the partisan guerrillas in *For Whom the Bell Tolls* was a fantasy close to his heart. He did not want an honorary commission to feed the U.S. propaganda machine, nor did he want to become a cog in some huge operation over which he had no control. In May 1942, he explained to Max Perkins that he was willing to go to the war, send his sons to the war, and give his money to the war effort. The one thing he could not do was write propaganda.[3] With the exception of his introduction for *Men at War*, as Ernest reminded his editor and his publisher, he had not written anything in three years. This hiatus, the longest of his career, made him prickly and short-tempered, which did nothing to improve his relationship with Martha.

A year earlier, in response to an irritating inquiry as to what he was doing for the war effort, he replied that in 1945 he would be glad to match war records with the questioner "for a nickel a side. We can also put in all our children's war records at a nickel apiece (ones who get killed count a dime). At that point we will also match Martha's war record (all time) against Mrs. Grovers. Then we will take all the nickels and melt them up to be cast into a medal to honor the winner."[4] He told Archie MacLeish that he once considered asking for a commission as friends of theirs had done, but gave it a pass, preferring to operate without any officer's insignia on his collar. Due to the secrecy of his patrol and wartime censorship (the FBI was reading some of his mail), he could not tell Archie about the *Pilar*, but after the coming summer he thought he might "be of some use in China."[5] In August, Hemingway asked MacLeish if there was any possibility of the government sending writers to war, not to write journalism or propaganda, but to gain the firsthand experience to write the books that needed to be written when the war was over. Maybe the Library of Congress could send him over as its correspondent?[6]

All of August and September, Ernest fretted over the redeployment of the *Pilar*, but one delay after another kept him ashore, where he listened to war news on the radio and answered letters in which he was frequently talking to himself. To a fellow writer who recently broke through an inactive period to write again, Ernest quoted Martha saying that "stalled" periods were an occupational hazard. All a writer needed to do to feel right about himself at day's end was to write well that morning. "Biting on the old nail never feels good," he advised, "[but] that is what we have to do and if we do not do it we end up as bad fathers and everything else."[7] The "old nail" of which he spoke was three years rusting on his writing desk, and two more years would pass before he put it between his teeth again.

At the beginning of September, Jack Hemingway, a newly commissioned lieutenant in the Military Police, visited briefly at the Finca before going on to his first duty station at Fort Custer, Michigan. At the same time Ernest was receiving letters from Oak Park neighbors advising him that his mother, Grace, was sick and becoming worse. "Your mother does not feel she is going to get well," a friend of his mother told him. "If it is at all possible for you to come, do so. A mother's first born son has a very close place in her heart." By the time Ernest received clearer information, Grace (seventy-one) had been in and out of a coma and was on her way to recovery, but the reminder of being her firstborn son produced the usual equivocal responses in Hemingway.[8] His mother, whom he blamed for his father's suicide, whom he reviled as an "all-American bitch," and from whose creative nature came much of his own drive, was a constant irritant to Hemingway. Scarcely a friend or passing stranger escaped without hearing of his horrible mother. If he resented ambitious, creative, independent women, that resentment linked directly to his feelings about Grace. That he married just such a woman in Martha was a conundrum, as were so many of his mixed feelings about married life. He wanted a home, but spent little time there. As soon as a passionate woman became his wife and mother to his children, he began to feel trapped; but should that woman leave him alone for longer than a week, he became morose, vulnerable, and began to speak of his own death. If he exploded in senseless arguments with Martha, he first learned that behavior listening to his parents in the far room, his mother usually dominant. What young Gregory witnessed that summer at the Finca were arguments rooted in Oak Park.

On September 20, Martha left for New York to begin her *Collier's* assignment, and the *Pilar* should have put to sea soon after, but Ernest and Martha both faced delays. It took Martha a full month of bureaucratic red tape before she could depart for England. In New York, while she waited, she saw the film version of *A Farewell to Arms*, and while visiting Eleanor Roosevelt at the White House, she saw a private showing of *For Whom the Bell Tolls*, with Gary Cooper playing the leads in both films. Before leaving New York, she wrote Ernest a long letter, professing her love for him and hoping that she was not too bad a wife. She was happy to be back in the thick of things, but "like woman, and your woman, am sad; only there isn't anything final, is there? This is just a short trip and we are both coming back from our short trips to our lovely home . . . and then we'll write books and see the autumns together and walk around the corn fields waiting for the pheasants."[9]

That October in the Gulf Sea Frontier, fifty-three convoys passed back and forth without a single loss, in fact, without a single attack. The Command lost seven planes and two blimps to the usual kinds of errors in judgment, but raised not a single German U-boat.[10] War in the Gulf of Mexico, which only a year before was irregular and dangerous, had become systematic and boring, but demanding no less vigilance. Hemingway looked elsewhere for action. Walking down Obispo Street to wait for Winston Guest at the Floridita, he was not eager to tell his executive officer that the *Pilar* still lacked clearance from the U.S. Navy and the embassy to begin its patrol. With nothing happening in the Gulf, they had requested permission to operate the *Pilar* in Caribbean waters, using the base at Guantanamo for supplies. They should have been on their way at

the end of July. Now, three months later, Ernest and Wolfie were
still ashore winning side bets at the skeet and pigeon range. All the
exciting possibilities came to nothing. They led a makeshift crew
out for short cruises in early November, but the patrol log of the
Pilar was closed, never to reopen.

With no more sailoring to do and left too much alone at the
Finca, Ernest was not at his best. Facing a Christmas Day without
his wife, he lived in an empty house with cats his only company.
Drinking too much, too often, and feeling too sorry for himself,
Hemingway complained to almost every correspondent about
Martha's absence. The day after Christmas, he told Archie
MacLeish that being without Martha was like having his heart cut
out. With so much of his love invested in her, he "would be in a bad
place" should anything happen to her.[11] Unfortunately, he was less
tender in his letters to Martha. In London, weak but recovering
from multiple viruses, Martha still hoped to hear that Ernest was
coming to the war zone. Everyone she met asked about him, wondered where he was, when he would be there. Every time she
begged Ernest to come be with her, he responded that he was doing
his assigned job in Cuba. She predicted that he would regret his
decision later, but she would not ask again. "I have to live my way
as well as [you] yours or there would not be any me to love you
with. You really wouldn't want me if I built a fine big stone wall
around the Finca and sat inside." Nine days later, after reprofessing
her love for him, Martha admitted to Ernest that life at the Finca
now seemed to her "remote and somehow awful." Dreading it, she
compared it to being strangled "by those beautiful tropical flowers
that can swallow cows!"[12]

Whatever the reasons, the equation for Hemingway changed:
the Gulf Frontier Command no longer needed an irregular Navy;
the Allied invasion of France was clearly going to happen; and
Martha was not coming home soon. Winston Guest, at the age of
thirty-seven, joined the Marines; John Thomason was in the
Pacific; Jack Hemingway was transferring from the Military
Police to a newly formed group called the Office of Strategic
Services (OSS) where Winston's brother, Raymond, and David
Bruce were players. On January 13, 1944, Ernest grudgingly wrote

Martha that he was closing down the *Pilar* patrols, closing down the house, and coming to England as soon as his present cruise was completed.

After playing in the outfield of the war game, albeit a very remote outfield, going back to journalism was like throwing down his glove to take a seat in the stands. Her arguments for being in the war zone were, he agreed, all sound for her, but as for being a part of history, well, fuck history. When the war began, he said he never thought he would outlive it, or that he would ever have to write another book, implying that a death foreseen awaited him, if not on patrol then perhaps in Europe.

She should blame his bitterness on his inability to sleep soundly, his enforced celibacy, and his frustration of having to give up active participation in the war. When he did sleep, his dreams were filled with frustration. Recently he dreamed that her luggage was left at a metro station where she was embarking on a ship. He cut across the electrified rail, picked up the luggage and with great effort got it to Martha, who was unimpressed, aloof, and critical, telling him that if he wanted to be with her that he needed to respond quicker. He signed the letter as her loving husband.[13]

Seventeen days later, the *Pilar* returned to Cojimar, her career as a clandestine naval auxiliary finished. The following day, Ernest wrote Martha, repeating that he would soon be joining her, but not to expect him to take any special interest in the venture. He was like an old horse being forced to take the steeplechase jumps against his better judgment. Being a professional he would jump as well as he was able, but he would take no joy in it. Had she allowed him to remain on patrol, a fine novel would have come out of his experiences, but now he would lose the story, for journalism would erase it from his head.[14]

Two days later, writing to an old friend, Hemingway casually announced that he expected to be in New York in about two weeks, for he was too lonely at the Finca without Martha. "Now I hope I will meet her where I go," he wrote, without saying where he was going. As soon as he took care of the thirteen cats, five dogs, fighting cocks, and pigeons, he would be on his way. The anger inside him, at a boil without a focus, needed direction. A married man with family responsibilities could not afford "the luxury of being killed," he said, unless he left his dependents well provided.[15]

Ernest's deliberately oblique and vague references to his plan for getting to the war are puzzling. He may have already begun his negotiations with *Collier's* magazine to sign on as their front-line correspondent. Who made that first contact is not clear, but for certain the possibility was discussed with Charles Colebaugh, Martha's editor at *Collier's*, and Martha must have known about it, if not in London, certainly in New York when she passed through en route to Cuba. On March 10, Colebaugh wrote Hemingway that he would have to embark for Europe via New York, but it would take two weeks in the city to arrange all the documents.[16]

The week of March 13, when Martha returned to the Finca, her husband's unfocused anger found a target. For public consumption in *Collier's*, Hemingway remained his wife's professional admirer: "When she is at the front or getting there, she will get up earlier, travel longer and faster and go where no other woman can get and where few could stick it out if they did. . . . She gets to the place, gets the story, writes it and comes home. That last is the best part."[17] With Max Perkins he could make rough jokes about how a bossy woman, once given the rank of captain, would never give it up; his only choice was to get a higher rank so he could say, "Roll over captain, a period of strenuous calisthenics is about to begin."[18] In the privacy of their bedroom, his demeanor was alarmingly different. Having sent her succinct telegrams—"ARE YOU A WAR CORRESPONDENT OR MY WIFE IN BED"—he now opened up with heavy artillery. As Martha told Bernice Kert some years later,

> Ernest began at once to rave at me. . . . He woke me when I was trying to sleep to bully, snarl, mock—my crime really was to have been at war when he had not, but that was not how he put it. I was supposedly insane, I only wanted excitement and danger, I had no responsibility to anyone. I was selfish beyond belief . . . it never stopped. . . . I put it to him that I was going back, whether he came or not.[19]

Having never seen her husband behave like this, Martha, even at several years remove, did not consider that Ernest might be suffering from something other than loneliness. The charges of being insane, of seeking out danger, or acting selfishly and irresponsibly applied as much to himself as to her. His son Gregory firmly believed that his father changed during that 1943–44 period into a different person. Hemingway's last wife, Mary Welsh, would experience the same sort of abuse that Martha reported. It was as if some inner, furious animal was set loose, an animal over which Hemingway had some control in public, but little at home. Anyone looking backward from 1960–61 might say that his behavior was a manifestation of the depression that eventually destroyed him. But that March of 1944, no one around him, least of all Martha, had the experience, training, or clinical knowledge to understand Hemingway's behavior as anything but outrageous and intolerable.

At the end of March, Hemingway wrote Colebaugh at *Collier's* that he and Martha were booked to fly into New York on April 23. In the letter he enclosed a commendation from Ambassador Braden, thanking Hemingway for carrying out "highly confidential intelligence activities" which he could not spell out until the war was over. Braden went on to thank Ernest for doing "certain other work, likewise of a confidential nature, involving personal risks and ever-present danger." Ernest asked Colebaugh to keep the letter confidential, for he wanted no publicity for this work.[20] When the syndicated columnist Earl Wilson found Hemingway in New York—fully bearded and overweight at 220 pounds—working out with the trainer, George Brown, Ernest was all sweetness and light with regard to Martha.[21] Like many manic-depressives, he could be as nice as pie in public and a son of a bitch in private. He could also keep a secret. Neither Martha nor Colebaugh knew that Hemingway had volunteered for assignment to the recently formed OSS, perhaps offering his journalist's credentials as his cover story—a scenario imagined seven years earlier in his play, *The Fifth Column*. On May 1, that offer was declined in a once secret document that read:

MECATO 3> OSS Will Not Use Hemingway. (GB-002-425, Shepherdson to Joyce.) Decided in the negative about

Hemingway. We may be wrong, but feel that, although he undoubtedly has conspicuous abilities for this type of work, he would be too much of an individualist to work under military supervision.[22]

When the Hemingways arrived in New York, Ernest became *Collier's* front-line correspondent—each magazine was limited to one—and Martha took an assignment that confined her, in theory, to the rear of that line. Later Martha would say that Ernest "automatically destroyed my chances of covering the fighting war."[23] If that was Hemingway's intention, Gellhorn's credits with *Collier's* in 1944–45 document his ineffectiveness. Martha forgot to remember the War Department ruling that female correspondents could "go no farther forward than women's services go," restricting Martha and fellow female correspondents to hospital areas. "Women were accredited to the war zones. They did not have accreditation to military units, as required for admission to press camps at the front." To defy these limits made a female correspondent liable to lose her credentials and even face court-martial. The U.S. Army, which had not wanted any female correspondents in Europe, specifically forbade them from covering the Normandy invasion. When Martha was on the beach with a hospital unit at D-Day +1, the Army press officers punished her for defying orders by not allowing her to accompany the other women when they were finally allowed ashore.[24] Ernest or no Ernest on their payroll, *Collier's* could not send Martha to the war as their front-line correspondent; had Colebaugh not hired her husband, he would have hired some other man.

If he did not exactly take her job, Ernest certainly did his best to punish Martha for being Martha, who acted, he claimed, with the willfulness of a spoiled child, but "always for the noblest motives."[25] When he refused to arrange a seat for her on his scheduled flight to England, Martha, angry and determined, found passage on a dynamite-laden freighter leaving New York on May 13. Ernest spent the following afternoon at Port Jefferson, Long Island, in writer Dawn Powell's beach cottage, where she noted in her journal: "Hemingway down all day yesterday—exhausted by his immense gusto—someone who gives out more in six hours than most people do in a lifetime—leaves you groggy."[26]

Arriving by military plane in England on May 17 two weeks before Martha's freighter docked, Hemingway quickly caught the war fever that made each moment potentially the last, each embrace a possible farewell.[27] In New York he had berated Martha, saying he would probably be killed in Europe, hoping that would satisfy her.[28] But at London's Dorchester Hotel his old journalist friends found him affable and expansive. Meanwhile, Martha was experiencing frugal life aboard a wartime freighter slowly convoying its way across the still dangerous Atlantic, where Nazi wolf packs were decimated but not yet out of business. In her notes she called the eighteen-day voyage "a fine rest cure," but she also remembered the food was terrible; there was nothing alcoholic to drink; with a habit of two packs of cigarettes a day, she, the only passenger, could not smoke. If she arrived in London a bit testy, there were good reasons.[29]

While Martha was at sea, Hemingway was busy cultivating RAF pilots for a story about their night raids on German targets. He was also cultivating a small, lovely, American journalist whose British husband was out of the country. In those last, mad days before the great invasion, Mary Welsh, whose by-line appeared in both *Time* and *Life*, did not lack for male attention. Novelist Irwin Shaw and *Time/Life* correspondent Bill Walton were both her frequent companions at the White Tower restaurant, and more than one senior officer was taken by her midwestern confidence, curly hair, and blue eyes. One day at lunch, Shaw pointed out the bulky figure of Ernest Hemingway across the room. Mary, whose sweater made it clear she was wearing no bra, was being greeted by every passing male acquaintance: "Nice sweater," or, "The warmth does bring things out doesn't it?" When Hemingway, who knew Shaw, came to their table asking for an introduction, Shaw obliged, and told Mary afterward that it had been nice to know her. She didn't understand, but she soon would. Before Martha Gellhorn ever stepped ashore in England, Ernest was telling Mary Welsh, "I don't know you, Mary. But I want to marry you. . . . I want to marry you now, and I hope to marry you sometime. Sometime you may want to marry me." [30]

Mary did not know what to make of his sad face or of his voice filled with loneliness, nor could she imagine the emotional maelstrom into which she was being drawn.

At three in the morning a few days later, Hemingway pulled his face back from the shattered windshield of a friend's car to find warm blood running into his eyes. Drunker than he should have been but no drunker than the driver, neither of them saw the steel water tank in the blacked-out London street. Hemingway's scalp was neatly parted in a shallow but ugly gash that put him once more in a hospital emergency room. Already he carried plenty of scars from other woundings: his right foot and knee were scarred from the 1918 trench mortar shell on the Piave River; his forehead bulged from the night emergency-room visit in 1927 Paris when he accidentally pulled the bathroom skylight down on top of himself; beneath his beard there was a scar from the veterinarian stitching up his face when his horse bolted through the Wyoming thicket in 1930; and his right arm bore scars from repairwork to a compound spiral fracture from a 1930 auto wreck outside Billings, Montana.

Arriving at Liverpool on May 31, Martha soon discovered that Ernest was a London patient in St. George's Hospital. The first news releases reported him dead, but the next day, May 25, *The Times* said he "was slightly injured early yesterday . . . when a car crashed into an emergency water tank at Lowndes Square." The slight injury required over fifty stitches, not to mention the ear-ringing concussion that Hemingway carried with him for weeks afterward. But when Martha arrived at his hospital room, she found her husband holding court with a roomful of visitors who were making ample use of his liquor supply, reconstructing his Milan hospital room from a world war earlier. Having had plenty of time at sea to review their relationship, Martha entered the room half sure their marriage was over; when she left, she had no doubts. "If he really had a concussion," she explained to Bernice Kert, "he could hardly have been drinking with his pals or even receiving them. He did not look the least ill anyway."[31] The concussion was real enough, and drinking was a sure way to make it worse. Ernest, garrulous and full of male-bonding jokes ("I never had a WAC shot out from under me"), was with Martha in the war zone as she had so fervently desired, but it was a husband she hardly recognized. If war released her from life at the Finca, it set Ernest free in ways she had not imagined. Before the ground war began on the beaches of Normandy, the private war between Martha and Ernest was finished. There was no acknowledgment of defeat by either party, but that was only a formality.

CHAPTER 6

Putting on the Ritz

June, July, August 1944

In the predawn hours of June 6, 1944, Hemingway was wide awake, his head still ringing from his recent concussion, his scalp wounds not yet completely healed beneath the bandage. He was not the only man wide awake aboard the *Empire Anvil* and the hundreds of other transports crossing the English Channel toward France. The great crusade to liberate Europe, the most complex military maneuver in history, was closing on the beaches of Normandy, its outcome uncertain. Like his shipmates, Hemingway's view of the operation was limited to his line of sight. He could not see the incredible size of the Allied armada, but he could hear salvos from battleships, cruisers, and destroyers pounding the German fortifications. On Hemingway's briefing map, the Normandy beaches were labeled "Sword," "Juno," "Gold," "Omaha," and "Utah." The narrow sector on which Hemingway focused was labeled "Fox Green" on the left flank of Omaha Beach, where 34,000 soldiers were about to go ashore under fire.

His head wound still fresh and with both knees swollen, Hemingway climbed down his ship's rope ladder into a landing craft, only to be transferred to another ship, up and down another rope ladder, and finally into the small, crowded landing craft. Here his vision was even more limited. In the first gray light of dawn, hundreds of landing craft wallowed in the rough sea, trying to group for the charge toward the beach. Hemingway described the scene for his *Collier's* readers:

As the boat rose to a sea, the green water turned white and came slamming in over the men, the guns and the cases of explosives. Ahead you could see the coast of France. The gray booms and derrick-forested bulks of the attack transports were behind now, and, over all the sea, boats were crawling forward toward France.[1]

Some men were praying, some seasick and puking, no one was talking. On that same sea 5,000 ships were sending 150,000 men onto beaches from which there was no retreat. If they could not break through the German defenses, they were lost souls.

On paper and in practice sessions, the Normandy invasion went smoothly enough considering its complexity, but in briefing rooms the sea was calm, no smoke obscured key landmarks, and there was no confusion among the landing craft. At the Fox Green sector of Omaha Beach, reality was far removed from theory. As naval historians later assessed:

> The resulting difficulties of the boat teams were heightened by the frequent separation of sections of the same company. Whether because of delays suffered by individual craft, straggling on the way in, or disagreement between coxswains in recognition of landmarks, some unit formations of landing craft were broken up enough to result in widely scattered landings. Under conditions prevailing at the beach, separation of craft by as little as 200 yards could easily bring about the complete isolation of a section.[2]

Before that day was done, one thousand soldiers died on Omaha Beach. Some were wounded to drown in the surf. Some were blown up with their landing craft. Many died facedown in the sand of Fox Green and Easy Red where German gunners had easy targets.

From the landing craft Hemingway scanned the horizon with his field glasses, picking out the Coleville church steeple as a guide. The coxswain could not decide if the route into the beach was clear of mines; the lieutenant was not sure if this was Fox Green or if they should put ashore. Finally, confused and frustrated, they began the run into the beach where Hemingway could see that "the first, second, third, fourth and fifth waves [of landing troops] lay where they had fallen, looking like so many heavily laden bundles on that flat pebbly stretch between the sea and the first cover." When the German machine-gun fire picked out their landing craft, Hemingway dropped down, and the lieutenant took the LCVP back out to sea. If that was Fox Green, it had not been cleared of mines in the water, nor had the tanks, two of which were burning on the beach, done their job. Later, when Navy destroyers blasted out some of the German guns, Hemingway's landing craft finally got its men and supplies into the surf and quickly backed out again, picking its way through underwater obstacles tipped with contact mines. Bearing evidence of the German machine guns, the LCVP made it back to the *Dorothea Dix,* where Ernest climbed back up the rope ladder unscathed.[3] Ten other landing craft that morning were blown up in the water before reaching shore.

Because of the uncertainties of the Normandy invasion, few correspondents were allowed ashore that first day. Late that night, Hemingway and most of the correspondents returned to English ports and from there to London. Ernest, not yet assigned to a specific unit, had yet to fulfill his commitment to *Collier's* for a story on the RAF's sky battles with the Germans. Working out of the Dorchester Hotel, he talked to RAF pilots based on Salisbury Plain about their secret aircraft, the Tempest, which flew fast enough to intercept the V-1 German buzz bombs that were now falling on England in random patterns. At Dunsford, on June 15, Hemingway was in the officers' mess of the 98th Squadron when a V-1 dropped out of the sky at the edge of the base. Flight Lieutenant R. G. Teakle soon received a reprimand asking him to be more careful regarding security matters, for the group captain had learned that "certain parts of a Flying Bomb were taken by Mr. Ernest Hemmingway [sic] while he was under your charge. I now learn that the parts have been restored to the Security Branch."[4] A few days later Hemingway was flying with the 98th on an afternoon mission to bomb V-1 launch sites at Drancourt in France. Eight groups of six B-25 Mitchell bombers came in low enough that Ernest could see plane wreckage left behind by earlier attacks, and then the black flak bursts from antiaircraft guns began blossoming alongside Commander Lynn's aircraft. Ernest watched the nearest

B-25's bomb bay open, and "the bombs all dropped out sideways as if she were having eight long metal kittens in a hurry." When he asked Lynn to go back over the target to check the damage done by the 500-pounders, the commander refused, of course, not willing to risk any more flak. The leading bomber in the second group was reported shot down at the target.[5]

On June 29, flying with RAF Group Captain Peter Barnes, Ernest went up on a practice flight in a Type-VI de Havilland "Mosquito," whose Rolls-Royce engines could push the aircraft to almost 400 miles an hour. Built of specially treated plywood, the plane relied on speed and maneuverability, not armor, to stay alive. Late that night Barnes took Hemingway on a coastal patrol run which came across several V-1s inbound for Portsmouth. At Hemingway's urging, Barnes dove on one of the buzz bombs from above, but was unable to get into position before they were in the middle of the Portsmouth antiaircraft barrage. Barnes fired a short burst from his 20mm guns, and then

> pulled away before we reached the barrage balloons. Ernest seemed to love the fireworks bursting all around us, and urged me to press on. . . . I was already in a state familiar to those who tangled with Ernest—I was acting against my better judgment. . . . I knew I was supposed to keep Ernest out of trouble. If you did blow one up, particularly at night, it was touch and go for yourself. . . . We dived even more steeply on the second V1 ... gave it two long bursts ... and then we were in the Portsmouth barrage again. I pulled away in a confusion of search lights and intensive flak. As we winged over, there was a huge flash behind us, and the aeroplane danced around like a leaf in a whirlwind. Someone got the V1, but not us. . . . Ernest seemed to have loved every moment of it.[6]

Unwinding after their return to base, Hemingway and Barnes got into a deep discussion on stress and strain, courage and bravery—conditions and traits about which Barnes knew too much from over four years of combat experience. When Ernest claimed that combat fatigue was a lack of courage, Barnes told him he had a lot to learn.

Hemingway was not the only correspondent who flew bombing

missions or risked his life at Normandy, but he may have been the most prominent. To the combat troops and RAF pilots, he seemed almost shy, a man asking questions, listening intently to their answers. Anyone familiar with his depressed and petulant moods at the Finca would not have thought him the same man. On the surface it would seem that his concussed and bleeding head had somehow pushed his demons back down below the surface of his mind. The soldiers and airmen admired the cool eagerness with which he faced the dangers they encountered, but they sometimes wondered why a man so famous would take such risks. That question had no easy or simple answer. Part of Hemingway wanted to be the warrior he imagined himself as a young boy listening to his grandfathers' stories of the Civil War. Part of him was half in love with an honorable death, not one that he sought, but one that found him. Yet another part of him simply no longer cared if he lived or died. This year or next, as Shakespeare said, a debt owed to God that he would be quit of. Were this not wartime, his behavior would have raised more questions. Because it was wartime, no one was dumbfounded by his acts, nor did any one think it strange that this famous and married man returned to Mary Welsh's bedroom, behaving like a figure from a romantic novel.

Twice married, once divorced, Mary was no novice in the field of love; her current husband, the journalist Noel Monks, was sent to France immediately after D-Day, leaving her a "target of opportunity," as Ernest described his own heart at the time. Exactly when they became lovers is a movable date, but maybe it happened as he described it in his first poem for Mary. He is sitting lonely and alone in his hotel room, watching the electric clock move "toward the hour when she will come opening softly with in-left key. Saying 'May I come in?' Coming small-voiced and lovely to the hand and eye to bring your heart back that was gone; to cure all loneliness and bring the things we left behind upon the boat."[7] That they were lovers was nothing strange in that London of 1944, nor, if rumors have any substance, was he her first or only lover. She also did not seem to be bothered that his hotel room had evidence that other women came and went.[8]

The first week in July, Hemingway shaved off his sub patrol

beard, leaving only a mustache. On his head, stubble was growing back after the hospital stitching. Catching a seat on a small plane flying into the half-cleared Cherbourg peninsula, he gathered there with fellow correspondents Bob Capa, Bill Walton, Charles Collingwood, Bill Paley, and others. After a rainy week spent visiting liberated villages—Ste. Mère-Eglise, Valgones, Barfleur, and others—he and Collingwood paid their homage at Château de Tocqueville, where *Democracy in America* was written and where the two correspondents left their initials—EH CC 7 44—"etched discreetly in the soft stone to the left of the main door of the *Pavillon* wing."[9] Still assigned to covering the RAF, Hemingway returned to London, where he soon got himself reassigned to George Patton's Third Army grouping at Néhou, well behind the front line. Flushed with the initial success on the Normandy beaches, the Allied armies were now engaged in bloody hedgerow fighting against well-trained, entrenched German troops. It was not yet clear that the invaders would be able to move off their several beachheads. A month after the D-Day landings, they were less than ten miles inland; somewhere along the loosely connected seventy-mile-front an opening had to be blasted.

When Hemingway arrived in France on July 18, General Patton's tank corps was being held in reserve while General Omar Bradley's First Army was assigned to force a wedge in the German defenses at St. Lô. On July 24, Hemingway transferred to the First Army at the very moment Bradley's forces broke out of their coastal confinement. That afternoon and the following morning, Eighth Air Force bombers, laying down a wall-to-wall carpet of fragmentation bombs to open the German lines, misread the bomb line and bombed their own troops, killing 136 and wounding over 500 American soldiers. Later, Hemingway's bitter character Colonel Cantwell recounts what happened when the wind blew the smoke marking the bomb line back into the American positions: "They bombed us the same way they bombed the Krauts. First it was the heavies, and no one need ever worry about hell who was there that day." [10]

Four days later, Hemingway found his semipermanent field home with the 22nd Infantry Regiment whose commander,

Colonel Charles "Buck" Lanham, was too busy fighting the war to worry much about what Ernest was doing or where he was going. That was just as well because from that point forward Hemingway was sometimes a journalist, sometimes an irregular soldier, and sometimes a gatherer of intelligence. His driver, Archie "Red" Pelkey, would take him anywhere, no matter what the road conditions. Their jeep carried rifles and grenades; Ernest was never without his Zeiss field glasses or his liberated German case full of battle and road maps. He was there in the France that he knew and loved early in his career, coming back now in the crusade to free her, following the old pilgrimage routes toward Paris.

On July 30, Hemingway liberated for his own use a German motorcycle with sidecar, and a Mercedes convertible, which was immediately repainted olive drab; he also liberated a well-stocked château's wine cellar: Château Lafité, 1915; Châteauneuf du Pape, 1929; Rudesheimer, 1915, which he, Ira Wolfert, Duke Shoop, and other journalists enjoyed that night, washing down K ration chili with rare vintages.[11] The following night in his letter to Mary in London he sounded tired but happy, fighting the war as best he could and to the extent his circumstances allowed. His headaches, he said, were much better.[12] On August 3, Reuters news service reported that Hemingway and Pelkey captured six German prisoners: "The private, with Mr. Hemingway, tossed hand grenades into the house and six of Hitler's supermen piled out and surrendered to Hemingway."[13] That same day, as the 4th Division mopped up German resistance at Villedieu-les-Poêles, Colonel Lanham remembered seeing Hemingway at a street corner, "standing poised as always on the balls of his feet. Like a fighter. Like a great cat. Easy. Relaxed. Absorbed. Intent. Watchful. Missing nothing."[14] With rifle and machine-gun fire only buildings away, Hemingway's street corner stance put him once more in close proximity to death. He was either very sure he would not be killed (a foolish thing of which to be sure), or he simply did not give a damn.

Two days later, at the outskirts of St. Pois, he lay flat in the ditch, head throbbing and ears ringing beneath his steel helmet pulled down tight. His liberated German motorcycle with sidecar was upended in the middle of road. Somewhere ahead, he could hear

Germans talking, but he did not raise his head to look because the first time he did, machine-gun fire splattered dirt in his face, and the antitank gun that knocked him there let loose with more rounds. For two hours he lay, not moving, listening to the noises in his head, and knowing the London concussion was back in business, not that it had ever gone far away. The rest of his band was safely hunkered down behind the protective curve in the road, watching the exposed inch of his butt sticking up from the ditch. It was a long afternoon.

The news story said the first German shell "fired at point-blank range exploded in the middle of the road three yards from Hemingway, who was blown into the ditch." Robert Capa (one of the men behind the protected curve) thought the first shell hit about ten yards in front of the motorcycle. Three yards or ten, it did not matter much to Ernest in the ditch. Capa, well known for his stunning battlefield photographs from the Spanish Civil War, was said to have "continued to take pictures until a second anti-tank shell swished close to him. Then he also took cover." [15] Capa remembered only the tracer bullets hitting the dirt above Hemingway's head, "and the popping, which came from a light German tank . . . continued without let up." When the tank pulled back, Hemingway ran to join Capa and his driver, Red Pelkey, and two other soldiers. Capa wrote that Hemingway "was furious. Not so much at the Germans as at me, and accused me of standing by during his crisis so that I might take the first picture of the famous writer's dead body." [16]

Traveling that unsecured back road into St. Pois, Hemingway was taking the sort of risk that became his trademark all that year in France. When he first showed Capa the way into St. Pois on the map, the photographer was dubious. "Papa looked at me in disgust," Capa wrote later, "and said I could stay behind. I couldn't do anything but follow him, but . . . I told him that Hungarian strategy consisted of going behind a good number of soldiers, and never of taking lonely short cuts through no man's land." [17] Hemingway would take more and more shortcuts, pushing the laws of probability to their limits.

The next day, Hemingway and Bill Walton were crossing the

mile-long causeway connecting the mainland of France to Mont-St.-Michel. Rising up out of the tidal flat before them was the ancient abbey with its Gothic visage and its surrounding ramparts. The register of the Hôtel de la Mère Poulard was filled with the names of recently departed German officers, le Mont having been liberated only five days earlier.[18] By the time reporters John Carlisle and Charles Collingwood arrived, Ernest seemed to be in charge of the place, having completely charmed the *patronne*. Collingwood said, "He chose the wine, decided on menus. He had great force of personality and a gift for organization."[19] For Carlisle, Ernest was "one of the happiest men I ever knew, a guy with a great zest for life and who enjoyed every minute of it." Bill Walton, who loved and admired Ernest without overlooking his faults, found him always "marvelous company. . . . He made me laugh more deeply than anyone else I'd known." John Ford's camera crew caught Ernest dining with A. J. Liebling. Not every fellow correspondent was so taken with Hemingway's ability to be always at the center of the action, to speak with commanding officers like Buck Lanham in their own language, and to speak with the locals in their own patois. For William Randolph Hearst, Jr., Ernest was "a pain in the ass" and no gentleman. "He was only a reporter the same as us, but he thought he was the Second Coming and acted like it. . . . I don't think anyone liked him."[20] Some, like Hearst, resented Hemingway's freelancing out along action's edge. Some accused him of "playing soldier."

They could not have been more wrong about Ernest Hemingway, who had not "played soldier" since he was a small boy armed with a wooden gun. After his wounding in World War I, Hemingway viewed armed combat as the most central experience of his century. Here a man could see his species stripped down to a primal level; here he could test his own emotional resources. This was Hemingway's fifth war since 1918; when not at the front lines, he was continuously reading the masters of war from Caesar to Clausewitz. Years of hunting in broken fields and rough terrain, facing dangerous game in tight places, all of it was good practice for the hedgerows of France and the forest at Hürtgen. His ability to read a topographic map as if it were a three-dimensional photograph let him anticipate where the Germans would or would not move. His familiarity with weapons, his proficiency in French, and his ability to shut down the normal response of fear made him invaluable to officers like Buck Lanham and a source of worry to officers more bound to the official book of war.

Soon after leaving Mont-St.-Michel, Hemingway himself threw away the book. At St. Michel he had made contact with an OSS officer, and by August 15, Hemingway carried a brassard of the Free French of the Interior (FFI) inscribed: "A Mon Ami et liberateur, un Francais Reconnaisant." By the time his old Havana embassy friend and now OSS colonel David Bruce met him outside Chartres on August 20, Ernest was working under contradictory compulsions: as a correspondent he was supposed to be a noncombatant gathering printable war news; as unofficial liaison officer with the French Resistance while working with the OSS, he was an irregular combatant who must never write of his activities. Much later, one who was there confirmed that "Hemingway was fighting with the Resistance before the liberation of Chartres. I saw him with the FFI right after we left le Mont." An OSS operative saw Hemingway in Chartres "during the liberation battle, at the site of a mass grave while the fires were still burning and the last Germans surrendering."[21] Between August 18 and 20, Hemingway was back and forth between Chartres, which was being liberated, and Rambouillet, which controlled one of the routes into Paris and which was tenuously held by handful of Maquis, French Resistance fighters.

When David Bruce regrouped with Hemingway at the command post of the 5th Division, Ernest was carrying a handwritten note directing dynamite units to "provide Mr. Ernest Hemingway with small arms, grenades or other captured articles he desires." It was signed by a major from Army Intelligence.[22] Although General "Wild Bill" Donovan, founder of the OSS, was said to be arriving in Chartres that evening, Bruce thought it more important to join Hemingway in Rambouillet. If the town were as vulnerable to German counterattack as Hemingway said it was, firsthand intelligence would be needed by the forces at Chartres where the liberation of Paris was being planned. One of the two routes into the French capital ran through Rambouillet. Any rearguard action the

Germans might mount there would cost lives, delay the highly charged and symbolic liberation, and embarrass its planners.

When Bruce arrived at the Hôtel du Grand Veneur, he found Ernest's two rooms on the second floor were an arsenal for the Maquis as well as a reporting point. "Agents and patrols kept rushing in with reports, some of them contradictory, but all indicating that the Germans were laying mines . . . about eight miles away with a force of approximately 150 men. . . . there were no American troops in Rambouillet." Bruce set off to gather reinforcements from the Resistance group twenty-two kilometers away at Maintenon. By midnight, Rambouillet was occupied by thirty volunteers, "including two very drunken AWOL paratroopers, ten Resistance people, fourteen gendarmes, and a few machine guns." Around midnight, Bruce organized the night patrol, password "France-Orléans," and bedded down in a private home to the sound of heavy rain on the roof.[23]

The next day, wet and overcast, Bruce and Hemingway were holding the town and "sending out small patrols along all the roads." The American reconnaissance team was gone, leaving Bruce and Hemingway defending the key crossroads with a handful of OSS men and a few Maquis. Both men found it incredible to be thirty miles from Paris with reports "that even a very small task force could easily move in," and to be forced to wait for unstated reasons. The report in Paris of imminent liberation caused Resistance fighters to rise up prematurely, resulting in "considerable losses." (Over the next five days, 901 Free French of the Interior and 582 Paris civilians were killed in the liberation, another 3,500 wounded.)[24] That afternoon Bruce moved into the Hôtel du Grand Veneur, where he, Hemingway, and a French secret service operative, Mouthard, interrogated patrols, settled local disputes, and received German prisoners brought in by armed civilians. That night the three combatants led an excursion to receive an arranged air drop of munitions, returning with "a number of bazookas, rifles and grenades."[25] For the next two days, Bruce, Hemingway, and Mouthard provided some semblance of order in the confusion that was Rambouillet, where German forces were still active on the perimeter. Later, Bruce recalled the scene in Ernest's bedroom:

Within, Ernest, looking like a jolly, dark Bacchus, dispensed high, low, and middle justice in English, French and broken German. His language was strong, salty, and emphatic. Army gear littered the floor. Carbines stood in each corner, revolvers of every nationality were heaped carelessly on the bed, the bathtub was filled with hand grenades, and the basin with brandy bottles, while under the bed was a cache of Army rations and whisky. . . . At one point we had a Polish private, a Ukrainian corporal, and an Austrian sergeant all shivering before Ernest. He dealt with them in summary fashion—the Pole was sent to the kitchen to peel potatoes, the Russian to a broiling greenhouse under guard, and the Austrian to clean jeeps.26

On August 22, Bruce recorded in his diary that "ten German tanks up the road were active again today. One of our Resistance men was killed, another captured, and they [Germans] took fifteen hostages away with them." The following day, correspondents poured into Rambouillet, hot on the track of General Jacques Leclerc, who arrived that afternoon at Château de Rambouillet, the summer residence of the president of the republic, to command the French column that would officially liberate Paris. Bruce recorded that General Leclerc was "tall, spare, handsome, stern-visaged, and a striking figure. . . . I was . . . asked by him to give all the intelligence I could to his G-2 Commander Repiton. This, with the assistance of Hemingway, Mouthard, and Mowinckle, I did."27

Early the next morning, August 24, Bruce and his OSS compatriots joined Leclerc's move toward Paris. On the outskirts of Versailles, they "found Hemingway and the Private Army, including Mouthard, had been engaged in a battle between French tanks and two Bouche 88 guns. The latter were demolished, and prisoners taken."28 (Ernest's account sounded less heroic: when the German 88s opened up on the column, he dove for cover.) In Hemingway's shirt pocket was a ragged-edged note ripped out of Bruce's memo book. Written the previous night, it directed Hemingway to arrange transportation for the Resistance men into Paris, where Bruce would pay their reasonable expenses. "I feel," Bruce wrote, "that it is important to keep them together to be used for certain future purposes that I have in mind."29 In the early afternoon of August 25, the feast day of St. Louis, patron saint of France, General Leclerc's column crossed the Seine and entered a Paris gone crazy with joy. By late that night, having weathered the thousands of Parisians who besieged them with flowers, kisses, and wine, having come through the sporadic sniper fire from rooftops and the celebratory firing of weapons in the streets, Bruce, Hemingway, and his band of men settled down in the Ritz Hotel on Place Vendôme, where the manager provided them first with an enormous round of martinis followed by a superb dinner. Outside, as Bruce recorded in his diary, "the streets are really dangerous, for everyone with a firearm is trying to use it."[30] The following morning, Hemingway and the FFI paid a call at the Shakespeare and Company bookstore where the younger Hemingway's Paris education began twenty-two years earlier. Sylvia Beach, the owner, came running down the stairs to greet him, and her enduring friend, Adrienne Monnier, offered wine to the men and her next-to-last bar of soap to Hemingway. The bookstore itself, earlier under threat of confiscation by the Germans, was bare, its five thousand books, photos, letters, and records spirited away to safekeeping.[31]

While Hemingway enjoyed the liberation of Paris, readers of the *New Republic* a world away caught the first wave of the postwar Hemingway critical industry—Malcolm Cowley's "Hemingway at Midnight." While editing the Viking *Portable Hemingway*, Cowley, a member of the Lost Generation turned critic, spun off essays that brought Hemingway's work into a clearer focus for general readers and young college instructors, who would, in turn, write their own academic essays. Cowley, seeing the patterns emerge, linked Hemingway to "the haunted and nocturnal [American] writers, the men who dealt in images that were symbols of an inner world." That there was an inner world to Hemingway, a world beneath the surface of his fiction, that one needed to read all of his stories to see it—these suggestions moved Hemingway's work out of the category of popular fiction and up to the level of American classics. Cowley, of course, did not get it all right the first time out, but here was the start of something new.[32]

Hemingway was too busy living in the intensity of Paris revitalized to be concerned by his literary reputation. Very quickly the appetites of its liberators reduced the Ritz kitchen to paltry fare, but its magnificent wine cellar continued to produce a steady flow of champagne. Most legitimate restaurants were closed while black market cafés flourished; the Métro remained immobile; and electricity was scarce. The swarm of American correspondents were billeted at the Hôtel Scribe, where an Army kitchen was set up to feed them, but Hemingway and his FFI men remained at the Ritz, operating out of room 31. That's where Mary Welsh found him with a half-finished letter to her on the table, telling her that he felt his luck had run out and asking her to find a *Time/Life* assignment in Paris, which she had already done without his urging.[33]

Mary registered for room 86, but as often as not she and Ernest either shared his bed or hers, a liaison which did not escape the eyes of Mme César Ritz, the proprietor's mother, who refused to recognize Mary's presence. The lovers rediscovered the Hemingway haunts from his early Paris days—old Montparnasse and St. Germain cafés, the Luxembourg Gardens, the St. Sulpice apartment—the two of them walking alone through all his old familiar places. The Louvre and other museums were closed; Gertrude Stein and tiny Miss Toklas were in the country; and at Cafés Select, Lilas, and du Dôme the answer was the same: no whiskey, no gin, no cognac. They found Picasso alive and painting in his chilly studio, undaunted by the Nazi occupation. For Ernest, those Paris days with Mary were a re-creation of his affair with Martha Gellhorn eight years earlier in Madrid. He was back in a grand hotel, in a war-ravaged capital city, sleeping with a lovely young woman while married to someone else. Not only was Mary sexually creative, she was also, and even better, a woman who had not heard all his stories of being poor in Paris. They lived existentially: "This is it," he told her, "our one and only life."[34]

CHAPTER 7

Down among the Dead Men

September to November 1944

A small but well-armed Hemingway convoy—two cars, two jeeps, and a motorcycle—left Paris the morning of September 7 with Archie Pelkey once more assigned as Ernest's driver. With them were three of the remaining FFI men, one Army officer, and two other correspondents, all en route to rejoin Lanham's 22nd Infantry Regiment for the push into Germany. The rest of September was a blur of road blocks, blown tires, friendly villagers, and retreating Germans. That Hemingway's convoy came unscathed through minefields, dangerous crossroads, and the possibility of German ambush is a matter of sound maps, good fortune, and battle-tested judgment. As they reached the Belgian border, Germans were counterattacking a few kilometers ahead at Paliseul, leaving ten Americans dead and twenty-three wounded. Ernest is warned to expect increased ambushes and traps, for Germans with captured American battle plans are trying to get their retreating troops and artillery safely behind the vaunted Siegfried Line of defense. Before sleeping that night, Ernest writes Mary, professing his love, wishing her good luck, and hoping that he is not in too much trouble, for he knows that disgruntled journalists have filed charges accusing him of carrying and using weapons at Rambouillet. If a full-blown court-martial results, he could be stripped of his correspondent's credentials and summarily sent back to Cuba.[1] When Ernest wakes in the night to a mortar's cough, he writes Mary that he thinks of Tom Welsh's lovely daughter, the look, touch, and feel of her. His almost daily letters are ardent and insistent, increasingly so, as he re-creates the paper passion of earlier separations from his previous muses—Hadley, Pauline, and Martha. Since meeting Mary in London, he has forgotten Martha except when drinking enough to bring out his wicked tongue. Once again he is living by his own rules of behavior, rules he will soon be calling tribal.

On September 9, Lanham's forward command post was situated on a hillside overlooking the Belgian town of Houffalize; the 22nd's tank destroyers were picking off retreating German armored vehicles as they crossed the town's bridge toward Liège. German artillery, in turn, was laying down protective fire on the approaches into the village. In the woods to the left, one of the 22nd's tank destroyers hits a mine: two men are wounded. On a foolish bet as to who can reach the village center first, Lanham and Hemingway depart on separate routes: Ernest, with Pelkey driving, follows another jeep of FFI men down the main road; Lanham's group takes a back route following a goat path. Delayed by a series of felled and booby-trapped trees blocking the road, Hemingway's group divides, Ernest and Pelkey going one way, the FFI jeep another. By the time Ernest arrives, the Germans have blown the bridge and Lanham is staring across the swift stream at the retreating enemy. He and Ernest, perched on a fence, survey the situation. It will be nightfall before his engineers arrive to repair the bridge, and Lanham is not going to advance on foot without his armored support. Once the liberated villagers understand the problem, they begin clearing debris, building buttresses, hauling and nailing plank flooring: in forty-five minutes they put up a wooden bridge that supports jeeps and tank destroyers.[2]

Three days later, the 22nd Regiment splits into two columns, entering Germany to seize the high ground above Hemeres. Hemingway follows the northern column through heavy woods, making his way up a high hill to see two German tanks racing out of the village chased by artillery shells sending up yellow clouds of smoke. Down the hill and across the slabstone riverbed, Hemingway touches down on German soil to be greeted by two villagers offering him schnapps while others come out with hands above their heads to surrender. On the right flank, Avel is burning, and the 50-caliber machine guns hammer away in the distance. Outside the village, Hemingway stops for the night at an abandoned farmhouse. There in the kitchen, with artillery fire punctuating the conversation, Ernest watches the interrogation of prisoners. The first one has fine yellow dust covering his face, his long hair tangled and clotted with it. The youngest, barely eighteen, tells of desertions, of Panzer tanks firing on their own troops, forcing them to attack, and of American bombs leaving him partially buried. Outside the farmhouse, American P-47s are laying down close air support, driving off another German counterattack.[3]

For several days afterward, Hemingway retires to the warmth of division headquarters to clear up a chest cold while Lanham's troops fight their way through the woods of the Schnee Eifel. When Hemingway returns to the front on September 18, Lanham walks him over the battle terrain, pointing out where the German 88mm opened up on his troops, explaining how he and Captain Blazzard rallied the men and took the hill. Ernest listens hard, interviews Blazzard, taking detailed notes, and writes it up as "War in the Siegfried Line," which due to *Collier's* editing sounds as if he were actually there as an eyewitness.[4] (From years of writing based on numerous sources, Ernest can take his reader into places he has never been, and everyone is certain that it is firsthand experience until anomalies appear.) That night at Buchet, where Lanham has set up his command post in a large farmhouse, Ernest is invited to a steak dinner celebrating his return to the regiment.

When the first German shell comes through one wall of the farmhouse and out the other side without exploding, ten of the twelve men at the dinner table disappear into the potato cellar. At the door Lanham turns back to see Hemingway "quietly cutting his meat." The colonel orders him into the cellar, but Ernest refuses and they begin arguing.

> Another shell came through the wall. He [Ernest] continued to eat. We renewed the argument. He would not budge. Another shell went through the wall. I told him to put on his goddamned tin hat. He wouldn't so I took mine off. . . . We argued about the

whole thing but went on eating. He reverted to his favorite theory that you were as safe in one place as another as far as artillery fire was concerned unless you were being shot at personally. I pointed out that was precisely what was being done.[5]

When the shelling stops and the dinner guests, officers and correspondents, return to find Lanham and Hemingway still sitting at the table, some call their behavior bravery. Lanham called it foolhardiness, emphasizing that he and Ernest knew the difference between the two.

There in the village of Buchet within a thousand yards of Hitler's Siegfried Line, Hemingway added to his legend without revealing anything about his inner condition. If he believed, as he told Mary, that his luck had run out, his act could be seen as suicidal. Externally, he appeared during this entire period to be extraordinarily happy, and said he was in letters—happy to be with frontline fighting troops, happy to see and understand the battlefields. He also continually took risks that amazed and worried the 22nd's riflemen. In a poem for Mary, he wrote:

> Repeat after me.
> Do you take this old whore
> Death for thy lawful
> Wedded wife?
> Repeat after me
> I do, I do, I do.[6]

After returning from division headquarters, where he may have heard more bad news about the investigation into his Rambouillet activity, Hemingway's letters to Mary became more ardent and more lonely. Words are repeated over and over—away from her, he is sick, lonesome, missing her, loving her, writing sad, dull letters, needing her letters, needing her next to him in bed desperately. She is his "Pickle" or his "Small Friend," as bomber pilots refer to their fighter escort as "Little Friend."

At Buchet the advance of the 22nd stalled for lack of supplies, ammunition, and gasoline. For almost two weeks, Lanham's troops laid mines and booby traps to protect their overextended lines, but still the Germans slipped through at night to lay their own mines. Vulnerable and a long way from home, it was a narrow time for the 22nd and for Hemingway. Lanham said later that he and Ernest were "both convinced that the Germans would jump us some dark night and would be back in our rear areas in nothing flat. . . . [Hemingway] told me repeatedly that he slept with his clothes on and his weapons beside him." During those tense evenings, sweating it out, Ernest and the colonel told each other tall tales of their youth. Lanham remembered hearing about Ernest's mother, Grace, "whom he hated and to whom he invariably referred as a bitch." He listened to Ernest's increasingly elaborate story of how his first wife, Hadley, "lost his volume of short stories. . . . He said it nearly did him in. Even in the retelling of the story I could see his rage mount." When Ernest told Buck about his married life with Martha, "his hatred of her was a terrible thing to see."[7] Increasingly, Hemingway's life was becoming his story, which he rehearsed and refined, embedding it with such vivid details that it would be difficult later to sort out his fictions.

On September 23/24, writing to Mary, he still worried about charges filed against him, furious to be in trouble over action of which any man should feel proud. The "liars" and the "phonies" are ganging up on him while the politics of war sicken him. After fourteen pages the letter breaks off, followed by two more pages the next day, and stuffed into an envelope marked: "Please Deliver (In case of CASUALTY)." In those added pages, he says no matter who has loved her, he loves her more; please love him, trust him.[8] On September 26, Ernest received permission from 4th Infantry Division to "be present in Paris an indefinite period for the purpose of writing articles for Collier's Magazine."[9]

Returning to the Ritz, now reserved by the military for Very Important Persons only, Hemingway had no trouble in securing a room while continuing to share Mary's bed. She soon made clear her misgivings about their relationship. In a letter to Ernest, she admitted that her second marriage was finished. Noel had written that he was sorry he "had not the qualifications to stay the distance" with her. She, in turn, was made to feel inadequate by Ernest, whose manic ardor at times overwhelmed her, demanding nothing less than everything. She admitted having avoided him at the Ritz one day, "wanting [a] four hours pass from your domination because you are so big and you absorb me so that I lose myself, wanting only the soft easy business of flattery and admiration and gaiety that matters not, and nothing intense, a whole evening cut right down to my small stature with no effort and nothing at all clutching at my throat and chest and stomach."[10]

On October 3, orders came from Supreme Headquarters Allied Expeditionary Force (SHAEF) directing Hemingway to report to the Inspector General, Third Army.[11] There was no need to specify the reason: charges of being an armed combatant had come home to roost. On October 5, at Nancy, officers Ernest knew on Patton's staff advised him to deny the charges. The Inspector General's hearing on October 6 was an inquiry to determine if the charges had any merit; it was not a court-martial. The hearing began with Ernest's rehearsed and sanitized version of Rambouillet, where he served only as an interpreter and conduit between the handful of OSS officers and the French Maquis. When Colonel Bruce arrived, Ernest said, "I offered my services to him in any way in which I might be useful provided that my actions did not violate the Geneva convention or that any of them should in any way prejudice my fellow war correspondents." In helping with the problems Bruce faced, Ernest said that he "served only in an advisory capacity to Colonel Bruce . . . I did not command troops nor give orders but only transmitted orders." The Inspector General then listed the specific charges:

> That Mr. Hemingway stripped off correspondent insignia and acted as a colonel [of] French Resistance troops; that he had a room with mines, grenades and war maps; that he directed resistance patrols.

Hemingway admitted to being without his correspondent's insignia only when he was in shirtsleeves in the warm August weather. As for being called a colonel, "it was in the same way that citizens of the state of Kentucky are sometimes addressed as colonel without it implying any military rank." Any arms seen in his room were "stored there by French Resistance men who were operating under orders of the proper authorities." As for war maps, he always traveled with maps, and he never directed any patrols.

> Q. Were there mines in your room?
> A. There were no mines in my room. I would greatly prefer not to have mines in my room at any time.

When asked if he ever "fought with the men," he responded somewhat mendaciously that he "didn't fight with the men."[12] As he explained years later,

> I swore I was not armed in Rambouillet. There was not need to state I was armed outside of the city limit. I swore I did not "fight with the men." Who would fight with the men, i.e. not get along with them. Not me. . . . I denied and kidded out of all of it and swore away everything I felt any pride in.[13]

Ever since the summer of 1915, when he was pursued by a game warden for shooting a blue heron and eventually standing before a county judge to pay his fine, Hemingway had a profound, almost irrational fear of the law, its enforcers, and the courtroom. He might joke about his sworn testimony at Nancy, but at the time there was nothing humorous about it until the Inspector General found no cause to pursue the charges. When Ernest sent *Collier's* his story on the 22nd attacking the Siegfried Line, he wired changes to a photograph, advising them to paint out the protruding ammunition clip from his pocket, which he was carrying for a sergeant and which "might be misconstrued."[14] By the end of the day, the Inspector General could report that there were no grounds for a court-martial, letting Hemingway off the hook. The finding should have elated Hemingway; instead it left him dark and moody, angry with the "phonies" and suspicious of higher authority.

His erratic behavior on returning to Paris may have been related to the interrogation. At the Ritz with Mary and his old friend, Marlene Dietrich, Ernest alternated between considerate, boyish lover, humming tunes off-key, and the dark, violent man who slapped Mary for insulting his drunken friends from the 22nd. She carped too much; he drank too much. Mercurial, impulsive, but eventually and always endearing, Ernest was never boring that

October in Paris. Then, as the month was ending, he was told that his son Jack, while on an OSS mission behind enemy lines, had been shot, captured, treated, and moved to a German hospital in the Vosges. Ernest was helpless, fuming, determined to effect a rescue while knowing such action would further endanger his oldest boy. The next day he convinced Mary to use her connections to apply for front-line coverage in the Vosges so that she might find better information about Jack. At the same time, he began packing up to rejoin the 22nd Infantry, leaving Paris on November 9.[15]

The day was drear when Ernest walked back into Lanham's command post, a plywood trailer in a far field facing an impassable forest. The 22nd's battalion commanders were already briefed for the morrow's attack on the Hürtgenwald, a battle from which none who were there would emerge whole. Lanham was happy to see Ernest's face. Over bottles of wine supplied by Hemingway, the two men talked until almost three in the morning. Lanham said, "We told each other about our childhood[s], our parents, our dreams, our hopes, our education, our women, our friends, our enemies, our triumphs and our disasters. . . . It was one of those rare occasions when two human beings suddenly find themselves in complete rapport and their separate worlds meet and merge."[16] Lanham, short and thin, was the field commander that Ernest would like to have been. In the Schnee Eifel, when his troops began to fall apart under murderous German fire, Lanham, armed with a pistol, led them back into the fight, telling them, "Goddamn, let's go get these Krauts. Let's kill these chickenshits. Let's get up over this hill now and get the place taken."[17] Hemingway, large in manner and bulk, was the writer that Lanham, who wrote poetry, would like to have been. They made an unlikely pair that night, each needing the other to be whole, a Laurel-and-Hardy tableau without slapstick, a "species of brotherhood," Lanham called it. It was a night spent whistling past the graveyard, for the soldier and the writer both knew the pending battle would be a bloody one.

The next morning, before the attack began, Hemingway wrote a quick note to his editor at *Collier's*, naming Mary Welsh as the sole beneficiary of the magazine's insurance policy on him. Martha, he said, was "fully provided for."[18] Shortly after noon on November 16,

Hemingway watched the first riflemen of the 22nd Infantry wade across the Roter Weh and into the dark woods of Hürtgen Forest. Lanham's men who went across the stream and into the trees were a tight unit, battle-tested, operating smoothly with confidence in their leadership and in their own abilities. About three miles away lay their objective, the tiny village of Grosshau. Thirteen days later, when they pushed into the village, 87 percent of the men who crossed the Roter Weh were casualties, and those few who remained, including Ernest, could not say why.

Across the stream, the infantrymen made their way up the facing hill to the Rabenheck (Raven's Hackle), where terrain and German fire stopped them by sunset. Firs and hardwoods in orderly, tightly packed rows were impossible to see through. Firebreaks and logging roads were puddled with rainwater and deep with mud under which German mines were planted. Private First Class John L. Page, squad leader, said: "I never dried out, and neither did most of the rest of us for the next two weeks. The heavy mud caused most of the boys to throw away their galoshes and the constant rain and sleet made us that much colder and wetter." The gorge below their front line was filled with chest-deep water of the Weisser Weh; in the draw to their left was a German pillbox surrounded by log bunkers and barbed wire. That evening, the 22nd took out the bunkers and the pillbox, leaving twelve dead Germans and taking four prisoners. Lanham's losses that day were four officers and sixty-nine enlisted men. That night, riflemen carried their wounded back one thousand yards through inky woods to the closest transport, at every step hoping they were still on the mine-cleared path.

Then rain began to fall, turning to sleet, and the German artillery barrage began to burst in the treetops, sending splinters and shrapnel slicing through the Americans below. Technician 5th Grade George Morgan said,

> You can't get protection. You can't see. You can't get fields of fire. The trees are slashed like a scythe by artillery. Everything is tangled. You can scarcely walk. Everybody is cold and wet, and the mixture of cold rain and sleet keeps falling. They jump off again and soon there is only a handful of the old men left.

Every trail is mined, every intersection zeroed in upon, every night a nightmare. Some men break down from the noise, some from the blood, some from fear. Replacements pouring into the staging area are frequently dead men before ever reaching their platoons. Battalion commanders disappear at an unsustainable rate; lieutenants go down like birds in a shooting gallery. Field commissions raise sergeants to the officer ranks where they are chewed up as so much fodder. On the second day of the battle, the 22nd lost 10 officers and 129 enlisted men without advancing across the Weisser Weh. Each day ended with the thought that the fighting could not get worse, and each morning that hope faded.

The men of Fox Company, reduced to fifty riflemen, no sergeants, and two lieutenants, were looking across a hundred yards of open ground to the wood line beyond.

> Lieutenant Fitzgerald stood up and shouted, "Come on all you riflemen, let's go," and about thirty followed. This poorly organized group of soldiers reached the edge of the woods without opposition, but instead of holding there continued into the woods, became disoriented, and turned to the south. In a draw outside the battalion sector, Fitzgerald halted the platoon and had the soldiers begin entrenching. Just as they began to dig, a small German unit counterattacked them. Only four of the platoon made it back to the main body of the company.

By the time the report reached Lanham, all that remained of Fox Company were two officers and twelve enlisted men.[19]

Each day Hemingway writes Mary about close encounters with that "old whore, Death," unable because of the military censor to give details. Each day his notes to her become grimmer, as the woods deteriorate into a shamble of splintered stumps, shell holes, and body parts of dead men. To take his mind off mortar bursts that seem continuous, he writes about their future life in Cuba, living at the Finca, fishing on the *Pilar*, writing well, being a good husband and father. A recent hurricane that devastated parts of Cuba could not have destroyed everything; the Finca will be their command post. Mary's first letters back from the Vosges tell him that his son Jack is a confirmed POW with a shoulder wound that is not serious. She has applied for extended leave to return with him to Cuba, telling her boss that "we thought we had something that deserves a chance." Not so emotional as his letters to her, Mary's closes with: "I am your woman my dearest Only One for as long as you'll have me, and I will try to make that forever."[20]

The next day she told him of encountering Martha while lunching at the Hôtel Scribe. As Mary walked the length of the dining room, she passed Martha's good friend Virginia Cowles on one side and Mrs. Hemingway on the other. When Bob Capa was asked where Mary was sitting, he said, "Just follow the daggers," referring to the looks given her by the two women. It was Mary's first encounter with Martha, whom she fairly assessed as "very pretty . . . the line of her nose was quite different from mine, and her skin nicer. It made me wish I were a tall slim sultry brunette . . . for you must be a little tired of blondes. And knowing she is very slim and straight-legged and lovely, I was terribly conscious of my damned old can. There was no face-to-face nonsense or anything stupid like that."[21]

Ernest had little time to savor Mary's account. Eight days into the woods, Lanham's command post trailer was now sitting on the edge of a firebreak, unsafe from artillery fire by day and from an unlocated German mortar by night. Returning one day from the area dubbed "The Valley of Death," Lanham found a rearguard fight going on in his clearing. "Men were firing and advancing and dropping and firing . . . then I saw E. H. . . . He was standing bolt upright watching the fight with intense interest. He was moving with the moving wave but I never saw him hit the ground. And this time there was no question at all that he was armed and using those arms."[22] That night Ernest tried to explain to Mary the cleansing effect of the violence surrounding him:

> You know how I was spooked of it [the battle] before it started. . . . But then about yesterday and the day before just like a gift . . . I get the old feeling of immortality back I used to have when I was 19—right in the middle of a *really* bad shelling—not the cagey assessment of chances—nor the angry, the hell with it feeling—nor the throw everything away feeling . . . just the pure old thing we used to operate on.[23]

Thereafter his letters begin to speak more frequently of his future writing, of collecting information, observing closely, seeing again the telling details. Absorbing and digesting the experience, he will "be able to invent a good battle for a book sometime out of my knowledge."[24] His book will not compete with the new young writers coming out of battles like this one, the ones "that we hope will write better and sounder than we can. That we blast the trail for. . . . I will just take my small piece of a tiny part of it and buttress it with the forgotten sometimes punchy knowledge and the new will work the mess so the old magic will work—and then we will have [the] book, a day at a time."[25]

Hemingway spent his days with Lanham and his troops, sleeping at night in the relative safety of a woodcutter's hut closer to division headquarters. His mornings began with General Raymond Barton's daily briefing on yesterday's action and the plans for the day, an affair Ernest disparagingly called the "ballroom bananas." By the time the 22nd got out of the dark forest, "Tubby" Barton was being referred to as "Our Lost Leader," after he stopped coming to the front lines to see what was actually happening. After several profane conversations between Lanham and Barton, the general did his best to have his regimental commander relieved, sending a psychiatrist to probe for signs of combat fatigue. Caught between entrenched Germans in front of him and a less than supportive commanding officer to his rear, Lanham sorely needed Hemingway as his "bitching post." The disparity between the infantrymen dying in the splintered, dripping forest and the military politics going on at division headquarters left a permanently bitter taste in Ernest's mouth.

Hemingway's own encounter with the psychiatrist did nothing to improve his attitude toward the profession or General Barton. Fellow journalist Bill Walton remembered the psychiatrist calling courage and cowardliness false values with which people kidded themselves. An argument developed, which led to the psychiatrist saying, "Every damn one of you is going to break sooner or later. . . . Including you, Hemingway!"

Hemingway exploded. He flushed deep red and pounded on the table so hard the wine bottle jumped around. . . . The captain was an ignoramus, an uneducated fool, a pervert, an enemy spy, and anything else unpleasant he could think of. . . . Something that was very deep in him had been touched. He couldn't forget it.[26]

On November 26, eleven days into the death factory, the 22nd Regiment finally reached their second-day objective: the village of Grosshau. The next two days were a horror show: infantry crossing an open field caught in murderous fire from entrenched Germans. Baker Company stalled at the edge of the woods, losing fifty-four out of seventy-nine soldiers. Suddenly, in one of those selfless acts that sometimes happen in battle, Private First Class Marcario Garcia went into the woods alone to destroy the enemy machine gunners with hand grenades and his rifle. Wounded in his assault, he nevertheless wiped out a second machine-gun pit, allowing what remained of his company to reach the woods. When Easy Company arrived with fresh support, they found "a picture of real carnage—arms, equipment, dead and wounded, Jerrys and GIs strewn all through the woods. Blasted trees, gaping shell holes, and the acrid smell and smoke of small arms and mortar fire completed the terrain. Company B remnants—2 lieutenants and 15 to 20 enlisted. . . . This was no picnic."[27]

Eventually Grosshau was taken by the 22nd in bloody house-to-house fighting that further diminished Lanham's already weakened regiment. For days afterward German artillery continued to bombard the American troops occupying the village until little was left above ground but rubble. When the 22nd was finally relieved from front-line duty on December 3, the regiment had cleared the enemy from six thousand yards of forest and one small village while sustaining over 2,700 casualties. The 22nd Regiment's Chaplain Boice said, "A part of us died in the forest, and there is a part of our mind and heart and soul left there." Two days after the 22nd stood down, Ernest wrote a bleak, tense letter, clearly disturbed by the Hürtgen experience, telling Martha that she had destroyed him with her demands to be free of him. In passing he said that a fellow correspondent related that Martha told him that Ernest's taking away her *Collier's* job was the worst thing ever done by one journalist to another. Ernest said the man would not believe that she had sent him to *Collier's*.[28]

Hemingway, Pelkey, and Walton were almost added to the list of those who did not get out of the woods. On the last gray, chilly day, driving down an exposed stretch of muddy road, Hemingway told Pelkey to stop the jeep. Listening to a faint hum, Ernest yelled, "Oh, God, jump!" The three went crashing face down into the muddy ditch, Ernest on top of Walton, while overhead they heard a plane stitching their jeep with its machine guns. In the dead quiet that followed, Ernest sat up and unhitched his canteen, offering Walton and Pelkey a roadside gin. They were alive only because Ernest recognized the aircraft motor from the Spanish Civil War. While they remained in the ditch, the plane reappeared out of the overcast sky to riddle the road one last time.[29]

PART TWO

A Fall from Grace

1945 TO 1952

You think it horrible that lust and rage
Should dance attendance upon my old age;
They were not such a plague when I was young;
What else have I to spur me into song?

> William Butler Yeats, "The Spur"

Like one
Who having into truth, by telling of it,
Made such a sinner of his memory,
To credit his own lie.

> William Shakespeare, *The Tempest*

CHAPTER 8

Starting Over

March to December 1945

With the war in Europe moving toward its now inevitable conclusion, Hemingway was suddenly eager to return to Cuba where Mary agreed to meet him for a trial union. On March 6, 1945, in her Ritz Hotel box she found his hasty farewell note promising to be faithful to her and love her always. He was her Mountain; she was his Kitten. A week later from New York, he sent her detailed instructions for getting to Cuba, where he would meet her at the airport. Displaced and out of step with the home front, he was discovering the chasm separating combat vets from state-side civilians: they no longer spoke the same language. Those who had not been there did not understand about Hürtgenwald. When not with others like himself, he felt strange and vulnerable. After a week in the city tending to chores—his publisher, his lawyer, his banker, his former wives, his children—he was on the train to Miami with sixteen-year-old Patrick, and from there to Havana. With him he carried two new shotguns and his bank statement showing a $20,000 balance.[1]

He was returning to domestic problems long deferred and to a life so quiet by comparison to the Schnee Eifel or to wartime Paris that it seemed hardly to move at all. By the time he reached the Finca, he had lost his temper twice with his second wife, Pauline, in phone conversations about their two boys. By letter she asked him to erase their arguments; she would be more considerate of his time if he would do the same for her. Knowing how incapable he was of dealing with a woman as an equal, she gave in on which boy would be with her for Easter. Pat was already with him; Greg would join them in Havana in a week.[2] Assessing the damage to the Finca and to himself, Hemingway found his numerous cats starved thin, many of his mango trees destroyed by a hurricane, and a good night's rest requiring a sleeping pill. Cats could be fattened and trees replanted, but his writing or the lack of it was a more difficult problem. For five years now he had written no fiction. In his writing room was an almost forgotten fragment of a Bimini story that referred back to the island's heyday as a rumrunner's haven during prohibition. Other than that, he had used up most of what he knew from the previous decade, but his recent war experiences were filled with usable material. So the difficulty was not the subject matter, it was the act itself—sitting down alone with pencil and paper to put down words in their effective order. It was an old problem that he had solved several times before. After each of his novels, he had experienced that emptiness that comes with having completed the work, followed by uncertainty of what to write next. Sometimes it had taken him as long as six months or a year to return to his trade, but never had he gone five years. It was going to be very difficult, he wrote Mary, but somehow he would get through it. The writing appeared impossible, but he would get in shape to fix that. He promised her that he was not drinking at night to fight off loneliness, nor was he drinking in the morning. For a man who began his mornings in Paris with a bottle of champagne, this was a large promise.[3]

On April 12, with the defeat of Germany in sight, Franklin Delano Roosevelt died of a massive hemorrhage, shrouding the nation in a cloak of mourning. Across the United States there were banner headlines, grieving civilians, special church services, and flags at half-mast, but at Finca Vigía, Hemingway did not weep. Despite having once met and dined with the president at the White House for a private showing of *The Spanish Earth*, Hemingway always resented what Roosevelt's programs had done to Key West. The quiet fishing village which was Ernest's haven went bankrupt in 1934, turning itself over to the Federal Emergency Relief Act. The island was transformed into a tourist resort, completely managed by federal bureaucrats and soon overrun with gawking main-landers looking for a glimpse of Ernest Hemingway. Two days after Roosevelt died, with Havana flying flags at half-mast, Hemingway went out to supper with a friend; in his several letters written that day, the only mention of FDR was to Buck Lanham:

> They talk about our Lord haveing [sic] a bad time on that tree and everyone in mourning for the death of the Chief Executive but nobody has ever been anywhere that hasn't been with Infantry. Catch him, men. Sentiment is about to over-come him.[4]

In those same several letters of mid-April, what Hemingway did not mention to anyone was the doubt that he could write a better book than *For Whom the Bell Tolls*. In the previous twenty years he had published three collections of short stories, a satire (*The Torrents of Spring*), a roman à clef (*The Sun Also Rises*), a semi-historical novel (*A Farewell to Arms*), a book of natural history (*Death in the Afternoon*), a safari book (*Green Hills of Africa*), a semiproletariat novel (*To Have and Have Not*), and a play (*The Fifth Column*). *For Whom the Bell Tolls* was his epic novel just as "The Snows of Kilimanjaro" was his epic short story: in both, he gave the reader a story within which was embedded an entire col-lection of short stories. The critics who said he repeated himself were missing the obvious. Always experimenting, always reaching beyond his last effort, Hemingway had never repeated the form, and he was not about to start. The bone upon which he gnawed was old, bearing teethmarks of every artist who ever created a master-piece: how to make a better one when the last one was the best he could make.

Following his old prescription for beginning again, Hemingway started by writing letters and reading background books: Buck Lanham's book on infantry tactics and the biographies of two gener-als—Nathan Bedford Forrest from the American Civil War, and Michel Ney, Napoleon's faithful field commander.[5] When his Havana doctor, José Luis Herrera, came by the Finca to discuss Ernest's recur-ring headaches and insomnia, Hemingway told him about his two concussions and their aftermath: a ringing in his ears, loss of verbal memory, temporary impotence, and sometimes erratic behavior.

After listening to his patient's symptoms, Herrera explained that his first concussion in London should have been trepanned and drained, and that his post-accident drinking could have triggered a fatal hemorrhage. The doctor recommended that Hemingway rest, do a little intellectual work each day, but not force it.[6]

Before Mary arrived early in May, Ernest had the Finca ready for inspection: the maid, cook, chauffeur, and gardeners at attention; the heavily chlorinated pool water as clear as possible; the house airy and bright; the Capehart phonograph restored to action. At Cojimar, Gregorio was almost finished with repairs to the *Pilar*, returning her from sub hunter to fishing boat. Having carefully prepared his bower, Hemingway was a little anxious: what if Mary did not like the house, his friends, the country, or his children? His loneliness, much detailed in every letter, sorely required a wife in bed beside him. He was convinced that Mary was ready to give up her career in journalism to be Mrs. Hemingway full time, to be the wife to him that Martha never was.[7]

Her arrival could not have been more propitious: on May 8, Germany surrendered unconditionally. The war in Europe was over. Simultaneously Ernest learned that his son, Jack, was safely liberated from a German prison camp. A month later, Hemingway told Buck Lanham how happy Mary was at the Finca, and how active they were together in bed: fifty-five times in May, he bragged.[8] When Jack arrived on thirty days leave for rest and reha-bilitation, he found Mary lovely to look at and supportive of his dad. Greg, at fifteen, was wary at first, having given his heart to Martha; but Mary won him over with her apparent devotion to fishing, her ability to command the Finca staff, and her quickness in learning to wing-shoot. Everyone agreed: Mary was the perfect fit for Ernest. She loved the Gulf Stream, enjoyed fishing, swim-ming, and boating, was taking Spanish lessons, and adored the Hemingway cats.[9]

In her journal, however, Mary chronicled a far less satisfactory life, one that she kept below the surface as well as she could. "Nothing is mine," she wrote. "The man is his own with various adjuncts—his writing, his children, his cats. . . . The strip of bed where I sleep is not mine. The room belongs to Marty—my heart belongs to Daddy." Martha's picture remained on the wall of Mary's bedroom because Ernest said he did not want to upset his sons who loved Martha. Martha's furniture filled the room, her presence hung in the air like perfume. "About your picture of Marty," Mary told him on an inter-house note, "I will try from now on not to be offended by such considerations for the children . . . [but] I cannot help but wondering whether or not you kept pictures of Pauline around for the sake of the children when Marty was here."[10] The Finca became for Mary "a lovely place for a prison," and her bracelets, gifts from Ernest, felt like "chains to this place by the wall." Alone in a strange country whose language she did not yet speak, she was terribly vulnerable and too aware of her differences, knowing nothing "of pursuit of fish, animals and birds," the house religion. Ernest wanted a daughter with Martha's blond hair; Mary resisted becoming "an old brood mare." She wept for the future "which looked good, tasted good and went sour in my stomach."

At the Club Cazadores, Ernest organized a shoot to welcome Jack back to Cuba, but Mary found the following luncheon raucous and disorderly, the only other woman in sight being some man's mistress. When a firecracker went off close to her ear, she burst into tears, and was driven home, where she wrote in her journal:

> Can only conclude I'd be an idiot to stay here and marry Papa. . . . Our values—most of them are antipodal. . . . He puts a premium on bad manners, on violence, on killing (man, animals, birds, fish), on toughness, on death. I begin to realize how highly I value gentleness, conversation, non-violence. . . . I'd better go while the going is possible and can be without too much bitterness.[11]

Without fully understanding how accurate his guess, Ernest referred to Mary's journal as her "Horror Diary."[12]

On June 19, Ernest wrote Mary's father, thanking him for the gift of religious books and professing his love for Mary whom he would marry as soon as possible. The next day, Ernest drove Mary to the airport to return to Chicago to complete her divorce from Noel Monks. On the mud-slippery road, Ernest lost control of the Lincoln convertible, which left the road, smashing into a tree.

Ernest's forehead banged into the rearview mirror, four of his ribs were damaged against the steering wheel, and his left knee was badly hurt. Jack was safe in the backseat, but Mary was covered with blood streaming from her left cheek. At the hospital, Ernest quickly arranged for a plastic surgeon to repair Mary's face, but could do nothing about her placement in the women's ward where the cries of those in labor went on all night long.[13]

A violent crash, bloody heads, wailing women: omens too ominous to dwell on, perhaps, but a determining accident nonetheless. Given her state of mind, had Mary left Cuba that day, she may never have returned. During the extra two months she remained at the Finca, Ernest was more solicitous of her well-being, listening to her ideas for organizing the household and to her requirements for a more orderly life. By the Fourth of July, Mary was writing to Pamela Churchill that life at the Finca was "so idyllic, so lush, so leisured, with everything so plentiful" that she sometimes felt guilty. "I can sun in the altogether with only the Finca dogs, cats, servants, and children to disturb my privacy." There were, she said, twenty cats, five dogs, and a parrot who said, "Wanna be a fighter pilot." She ended the letter saying, "I know why they always have the films ending with the two lovers riding into the sunset . . . felicity is so dull to all except its immediate participants."[14]

Before leaving at the end of August to complete her divorce, Mary wrote Ernest a good-bye note that pledged her love no matter what adjustments they needed to make.[15] While she was gone, Ernest bombarded her with letters and gifts pledging his ardor and his good intentions. She was his full partner in the Hemingway venture, and his best lover always. Her suggestions for the Finca were underway: gutters were being improved to gather water; the cats would no longer sleep all over the house; the new furniture she wanted to replace Martha's was being built.[16] The two of them, he said, were a country of their own beyond the rules and prejudices of institutions. Needing no organized religion to guide them, they must only believe in each other. As always, Ernest was a more persuasive swain on paper than in person; his written words, which were his art, were always able to move a woman's heart closer to his own.   .

Mary returned in October, her divorce final and her previous unhappiness at rest. She found Ernest to be constantly polite, loving, and open to her needs to work. She would help him with his typing, take care of marketing, oversee household expenses, learn the routines of gardens and pool, and most importantly keep Ernest's "privacy absolutely intact for whatever hours each day he works and let nobody get at him." After six weeks in Chicago, the Cuban weather, the ease of country life complete with servants, and the beauty of the Finca were a soothing balm.[17] One of the first things she did was answer a telegram from Time/Life asking if she planned to return. She telegraphed back: "With much nostalgia for Time . . . I [am] nonetheless eager [to] continue current career of loafer fisherwoman housewife . . . so strike me off the rolls."[18]

Her euphoria lasted about a week. Soon she complained of Ernest's need to control all that he surveyed. He might speak of sharing, but in fact he continued to make most of the everyday decisions: what food to buy, what meals to prepare, what jobs needed to be done. He even took to "supervising" Mary's letters to her parents. In her journal, she noted:

> Whatever else the critics say about him, they certainly [are] right about him and women—he wants them like Indian girls—completely obedient and sexually loose. That I think I might learn to handle. But the . . . criticism and long intelligent speeches about [the] inadvisability or expense of something—after about 3 samples in one day—I get that smothered feeling. . . . I wish the hell I were out of here and running my own household and my own life—with no dictatorship. . . . This is like being a high-priced whore.

It was that kind of relationship—erratic and volatile, with little middle ground between adoration and revulsion. On a bad day in October, Mary could find fault with everything about her circumstances:

1. On being alone 5 out of 7 mornings.
2. On cultivating sports which bore the shit out of me.
3. On having so little company I don't know why the hell I try to stay here.[19]

At this same time, Mary wired Time/Life asking if her position there, which a week earlier she had given up, might be reinstated as a leave of absence until December.[20]

Yet in December she remembered the previous two months as idyllic as she gradually understood that Ernest's "supervision" was largely to protect her until she became confident in this other country. To please Ernest, she bleached her brown hair blond, painted her nails a darker red, and exercised herself thinner. She swam daily, read his writing regularly, criticized little, manicured his hands and feet, and cut his hair. She was going to Spanish classes, learning to wing-shoot a 20-gauge shotgun, studying navigation, and cooking Sunday-night suppers when the kitchen staff was off. Ernest was "seldom over-drinking," and "in bed he has certainly been better for me than any man I ever had."[21] He was also a mercurial man whose temper could explode without warning, a demanding man given to emotional highs and lows. A part of him could spend money without a second thought. The same man wanted a detailed accounting of every penny spent on the Finca. It galled Mary that he gave her money as a gift, as a reward, as a bribe. It doubly galled her that, unlike his first three wives, she had no income of her own, nor would she ever if she gave up journalism.

As the sultry heat of summer faded and the hurricane season passed, life at the Finca settled into a reassuring if unexciting routine for Mary. Whatever money worries there had been disappeared when the film rights for Hemingway's "The Killers," and "The Short Happy Life of Francis Macomber" sold for $112,000. Even with the staggering monthly upkeep of the Finca at $3,000, they had a comfortable margin. Mary might complain that she did not see Ernest in the mornings, but it was because he was rising early and writing, which meant he was completely happy for the first time since returning from Europe. After seven months of "getting in shape," and beginning rough starts that floundered, Hemingway was writing easily once again. A year earlier, riding the rush of the Paris liberation, he told Max Perkins that he would write a war novel encompassing sea, air, and land action, but his attempts to begin that epic did not jell. This time he began with a war correspondent, called Hudson, who looked a lot like Ernest Hemingway, complete with concussed head and healing wounds, who covered RAF raids along the Somme. The story quickly turned into conversation, and the action moved to London where Mary, the Irish maid at the Dorchester, could barely wait for Hudson to bolt the door of his bedroom before undressing.

He wrote two drafts of another story called "The Faker," which never got past its opening few pages once more set in London. At the White Tower, Hudson introduces a British flight surgeon, Blakley, to two female correspondents—Pam, short and dark; and Jan, a tall blonde with long legs who sounded a lot like Martha. In the course of their acidic conversation, it becomes apparent that Hudson and the blonde have known each other for some time, and coincidentally Blakely performed a curettage on her when she miscarried after a jeep accident in Greece. The accident for Martha was actual, but not in Greece, and the miscarriage was a fictional reminder that Martha did not give him the child he wanted from her.[22] Despite a friendly exchange of letters with Martha, Ernest had not yet forgiven her, as he saw it, for leaving him.

From a brief meeting with her in London on his return trip to the Finca, Hemingway also knew that Martha and Virginia Cowles (a dark-haired journalist) were writing a play about male and female correspondents during the war. Under various trial titles— *Men Must Weep, Take My Love Away*, and finally *Love Goes to Press*—the comedy centers on two female journalists—Jane Mason (blond and British) and Annabelle Jones (dark and American)— who connive to prevent Annabelle's onetime husband, Joe Rogers, from marrying a touring British movie star. Annabelle tells Jane that Rogers married her "to silence the opposition," by stealing her stories. "You can't tell from the outside that he's got the character of a cobra," Annabelle explained. "From the outside he's a beautiful, funny, fascinating man."[23] Nor could you tell from Martha's letters to Ernest that she still smarted from his treatment of her.[24]

Having flown only a few actual missions as an RAF observer, Hemingway found he did not know enough to write the air war, and put it aside about the same time that Mary returned from Chicago in October.[25] With his drinking cut down to a minimum, his weight down to 202 through his daily regimen of thirty laps in the pool, he returned to the Bimini story begun before he went to England. The eight typed pages started with a narrator questioning whether the story he wants to tell will hold together. An odd story, some of it unprovable, its beginning known to only a few people and its conclusion confused, it was still a story worth telling, he assured the reader, once he straightened it all out. Picking up the thread of the story, Hemingway continued, writing quickly and easily. Within a week he had forty-seven pages done; five days later, more than seventy pages written. By the end of the month, he reported to Max Perkins that he averaged 750 words a day through October. By then he knew he was writing a novel, but had no idea where it would end. It was a strange enough story, mixing memory and desire on the cool sea breeze coming through the open doorway and windows of a painter's island cottage. The time is 1936; the two male characters—the older painter and the younger novelist—are old friends who carry heavy personal baggage. The theme was remembrance of things past, but most particularly it would detail the condition of the artist played out against the backdrop of twentieth-century conflicts. In fact, it was a story he had been writing obliquely for some time now, and would continue to write for the rest of his life.[26]

By December, Mary's nostalgia for the "helter-skelter of journalism and politics" was fading as she became more accustomed to life at the Finca. Although Ernest had no love of Havana night life, he did take Mary to an occasional concert, including one given by Yehudi Menuhin. Jack Hemingway, who was visiting his father, took Mary to the Sunday-night movies in the tiny adjoining village of San Francisco de Paula. Ernest's divorce from Martha was now final, making Mary feel more like a fiancée than a camp follower. Patrick and Gregory, who seemed to accept her without question, were arriving on December 28 for a delayed Christmas, for which Mary was desperately trying to translate holiday recipes for the Chinese cook.[27]

CHAPTER 9

Rules of the Game

1946

Despite recurring arguments with Mary and internal conflict with his own erratic moods, Hemingway in the new year wrote like a man possessed. Going to sleep at night with two Seconal tablets, he woke before dawn and was at his writing pad when the light broke. Remembering all the monumental authors he ever read—Homer, Proust, James, Joyce—Hemingway loosely envisioned a book that would bring together everything he had learned about structure, landscape, and character. The first part—Bimini before the war—was begun years earlier. Returning to it now with a more complex vision, he would use Bimini as the foundation for a multivolume work that would span the decade 1936–46, encompassing the land, air, and sea war—earth, air, water, and fire. What started as a monumental but straightforward project became over the next fifteen years more complex and introspective. In its metamorphosis, the sea war became what is now called *Islands in the Stream* and *The Old Man and the Sea*. The air war was eventually abandoned, and the ground war would become the memories of a bitter Army colonel dying in Venice—*Across the River and into the Trees*.

He poured himself into the fiction, reliving the summers on Bimini with his sons, catching and losing the big fish, scaring hell out of himself when the boys were in the water with the feeding shark. Embedded were memories of early days in Paris where the artist learned his trade. For the next fifteen years, Hemingway's memory and his fiction would return again and again to the apartment above the sawmill on rue Notre Dame des Champs where he first found his voice. Finally, remembrance of things past would produce his Paris memoir—*A Moveable Feast*. Out of the same matrix came a different story of a Paris writer, David Bourne in *The Garden of Eden*. By July 1961, the book that began as a study of the artist at war had become a multivolume portrait of the artist/writer in the first half of the twentieth century, "complete with handles," as Hemingway might say.[1]

While his Bimini painter and the visiting writer had their problems with fictional ex-wives and new lovers in Hemingway's writing room, Ernest's attention was continually distracted by Mary's unhappiness. With his previous three wives, each marriage entailed a change of venue: with Hadley he left Chicago for the Latin Quarter of Paris; with Pauline he moved into the St. Germain area and then to Key West; with Martha he moved to the Finca in Cuba. With each marriage he had given up certain favorite spots and more than a few friends closely associated with the receding wife; none of the first three wives was asked to live in the house of her predecessor. With Mary, none of the above applied: she moved into Martha's house, ate off Martha's china, looked at Martha's photograph on the wall, and lived with Martha's servants. Every old friend of Ernest's who came to the Finca was once there while Martha was wife; every Havana bartender made unspoken comparisons. The only place Mary did not feel like an intruder was on the *Pilar*, which had survived Pauline and Martha because it was always Ernest's boat.[2] Wherever she turned, except in bed, she felt inadequate: she was not the lady from St. Louis as were the first three wives, nor was she able to give Ernest children as Pauline and Hadley had. She did not know the Paris of the 1920s, had not read all the books, met all the famous faces. She did not have Hadley's or Pauline's trust fund; she did not have Martha's poise or stunning beauty; she did not bring a rich uncle to marriage as had Pauline.

In Mary's recurring dream, she is in a large house filled with people "all jolly and gay," eating from tables of food. Suddenly the guests all depart for a picnic, leaving Mary behind, uninvited. Wandering through the house, she finds Ernest and "another woman, unidentifiable, but older and bigger" than she, sitting on a stone bench. Ernest and the woman go for a walk, asking Mary to join them:

> We walk along a sort of country road with deep smooth ruts, and you and woman take the ruts. . . . You are very tall and your legs are very long and because you are both much taller than me, I cannot keep up with your conversation because you talk across my head, and I cannot keep up with you in speed because you are walking fast and you have good foothold in the ruts, and I am walking between the ruts, and the ground there and the fields beside the road are of shiny slippery white porcelain so that I slide back with every step.[3]

It is not surprising that their relationship was filled with misgivings, misunderstandings, and violent arguments.

As was his habit learned early as a boy in Oak Park where angry parents left notes for each other, Hemingway preferred to state his case or make his apologies in letter form. Throughout the mild late winter of Cuba and into early spring, the interhouse mail was in steady use. Please forgive him, he asked, for he could not imagine why he behaved so badly over the glass of water. He was both ashamed and apologetic for smashing the glass, and would try very hard to be good. Ernest's fierce temper was liable to explode when Mary was least expecting it, sometimes scaring her with its violence. When their milk cow died and no one came to haul the carcass, he turned on her, having no one else to yell at, and afterward wrote another apology. These abject, remorseful exercises sounded more and more like the young boy in Oak Park writing out his apology to parents for misbehaving at a church function. Always he would do better. Mary accused him of making her into a bitch, but he claimed it was just not so. When he wanted to hurt her, Ernest paraded the men in her life before her—Noel Monks, Irwin Shaw, the General—they all loved her, maybe not as completely as he did, but then it was not his fault that the General found her in bed with Shaw while she was still married to Noel. What seemed like a non sequitur was a reminder of Mary's recent history of fornication, implying Ernest was not alone in contributing to her bitchood.[4]

At the end of February 1946, Hemingway wrote Buck Lanham

that he was deeply depressed, "black ass to end all black ass," what with Bumby's unsuitable girlfriend and Mary being more difficult that he ever anticipated.[5] Mary's misgivings about their relationship, in which she bore the brunt of his "black ass" moods, had steadily increased. No, he argued, he was not jealous of her friends, was not keeping her from seeing them, nor was he trying to be anything but gentle when he woke her in the morning. To prove it he paid for her week's trip to Miami in January to see old friends and shop for clothes. Meanwhile, he said that he would find a way to cope with the terrible loneliness her absence caused in his heart. In fact, he would not even mention it because that would be whining.[6] She quickly answered that she also was missing him badly, wishing "very much could curl into your arm and leg and neck and be very close to you. Please don't stop loving me dearest and please let's give ourselves another chance to both be good."[7]

Before their marriage that spring, they had, through several rounds of play, established the house rules for this game of love: Ernest initiated the attack; Mary retaliated; Ernest apologized; Mary, if unmollified, threatened to leave him; Ernest begged her to stay; Mary professed her continuing love. It was a game heavy on manipulation, with each player aware of the other's vulnerabilities, a game Ernest had played successfully with earlier wives. His arsenal of verbal abuse included irony, sarcasm, ridicule, vulgar insults, public embarrassments, and temper tantrums. When all else failed, he relied on petulance and sulking before playing the last card in his hand, the threat of suicide, which he used so often that his friends became inured to it. When he wanted to repair the damage, he wrote loving in-house letters, made sure that Mary slept late and undisturbed, gave her money, or, after seriously behaving like a bastard, gave her an expensive gift. These various tactics worked well with his first wife, Hadley, and his second wife, Pauline. Martha simply refused to play the game. Mary, who was more of a street fighter than her earlier avatars, played the game as if she had invented it. To spectators, the game was embarrassing, but they were not privy to the excitement each round could produce later in bed.

To call this serve-and-volley relationship a game is to minimize the hurt of any actual moment, and at the start, with no pattern established, Mary's distress reached intense levels. On March 13, the day she and Ernest were to pledge their brief wedding vows before the Cuban civil authority, she told him that she did not want to marry him. With plans set, a few select guests invited, his fishing and sub-hunting friends Tommy Shevlin and Winston Guest in attendance, Ernest was furious. Mary, finally relenting, went through the civil ceremony, while Ernest was barely civil and guests cringed. In her journal at 3:00 a.m. on their wedding night, Mary recorded her impression of the day:

> He came out with only a few of the nasty ironic resentfulness he usually accords me, then spent most of the day giving me that highly formal treatment, pretending I would be unreasonable about everything—thus clearly indicating to Tom Shevlin and Bumby what a heel I am. So phony, so cheap, so chickenshit. . . . But pinched by circumstances (Wolfie being here) we went to the lawyers and signed declarations to marry. I was certainly not gracious, and from then on he took it out on me—making jokes as we went back to the Florida about "Have a glass of hemlock"—and on the way home working himself into a fine rage and calling me "Rather-Out Welsh!" . . . What infuriates him most apparently is that he thinks of our life as some kind of ~~game~~ war and tonight that he thought I had won it. That was what started him. Tonight he has made the concession of allowing me to sleep alone—which is a relief.[8]

The next morning when the sun rose over the grounds of the Finca, the woodpecker was busy digging insects out of the huge ceiba tree, Ernest was at his writing pad, and Mary slept late. When they and their houseguests gathered later beside the pool, it was as if the previous night's embarrassment had not happened. Two weeks later, Mary was writing an ecstatic letter about the "simple-minded happiness" of her life with Ernest.[9]

Over the next three months, Hemingway's routine did not vary: wake early, write through the morning, swim in the afternoon or take the *Pilar* out from Cojimar to fish, return to an early supper, listen to music on the Capehart, and retire early to read. It was not an exciting life for Mary, but at least there was some harmony in the garden over which she was now the mistress. Gradually she brought about needed changes: the cadre of house servants and gardeners was somewhat reduced; the expense receipts were organized; the vegetable garden planted; and cows were brought in to produce milk for the family, the staff, and the cats. Within a month Mary was confident enough in her new role to write Martha about shipping to London the Gellhorn monogrammed silver, china, and crystal left behind. Light of voice and pleased to bring her former life to a distinct close, Martha replied that she was looking forward to the shipment.[10] Two months later, her china and silver having arrived in London, Martha replied to Mary's questions about other possessions. There was no need to be facetious, she said, about sending things as mundane as a box of corn pads. If Ernest thought he could needle her with the suggestion, he was wrong. "I feel," Martha wrote, "that I have been completely mild and entirely modest, though I know how prone E is always to feel that he is being robbed. In all cases, let us cut out such nonsense, as it is a bloody bore all round." As for her papers at the Finca, her letters to Ernest had been returned long ago. "He wants the record, I do not."[11]

At the end of April, another woman out of Ernest's recent past appeared at the Finca to undermine Mary's self-confidence in her newfound role as Mrs. Hemingway. Slim Hawks, wife of renowned movie director Howard Hawks, called from Nassau to tell Ernest that she was a new mother and an unhappy wife. Urging her to fly into Havana, Ernest said, "You need to be with people who love you." He was speaking for himself, for Mary did not love the tall beauty who walked into the Finca trailing clouds of Hollywood gossip. Nor was Slim particularly taken with Mary, whom she found to be

a fidgety banty hen of a woman, always scurrying around, doing needless things that she thought made her indispensable . . . she didn't have a clue how to run a house with Ernest Hemingway in it. She was tatty-looking . . . [with] a deep, affected voice that wasn't hers at all. And she wasn't sophisticated enough to disguise her displeasure at my having been invited to Cuba because of her husband's great affection for me.

Having appeared on the covers of several fashion magazines and recently been named "Best Dressed Woman in the World," Slim Hawks, with her natural blond streak, her wit and carriage, and her long list of prominent friends, was Mary's antithesis. Slim prided herself on never having worked in her life; Mary was born working and felt diminished when she was not.

Bemused by Hemingway's disregard for his newly married wife's feelings, Slim enjoyed his attention. When she returned to him a borrowed shirt, he gallantly told her that he would never wash it, for now it smelled like her. It did not take Slim long to figure out what Mary was learning the hard way: Ernest needed a wife and needed another woman with whom to flirt: "He didn't have to consummate the flirtation; in fact, it was the key that he didn't . . . although he might be having a silent love affair in his head, he was faithful to his wife."[12] From his first marriage to his last, Hemingway needed the presence of more than one woman within range of his magnetism. His wives were not always at ease with this need, but all coped to varying degrees. Before his first marriage with Hadley Richardson, she asked rhetorically, "Ernest, you don't have lots of infatuations do you? What could I do if you did? 'Course if you do I guess you can't help it."[13] The one gift that neither Hadley nor Pauline nor Martha was able to give Ernest, the one gift by which Mary could consolidate her position, was the gift of a daughter. By the time Hemingway met Mary, he was calling any woman younger than himself "daughter." As soon as their vows were spoken, Mary did everything her Chicago doctor advised in order to become pregnant. When she did not miss her April period, she wrote Dr. Gough for further advice, saying his pills were no help.[14]

As a largely absentee father, Hemingway went for long periods without being particularly concerned about his three sons. Then, on a mood swing, he could become overly parental. On June 21, Ernest's concentration on his writing was broken by his concern for his three sons, who were driving cross-country with Jack at the wheel bound for a California vacation. Angry to be told so little about their plans while he was trying to organize a family rendezvous at Sun Valley in August, Ernest wrote them that they needed a little discipline, which he was happy to provide: from this day forward he expected two letters a month (written on the first and fifteenth) from each son—letters neither hurried, sullen, nor forced. Further into the letter he changed the dates to the first and third Sundays of the month, coupling this duty with Pat and Gregory's religious duty to attend Mass. If these letters were not forthcoming, Papa Hemingway threatened that steps would be taken. As he was writing his sons, his mother in Oak Park was writing him in care of his publisher, for she had no idea what his Cuban address was.[15]

Two days after he began his letter to the boys, Mary precipitated another argument, locking herself in her bathroom and refusing to speak to him. Afterward in writing she explained to him her sense of diminished worth and entrapment resulting from her total dependency, a condition she had never before experienced. She knew that financial provision for her aging parents fell entirely on Ernest's largesse, for she was earning no money of her own. She was lonely, insecure, and bored. "I have no life of my own," she wrote, "only odd functions which provide you with companionship . . . and release of your sex functions which has long been almost totally mechanical." For the past month, Ernest had gone directly to bed after supper, leaving her too much time to consider her situation. Having given up her independence and her profession to face the challenge of being Mrs. Hemingway, she realized her job's longevity depended solely on his whim.[16] Whether it was Mary's despondency causing Ernest to pay more attention to her or the doctor's pills, a month later, a delighted Hemingway told Buck Lanham that Mary thought she was pregnant. Maybe this time he would get the daughter he longed for, and by the time she was old enough to be trouble, he would be dead.[17]

By July 21, Hemingway had almost a thousand pages of manuscript, revisions, and inserts done on the book that he refused to plan. As he explained to Lanham, he never knew precisely what was going to happen in any book he wrote; whatever plans he had always went astray when the story got away from him. So he lived in the book, inventing it day by day, letting it develop organically. If it did not "get away" from him, he would be worried.[18] Taking a day off from writing, Hemingway celebrated his forty-seventh birthday at sea on the *Pilar* with Mary and one or two friends, followed by a small gathering at the Finca. On that same day, his mother, vacationing on Walloon Lake with his sister Marcelline's family, wrote her son a birthday letter, reporting on the condition of the Hemingway cottage where Ernest spent his first eighteen summers and which was the setting of his first mature fiction. Years earlier, his mother had transferred ownership of the lake property to Ernest's name. Not having seen the cottage in four years, Grace was upset by what she discovered.

> I walked over to Windemere, and thought of all the happy days we spent there. I grieved to realize that you cared nothing for the place and had never been even to see it in the past eleven years. I left it clean and perfectly furnished to the last detail. . . . For some time it was broken into almost every winter by marauders . . . the mice have gnawed holes in the house . . . the front porch floor and roof are fast disappearing. The steps . . . have rotted away. The neighbors call it the haunted house.[19]

Windemere was, indeed, filled with ghosts from Hemingway's youth, memories still tender on the mind. There his father taught him to hunt and fish, taught him about the woods and the water, taught him to be resourceful. There on his birthdays beside the decorated birthday tree, his father would ceremoniously give him the five-dollar gold piece, heavy in his hand. In the lake shallows at the foot of the cottage, Ernest and his young sisters bathed naked in the water. Windemere was his first Eden, the clearest part of his life. And like Eden it was lost to him in various ways, some his own doing. When he was twelve, his father Clarence stopped coming to the lake during the summer as he retreated into progressive depressions that the young boy did not understand then and the man did not want to understand. When Ernest was twenty-one, Grace threw him out of the cottage, calling him a menace to youth, telling him not to return until he cleaned out his mouth and could respect his mother. Two years later, he and Hadley spent their wedding night at Windemere, the last time he was in the cottage. In his dreams and fiction, he returned there more often than his mother could know, nor would he tell, for he had nothing good to say to or about Grace Hemingway, holding her responsible for his father's strange moodiness and eventual suicide. Grace, he said, would be more dangerous dead than most women alive. If he ever went to her funeral, he would fear she was booby-trapped.[20] The older Hemingway became, the larger his mother's guilt grew in his mind; from Normandy to Hürtgenwald, he told friends and strangers that he was, in truth, a son of a bitch.

A week after Hemingway's forty-seventh birthday, he learned that Gertrude Stein, his literary mother and godmother to his first son, had died in Paris, leaving tiny Alice to nurture her memory. Cancer took the "mother of us all," leaving the garbage pickers of history her literary remains and the memories of those who once paid her homage. Sweet, sweet, sweet Gertrude, as a doer she was done. Having had her say on Ernest in *The Autobiography of Alice B. Toklas*, she made the singular mistake of leaving him alive after her passing, for he too would have his say, as he often promised. The following Monday, a biting letter arrived from Martha that caused Ernest to explode in a three-page typed diatribe, berating Martha for her ingratitude, reminding her that he titled her books, *A Stricken Field* and *The Heart of Another*, and wondering if he should copyright "A New Slain Knight" before she stole that one. He wished her luck in finding someone of his caliber to correct, rewrite, replot, and tone down her penchant for melodrama as he had. Having vented his spleen, he said, in a metafictional moment, that he would not send the letter, for it was too fine a piece to waste on her. He signed off, calling her a phony, pretentious bitch, and never mailed the letter.[21] There was more than one way to make his point for future literary historians.

On August 7, with a thousand pages of drafted manuscript in hand and Mary two months pregnant, the Hemingways left Cuba for Sun Valley, Idaho, where they would be joined by his three sons for a fishing and hunting vacation. Having wormed his way through the Cuban restrictions on moving guns or ammunition in or out of Cuba, Ernest checked a small arsenal in baggage and boarded the Pan-Am flight to Miami, where their Lincoln convertible was being road-checked and outfitted with five new tires, difficult to find in an America not yet returned to prewar conditions. It was the summer of a deadly outbreak of polio and the disappearance of most of the Bikini atoll during the testing of a new atomic bomb. The trip was one of rediscovery, for Ernest had not driven the route since 1941. On the highway and in the small towns, not much had changed except around military bases where Quonset huts had mushroomed along with nearby signs for used cars, cold beer, and hamburgers. The cars on the road were all prewar vintage, for new models were not yet in production. Prices for goods and services were in flux. The Office of Price Administration (OPA), which froze prices and imposed ration stamps on basic goods during the war to prevent inflation, was gradually letting America return to a free marketplace.

As the price of everything from sugar to silk began to rise, organized workers demanded better pay. Rail travel was in chaos due to a Pullman porters' strike; in Detroit, Packard automobile was closed by union strikers. Everywhere they stopped for food, gas, or a night's sleep, they found returning servicemen trying to assimilate into the almost too quiet life of Wabulla, Apalachicola, and other sleepy towns all across the South. On static-ridden radio stations and nickel jukeboxes, songs from the war years were giving way to new nonsense—"hubba, hubba, hubba" and "hey baba rebop." The long cross-country Route 66 that once carried the dust-blown and destitute west during the Depression was now being immortalized as the place to "get your kicks." Skinny Frank Sinatra pleaded with someone for "only five minutes more" of her kissing, while others, bags and reservations in hand, were "gonna take a sentimental journey home." Franklin Roosevelt, dead and buried, left his little known vice president, Harry Truman, to deal with out-of-work veterans, Russians in Berlin, higher Social Security taxes (now 1%), and a resurgence of the Ku Klux Klan.

On the road again, Ernest was not bothered by the stifling August heat burning West Texas and southern Colorado dusty brown, nor by the Lincoln's occasional vapor lock as they gained altitude. In no particular hurry, they drove up through Denver and Cheyenne and on to the open Wyoming plains, stopping August 18 in the Mission Motor Court's tiny, un-air-conditioned room in Casper, Wyoming. From Casper through Yellowstone National Park to Sun Valley, where they were scheduled to rendezvous with Ernest's sons, was an easy drive, but they would not reach the resort until almost a month later. On the morning of August 19, Mary woke alone in the cabin with an excruciating pain in her stomach, tried to stand, and doubled over screaming. Ernest, outside the cabin packing the car, found her writhing in pain. An emergency ambulance carried her to the county hospital, where the doctor on duty determined she was hemorrhaging from a burst fallopian tube resulting from an ectopic pregnancy. The hospital surgeon, away on a fishing trip, did not arrive until that evening, by which time Mary had been given several transfusions of whole blood and plasma. Finally, late that night, as she was being prepped for surgery, Mary's veins collapsed on the operating table. The doctor told Ernest it was hopeless; if he operated, Mary would die from shock. It was time to tell her good-bye. Ernest, who had seen enough battlefield transfusions in Hürtgenwald to know what he was doing, took charge. He ordered the intern to cut for Mary's vein and insert the needle, but the plasma would not flow. Ernest "cleared the line by milking the tube down and raising and tilting" until he got it flowing. With a fresh pint in her, Mary fluttered back to life, and Ernest told the surgeon to operate. Four bottles of plasma later and her ruptured tube removed, Mary was out of danger. Before dawn, she received two more blood transfusions under an oxygen tent, where she remained for a week.[22]

Quite literally, Ernest's quick and effective decisions brought Mary back from the edge of death. As ample evidence attests, he could be an impossible man to live with, a sarcastic drunk, a self-centered adolescent, but no one was better in an emergency than Ernest. For all their bickering and all of Mary's threats, past and future, to leave him, she never forgot that he saved her life. For the following two weeks, when Mary woke from her drugged sleep, either Ernest or a private nurse was at her bedside. Nine days after the operation, her stitches were removed, but Mary remained in the hospital until September 3 and could not travel for another week after that. As she gained strength and was clearly recovering, Ernest became restless and bored in Casper. He bought a Royal portable typewriter to write letters, but did not want to work on his novel until he could give it his full attention. At the end of August, he went fishing, probably with Mary's surgeon, but mostly he was taking care of his wife. After a week back at the motor court, Mary was finally able to travel. With Ernest driving and Mary napping in the Lincoln's front seat, they left Casper the morning of September 12, crossing through Yellowstone bound for Sun Valley and his sons.[23]

Sun Valley Lodge was not yet returned to service from its war duty as a rest and rehabilitation center for wounded soldiers. Instead, the Hemingways booked into two of the McDonald log cabins, which included a small kitchen, a fireplace, and a separate writing room for Ernest, where he returned to the novel he now titled *The Island and the Stream*. Although the Lodge was not yet back in the entertainment business, most of Hemingway's Ketchum friends remained in place, and the local bars and eight gambling establishments were wide open. Ernest, who would place or accept a bet on almost anything, favored the Alpine ("homey and nice"), where he claimed to be "well ahead." The bird season was abundant with quail, Hungarian partridge, and pheasant in the fall fields and ducks on the irrigation canals. Patrick Hemingway, who remained on in Ketchum when his brothers returned to school, added to the larder with a prime buck, his first big game kill. Between afternoon bird hunts, late evening suppers, and visiting friends, Hemingway's writing mornings were shorter than usual and less productive. At the Sun Valley theater, producer Mark Hellinger premiered for invited guests a director's cut of his film based on Hemingway's short story, "The Killers." Hemingway, who hated most films made of his work, so enjoyed this one that he acquired his own copy to run at the Finca.

In the hunting fields, with a cold wind blowing and stubble dry underfoot, Ernest and Mary shared their days with Gary and Rocky Cooper, with Hemingway's old mentor Charles Sweeny, and with Slim Hawks, who arrived at Ernest's invitation to escape the gossip columnists hot on the trail of her adultery with Leland Hayward.

Hemingway advised her to answer no questions, ignore the publicity, and take none of it seriously. She should escape to Ketchum, where he would put her up in the cabin he used for writing, asking her to bring "a little seconal for Papa."[24] Mary, more secure in her relationship with Ernest after her ordeal in Casper, was less resentful of Slim's presence than she had been at the Finca, and could not have anticipated the near horror that Slim almost wrought. Returning to Ketchum with a nice bag of partridges, Hemingway suddenly stopped the Lincoln when he spotted another partridge; he, Mary, and Slim piled out, loading their shotguns, but no wings beat the air. Slim, sitting on the fender of the car, pumped two cartridges out of her 16-gauge automatic, forgetting that she had removed the plug to allow more shells. Thinking the chamber empty and not wanting to leave the weapon cocked, she pulled the trigger. Just as Ernest was bending over to tie his shoelace, the gun fired, sending a load of birdshot zinging past his head, singeing the hair on the back of his neck. He rose up livid with anger just as Slim shrieked and began to cry. Ernest quickly swallowed his anger to console her, trying to make a joke of the near miss, but no one was laughing.

By early November, snow was falling in the Idaho high country. Knowing that the two-lane roads south would soon become dangerous or impassable, Ernest and Mary, completely recovered from her near-death experience in Casper, drove south to Salt Lake City. There they hunted briefly with Charles Sweeny, who had fought in a half century's worth of revolutions and wars. From Utah, the Hemingways continued south to Arizona, spending the night of November 19 at the Grand Canyon on their way to Tucson. Turning east, the dusty road followed the old trail through Apache country into Lordsburg and down to El Paso. A long, hard day's drive south and east took them across Texas and then into New Orleans for Thanksgiving. Mary's parents, plain and basic folk, were charmed by their new son-in-law, who provided a complete turkey meal served in their spacious hotel suite. By train, Ernest and Mary traveled on to New York, where they booked into the Sherry-Netherland on December 1. It was there that Buck Lanham found a Hemingway much altered from Hürtgenwald days. Unshaven and overweight, his paunch bulging over his German belt buckle,

Hemingway was dressed in bedroom slippers, tight pants, and a loose shirt with missing buttons. Speaking in what sounded to Lanham like Indian dialect from a bad western movie, Ernest was clearly drinking too much and behaving badly.

Contrary to his usual policy of refusing to talk to unknown reporters, Hemingway was feeling so good about his writing that he gave three interviews, each filled with inaccuracies, many of his own making. Mary Harrington erroneously reported that Hemingway ran away from home to become a prize fighter, but was persuaded to finish high school by his father. At the Stork Club with Mary, the columnist Leonard Lyons, and Buck Lanham, Ernest saw the prominent actor Charles Boyer seated close by with Ingrid Bergman. Ernest, residually possessive of any attractive woman who passed through his province, began "to ask loudly whether or not he should give that small green-faced character [Boyer] the back of his hand." Before the week was out, he left a pointed message for the editor of *New Masses*: "Tell Mike Gold to go fuck himself."[25]

After a miserable duck shoot with Winston Guest and Lanham on Gardiners Island, a short distance from the city, Hemingway returned to New York, where he gave interviews to the *Herald* and the *Post* at the Sherry-Netherland. Yes, he was working steadily on a long book that would "touch on the war." With twelve hundred pages of manuscript finished, it might take another nine months. "It's a big book," he said, "I've broken the back of it now." The war novels he anticipated would not be the "disillusioned realism" like that of the Twenties. "Some very excellent writing is going to come out of this war by writers who are completely unknown right now," he said, "but it's going to be entirely different from what we had before." He recommended Jean-Paul Sartre's *The Wall*, but backed shyly away from accepting the compliment of being "the best living American writer." He said that "William Faulkner is the best living, and Nelson Algren." Soon afterward *The New Yorker* caught up with him for a martini and snails lunch:

His resemblance to a handsome, playful, and potentially violent bear was heightened by the way his hair ran down over his

coat collar like a shaggy gray pelt . . . he looks and acts inde-
structible—a state of affairs that neatly supports his theory that
no Hemingway ever dies a natural death.[26]

By the time the interviews were in print, Ernest and Mary were
back in Cuba putting away the remains of Christmas celebration at
the Finca. On the desk was a gossipy letter from Paris telling them
that Ernest's journalist friend from Hürtgenwald, Willy Walton,
was now involved with Martha Gellhorn.[27]

CHAPTER 10

Year of the Dog

1947

Forty-seven years old and aging quickly, his hairline receding, his liver slowly betraying him, Hemingway had not published a book in six years and would not for another three. In 1940, he was a lion among writers; in 1947, he was becoming an historical artifact, a relic from the Lost Generation whose early work was entering the academic literary canon. Soon biographers would be at his door, ready to entomb him. Elsewhere, a new moon was rising on the cultural landscape of America. On the dark side of New York the Beat apocalypse of Allen Ginsberg, William Burroughs, and Jack Kerouac was evolving underground. In Chicago, Nelson Algren was about to take a walk on the wild side, and in Brooklyn, a young veteran named Norman Mailer was finishing *The Naked and the Dead.* In his studio reeking of automobile paint, Jackson Pollock was dripping abstract colors in wild profusion, making ancient Miró's *The Farm*, which presided over Finca Vigia. Fats Waller with his rolling eyes was dead, and the new young beboppers were playing a jazz the white boys could not steal. "Papa, papa," pleaded the pop recording, "won't you dance with me? Won't you dance?"

Ernest did not bother to answer. Having gone his own way always, he was confident in the long book piling up on his work table. A thousand pages into it, he began revising, typing the opening section to see how it looked, paring down the manuscript. He had not yet reached the air war over England, much less the invasion of France, but was under no pressure to hurry. Mark

Hellinger, pleased with the money made from his film *The Killers*, was offering Hemingway a lucrative deal on four unwritten short stories: $50,000 a year for four years, plus 10 percent of the film profits, guaranteed minimum $25,000 per film.[1] Scribner's was about to reissue his three best-selling novels—*The Sun Also Rises*, *A Farewell to Arms*, and *For Whom the Bell Tolls*—in a boxed set, perhaps with illustrations. *A Farewell to Arms* was coming out in a college edition with an introduction by Robert Penn Warren, and Jonathan Cape, Ernest's British publisher, was keeping his work in print. Publishers in Germany, France, and Russia were returning to the marketplace with Hemingway translations, all of which would provide steady income for the rest of his life.[2] Despite the high cost of maintaining his lifestyle at the Finca and his penchant for equally expensive travel, Hemingway could afford to lay down books in his bank vault if he chose, leaving them to his heirs to publish.

He was also leaving heirs, friends, and scholars the complex and contradictory legacy of his life. It was never the same story twice, never quite the same mood. Chiding William Faulkner for writing while drinking, he prided himself on not taking a drink before noon when he was working. For a man who belittled alcoholics, Hemingway spent a lot of time in letters congratulating himself on not being one. At eleven in the morning when he was through writing for the day, one of the servants would bring to poolside a shaker of martinis—"Montgomerys," Ernest called them in sarcastic reference to Field Marshal Montgomery's need for a fifteen-to-one advantage on the battlefield. Hemingway would tell a guest, "Eleven o'clock. What the hell it's noon in Miami. Let's have a drink."[3] When he drank too much, which was more and more often, he was liable to say almost anything to anyone, and the less he respected someone, the more outrageous his mouth became. How many Germans did you kill, Papa? The number increased in direct ratio to his drinking. When the figure went past one hundred, most listeners stopped believing the stories. Thus he denigrated and devalued his long days on submarine patrol, the tense moments at Rambouillet, and the dark night of Hürtgen. Unable to explain his sudden mood shifts and excessive drinking, those who loved him looked the other way, made excuses, remembering always the man sober, intense, and magnetic.

Yet in an emergency, he remained the one the who never panicked, the cool head who assessed the situation quickly, organized the response, and took control. In April at the Finca, he was faced with a tense and emotional crisis when his son Patrick arrived from Key West with an undiagnosed concussion from a car accident. As Ernest explained to Mary, who was in Chicago where her father was undergoing hospital tests for prostate cancer, Patrick's behavior exhibited all the signs of mental disturbance: excited and slurred speech, disjointed conversation. That evening, when Patrick explained about the accident, Ernest was certain he was suffering from a concussion. Five days later, with Patrick running a high fever and behaving violently, doctors were running blood tests, and Ernest was organizing all available hands for round-the-clock watches, he himself sleeping outside Patrick's door. Patrick's mother, Pauline, came from Key West to help with the nursing and cooking, glad to be of use and pleasantly surprised by Ernest's considerate behavior. Erratically better, Patrick had brief lucid periods followed by relapse; for three weeks, the Finca team kept watch, feeding their patient, bathing him daily, and restraining him when violent. In his deliriums, Patrick fought valiantly with the devils he found at his bedside. When lucid, he did not remember the fiends who tormented him. By May 2, Ernest was worn out from going sleepless and from worry; he passed in and out of dark, gloomy periods, but his responsibility for Patrick kept him from going over the edge.[4]

Unable to work with any consistency on the prewar Bimini novel, he wrote daily loving letters to Mary, assuring her that he could pay her father's hospital bills and giving her detailed medical advice on prostate cancer. From his recent reading of Paul DeKruif's *The Male Hormone*, Ernest explained that injections of testosterone would sometimes arrest prostate cancer. (Soon he would be taking injections himself for his flagging energy level.) He also reported on Patrick's slow progress and life at the Finca. Blue poinciana and eucalyptus were flourishing; alligator pears were forming on branches by the hundreds. His letters frequently carried some private reference to their sexual life which he and his penis—"Mr. Scooby"—were eager to resume. Much of the eroticism was connected with Mary's brown hair, now bleached and dyed blond. While in Chicago, he urged her to go to a professional beautician to turn it smoky silver, which would complement her tan. She could tell how excited he was about her return, he said, because he usually did not write about their private sexual games. She might, he suggested, really surprise him by returning as a redhead, which would please Papa as well as *Catherine* and *Pete*.[5] The latter two were the names they invented for the characters they sometimes assumed in bed—he was "Catherine," Mary was "Pete." Her girl "Catherine," he wrote her, had not been around much since she left, but he was certain she would turn up as soon as "Pete" (Mary) returned."[6] Eight days later, Ernest turned his own hair a bright copper tone to amuse Mary on her return to the Finca. Trying for the color that "Catherine" wore, he was shocked the next morning to see the results in the mirror. He wrote Mary that so long as their games hurt no one, it was nobody's business but their own. Then her letter came, asking him to bleach his hair exactly as he had already done it.[7] Soon these games would become part of his fiction, which in turn would enrich the games. In the beginning he could move easily back and forth between the fictional world of his characters and the less fictional world outside his writing room. Later that dividing line became so porous that it was difficult to say on which side of it he stood.

On May 18, Mary returned to the Finca, and Pauline, who had taken a break from nursing Patrick, returned five days later, for her son was not yet "lucid" and still required constant care. Bemused, delighted, and sexually stimulated to have both women in the house at once, Ernest wrote Buck Lanham on May 24, "that he and Mary had made love eighteen times since her return."[8] Twelve days later, Mary came down with a virulent flu that put her in bed for two weeks running a high fever; Pauline again returned from Key West to nurse Mary so that Ernest would not carry the flu to Patrick, but also because she knew how the threat of flu terrified Hemingway ever since he listened to the death rattle of flu-stricken soldiers in World War I.[9] Mary, in her fever, tore off part of a brown paper bag to scrawl out a quick will stating she wanted her cremated remains to be dropped into a "clean part" of the Gulf Stream. She also assigned her London flat's contents to Pauline, with whom she was now close friends.[10]

Frustrated by the hiatus in his writing, worn out from nursing duties, Hemingway took another heavy blow on June 17 when Charles Scribner's telegram told him that Max Perkins had died suddenly from pneumonia. "What awful luck," Ernest cabled back, unable to say in a few words the magnitude of his loss. Max, the caretaker, was no longer there to run Ernest's long-distance errands, deposit the Scribner loans, and deflect Hemingway's angry outbursts after each book was published. For twenty years, Max was there for Ernest, mediating between the needs of the author and the exigencies of the publishing house, counseling wisely and always sympathetic. For Max's leaving, Hemingway was the poorer, having lost a voice of reason that no one could replace. Missing Max with his well-worn hat, Max so proper in the face of whatever nature sent his way, Ernest had no one left from the old days to lean on, to talk the literary talk. By deaths and disputes more and more isolated from his old literary friends, Ernest was vaguely aware that the postwar age was passing him by. Always overly sensitive to constructive criticism, his tolerance for it was now almost nil.

On June 26, Ernest put Mary, still feverish, on the plane to Key West, where she recuperated for another two weeks with Pauline, who moved back and forth between the two sick bays. On July 7, Patrick began new treatments three times a week, which immediately improved his condition.[11] Through all of the late night watches, worry for his son, lost sleep, and the strain of remaining calm, Ernest's own physical condition was deteriorating. With only erratic exercise and almost no fishing, his weight ballooned up to 256 pounds, and though he did not yet know it, his blood pressure was approaching fatal numbers. When, in a "black ass" mood, he read a William Faulkner statement seemingly questioning his courage, Ernest was stung to the quick. Rather than respond himself, he asked Buck Lanham to send Faulkner a detailed testimonial to Hemingway's behavior under fire and in close quarters. Faulkner had, in fact, used the word "coward," saying that of the leading

American writers, Hemingway took the fewest risks in writing, not trying for the impossible. Chagrined by Lanham's lengthy documentation of Hemingway's courage, Faulkner wrote directly to Ernest, apologizing for not insisting on looking at the interview before it was published. "I have believed for years that the human voice has caused all human ills," it said, "and I thought I had broken myself of talking. Maybe this will be my valedictory lesson."[12]

Hemingway's friendly response said he was sorry Faulkner had been misquoted, and that nothing Faulkner said mattered now that he knew how it happened. That was on a good day. Time and again, when the paranoia, lurking beneath the surface of his reason, became full blown, he would come back to Faulkner's inadvertent insult, reopening the old wound. Faulkner took Hemingway's letter at face value, saying he hated literary gossip, particularly having started it himself by testing out an idea of no value anyway. Some of Hemingway's stories, like "An Alpine Idyll," were so complete that there was "nothing more that even God could do to it; it's hard, durable, the same anywhere in fluid time; you can write another as hard and as durable if you are good enough but you can't beat it. . . . I wish I had said it that way . . . what I wish most is I'd never said it at all."[13]

Slightly miffed that Faulkner chose an early story rather than something more recent to declare durable, Hemingway pointed out several parts of *For Whom the Bell Tolls* where he was taking the sort of chances that Faulkner praised Tom Wolfe for attempting and failing. But the real test was not their contemporaries, but the durable writers from the past: Dostoyevsky, Turgenev, De Maupassant. Faulkner was, Ernest said, a better writer than Fielding; they both had beaten Flaubert, the "honored master." Filled with military metaphors and earthy language, the letter played more to Hemingway's public image than to that inner part of him where the writer lived.[14]

On September 20, in a year already filled with pain, worry, and loss, Hemingway received news of the death of his old friend, Katy Smith, the wife of John Dos Passos. Driving westward into a setting sun, Dos crashed headlong into a truck parked on the road's shoulder; when he regained consciousness, he found his car's top almost sheared off and Katy dead in the seat next to him. Dos himself was badly bruised, and his right eye permanently damaged beyond repair. Hemingway sent a telegram of sorrow and loss, silently remembering the long-ago summers at Walloon Lake when Katy, with her teasing eyes, was the sexiest woman he knew.[15]

All that summer and into the fall, while Hemingway's attention was largely familial, the political intrigues of the Americas were bubbling on all sides of him. In Costa Rica, violent labor strikes left dead and wounded in the streets. In Paraguay, a civil war was raging, and in Chile, civil liberties were suspended to deal with communist-led strikes. In August, a bloodless coup replaced the president of Ecuador; in September at Rio de Janeiro, President Harry Truman was one of the nineteen endorsers of the Inter American Treaty of Reciprocal Assistance, but on the same day the new dictator of Ecuador was himself overthrown. On September 12, an armed coup attempt in Venezuela was suppressed.

Then came the Dominican Republic fiasco. The first story broke in Havana on August 6, when the minister of defense announced the capture of four pilots and their airplanes presumably belonging "to the group that is preparing the much publicized revolutionary expedition against Santo Domingo."[16] Two weeks later the recently reelected president of the Dominican Republic, Rafael Trujillo, asked Cuba "to intervene to stop revolutionary preparations . . . being made in Cuban territory against the Dominican Republic."[17] There was, in fact, a ragtag army being formed and trained to overthrow Trujillo, and one of the revolutionists' supporters was Ernest Hemingway, who had foolishly given money to the cause in the form of personal checks. As with any political activity in Cuba, someone in the government had to be complicit in the effort, either for money or for idealism, for it to succeed. In this case the minister of defense had given guarantees that Cuban President Ramón Grau would be kept uninformed of the revolutionists and that the government would not interfere. Either not enough money changed hands, or the minister found it more advantageous to betray the project. Whatever his reason, his betrayal left Hemingway liable to arrest as soon as his checks surfaced. His doctor, José Luis Herrera, could not believe that Ernest had been so naive as to give them checks, or to have ever believed that the minister of defense would keep his word. Had Hemingway not noticed that none of his Cuban friends who hated Trujillo were involved in the plot? Herrera assured Hemingway there would be arrests: he must flee the country immediately. If they hurried, they could just get him on the afternoon flight to New York. René, who oversaw the Finca staff, packed a suitcase, while Ernest left hurried advice for Mary, who was remaining at La Vigia along with Pauline, Patrick, and Gregory.[18] Cursing the politicians, Hemingway was driven into town by his chauffeur, Juan Lopez, reaching the airport just in time to trot up the boarding ladder.

On September 26, the *New York Times* reported that Cuban military and naval units had trapped "about 1,500 Dominican revolutionists on Confite Key off the north coast near Nuevitas . . . former United States fliers, said to have been engaged to pilot planes, now are reported to have been returned to the United States." Four days later, a front-page *New York Times* story confirmed that eight hundred revolutionists had surrendered and were now in Cuban prison camps. They were now being charged with "action against the security of Cuba," and the minister of education was under arrest as a conspirator. "Large quantities of arms and ammunition were captured."[19] It was rumored that the government sweep missed one of the organizers, young Fidel Castro.[20]

When the Cuban government finally admitted the suppression of a plot on Cuban soil to overthrow Rafael Trujillo, Hemingway, with Toby Bruce driving, was miles north entering Yellowstone National Park en route to Sun Valley. [21] Thus he was not at the Finca when the *Diario de la Marina* said that the planning committee met at Finca Vigia where Hemingway reportedly held out for token bombing of the Dominican capital. A second story said that Ernest was heading a revolution against Cuban President Grau.[22]

When further details were made public, Hemingway's name was prominently featured:

> [Mercenary pilots] were given lodging in the home near Havana, Cuba of the American novelist, Ernest Hemingway, who on several occasions acted as spokesman for the revolution-

aries. The American aviators implicated in the plot . . . [said] that although they had been well fed and provided with drink in Hemingway's home, they had not been paid the sums they had been promised for their part in the adventure . . . an agent of the Dominican government was informed by the revolutionary spokesman, Ernest Hemingway, that the invasion army "had grown to seven thousand men," and that their training was being carried out publicly in several places in Cuba.[23]

How involved Hemingway actually was in the failed revolution depends upon who is telling the story. One of his doctors said, "Hemingway gave some money for the Confites thing. But we heard he was going to be arrested, so I . . . got him a ticket for Miami. . . . We got to the airport just a few minutes before the plane's departure."[24] In a letter to Buck Lanham, Hemingway's knowledge of the foiled plot indicated that he had inside information: the group had no security, pitiful logistics, and no sense of priorities. He himself was too busy nursing Patrick to become involved, but was tempted because it would have been easy to bring off. All he did was give advice and make recommendations.[25] Whether Hemingway left Cuba on the run, or leisurely as planned, did not matter to Mary when Lieutenant Correa and his squad arrived to search the property and question Ernest. When she ordered Correa out of the house, he pointed his pistol at her as if to shoot. Mary quickly invented a pregnancy and a U.S. Army captaincy to protect herself. Not finding Ernest, the lieutenant and his men confiscated all weapons, but returned them next day. On October 3, speaking to Mary through a patchy phone connection from Sun Valley, Ernest learned about the frightening house call, and apologized to her for having to go through it alone. Guilty or not, his known interests in revolutions made him a likely suspect; but five months later when he returned to Havana, the whole affair had blown over.

When Mary arrived at the Sun Valley Lodge, she found her husband dieting, restraining his drinking, and exercising daily in the hunting fields, but his blood pressure (215 over 125) remained high, creating a steady, irritating buzz in his ears. Comfortably ensconced in the "Glamour House" suite with two bedrooms, a living room with fireplace, and two sun porches, each morning Ernest was up early, invigorated by the altitude and the perfect Indian summer weather. For the first time in months, he was once again writing steadily on the Bimini book. With a rich supply of ducks on Silver Creek, fat pheasants at Dietrich, the World Series on the afternoon radio, he was happier than he had been for many months. The string of deaths, sicknesses, and setbacks seemed at an end. At Thanksgiving, he urged Mary to accept Pauline's invitation to join her in San Francisco for Christmas shopping, which she did. There was no problem about money because the second payment of $25,000 was due from Mark Hellinger. By mid-December his weight was down to 220, and his blood pressure, with the help of Nitrotonal pills, fell to 150 over 110.[26]

When his three sons arrived for a Ketchum Christmas, Ernest moved the entourage into three of the McDonald Cabins, where they were joined by Juan Dunabeitia and Roberto Herrera, who were there as Hemingway guests, their reward for having faithfully helped when Patrick was sick. Mary cooked and baked, listened and laughed, correcting her husband's exaggerations and keeping track of expenses, which were significant. Mark Hellinger's check arrived, which, even after setting aside $20,000 in his tax account, would leave the Hemingways in reasonable financial shape. Because of the high tax rates imposed during the war and not yet rebalanced, Hemingway's seemingly large tax reserve was not without reason, for he was in the 90 percent bracket. Unfortunately, a few days before Christmas, Hellinger died and Hemingway returned the uncashed check to his widow.[27] The long-term deal promised by the Hollywood producer went up in smoke along with any future payments. It was an appropriate end for a year filled with disappointments and loss. New Year's Eve at Trail Creek Cabin, Ernest in coat and tie took up a defensive position in a corner of the room, where he spent most of the evening talking with Ingrid Bergman and Gary Cooper. There was a good deal of joking about the lovemaking in the sleeping bag scene in the For Whom the Bell Tolls movie, but by midnight, levity was muted. Watching the limbo dancers trying to slither under the low bar, Hemingway told Bergman, "Daughter, this is going to be the worst year we have ever seen."[28]

CHAPTER 11

Enter Biographers, Stage Left

December 1947 to September 1948

As Albert Camus was beginning to formulate, there comes a midpoint to a man's life beyond which time is no longer on his side, a point at which he knows, perhaps for the first time, the absurdity of the universe. Uncommonly aware of this absurdity since being blown up at eighteen, Hemingway was existential long before the word was current. When drinking with people he knew, he often regaled them with scenarios of his own death, sometimes demonstrating with an unloaded rifle or shotgun exactly how he would place the muzzle against his palate and trigger the shot with his naked toe, or any object at hand. That friends were not amused by this demonstration in no way lessened the delight he took in the performance. The specter of his own death was never far from his consciousness; "the old whore," as he called her, was always there, rocking the cradle.

For the previous thirty years, this relationship with the absurd heightened his experiences, making them more valuable because they were momentary. One never knew if this was the last fish, the last Scotch, the last pretty woman, or the last book. Each time he changed wives, he moved on to new homes, new cafés, new territory—moving westward until he passed a different sort of midpoint than the one Camus would describe. The previous September on his way to Sun Valley, he took a long detour up the lower Michigan peninsula to the "haunted" cottage on Walloon Lake. Around the old store at Horton Bay, some say he stopped, asking directions, because everything was changed.[1] He had not been there since 1921, and this visit was the beginning of his many returns, going back to once familiar places: Fossalta where he was first wounded; Pamplona with the bulls in the street; the Serengeti of his first lion. Each return would be a disappointment. He should have listened to T. S. Eliot who said "old men should be explorers," not returnees. But by 1948, Hemingway stopped his explorations to revisit and reassess a life that was already a legend. The only newfound lands left to him were in his fictions. He entered, unannounced, into his final period, a holding action against all kinds of physical and emotional problems, but writing with renewed intensity.

This period was also characterized by the appearance of Hemingway's chroniclers, the first of whom, Lillian Ross, arrived at Sun Valley early the day before Christmas to gather information for a *New Yorker* "Profile" on Sidney Franklin, the Brooklyn bullfighter and Hemingway's friend. She met Ernest at the McDonald Cabins:

> He was standing on hard-packed snow, in dry cold of ten degrees below zero, wearing bedroom slippers, no socks, Western trousers with an Indian belt that had a silver buckle, and a lightweight Western-style sports shirt open at the collar . . . he looked rugged and burly and eager and friendly and kind. . . . I was absolutely freezing in the cold.[2]

Although dubious of her ability to write convincingly about a ritual for which she had no *afficion*, Hemingway was a gracious source of information. Ross spent most of the day with Ernest and Mary, talking, Christmas shopping, eating and drinking. In the process, she picked up interesting inside information on Hemingway as well as on Franklin, information that would lead eventually to her *New Yorker* "Profile" on Ernest a year later. No sooner was she on her way back to New York than those around Hemingway realized that Ross's appearance had upset him. Maybe it was his high blood pressure; maybe one of those sudden mood changes which were becoming more frequent. Ross, he said, was bright enough, maybe even a sound journalist, but he did not trust her. Forgetting that when she called, he had invited her to Sun Valley, he complained about outsiders disrupting his life, asking questions about his work. For several days afterward he worried about what he had said to her, concerned that it might look foolish in print.[3]

When the screen writer Pete Viertel and his attractive wife Jigee (formerly Mrs. Budd Schulberg) arrived at the McDonald Cabins, Hemingway quickly absorbed them into his "mob." The following evening, at Hemingway's invitation, the Viertels joined Ernest and Mary for supper. When they entered the Hemingway cabin, Blackie, an adopted stray dog, was stretched out by the fireplace, books and newspapers were piled on the floor, and Marlene Dietrich was singing sentimental German songs on the phonograph. The group went out to the Sun Valley Lodge, where they were joined by Gary and Rocky Cooper. Later, back at the cabin, Hemingway made some rough comment about Irwin Shaw, a good friend of Pete's and a recent collaborator with him on an unsuccessful play. Mary jumped to her former lover's defense, saying she "adored Shaw." Ernest told Pete of meeting Shaw during the war:

"Walking into their unit was a lot like reading Proust," he said, "the part where he describes all the fairies."

"Shaw's no fairy," Mary replied.

Not understanding the game in progress, Pete and Jigee watched perplexed at the ball going back and forth across the matrimonial net. Vaguely they realized that they were being tested, but without a clue as to the purpose of the test. Ernest's irritability alarmed Pete, who thought that Mary's constant corrections of his stories only provoked him further. The man was a contradiction: "his shyness, his hesitant speech, the apologies that nearly always followed one of his sarcastic, or even disagreeable, comments." Before the Hemingways left Ketchum, Pete Viertel "became aware that he [Ernest] was capable of sudden, extreme rages."[4]

At the end of January, Ernest and Mary began tidying up for the drive back to Key West. Pauline, who was in Havana to speak with Patrick's doctor, reported that the new tower Mary designed and contracted to have built was an architectural triumph. Like the swimming pool with which Pauline once surprised Ernest in Key West, the tower writing room was Mary's surprise for him at the

Finca. That Pauline knew more about the tower than did Ernest was further evidence of complicity between former and present wives which did not noticeably bother him. In fact, he and Mary intended to visit with Pauline in Key West before returning to Cuba. On February 1, Pete Viertel helped Ernest pack the Buick, filling the trunk and the entire backseat with luggage, maps, guns, books, bottles, fruit, two roasted ducks, and the stray dog, Blackie. Traveling east across snow-covered Idaho and into Wyoming, Ernest drove while Mary manned the maps and guidebooks to answer questions about the passing topography. Four thousand miles and thirteen days on the road brought them finally to Key West, where Pauline welcomed them to the familiar house on Whitehead Street.[5]

By February 20, Hemingway was back at the Finca, his weight down to 216, his mind at ease and ready to return to his writing, leaving behind a Key West that claimed to have been shocked by his visit. Earl Wilson, who happened to be passing through the town on his way to Havana, reported in his gossip column that the town was "aghast" because Mary and Pauline "have been acting like turtle doves." Visiting Hemingway at the Finca, Wilson, stepping over the twenty-two cats occupying the ground floor of the new tower, admired the view from the third-floor writing room. It was here, Hemingway told Wilson, that he would hide out from unwanted visitors while completing his novel in progress. "When you're going good," he said, "when words are falling on your paper like rain, you don't like to be stopped."[6]

Yet he stopped himself often enough, for he was forever inviting friends and chance acquaintances to visit the Finca. On March 7, he was waiting at the Havana airport's arrival gate to welcome Malcolm Cowley and his family. On commission from *Life* magazine, Cowley, who knew Hemingway briefly in the Paris Twenties, was there with Hemingway's consent to write what would be the first important biographical essay on the man and the writer. Already there was a sizable correspondence between them on the project, and more letters would follow their extended interview. It was the sort of in-depth public exposure which Hemingway had long avoided; that he was acceding to it at this point in his life coincided with his own return to places past and to his ongoing revision of his early life.

Housing Cowley, his wife, and son at the Hotel Ambos Mundos assured Hemingway morning writing time to work on the second part of his novel: the cross-country trip taken by the fictional novelist and his newly found love, Helene. Ernest and Cowley's afternoons were spent around the Finca pool or on the *Pilar*, where thirteen-year-old Bob Cowley became seasick, vomiting on the deck. "Hemingway stripped off his jersey," Bob remembered years later, "and wiped it up and threw the jersey into the sea . . . and went on fishing." The working visit was complicated by the arrival, by invitation, of Hemingway's younger sister, Sunny, and her son, Ernest, named for "Uncle Ernie," who despised being called "Uncle Ernie."[7] The usual gin and tonics at pool side, daiquiris at the Floridita, wine with supper, and Scotch afterward may have made Hemingway more than usually talkative about his past, both recent and distant, but what he told Cowley was not noticeably different from stories told to Lillian Ross in Ketchum. As a journalist talking on the record to another journalist for publication, Hemingway revealed details about the wartime patrols of the *Pilar*, his paramilitary engagement at Rambouillet, and the horrors at Hürtgenwald—subjects that heretofore he discussed only off the record.

No sooner was Cowley back on the mainland pursuing Hemingway friends for pithy quotes than Ernest fell into deep remorse for agreeing to the interview, for allowing himself to reveal personal information, and for possibly endangering his residence in Cuba. He asked Cowley not to write anything about the "Caribbean business" because it remained secret information. If the Cuban government found out that not only was he on military patrol while pretending to be fishing but he also operated as a counterintelligence agent for the United States, they would have good reason to suspect him of being a current American agent. Without telling Cowley about his alleged involvement in the Trujillo fiasco, Ernest said he would be in big trouble if his wartime activities were made public. When he was dead, Cowley could tell all; in fact, Ernest gave him the names of those still alive who could confirm and elaborate his stories. The more he pleaded for secrecy, the more he regretted ever agreeing to be part of what now smelled to him like a mortuary. To write a biography of a living writer was tantamount to placing him in the grave.[8] Then, four days later, Hemingway's alter ego was giving Cowley leads to follow up on his early years at Walloon Lake, and telling him the history of the machine gun he carried in the jeep across France and which he used on Germans during the attack on Lanham's command post.[9] In Hemingway's next letter he gave Cowley even more details of the battle in Hürtgenwald, including his temporary impotency throughout the battle. In July, Hemingway told Cowley further details on his life while refusing to read the essay in advance of publication. In fact, he asked Malcolm to state up front that he had not read the piece and would be delighted if the events described were all proved to have never happened.[10]

Cowley must have been perplexed by Hemingway's frequent and contradictory letters, taking away with the left hand what the right hand had given. But this behavior also kept Cowley asking questions, for each of Hemingway's responses would reveal some new piece of biography, some more fabulous than accurate, all provocative and somewhat paranoid. Unsolicited information was given about his father's suicide, not all of it true. About his wounding in Italy, Hemingway asked Cowley to say only that he was severely wounded and received several medals as a result; because he was in "bad trouble" in Italy, too much information might bring it up again. In fact it would be better if Cowley were to leave Italy out completely, for which favor Hemingway would leave Cowley a letter to be opened after he was dead which would explain the "trouble" that had no statute of limitations. Absolutely not to be used in *Life* was the story that there was Indian blood in the Hemingway family, or that one of his sisters was once in love with him. Then, in a rambling, repetitive manner, Hemingway went into great detail about his prowess as a driver of fast automobiles, an activity that he was forced to give up after five wrecks in which people were killed or hurt in all five; in truth, no one was ever killed in a Hemingway auto wreck, but he was a dangerous driver, particularly when drinking.[11]

Why Hemingway was making these revelations is speculative. From letters and other documents, he is clearly worried about his hypertension and his weight, for both of which he records every slight fluctuation. If he went to the war looking for an honorable death, or maybe just not caring whether he lived or died, it was because he did not know if he could ever write a better book than *For Whom the Bell Tolls*. Now, confident in his knowledge that he was working on a novel of such complexity that it would surpass *The Bell*, he felt that he was writing in the shadow of death, but the drugs he was taking to control his blood pressure had side effects which were potentially dangerous for a mind genetically pro- grammed toward depression and paranoia. For the remaining years of his life, his recurring worry was that he would die before finish- ing the "big book."

But he was also passively seeking the man to play Boswell to his Johnson. Mary, he knew, was keeping a daily journal of their wheres and whens, his ripostes and tantrums, the names of tourist courts and daily mileage. But Mary was not in the same league with Arthur Mizener, for example, who was leading the biographical glorification of Scott Fitzgerald. Perhaps Hemingway thought Cowley was such a man. In his September 5 letter, he gave Cowley permission to do the "book" on him which Scribner's would pub- lish. When "A Portrait of Mister Papa" appeared in *Life* magazine, most of the information Hemingway gave Cowley but asked him not to mention was part of the public piece: the sub patrols right down to armament and objective; the paramilitary activity at Rambouillet; and the battle at Hürtgenwald. By giving Cowley fas- cinating information, while denying him usage with one hand and directing him to other sources to confirm it with the other, Hemingway had it both ways. He liked having it both ways.

Consciously or not, Hemingway was complicit in the construc- tion of what would be the outline for future biographers: Hemingway the young boxer, the cub reporter, the wounded sol- dier, the novice writer poor in Paris, Ezra and Gertrude's pet. Turning points were highlighted: the lost manuscripts, the struggle to find a voice, the fight to keep his art uncorrupted, the break- through novels, Bimini days, marlin afternoons, African lions, the

Spanish war—all culminating in *For Whom the Bell Tolls*. The essay ended with Hemingway's commentary on his art in phrases borrowed from *Green Hills of Africa:*

> You can do it or not do it in that league I am speaking of. And you only have to do it once to get remembered by some people. But if you can do it year after year after year quite a lot of people remember and they tell their children, and their children and their grandchildren remember, and if it's books they can read them. And if it's good enough it lasts forever.[12]

Speaking in the prophetic voice, Hemingway gave Cowley the perfect conclusion, and in the process maintained some control of his public life. From his Paris days forward, he read deeply into the lives of the artists—Byron, Yeats, Lawrence the novelist, and Lawrence of Arabia—studying how their fame became them. A man might not control all the variables, but neither could he fail to try. For the next twelve years, with the postwar academic scholars in hot pursuit, Hemingway would continue to manage the revelation of his public and private lives.

No sooner were Cowley and family out the door than Hemingway was inviting Pete Viertel to visit again.[13] Viertel was collaborating with the Hollywood director John Huston on a movie script for *China Valdez*, a movie in which Cuban revolutionists attempt to assassinate President Machado. When the script stalled, Huston decided to go to Havana for possible locations and inspiration. Viertel, knowing something of both Huston and Hemingway, was anxious about their meeting: both were dominant males, both could be provoked to violence, and both were heavy drinkers. Their first meeting was an afternoon outing on the *Pilar* in a heavy sea that quickly took Huston's young wife, Evelyn Keyes, to the verge of nausea.

The following evening, Pete, Jigee, John, and Evelyn were supper guests at the Finca, where introductory martinis and dinner wine were followed by terrace conversation which turned to boxing. When Huston mentioned that he had once boxed professionally as a light heavyweight, Hemingway quickly suggested they put on the gloves and spar a few rounds. Viertel was rightly worried: "I could imagine nothing worse than John and Papa stepping a few fast rounds on the terrace. Mary Hemingway was equally appalled about the prospect of her husband taking on one of his guests. 'Pete . . . do something to stop Papa,' she whispered in my ear." Viertel found Hemingway in the bathroom, stripped to the waist, mumbling, "I'm just going to cool him quick, Pete." Viertel finally persuaded Ernest that both he and John had drunk too much, and the match was avoided.[14]

Huston's two-week stay at the Hotel Nacional ended with a going-away party to which John invited the American consul and the Hemingways, including Pauline, who arrived that afternoon to visit Mary. Meeting in the Huston suite, the gathering was pleasant enough until Huston asked Hemingway about Joris Ivens and the filming of *The Spanish Earth*. Having made documentaries himself during the war, Huston seemed honestly interested, complimenting Ernest on his narration and asking him why he had read it himself.

> "Orson Welles was supposed to do it," Hemingway said.
> "Orson, eh?" Huston said, nodding. "And why didn't he do it?" Everyone in the room was listening by this time.
> "Well, John," Hemingway replied in his gravelly voice . . . "Every time Orson said the word 'infantry' it sounded like a cocksucker swallowing."

Huston managed to laugh, but to his guests, unaccustomed to sexually explicit language in mixed company, Hemingway's statement "was like a hand grenade going off" in the suite. The U.S. consul and his wife made their excuses and left. The Hemingway party departed soon after for the Finca, pleading that Ernest never ate supper out. The next morning, the Hemingways put to sea on the *Pilar* for a week's fishing trip that lasted to the end of March.[15]

Returning refreshed to his novel, Hemingway wrote ten out of the first fifteen days of April, taking time off only to answer letters. He did have a cash-flow problem, which was resolved when his lawyer, Maurice Speiser, arranged for the film sale of "The Snows of Kilimanjaro" for enough money to repay a $12,000 Scribner loan and to plan an extended European trip in the fall. After two fall seasons in Ketchum, Ernest was ready to find new country. As he told

Pete Viertel, when they started putting your picture up in the local real estate office as a reason to buy a house, it was time to move on. He and Mary were booked in September on a small ship bound for Italy, where he asked Viertel to join them if he was interested in working on a joint project. Ernest had imagined a wonderful story to write, but it needed a collaborator: A disabled German submarine is abandoned by its crew, who take over a Cayo Lobos lighthouse where the wartime *Pilar* crew find them. Ernest knew the *Pilar* side of the story; he wanted Viertel to research and write the German side. It would be a short book, which should go well as a movie, but would nonetheless be written as if it were the last book either could write. They could write together in Paris and then, when the snow fell, hole up in the mountains where Pete and Jigee could ski and he could write.[16] It was an uncharacteristic offer for Hemingway to make, one he would never have made on an earlier book. Viertel, uneasy about working with Hemingway, told Ernest he was not the man for the job, pleading that he was not yet sure enough of himself as a writer. He might serve as a research man, but not a collaborator.[17]

Hemingway did not give up on the idea. In a long, rambling, repetitive letter, he renewed the offer, saying if not in the fall then why not late winter. Of course if Pete had commitments, he had commitments, but he needed to see the island setting before he started writing on the project. Ernest assured him, he was not trying to pressure him about the collaboration. Embedded in an already curious letter was an even stranger, unsubstantiated account of Ernest's activity during the Spanish Civil War. Helping others to execute a camp of war prisoners, he claimed he spent the night pulling a trigger that left water blisters on his finger and murder on his conscience. Two months later he told Archie MacLeish that he personally killed twenty-six Germans and extended his World War II combat time from five months to eight. The truth was never enough.[18] In the June letter to Viertel, he admitted to being obsessed by war, but promised to resolve that issue by writing about it.[19]

More and more in his letters, Hemingway was rehearsing his biography, modifying here, exaggerating there, leaving a confusing trail of truths, half-truths, and outright fantasies. At forty-eight, he began saying outrageous things to complete strangers, things he would never have said earlier. What appears at times to be mania can also be read as his response to the canonization of his generation already dead: Tom Wolfe (1938), Scott Fitzgerald (1940), Gertrude Stein (1946), Max Perkins (1947). After reading W. G. Rogers's Gertrude Stein biography—*When This You See Remember Me*—Hemingway wrote an unsolicited letter, telling Rogers how much he enjoyed the book, and how much he loved Gertrude. His only ambition had been to write well. Too bad she had so many ambitions. He "used to listen and learn," and he "always wanted to fuck her and she knew it and it was a good healthy feeling."[20] To Lillian Ross, whom he barely knew, he was writing long letters filled with "fucking" this and "fucking" that, telling an apocryphal story about being a 1920 precinct election judge in Oak Park where he cast the only vote for Eugene Debs, the Socialist presidential candidate serving a prison term for World War I pacifism. It made a good story, but Hemingway was not living in Oak Park at the time, and none of his daily letters to Hadley Richardson during November 1920 mentioned the election.[21] Sometimes these stories were meant to be humorous, but they also had a manic edge to them.

In the June letter to Pete Viertel, which Hemingway knew that Jigee would read, he repeatedly spoke of his sexual prowess. White turtle eggs, he said humorously, were better than testosterone injections or Oreton-M. After eating them plentifully in Bimini, he would walk about with such an erection that natives, passing in the street, would salute it. And he would tell them if they knew someplace better to keep it than in his pants, they should tell him. Both Ernest and Mary sent the letter off with their love to both Viertels.[22] In his next letter to the Viertels, Hemingway sent his love to Jigee, about whom he enjoyed thinking. He said there were at least twenty-two ways he remembered her looking, which was a high score for any woman.[23]

While Viertel was composing his rejection of Ernest's offer, Hemingway's future walked into the Floridita where by appointment he met with the young assistant editor from *Cosmopolitan* magazine. Aaron Edward Hotchner arrived in Havana to persuade the famous writer to participate in a survey on the Future of Literature. After blitzing Hotchner with "Papa Doble" daiquiris and blistering him the next day fishing on the *Pilar*, Hemingway said he was interested in the project if the magazine would also commit to two short stories, as yet unwritten, at a total price of $15,000, and a tacit agreement to serialize the first volume of his long novel, the Bimini story, which was complete in draft.[24] The fee was lower than he might have asked, but contracted pieces written by nonresident citizens while out of country for six consecutive months were tax-free, an enormous savings given Hemingway's high tax bracket. In order to pay for his European trip, Hemingway needed the *Cosmopolitan* money to pool with the *Holiday* magazine fee for an essay about his life in Cuba. It was writing for hire, which part of him despised, but which he could not pass up. Making $15,000 tax-free from *Cosmopolitan* was for Hemingway the equivalent of making $75,000 taxable dollars. On June 27, just before leaving for a Bahamas fishing trip with his sons, Hemingway returned the signed *Cosmopolitan* contract for stories unwritten and an essay, for which he had no appetite. Fortunately, a change of editors at *Cosmopolitan* scuttled the Future of Literature series, but the magazine honored its contract with Hemingway, asking him to write an essay of his choice. Finally, his choice was not to write an essay, which Hotchner cabled him was fine with the magazine. If he ever had a good idea for one, they were standing by; if not, it was not a problem. The check for $15,000 was being cut anyway for the stories, which Hemingway promised would be the best he could write.[25]

All through July and into August, both Ernest and Mary worked on the Viertels to join them on their European trip so that Pete could collaborate on the book, but to no avail. With his weight down to 210 and his blood pressure at 180 over 100, Hemingway felt he had cheated death once again. The blood pressure was still dangerous, but not as lethal as it had been. Others around him continued to be less fortunate. On August 9, he learned that his longtime lawyer, Maurice Speiser, was dead from prostate cancer. Turning over his tax problems to Speiser's junior partner, Alfred Rice, Ernest refused to be daunted by whatever bad news the mails delivered. Not even his six-month Scribner's royalty report ($7,271 minus $3,000 for Pauline's alimony payments and $1,168 to the Scribner Book Store) could depress him, although he added a sarcastic note to its margin: "Of this Pauline will take $2,000 at 500 per month for Sept–Dec. which is not a bad take for a woman you slept with last in 1937."[26] The afternoon of September 7, Ernest and Mary waved good-bye to friends and retainers as the *Jagiello* pulled away from the Havana pier to take Hemingway back to Italy. Ernest was eager for it; Mary, "the short, happy wife of Ernest Hemingway," as she sometimes called herself, was delighted. Neither could have anticipated how this return to places past would change their lives.

CHAPTER 12

Sentimental Journey

September 1948 to May 1949

Hemingway was always going back to places better left in the past. In 1921, when he married Hadley Richardson, he took her around Petoskey, Michigan, to meet his former girlfriends, which only perplexed her and angered the old flames. Within a year he was telling readers of the *Toronto Daily Star*:

> Don't go back to visit the old front. If you have pictures in your head of something that happened in the night in the mud at Paschendaele or of the first wave working up the slope of Vimy, do not try and go back to verify them. It is no good. . . . It is like going into the empty gloom of a theater where the charwomen are scrubbing.[1]

That was after taking Hadley back to the Piave River site of his night wounding; now, twenty-six years later, he was misguidedly taking Mary back to the same place.

The trip across the Atlantic was leisurely and informal on the Polish liner. Every night there was champagne at the captain's table, but in their stateroom, the toilet was as erratic as the ship, sometimes blowing its contents out of the bowl. Once the ship's engines stopped at sea while officers and engine-room stokers argued in different languages about who was to blame. But there was a well-stocked bar that Ernest and Mary enjoyed, as did the ship's officers, one of whom got into a drunken argument with Ernest. When they docked in Genoa, Mary recorded that Ernest was too tight on martinis to deal with bringing their Buick through customs, leaving the chore to her.[2]

Four days later, on September 25, with Richard, their hired driver, at the Buick's wheel, Ernest and Mary drove north to Stresa, where thirty years earlier Ernest on leave hobbled about the village with a cane. At night from the hotel's window one could see across the calm surface of Lago Maggiore to the lights of Palanza, the same lights that the fictional Frederic Henry and the pregnant Catherine Barkley once searched for that stormy night rowing up the lake.[3] But that was in another country of Hemingway's mind, that fictional country where he could control the forces at work. He told Mary he was never able to bring his "girl" to Stresa, never took her to Palanza.[4] That was when he was nineteen and in love with his nurse eight years his senior, the nurse he never forgot or forgave for dismissing their relationship as puppy love.

Swept along by nostalgia, Ernest continued to entertain Mary with stories of his past, stories at least half true. She learned of the Hemingway and Hall family history: Grandfather Hall's Civil War Minié ball that he carried in his hip from fighting Quantrill along the Missouri border; Grandfather Hemingway's inability to sit at the same table with a Democrat. As a young boy in Oak Park, Ernest told Mary that he once caught a robin by salting its tail with one hand and grabbing it with the other, told her that between the ages of nine and fourteen he helped forge horseshoes in Jim Dilworth's blacksmith shop at Horton Bay. "Papa remembers" was how the entries began, as Mary recorded them in her journal for some future use, which may or may not have been spoken between them, but Ernest knew she kept these records. He was laying down the tracks of a future biography, supplementing and enlarging upon themes he established in Malcolm Cowley's essay. At the time he thought Malcolm might do the full treatment, but when Cowley questioned Ernest's high school athletic ability, Mary wrote him a furious letter, insisting that her husband was a star athlete. (It was not true, but she thought it was.) Clearly if Mr. Cowley could not get that simple point right, he had no business doing the biography. Ernest, having it both ways, told Cowley that he was tired of such questions about whether or not he was a high school football star. A man should be allowed to die before such questions were asked.[5]

In one entry it is clear that Mary thought of her journal as a source for a book—whether her own or Ernest's is not clear. After recording several pages of notes on the Hemingway children, Mary's next entry begins, "A better *chapter* than this—when under indictment for killing blue heron & had to leave home & live with Ojibway & later came back to plead guilty at Boyne City in order not to go to reform school [my emphasis]."[6] As with so many of his memories, it was never the same story twice, and each retelling tended to create new details. Before the trip was completed, Mary would have the stories of the bitch mother, the Indian girl, the cowardly father, the adoring sister, the blue heron, the night wounding, and the lost manuscripts memorized.

One area of his shadowy past that he wanted Mary to understand clearly was the situation between his father and mother, and how they destroyed the secure home life of his early years:

> Papa remembers well how . . . he was an extremely obedient little boy, thought his parents always right & their decisions unquestionable. But as he grew up he was increasingly disturbed by their quarrels when many nights his father revised his will, and they both charged him with family responsibilities beyond his capacity. In the morning they were friends again and looked on him as the only spectator of the quarrel, with hostility. . . . Ernest grew increasingly disillusioned about his parents, chiefly because of their constant quarreling, always calling him in as a witness. He learned that none of the children were made by accident—his parents never made love except to produce children, a restriction laid down by his mother, who was a high church Episcopalian. Papa says she was just a "put-off" of other good fucking ancestors.[7]

Never completely understanding Ernest's storytelling mode of mixing fact and fiction, Mary accepted this account at face value.

Like her predecessors—Hadley, Pauline, Martha—Mary Hemingway listened to story after story of Grace Hemingway's malfeasance as a mother. She wasted family money on her own extravagances, buying a $135 hat in 1905 when his father was so poor he had to let his secretary go. (No one but Ernest remembers such a hat or Dr. Hemingway ever having had a secretary, and his mother's income, which was considerable in 1905, was hers to spend.) She listened to his account of how much he and his siblings enjoyed themselves when Grace was hospitalized with typhoid fever. "We had no discipline at all by that bitch," he told Mary, and the children never visited her. "We had complete anarchism in the house," he said.[8] If Mary was listening closely, she should have gotten a better understanding of Ernest's perplexing temperament: ardent lover before marriage, turning into argumentative husband. The arguments between Clarence and Grace Hemingway that were forgotten next day should have reminded Mary of Ernest's need to provoke similar arguments, which resulted in long in-house letters of explanation. His descriptions of Oak Park life might also have provided clues as to why he was usually more comfortable on the road, in a hotel, or in rented quarters than he ever was in a place called "home."

From Stresa, the Hemingways drove slowly past the northern Italian lakes, stopping at Bergamo, where Mary pulled a reluctant Ernest into the opera house. Late that next morning they continued on through the fall countryside to the fabled lake of Dante and Pound—Lago Garda—making a pilgrimage stop at Gardone Riviera where Ernest's early hero, Gabriele D'Annunzio, was buried. In 1919, when Ernest returned from his brief but traumatic Italian war, he gave copies of D'Annunzio's *The Flame* to every young woman of interest, including his first wife, Hadley Richardson, before their marriage. Set in Venice, *The Flame* tells of the bright-burning, all-consuming love of an aging actress for a younger poet, who passionately adores her and with equal passion maintains his independence. That he can never marry her does not matter to the actress, nor does his interest in a younger dancer bother her. Theirs is an affair from the courtly love tradition in which only amorists outside marriage can achieve love's heights, and, like a flame, the relationship is a self-consuming artifact.[9]

Three days later they arrived in Cortina d'Ampezzo in the heart of the Dolomite Mountains. Hemingway's last visit to the mountain resort was in April 1923, returning from a *Toronto Star* assignment in the Ruhr to retrieve Hadley, who waited there for him.[10] Untouched by war, Cortina remained much as Ernest remembered it, sunny, surrounded by mountain ski slopes, and with good restaurants. So pleased was he with the resort village that he sent Mary off looking for winter rentals for the Christmas season. A mile and a half outside the village, she found Villa Aprile, which she stocked with cut wood, linens, and other necessities. When Ernest invited Pete and Jigee Viertel to join them in Cortina for the winter, he said that, as in Ketchum, they could make their own tribal rules.[11] The Viertels, with enough troubles of their own, were unable to accept the invitation.

With winter quarters secured, the Hemingways moved down to Venice, a city Ernest had never visited. On October 22, they signed into the Gritti Palace, the most expensive hotel in town. Ernest once avoided such elegant surroundings, preferring to get the most for his money, but after liberating the Ritz in Paris in 1944, he was a changed traveler. Now, he and Mary were living as if money did not matter. Bartenders became his old friends and newfound Italians, like the young Baron Franchetti, provided duck hunts without limits. Shooting newly purchased shotguns, Ernest loved being poled out by moonlight to sunken duck blinds in the marshes where his guide would put out the decoys along with two or three live callers. Widgeon early, later mallards and pintails, it was a duck hunter's dream. None of that four-ducks-and-you're-limited-out stuff as the hunt had become in Idaho.[12] Venice was his town and Byron's town, a place where rough writers like the two of them were taken to heart. At home they were calling him the American Byron, an epithet to which he did not object.

In Venice, Hemingway's stories of his World War I exploits continued to expand until he convinced even himself that while commanding Italian troops he was severely wounded in the marshes defending Venice from the Austrian Army. He took Mary back to Fossalta, almost within view of Venice, where nothing remained that he remembered, the once artillery-broken land now smooth and green. With ceremony, he buried a ten-thousand-lira note ($15) close to the spot where a mortar shell ruined his right knee and his night dreams. That he was, at the time, only a young Red Cross man delivering cigarettes and chocolate to the Italian troops disappeared from the story. There in Venice, he was casting a parable which would, when mature, bear the fruit of his next novel.

On November 1, the Day of the Dead, Ernest and Mary changed their travel plans of going to Portofino. After talking with Giuseppe Cipriani, owner of Harry's Bar, they moved instead into his comfortable inn, Locando Cipriani, on the relatively remote island of Torcello. The tiny community, only a thirty-minute vaporetto ride from Venice, was not a major tourist attraction. Once an important medieval center, it was now lost in time, an almost deserted village of duck hunters, fishermen, and a looming, square-towered basilica. Getting off at the wooden jetty, Ernest and Mary made their way up a grassy path along the canal, leaving their considerable luggage stacked at the dock. A bare, ruined vineyard on their right, ahead what once was the city center, now covered with dead grass crossed by footpaths, and not a sound anywhere except the fading engine of the vaporetto. At Locando they stepped back into the twentieth century: a garden, lovely rooms, porters for the luggage, and a fireplace against the damp chill.

Torcello was Hemingway's sort of place—excellent food and wine at the inn, medieval ruins, few people, and almost no tourists that fall. He would soon count as friends the village priest, Emilio the gardener and duck hunter, and Romeo the waiter.[13] The next day, walking about the small island, he entered the nakedness of Santa Maria Assunta, damp-stoned and musty, dim lit in weak sunlight, its altar unadorned, sanctuary light not burning, the gods departed. Then, having taken in its simplicity, he turned to leave, and there on the west wall, directly behind him, the jewel was embedded: a vast, dimly glittering *Last Judgment* done in Byzantine mosaic. At the fifth and highest level, a solemn, stern Christ pulled one of the saved to glory; layered beneath Him, the community of saints; then bands of angels gathering souls. At eye level were the saved, awaiting passage upward, and the damned being forked down into the floor-level hell, where fires burned and skulls gaped with snakes crawling from empty eye sockets. To leave the church he had to pass beneath the Virgin whose outstretched hands offered him the choice of salvation on his left or the fiery pit on his right.[14] Fallen-away Catholic Hemingway might be, but a peculiar Catholic yet. At the Finca, the Black Priest, Don Andrés, came regularly for food, drink, and conversation, and Ernest never passed up a cathedral. To live in Cuba was to be Catholic or to be nothing, for other religions did not signify. Here in Italy, where he had first encountered the Church, he was, if not a practicing Catholic, at least a passive one.

In mid-November, he sent Mary off in the Buick, with Richard driving, to see the sights of northern Italy. With her insatiable appetite for churches, plazas, and museums, Mary was, to Ernest's sometime chagrin, the typical American tourist. He, meanwhile, remained comfortably set up on Torcello, bonding with locals, looking and listening, absorbing it for future uses. Once a week, there were God's plenty of ducks to hunt, and any afternoon he could shoot the tiny, delicate sparrowlike birds feeding on the local grapes.[15] Mornings were reserved for writing; first letters, then the essay he promised *Holiday* magazine. He reconnected with David Bruce, who was now in Paris heading a special mission to France for the Economic Cooperation Administration, and wrote daily letters to Mary.[16] With no more letters to answer, and his pen point, as it were, resharpened, he sat down there in the late fall on Torcello, now the only inhabitant of the inn, and began writing about Cuba and the Gulf Stream.

Wherever he was, no matter how delightful, he was frequently elsewhere in his head, remembering, comparing, savoring. In his early Paris cold-water flat, he wrote about Nick fishing alone on Big Two-Hearted River. In the heat of Key West, Piggott, and Kansas City, he wrote about the northern Italian spring when Frederic Henry was blown up on the Isonzo River. In the Havana heat, he described snow falling in the Guadarrama Mountains of Spain. Now, in the weak Italian sunlight, he began telling *Holiday* readers why he lived in Cuba. Usually he gave a simple answer such as because "it is too complicated to explain about the early morning in the hills above Havana where every morning is cool and fresh on the hottest day in summer." Then he took his readers with him to the cockfights and the pigeon shoots, reminding us that on those cool mornings at the Finca, he wrote as well as any place he had ever been. It sounded as if he were there, with the morning breeze blowing, palm trees rustling. He had that touch, that ability to project himself into the setting remembered with a clarity and attention to telling details that carried readers with him.

There were, he wrote, many reasons to live in Cuba, reasons he usually did not tell strangers but he would tell us this once,

> the biggest reason you live in Cuba is the great, deep blue river, three quarters of a mile to a mile deep and sixty to eighty miles across, that . . . has, when the river is right, the finest fishing I have ever known.

With readers hooked on his bait, he pulled them into the *Pilar* for a detailed lesson on marlin fishing. While taking us out of Havana Harbor past the Cabañas fortress where "most of your friends have been political prisoners at one time or another," he told us about his fishing boat, his faithful mate, Gregorio, and how sometimes flying fish rise in a covey as you enter the stream. With the patience of a dedicated teacher, he described everything we needed to know. With outriggers baited and set, teasers zigzagging in the water, we see the dark purple of a marlin rise to the teaser. Quickly pick up the rod baited with the feather and pork rind just as the marlin hits it. If "he turns his head you hit him, striking hard" to set the hook.

> Then he feels the hook and jumps clear. He will jump straight up all clear of the water, shaking himself. He will jump straight and stiff as a beaked bar of silver. He will jump high and long, shedding drops of water as he comes out, and making a splash like a shell hitting when he enters the water again.

By the time Hemingway was finished with the essay, his readers knew what size rods and reels were needed, how much piano wire leader, how heavy a line, and what baits were used to pursue fish two and three times as heavy as the fisherman. He called the essay "The Great Blue River."[17]

At the end of November, when Mary returned from her excursion, filled with impressions of the Uffizi Museum in Florence and her meeting with Bernard Berenson, she found Ernest happy but fuming. She told him about paintings and meals; he told her about overhead shots made in poor light and the material Martha Gellhorn had stolen from him for her war novel, *The Wine of Astonishment*. After four years with Ernest, Mary might have been more concerned about his obsessions that he scratched and scratched until they bled. Martha, he claimed, had used everything he told her about Hürtgenwald, having never been there herself, then ruined the material by having her lover Jim Gavin, the great General, make corrections about which he knew nothing. Marty would always be an ambitious bitch, an amateur without discipline. To hell with her and her books. If she ever died by fire the way Zelda Fitzgerald had recently, he hoped she would take a deep breath and die quickly.[18]

Then there was Ira Wolfert, the journalist much with Hemingway in London before the invasion and later in France. Wolfert' s earlier books were reportorial accounts of fighting in the Pacific theater of operations. In 1948, he finished a war novel, *An Act of Love*, which was sent to Hemingway for a supportive blurb. Irrationally, Ernest felt that anyone writing fictively about the European War was invading his domain. The book was so terrible, Ernest said, that he simply could not tell the publisher what he thought. Maybe if he had a really good day with the ducks, he might say that clearly Wolfert did not steal the book because it was so god-awfully written. When he wasn't complaining about Martha or Wolfert, Hemingway was tearing into Mary's onetime lover, Irwin Shaw, and his war novel, *The Young Lions*, which Ernest had not yet read due to the maritime strike preventing books and magazines from reaching him, but about which he had firm opinions. For Shaw's agent to claim the book was better than Tolstoy was absurd: Tolstoy saw real action at Sevastopol while Shaw never killed anyone. If he could only get Shaw in the boxing ring, Ernest would teach him a thing or two about fighting, cut him up slowly until they stopped it bloody in the fifth round, or maybe just take him out quickly in the first. These fantasies were reviewed and revised, again and again—Ernest shadow-boxing in a darkening room.[19]

The cumulative effect of the war novels, which Hemingway said he was sick of reading, was to make him doubt the need for his planned sea-air-land novel beginning in Bimini in 1936 and ending after Hürtgenwald in 1944. Shaw, Wolfert, Martha, and Norman Mailer with his monumental *The Naked and the Dead* were all there ahead of him. Maybe, he told Charles Scribner, the war would only be a noise heard offstage. But when Scribner pointedly asked if that meant the end of the planned trilogy, Ernest quickly replied not to worry about the three-part book. The sea part was taking him longer because it covered two whole years; the air and land parts would go more quickly. He did not say that his attempts to write of Thomas Hudson flying with the RAF were a dead end. Charley should stop pushing him so hard on this subject. Had he not been taking nauseating medicine daily for his high blood pressure? Was he not still bothered by ringing in his ears? The ruthlessness of war was not yet purged from his system, so Charley must put up with his author's irritations. Had he not been blown up so badly the last time that he coughed blood for six months after returning to Cuba?[20] (Yes and no: he was coughing blood but not from being blown up.)

Angry about the explosion of war novels, about Scribner's pushing him to finish a book to which he did not yet know the end, Hemingway was furious as well with his new lawyer, Alfred Rice, acquired by default as the assistant taking over the late Maurice Speiser's practice. Apparently the IRS was auditing Hemingway's 1944 tax return, filed on the basis of being a nonresident all of that year. Unfortunately, he did touch down on American soil while en route to England and the war. Technically, those two weeks should have cost him his nonresident taxpayer status. Rice suggested a tax loophole whereby they were due a tax refund, to which Hemingway replied that Rice was never to take unilateral action on any Hemingway business. He, Ernest, not Rice, would "judge whether it is an honorable and ethical action to take, not simply legally, but according to my own personal standards. . . . I need money, badly, but not badly enough to do one dishonorable, shady, borderline, or 'fast' thing to get it. I hope this is quite clear." Then he spelled out in great detail all of his war duties in Cuba—counterespionage, submarine patrols—his war journalism for *Collier's*, the battles he covered, the injuries incurred in the line of duty, and being awarded finally the Bronze Star. "For two bits," he said, "I would quit writeing [sic] if I have to pay dough for what I did in 1944."[21]

The second week in December, the Hemingways closed up operations on Torcello, where Ernest now thought of himself as related somehow to the "tough boys" who once dominated the estuary. After moving back into the Gritti, Mary left him on December 13 to take possession and make ready the Cortina house. That same afternoon Ernest went to lunch with the Duke of Aosta's nephew and a "beautiful, jolly, nice, and ungloomy" girl.[22] He had met eighteen-year-old Adriana Ivancich two days previously while hunting at Baron Nanyuki Franchetti's lodge north of Venice. The Ivancich family, long established and respected in Venetian society, had lately fallen into difficult financial straits. Having sailed, served, fought, and prospered under one hundred and fifty years of Venetian Doges and leaders, the Ivancich family was sadly diminished by the European War. Their country villa near San Michele was destroyed by Allied bombers and their financial situation greatly reduced. When Adriana's father, Carlo, was murdered in the postwar infighting, family responsibilities fell to Adriana's brother, Gianfranco, and her mother, Dora, neither of whom had sufficient business acumen to restore the family to its previous glory.[23]

With long, lovely black hair, green eyes, and a thin Roman nose, Adriana stepped into Hemingway's fantasy close to the spot that Frederic Henry climbed out of the Tagliamento River on his way to rejoin Catherine Barkley. Wet with rain, she sat by the fire combing and drying her hair, probably not noticing the throaty quality of Ernest's voice as he watched her, but certainly aware she had his full attention. Recently graduated from the protection of nuns, Adriana was a lovely young woman about to discover her power over men. For Ernest, life, fiction, and fantasy were coinciding in ways that he did not stop to question. In *A Farewell to Arms*, he let an older Frederic fall in love with a slightly younger nurse, whose hair the wounded American found incredibly erotic:

> I loved to take her hair down . . . I would take out the pins and lay them on the sheet and it would be loose and I would . . . take

out the last two pins and it would all come down and she would
drop her head and we would both be inside of it . . . I would lie
sometimes and watch her twisting it up . . . and it shone even in
the night as water shines sometimes just before it is really day-
light.[24]

Now, by firelight, watching Adriana's black hair fall in waves, he
was the older man, and she the very much younger woman. That
he was thirty years older, paunchy, graying, with erratic blood pressure and ringing in his ears, did not matter to him. This was the
beginning of a Jamesian novel to be played out in Hemingway's
imagination. She was the muse he needed, the muse that Mary, for
all her sexual experience, was never able to become.

Dora Ivancich, the watchful mother, could not understand why a
man old enough to be a grandfather would be interested in her
daughter except for all the wrong reasons. Adriana assured her that
Hemingway's invitations to lunch, to drinks at Harry's Bar, to walks
about Venice were harmless. Her friends were always with her; they
made him happy. What did they talk about? Adriana was not always
sure because Ernest spoke an English that she had not learned in
school, but when he laughed, she and her friends laughed. He
called her "daughter," and he was the Papa. Dora Ivancich was not
reassured. Later, in her memoir, *La Torre Bianca*, Adriana said,
"For me he was a much older man, even though there was something of the big child about him. But 30 years [difference] was for
me a lifetime. I never thought of being in love with him."[25] But
that was not what she wrote at eighteen when she was full of poetry and pictures, forever sketching and dreaming. At eighteen, she
was flattered and intrigued by Hemingway's gentleness and the
unmistakable if unspoken sexual attraction he felt for her.

Leaving Adriana behind in Venice, Hemingway joined Mary at
Cortina before Christmas, where he settled comfortably into Villa
Aprile, while continuing to go on duck hunts only a few hours away.
On January 16, 1949, the lagoons finally froze up, making the trip
into the duck blinds heavy work. There, shooting against the full
moon setting, Ernest brought down fifteen ducks, the last of the
season. Five days later, Mary was carried down from the slopes by

the ski patrol, her right ankle broken from a spill in wet snow. Ernest went with her to the hospital to get the ankle set and plastered, telling Pete Viertel in a letter that the accident would end his writing for at least a month. The letter, with several appendices, continued to refight the Normandy invasion, complain about inaccuracies in Shaw's *The Young Lions*, which he had finally read, and declare he was nauseated by Cowley's *Life* magazine essay.[26] When he finished the Viertel letter, Hemingway cut bottom portions off three pages, his own "black ass," as he called his depressions. What remained was "black ass" enough: Shaw had no right to write about cowardly company commanders. The man should go out and hang himself. What he did not mention to Viertel was the veiled and unflattering presence in Shaw's novel of himself, Mary, and his younger brother Leicester.

Three days after Mary's accident, Hemingway was complaining to Cowley that the *Life* essay was going to cause him serious problems in Cuba, having revealed that the *Pilar* was carrying high explosives during the war and thereby breaching Ernest's elaborate security measures.[27] Apparently no one in Cuba noticed, but the level of Hemingway's chronic paranoia was rising. Later, he told Cowley to forget about writing a book-length biography while he was alive. It was too embarrassing to see himself in his son-of-a-bitch mode, and equally embarrassing to see himself behaving well. He added, darkly, that if the whole truth were told, he would be put in jail. Nor could he let anyone else write about his parents. His mother might be a bitch, but she was family. He cooperated with Malcolm only because, his doctors having convinced him that his raging blood pressure would surely kill him within a year, he wanted to set the record straight on several points, including his efforts during the war. Seeing his life in print was so unnerving and onerous that he would neither cooperate, authorize, nor consent to a full-scale effort. (All the while Ernest was telling Mary detailed stories of his life for her journal, assuming she would use them after his death.) Cowley's counterpunch did not reach Hemingway until he returned to Cuba: a young Princeton professor by the name of Carlos Baker was working on a critical book about Ernest.[28]

All that month of January, Ernest was by turns either gentle and caring, or absolutely miserable and vicious. When a perfectly friendly letter from Pauline told him his sons missed being with him at the Finca for Christmas, and that Greg had seen Bumby in New York, loaning him money for uniforms to return to Army service, Ernest responded in his vitriolic worst: she had sent him a packet of poison, no real information, a couple of letters a year but nothing else, probably due to her laziness or drunkenness. He was sick of hearing about money loaned by her or his sons. Either send him a bill or shut up about it. Then, twisting the knife, he told her that their marriage ended not because of Martha, rather because of coitus interruptus imposed by the Catholic Church when her twice surgically opened womb could not bear another child.[29]

Ernest's surliness was not entirely due to Mary's ankle, Shaw's novel, Cowley's essay, or Pauline's letter. Part of the cause was his own writing, which was not progressing. Having promised *Cosmopolitan* two stories by December 1949, he had nothing yet to send to Ed Hotchner, his go-between on the magazine. In March, he said the one story he'd finished was too "rough" for *Cosmopolitan*, but surely when he returned to the Finca he would have the two stories written on time.[30] The other and more immediate cause for his "black ass" moods was Adriana, with whom he was hopelessly and idealistically in love. For two weeks in January he returned alone to Venice on the excuse of business papers that he needed to sign. In March, he and Mary returned to the Gritti, where they dined one evening with Sinclair Lewis and the mother of Lewis's former mistress. Mary listened, taking mental notes: Lewis's face looked like "a piece of old liver"; when he ate, she could see blobs of food moving inside his mouth; his hands trembled, and his walk was "brittle." During the three-hour meal, Lewis seemed to grow older and more feeble, while Ernest became younger, boyish and shy. Mary was with Ernest at meals and in bed, but she was also much alone. On her mended ankle, she visited museums, went to concerts, seldom mentioning Adriana in her journal although she had to know that Ernest was spending afternoons with her.[31] Mary had seen it all before, from both sides of the scenario: as the younger woman for whom Ernest only had eyes, and as Mrs. Hemingway watching the younger woman being flattered by her husband. This infatuation, Mary was sure, would pass as had the others since their marriage. Nor was she confident enough in being Mrs. Hemingway to take a firm stand.

By the middle of March, Ernest and Mary were back at Cortina, where he was writing every morning about a fifty-year-old infantry colonel duck-hunting on the frozen lagoons with a surly boatman. "I must not let him ruin it," the colonel thinks, "I must keep it entire and not let him do it. Every time you shoot now can be your last shoot and no stupid son of a bitch should be allowed to ruin it."[32] For two weeks the story went beautifully, only to be sabotaged by Hemingway's own physical misfortunes, which followed him everywhere.[33] On March 28, his eyes became infected, turning into erysipelas that sent him to a hospital in Padua for ten days of penicillin injections and bed rest, his eyes swollen shut and his face covered with ointment.[34] By mid-April, when he was mostly recovered, it was time to close down Villa Aprile and return to Cuba. Colonel Cantwell's duck hunt and his three days in Venice were left suspended in Ernest's mind until he could get back to the Finca.

Before leaving Venice for Genoa and home, Ernest invited Adriana and her older brother, Gianfranco, to lunch with himself and Mary at the Gritti. Gianfranco was also soon to depart for Cuba, where employment was possible. Ernest told Adriana he would look after her brother's best interests. Mary noted later in her journal that her husband and the far too young Adriana "were busily launching a flirtation." That she thought the "flirtation" was only beginning says how well Ernest had kept Adriana's presence in his life to himself.[35]

The beginning and the end: Sun Valley Lodge, September 1940. Ernest, Gregory on his lap; standing: Toby Bruce and Jack Hemingway; Martha seated and Patrick cross-legged. *For Whom the Bell Tolls* is finished but not yet published. Ernest and Martha are in love but not yet married. World War II has begun but the United States is not yet in it. (John F. Kennedy Library/L. Arnold)

West of almost everything: Ketchum, Idaho, ca. 1940. Until the Sun Valley Lodge dominated the scene, Ketchum was a rough ranch and mining town with open gambling and several saloons. The sign for Jack Lane's Mercantile store, barely readable in the middle of town, marks the right turn toward the Lodge. Hemingway's house, bought in 1959, was located in the woods north and slightly to the left of Lane's. (UP Collection, Community Library, Ketchum, Idaho)

Sartorial author and the Blond Venus: December 1940, New York City. Ernest and his friend Marlene Dietrich, whom he called "the Kraut." In suit, vest, and tie, Ernest is dressed in his big city mode. Befurred and camera conscious, Dietrich carries a copy of *For Whom the Bell Tolls* under her left arm. (John F. Kennedy Library)

Celery stalks at midnight: December 1940, New York City. A month married and not yet antagonists, Ernest and Martha are sipping martinis at the Stork Club, Martha with her habitual cigarette. *For Whom the Bells Tolls* has become a bestseller, and they have booked trans-Pacific passage to the war in China. (John F. Kennedy Library)

OPPOSITE: From the far field: October 1940, Idaho. Ernest, Gary Cooper (guests of the Sun Valley Lodge), and Taylor "Beartracks" Williams, their guide, have a good start on their bag limit of ducks and snipe taken along Silver Creek, not far from Bud Purdy's ranch house. (Arnold Collection, Community Library, Ketchum, Idaho)

Over there: July 1944, somewhere in France. Ernest studies battle maps with his jeep driver after the breakthrough at St. Lô. Noticeable are his wire-rimmed reading glasses. Noticeably missing are any insignias designating him a correspondent. (John F. Kennedy Library)

Off-limits to troops: August 1944, Mt.-San-Michel, France. On the causeway leading to the famous abbey, MPs keep the enlisted men at bay while the VIPs enjoy the Hôtel Poulard's equally famous omelets and extraordinary wine cellar. Here Hemingway spent several days recovering from his St. Pois concussion. (John F. Kennedy Library)

The feast of St. Louis: Paris, August 25, 1944. Free French of the Interior, Maquis, and Paris resistance fighters, armed and wearing brassards, parade German captives down an avenue of Parisians. Elsewhere in the City of Lights, pockets of German resistance are being overrun. (John F. Kennedy Library)

Summer's lease runs out: September 1944, somewhere in northern France. Hemingway and Colonel Charles "Buck" Lanham at rest during the race across France toward the German-Belgium border. Ahead of them await the dark woods of Hürtgenwald. (John F. Kennedy Library)

The muse: Adriana Ivancich in Venice, Italy, 1948. (John F. Kennedy Library)

The Blond Venus reprised: ca. 1950. Mary Hemingway, her short-cropped hair bleached the smoky shade of blond favored by Ernest. (John F. Kennedy Library)

The eyes have it: December 1950, in the Floridita Bar, Havana. Gianfranco Invancich with his arm around Mary watches Ernest bask in Adriana's light; Mary Hemingway smiles at Adriana; Dora Ivancich looks back toward her son, Gianfranco, while Adriana looks elsewhere. (John F. Kennedy Library)

In the middle of the night:
late spring, 1952, Finca Vigia.
Scary photo of Ernest armed
and rampant at the Finca
during the period of break-ins.
(John F. Kennedy Library)

After the fall: January 23, 1954, near Murchison Falls, Africa. The remains of
Roy Marsh's Cessna after the first crash, from which Ernest and Mary walked
away relatively unhurt. (John F. Kennedy Library)

Illusion and reality: 1955 in Cojimar, Cuba. On the set for the filming of *The Old Man and Sea*: the *Pilar*'s mate and cook, Gregorio Fuentes, Spencer Tracy, and Ernest. Compare Gregorio's shirt, newly pressed for the occasion, with Tracy's shirt, carefully wrinkled for the filming. (John F. Kennedy Library)

News from the mainland: ca. 1957, Finca Vigia. In the living room, Ernest reads by the window's light. Copies of the *New York Times* are stacked on the low, filled book cases that line the wall. His loose shirt is typically Cuban. (John F. Kennedy Library)

The dangerous summer of 1959: Pamplona, Spain. Ernest in conversation with Valerie Danby-Smith, the young Irish woman who became part of the Hemingway *cuadrilla* that summer of the bullfights. (John F. Kennedy Library)

The artist in his studio: summer 1959, somewhere in Spain. The bull, carrying three perfectly placed *banderillas*, is turned in his tracks by Antonio Ordadrilla, who, on one of his miraculous afternoons, lures him back to the *muleta*. (John F. Kennedy Library)

An old man in a dry month: Finca Vigia. Ernest at sixty with the mounted kudu from his 1933–34 safari. (John F. Kennedy Library)

CHAPTER 13

Venice Preserved

May to December 1949

On the last day of April, the Hemingways left Italy carrying a mountain of luggage and Ernest's fledgling war novel. The duck hunter, Colonel Cantwell, was afoot on his three-day rendezvous with love and death on the stones and bridges of Venice.[1] Behind him stood a troop of forebears: Dante's burning lovers; Byron's gaudy life; Henry James's *Aspern Papers*; D'Annunzio's inflamed young poet and aging actress; Thomas Mann's *Death in Venice*.[2] Ernest knew them all, read and remembered them all, using them wherever needed. "Sometimes I am Mr. Dante," Colonel Cantwell would say, and mean it. By giving his crucial war memories and a good deal of his recent reading to the dying colonel, Hemingway was changing the outcome of his proposed sea-air-land trilogy, which already covered sixteen hundred pages of manuscript.

The slow trip home gave Hemingway leisure to work on the book, for the Polish ship made frequent overnight stops along the South American coast.[3] Almost four weeks at sea, he woke early as always, caught the morning light reflecting on the water before finding a quiet place to continue the Colonel's memories of wars long ago and recent, mixing the 1918 defense along the Piava with the recent debacle in the German woods where Cantwell lost so many good men, poor men, dead men all. Unable ever to dissociate love and war, Hemingway was working toward a different configuration than in his earlier two books, *A Farewell to Arms* and *For Whom the Bell Tolls*. Richard Cantwell's love for the young girl, first called Nicole and then Renata,[4] is hopeless not because of their age difference but because his heart is quite literally failing him. Both the author and his character take Seconal to sleep; both are taking mannitol hexanitrate—Ernest to control his high blood pressure; the Colonel to keep his heart pumping.[5] Old soldiers do eventually die, but they do not go gentle.

After reaching the Finca on May 27,[6] he hired Juanita ("Nita") Jensen as a part-time secretary to whom he dictated afternoon letters, gradually reducing the mountain of unanswered mail. That June at the Finca, correspondence, household chores, and planning a Bahama fishing trip made progress on the unnamed novel slow going. By June 10, Patrick, Gregory, Buck Lanham, and Nanyuki Franchetti from Italy had arrived, ready to board the fishing flotilla—Mayito Menocal's large, well-appointed yacht *Delicias* and Hemingway's *Pilar* with Mary's tiny *Tin Kid* in tow for shallow waters. The trip was well planned, but everything conspired against it: the weather turned rough; Gregorio, his longtime mate, was sick with a cold; Santiago, hired on as engineer, knew nothing of engines; and Gregory's appendix flared up requiring a Navy crash boat to take him into Key West for an emergency operation.[7] When Ernest returned to port, he found a letter from his arthritis-crippled mother, who was turning seventy-seven, telling him how furious she was with the *Life* magazine feature: "They stole the pictures of you and your family when I was not at home and got someone to write it up. We were most disgusted as we know you would be." She also told him to ignore any hospital bills sent to him by her doctors who had accepted her paintings as payment for service. But when they found out how wealthy Ernest was, they came asking for his address, which she refused to give. For her approaching birthday, she wanted nothing from him but his love.[8] Instead, he sent her a book on science and religion, hoping perhaps that it would counterbalance her penchant for supporting mystical religious groups.[9]

At the Finca there was never a shortage of fresh reading material—New York newspapers, current magazines, and stacks of new books, fiction and nonfiction. Before returning from Italy, Hemingway renewed fourteen magazine subscriptions through the Scribner Book Store, ranging from *Field and Stream* to *New*

Republic. His order lists were as diverse as his interests: new fiction, military history, books on the Southwest, the American Civil War, and the journals of André Gide in three volumes. In July, he received a twenty-four-volume set of Mark Twain's works, Philip Wylie's new novel, *Opus 21*, Dostoyevsky's *Diary of a Writer*, George Orwell's *1984*, and Eliot Paul's *Life and Death of a Spanish Town*.[10] Some who did not know him thought him an instinctive naif, a raw American product largely uneducated. Those who knew him well were amazed by the breadth and depth of his reading, by the large and growing Finca library and the diversity of his interests. Two to three hundred books a year passed through his hands— books as factual as guides to navigation, as fluffy as murder mysteries. Books arrived as gifts from known authors and complete strangers. He read deeply in biographies and letters of selected writers, including George Gordon, Lord Byron, whose Venetian sojourn echoed in Hemingway's head when creating Colonel Cantwell in the Venice of his imagination. About his own *Don Juan*, Byron had written from Venice:

> It may be bawdy, but is it not good English? It may be profligate, but is it not life, is it not the thing? Could any man have written it who has not lived in the world? and tooled in a post-chaise? in a hackney coach? in a gondola? against a wall? in a court carriage? in a vis a vis? on a table? and under it?[11]

Before Hemingway was finished, Byron's fornication in the gondola would reappear in his still unnamed novel.

From mid-July through the end of October, Hemingway worked on the Venice novel five days a week, always leaving himself two days for fishing. Riding what sounded like a manic high, he was amazed at the way the book was writing itself. It was as if he were twenty-five, not fifty, but knowing at twenty-five what he now knew at fifty. While the U.S. Congress spent the summer looking for spies and subversives in government, Hemingway looked for ways to speak of the war without refighting it. Colonel Cantwell's memories, provoked by Renata's continued questioning, are a catalogue of mistakes that killed, orders that maimed, and operational blunders by commanding generals who never saw the front lines.

Combining what he knew of Buck Lanham's and Charles Sweeny's careers, Hemingway created the officer who knew too much, was too aware of what had happened and why. Better never to have known, but Cantwell cannot avoid what he has learned at great cost, nor can he erase his memories.[12] Mixing his own observations with his reading of World War II histories and very specific information Lanham supplied from sometimes classified sources, Hemingway buried the war beneath the Colonel's bitterness. The book might be fiction, but its factual details were as accurate as he could make them.

While exhilarated by the flow of the story, living in it, making it up, Hemingway was also making up his own life in ways that are more difficult to understand. All writers, he once said, were liars who, when drinking, would lie to anyone, friends or strangers. He might have also said that fiction carried the connotation of making up events that never took place, in effect, telling lies. Since words can never reproduce reality, all writing, at some level, becomes fiction, making liars of us all. But Hemingway's life and his work were not the same, except for the fact that he was continually inventing both of them. Where once he was loath to speak of himself, the threat of death by aneurysm, hanging over his head since 1947, set loose a torrent of biographical stories, all of them verging at some point on fiction. For example, he told a newly made Italian acquaintance that he held no advance degrees, having barely made it through *military school*.[13] Colonel Cantwell, we learn, graduated in first draft from Virginia Military Academy and in revision from West Point, but Ernest graduated only from high school.

Some of his more wooly inventions were written to Charles Scribner, Sr. In July, with the novel settling down into a daily routine, Hemingway told Scribner that four of his ancestors went on the Crusades, and that he and his son Gregory had inherited genetic traits from his great-great-grandmother, a northern Cheyenne Indian,[14] a fable that amused his sisters. Exaggerations and inventions such as this one may have resulted from Hemingway's use of a newly acquired wire recorder, on which he dictated letters for transcription. Speaking to two audiences, the attractive young woman transcribing the recording and the recipient of the letter,

Hemingway was liable to say almost anything. But the deeper he got into the Colonel's character, the more Hemingway began to sound like his invention—rough, brusque, and violence-prone. He gave Scribner a detailed account of killing a "snotty SS kraut" who would not give up the German escape routes. When Ernest threatened to kill him, the German supposedly replied that he would not dare because Americans were "a race of mongrel degenerates," and it violated the Geneva Convention.

> What a mistake you made, brother, I told him and shot him three times in the belly, fast and then, when he went down on his knees shot him on the topside so that his brains came out of his mouth or I guess it was his nose.[15]

None of the evidence or the memories of those with him in France support such a story.

A year earlier, Ernest wrote Archie MacLeish that he fought for eight months as an irregular, killing twenty-six armed Germans.[16] To a college professor, Hemingway expanded his war record to include sixteen woundings to himself and one hundred and twenty-two men killed at five different wars.[17] Not even Charles Sweeny, veteran of numerous wars and revolutions, would have claimed to have killed that many men, not in wars where one usually never saw the results of a shot fired. To John Dos Passos, Hemingway said that seven concussions in one year were probably more than a writer should sustain.[18] In a dictated letter to Pete Viertel, after telling him about a new Havana prostitute whom he refrained from bedding, Ernest added, by hand, that he had given in, spent the night with the whore, drank seven bottles of Roederers Brut Champagne '42, and fucked all night, which was the reason he had written only 708 words that day.[19]

The question about these claims is not whether they are true or not, but why Hemingway felt compelled to invent and exaggerate them. That he killed or participated in the killing of at least two German soldiers—at Rambouillet's crossroads and during the attack on Lanham's Hürtgenwald command post—should have been enough. That he suffered two concussions, aggravated by whiskey and more head banging, should have been enough. Always one to tell wild and frequently funny stories, Hemingway was capable of exaggerations but not usually ones like these tales, all of which exposed his underlying need to establish that he was a warrior, an outlaw, a rough character capable of extreme violence. After being wounded in World War I, he immediately began using his ruined knee as visual proof of imaginary deeds. On crutches in Milan, he told a young British officer that he "had been badly wounded leading [Italian] Arditi storm troops on Monte Grappa."[20] By the time he reached Paris in 1921, he had transformed his Red Cross duties into regular Italian Army status. Now he was doing the same thing to his war in France: his status as a war correspondent was disappearing as Hemingway the leader of Free French of the Interior irregulars emerged. Killing increasingly larger numbers of Germans in his imagination until he actually believed it to have happened, he was purging, perhaps, the nightmares of war that haunted his sleep: The German tank at the window, himself with an antitank weapon, he pulls the trigger, but the projectile dribbles out the muzzle and onto the floor. He wakes before it explodes to kill him. Or maybe he could no longer tell the difference between what he imagined and previous reality. Or, more disturbingly, he was, perhaps, *becoming* his fiction.

All of his writing life he was said to create male characters in his own image. While every author is present to some degree in his fictions, Hemingway was more open to this analysis than most because more was known about his active life. However, when one looked closely at his earlier fictions, there were always significant dissimilarities between himself and Jake Barnes, Frederic Henry, or Robert Jordan. Now, at fifty, no longer able to drink with the metabolism of his middle years, and intensely aware that his erratic blood pressure could, at any moment, blow a hole through a major artery, Hemingway was existential to the bone, breakfasting with death as a tablemate.

The more intensely focused he became on his morning fiction, the more the fictive stories he told in letters began to mimic the life of Richard Cantwell, including their shared love for the nineteen-year-old Renata/Adriana. During the Italian journey of the previous year, Ernest had not been in prolonged contact with Adriana, but he was telling Patrick and Gregory that she was one of his "girls" they should visit during their 1949 European tour.[21] While his Colonel pledged his dying love to Renata only in the Finca mornings, Ernest thought of her more often, writing letters that went unanswered. In September, he complained of Adriana's silence to an Italian correspondent, knowing that she would speak to his young muse: "I think she understands plenty, but why not write and take a chance."[22] As if by magic, Adriana's brief letter arrived, saying she had seen his sons in Venice, and that she was going to Paris to study art. Ernest responded immediately. He would be in Paris in November, staying at the Ritz, where he would leave instructions for her calls to be put through to his room. He had "much nostalgia" to see her, particularly in Paris.[23] Having spent spring and summer devoted to her beauty, albeit restricted to the confines of his novel, Ernest was as deeply in love with his half-imaginary Adriana as Cantwell was with Renata.

It was not until August 24 that Ernest, in a note he labeled TOP SECRET, wrote Charles Scribner about the new novel, which he promised by the end of October. Two days later, thanking Scribner for the wire recorder, Hemingway reported that Mary was overwhelmed by the portion of the novel he let her read. So moved was she that she did not care about his whores or his three Italian countesses.[24] More exaggerations and fictions. As with everyone else he wrote that summer, Ernest asked Scribner to say nothing of the novel to anyone, particularly not to Martha. As a result of sowing this admonition on two continents, the word gradually spread through the publishing industry. By July, Hemingway was turning away an inquiry from *Ladies' Home Journal* about his new work, and an attempt by *McCall's* to interview his mother in Oak Park. But he was also writing Lillian Ross of *The New Yorker* about his book, including a list of possible titles: *A New Slain Knight*; *Our One and Only Life*; and *Over the River and into the Trees*.[25] By the end of August an Associated Press man was after Hemingway for an interview, and *Life* magazine was asking for information on the book's content and publication date. In September, Ernest let Ed Hotchner read sixty pages of manuscript as a teaser, asking if *Cosmopolitan* would be interested in it as a serial, an inquiry which

Hotchner said delighted his managing editor.[26] A month later, Hemingway announced the book to Al Horwits at Universal Pictures as a property that Al might want to film. Ernest spoke of the book in vague but glowing terms—he wrote it to put Shakespeare on his butt, as if writing were a contact sport.[27]

So sure was Hemingway of this still untitled book that he asked Charles Scribner for a $10,000 loan against it to buy Mary a mink coat. Having been such a bastard while writing the story, he wanted to make it up to her. A gesture, he called it, in the middle of their fight to show her it did not matter how the conflict turned out, he was hers. Without asking about the nature of the family argument, Scribner immediately cabled that the $10,000 was deposited in Hemingway's New York account.[28] Under pressure of his writing, Ernest was irascible and easily pricked. That August, when Martha and Pauline ended up in Venice at the same time, he fumed about what they might be saying of him in *his* town. In September, he sent Charles Scribner an unpleasant letter about Martha's anatomy and her Jewishness, neither of which alleged traits apparently bothered him during their four-year affair. Now he said the reason she was never pregnant by him was that he did not care to father half-Jewish children.[29] Unprovoked by anything Martha was currently doing or saying, these vicious remarks about her continued throughout the year and into the next. All his life he forced his wives to ask for a divorce, which was his way of getting what he wanted without taking the responsibility for it. With Martha, roles were reversed: he was the house husband while she went off on assignments; he was the injured party; and he filed for the divorce on the grounds that she deserted him. It all made him look foolish in his own eyes, and he never forgave himself or her for that embarrassment.

In September, Mary was in Chicago visiting her parents, leaving Ernest to his professed loneliness and the "wild life" he said he enjoyed when no one was there to maintain household discipline. Soon he was bragging to Pete Viertel about his all-night stand with the new whore he called Xenophobia. The very same day he wrote Mary how pleased he was with her purchase of a wild mink coat at Marshall Fields. He mentioned his recently written letters to Marlene Dietrich and Teresa, the Italian countess, explaining he was loving in his letters to these women, but it was Mary he loved, and her alone. He was always true to her and literature and war in his fashion. Simultaneously, he wrote Hotchner that he was out of the "doghouse" with Mary, without saying that it took the most expensive mink coat in Chicago to do it.[30]

While Mary was in Chicago, Ernest, to emphasize his "bad boy" character of which he was so proud, wrote Charles Scribner he was having Xenophobia out to the Finca for lunch. At seventeen, she was lovely, ambitious, and had a talent for her chosen profession. At night she worked her trade, but during the day she liked to hang around "us bad boys."[31] Roberto Herrera, apprentice factotum in Mary's absence, brought Xenophobia out to the Finca, where in the course of the afternoon he photographed her several times. Two days later, Mary returned with her mink, happy to be home with Ernest, but her joy lasted only as long as it took Roberto to get his photographs developed. Noticing that the girl was pictured in three different dresses, indicating that she had been at the Finca at least three times in Mary's absence, Mary exploded, furious with Ernest for allowing a whore into her house. To no avail, Ernest tried to lie his way out of the situation, but lying to Mary, he said, was a quick way to starve to death. He was back in the doghouse again.[32] For the rest of the month he worked to placate Mary, finish the book, nego- tiate the serial with *Cosmopolitan*, and settle on the title. Mary was the easiest part of the equation to solve, for she always forgave, at least on the surface. It was a curious relationship that puzzled Buck Lanham during his June visit. As he later told biographer Bernice Kert, he "was surprised by . . . Mary's increasing submission to Ernest's exhibitionism. Ernest would sit around the pool or at meals and brag about his sexual conquests (real or imagined), and Mary, covering her embarrassment, would act as though she were proud of his manliness."[33] In private, Mary was not nearly so submissive, or so forgiving. Like all of his wives, she suffered from Ernest's unpredictable mood shifts and his erratic verbal abuse; but when they were alone, she gave as good as she got, sometimes stunning him into silence with language unbecoming to a lady but necessary in her battles with Ernest.

In September, by his own count, Hemingway had written over

thirteen thousand words; in October, with publishers' deadlines at his back, he wrote another thirteen thousand. By the end of the month, with Scribner's planning a spring publication and the price set with *Cosmopolitan* for the serial to begin in February 1950, Ernest still had not shown any text to either camp, nor was he committed to a title. On October 12, to quiet rumors that this was Hemingway's "big sea, air, land novel," which had been discussed in gossip columns during the past year, Scribner's issued a press release saying that when told by doctors he had but a short time to live, Ernest put aside his "book of larger proportions" to write a shorter novel he knew he could finish. Hotchner was furious: the blurb in the *New York Times* implied that the new novel was written as something of an afterthought, making the public think they were getting something that was a warm-up for the "big book."[34] By the last day in October, Hemingway wired Scribner's and *Cosmopolitan* the title—*Across the River and into the Trees*—which Charles Scribner did not like. On November 4, Ernest air-mailed the first sixty-two pages and the chapter that introduced the girl, Renata, to *Cosmopolitan*. After "jamming" all summer and early fall, Hemingway's weight hovered around 205 pounds and his blood pressure was dangerously high: 180 over 105.[35]

On November 16, Ernest and Mary flew to New York, checked in without fanfare at the Sherry-Netherland, and spent two days making last-minute additions to their luggage for a return trip to Venice. Two days later, Leonard Lyons's newspaper column reported that Ernest was in town but could not visit with old friends, for he was busy finishing his novel, which was not quite true.[36] By arrangement, Lillian Ross met the Hemingways at the airport and spent the better part of two days with them. Mary in her mink coat was "small, energetic and cheerful." Ernest appeared

> bearish, cordial, and constricted. His hair, which was very long in back, was gray, except at the temples, where it was white; his mustache was white, and he had a ragged, half-inch full white beard. There was a bump about the size of a walnut over his left eye. He was wearing steel-rimmed spectacles, with a piece of paper under the nosepiece.[37]

Ross accompanied Hemingway about New York: buying a coat, supper in the hotel room with Marlene Dietrich one day, lunch there with Charles Scribner the next, and a prowl through the Metropolitan Museum of Art with Patrick, now a sophomore down from Harvard. To read her "Profile" of Hemingway was to read his most recent letters, for he told her the same things he was telling everyone else: a list of writers he had beaten in the literary "ring"; how he wrote *The Sun Also Rises*; advice on boxing; stories of Scott Fitzgerald's ineptitude; and old jokes. Taking it all down in her notes, Ross reproduced as accurately as possible the man in his setting, including three double bourbons at the airport bar, the several bottles of champagne in the suite, and the silver flask that he nipped at in the museum. In the background of the Profile, Mary flits in and out of focus, attending to their fourteen pieces of luggage, unpacking at the hotel, hanging up the coats of visitors, a lady in waiting as it were, almost invisible.

Before boarding the *Ile de France*, recently refurbished from a troopship to her prewar splendor, Ernest turned over not quite finished typescripts to Scribner's and *Cosmopolitan*. He was leaving behind a story far stranger than anything he had previously written, a novel book-ended by the Colonel's last duck hunt and filled with more allusions and arcane references than anyone expected to come from him. Mixing and inverting old stories—Dante's *The Divine Comedy* and D'Annunzio's *Notturno*, among others—Hemingway's account of his dying Colonel, reduced from his general's rank for some unnamed fiasco, was a war novel without any war, yet it was largely about the war. Having "moved through arithmetic, through plane geometry and algebra," he was now "into calculus." The book was "all done with three-cushion shots."[38] With a young and beautiful Renata as the novitiate and the Colonel as her guide, the two unlikely lovers enter a newly made hell of war, circling down into its levels of mistrust, incompetence, butchery, back-stabbing, and losses too terrible to recount. Their three-day journey, played out against the backdrop of Venice, is prodded on by Renata's questions. As Cantwell tells her of malfeasance in high places and muck-ups below, the Colonel fingers her three emeralds in his pocket, given to him to hold in trust, emeralds similar to the three stones given to D'Annunzio by his muse, Eleonora Duse. When not engaged in this painful remembering, Cantwell's impressions of Venice, in light and color, set an aesthetic backdrop for the story, a sensitivity to place worthy of Pater.[39]

Newer younger writers—Irwin Shaw in particular—might be able to write convincingly of combat and cohabitation, but could they write with this kind of complexity where the story reverberated on several levels? Would readers, fresh from the war and ready to return to civilian lives, want to be reminded of the remaining bitterness among professional soldiers? Hemingway was certain that *Across the River* was the best book he had ever written; certainly it was his most complex, with little action and much retrospection—not unlike the retrospective of his own life that he was pursuing. Charles Scribner, who finally got to read the typescript after Hemingway was at sea, was concerned that Renata did not appear until the reader was sixty pages into the story. Couldn't she appear sooner? The book, he said, was filled with "beauty, restraint and understanding," more so than in Ernest's earlier books. If Ernest wanted to rework any part of it, Scribner's would reset galleys and postpone publication to meet his schedule. In fact, Hemingway asked Scribner to hold off on setting type for the galleys until he was able to rework the last chapters of the novel in Paris.[40]

Ernest, Mary, and the entourage of Don Andrés, Ed Hotchner, and Jigee Viertel boarded the *Ile de France* together—ladies, gentlemen, and private priest off on a spree. Soon after they arrived at the Ritz Hotel in Paris, Ernest came into a windfall of $6,000 in back royalties from his French publisher. He divided the money evenly between himself, Mary, and Jigee to use as mad money on the town. Hotchner—there on *Cosmopolitan*'s expense account to bring back revised copy for the serial—stayed in a less expensive hotel but spent his days with the group. For almost a month, Hemingway worked early mornings revising Cantwell's last day in Venice while revisiting his own old Parisian haunts and keeping his hand in at the race track. No phone calls came from Adriana, who was still in Venice, but Jigee Viertel was close at hand, for Ernest had arranged special rates for her at the Ritz while insisting she use some of the windfall to pay for it. Mary, in public, was comfortable with the arrangement, but when Ernest spent an hour and a half one night in Jigee's room, she was hurt and furious.[41] When Pete Viertel arrived, Ernest was quick to reassure him that "We've looked after your girl." To his chagrin, Pete learned that this included the gift of almost $2,000; "pocket money," Jigee called it. It did not take long for Viertel to realize that Ernest was smitten with his wife, but Jigee assured him there was nothing to their mild flirtation. How could she be anything more than flattered by the attentions of an old gray man with a heavy paunch behaving like a well-mannered schoolboy?[42] Over the next two weeks, Pete was Ernest's new audience for yet another guided tour into the lost days of his Paris youth.

For the first time since the war, Hemingway was writing poetry, but hardly with the same lovelorn sentiments. Jigee at hand and Adriana in Venice, his newfound "girls," produced in Ernest a schoolboy reaction which Mary neither understood nor tolerated with grace, but she did tolerate it. Whenever an attractive female appeared the least bit vulnerable to her husband's magnetism, Mary became as unimportant as their chambermaid, suffering insults plain and oblique that would have sent a less determined woman to her lawyer. There in Paris, where Mary enjoyed the warmth of her mink coat, Ernest wrote about "the nigger rich . . . wild natural mink is on their backs/Their shoulders, sleeves, and on their flanks." "We leave them all quite easily," he wrote "when dislike overcomes our love." They were poems about Mary without being for Mary.[43]

In another poem, he urged,

> Now, Mary, you can face it good
> And face it in your widow-hood
>
> . . .
>
> So sleep well, darling.
> Sleep well, please,
> And know that I am at my ease.

"It" was death, his own death, holding heavy sway in a mind not quite right. At Auteuil, he watched the ponies run but thought about the war.

> Eternity is scarcely found
> Until we're underneath the ground
> Where thudding hooves will seldom sound.

The day before Christmas, Ernest and his irregulars left Paris by auto, making their way down the foggy Rhône Valley toward Provence.[44] Traveling in a Packard with trunk and roof rack jammed with a mountain of luggage, Ernest gave intermittent lectures on the passing countryside while the hired driver, Georges, took care of the road. At Nice, the Viertels and Hotchner returned to Paris by train, leaving Ernest, Mary, and their Basque-speaking priest to complete the trip to Venice. In his briefcase Hotchner carried the last three revised chapters of *Across the River*.[45]

CHAPTER 14

The Middle Parts of Fortune

January to October 1950

"Never lead against a hitter, and take everything he has to get inside. Duck a swing. Block a hook. And counter a jab with everything you own."[1] The advice he gave Lillian Ross, Ernest sometimes forgot, but Mary never did, which stood her in good stead over the next several months. No sooner was Jigee Viertel out of their lives than she was replaced in Venice by Adriana Ivancich, the muse who inspired *Across the River*. Dora Ivancich, mother of the muse, was even more worried than Mary about Hemingway's attentions to her headstrong daughter: "You see this man Hemingway too much," she told Adriana. "It is not normal, a married man, older than you. I don't forbid you to see him, but from time to time, not so many dates. . . . You have to consider what people might think."[2] Adriana was too young to care what people thought, but neither she nor her mother had yet seen the novel in which her identity was so thinly veiled. While Mary visited churches and museums, Ernest waited at the Gritti Palace for Adriana to meet him for lunches at Harry's Bar or slow walks along the narrow waterways.

Count Carlo Kechler, a new-made Italian friend, warned Ernest that his infatuation with Adriana, so apparent to anyone in their near vicinity, was dangerous for both of them. Ernest would not listen. She was his "Black Horse," the code name he gave her. He was Papa; she was "daughter." Mary, trying to ignore the game, maintained as much dignity as the situation would allow. When Adriana came to Cortina with the Hemingways in early February 1950, Mary wrote in her journal that Ernest was "weaving a mesh which might entangle and pain him," but nothing she could say could change that. When Adriana overstayed her second visit to Cortina, her mother summoned her home. Ernest gallantly volunteered to drive her to Venice while Mary remained in Cortina skiing. Before her errant husband returned, Mary was once more in a cast, having broken her left ankle on the slopes.[3]

Revitalized by Adriana's presence, Hemingway made more revisions to the book version of *Across the River* and added two new short stories to the several "black ass" poems written in Paris when his novel was in its death throes.[4] His Italian publisher said that Ernest was a sure bet for the Nobel Prize with his next book, which pleased Hemingway immensely. But with the reality of his Venetian story now hard upon him, Hemingway forbade any translation of *Across the River* into Italian for a period of two years, a gesture which proved no barrier to the scandal soon to break over the Ivancich family.[5] Without even a second cousin as chaperone, Renata and Richard Cantwell drink together at Harry's Bar, eat together at the Gritti Palace, and then ride the elevator up to his room, where they stretch out together on his bed. In Venice, where every act and every gesture carried political nuances at the local level, such blatant behavior in a book spoke volumes about the Ivancich family. Who would care that *Across the River* was a book about the politics of war when the Colonel bundled Renata beneath the gondola blanket and with his "ruined" hand found beneath her clothing "the island in the great river with the high steep banks"? Following her instructions to "hold the high ground," Cantwell brings the young girl to a sexual climax.[6] When the Italian press would link Hemingway's name with Adriana's what else would there be for the gossips of Venice to discuss?

In February, the first of five installments of the novel appeared in *Cosmopolitan*, where Ed Hotchner was no longer on the masthead as an assistant editor. He blamed the new editor, Herb Mayes. Years later Mayes said, "Hotchner's handling of the project for *Cosmopolitan* was so unfortunate that, in February of 1950, the very month we published the first installment . . . it became necessary to ask for Hotchner's resignation."[7] Without specifying the problem, Mayes may have become aware that Hotchner's loyalties were riding mostly with Hemingway in the contractual process, or he may have been upset with the content of the serial. As a young lawyer with a flair for journalism, Hotchner was a survivor who was never looking for a permanent home on the magazine.

As during the previous winter, Ernest and Mary made the Gritti Palace their home base. When he was not correcting galleys for the serialization of *Across the River*, he was shooting ducks, courting Adriana, and enjoying his status at the Gritti. Mary was behaving better than he had any right to expect. On the surface at least, she was friendly with Adriana, despite Ernest's frequent little insults and his public fawning over the young girl. "My god-damned heart," he wrote, "that target of opportunity, sliced straight in half like the judgement of Herod. Only they sliced mine as clean as with a butcher's cleaver and Herod held up the attack."[8] Mary and Dora Ivancich finally met at a lunch arranged by Ernest, who prevailed upon Mary to invite Dora and Adriana to visit them at the Finca. There they could spend time with Gianfranco, who was now working in Havana to restore the family's diminished fortune. Awkward in her walking cast, Mary was embarrassed and angry, but nevertheless did as Ernest asked of her, smiling and tolerant of Dora's hesitant English while mentally classifying the Italian woman as "gray of hair, eyes, manner and wardrobe."[9]

Mary did not speak of the letters from Nita Jensen, whom they left in charge of the Finca. No sooner had the Hemingways left Cuba than Gianfranco moved into their house on a regularly irregular basis, and Nita could not dislodge him, and would not sleep in the same house with him. One night when she arrived, Gianfranco "was here with several women in some fancy station wagon. . . . The following night . . . Sinsky met me and asked me who the man was who was using your room. I just about died. Every time René locked your typewriter away the Italian managed to find it . . . I'm convinced that he's purely a sponger and taking every advantage he can of you."[10] Later, Dora Ivancich responded to Mary's invitation with a cautious note saying she would consider the possibility of a visit. She did not say there was no money to pay for such an extravagance. Nor did she know that Gianfranco, temperamentally unsuited to tedious employment, was enamored with the seemingly carefree life of the writer.

After a self-hosted farewell supper in their Gritti apartment with Adriana's family, the Hemingways departed Venice on March 7 en route to Paris with stops in between at Nervi, Nice, and Aix-en-Provence. In Paris, registering once more at the Ritz, Ernest went to bed with one of his recurring bronchial infections from which he did not recover until Adriana arrived the following week to return to art school. About the same time that Adriana appeared, so did a letter from an almost forgotten person out of the past. Olga Rudge, Ezra Pound's mistress since the mid-Twenties, wrote to remind "Dear Mr. Hemingway" that Ezra continued to molder in St. Elizabeth's Hospital for the Insane in Washington, D.C., incarcerated there by the American government rather than putting him on trial for treason. During the war Pound had made a series of radio broadcasts from Italy urging British and American troops not to fight for their decadent capitalist employers. Olga reminded Ernest that he suggested a year earlier that Ezra might be granted amnesty. Was anything being done about it? The controversial awarding to him of the Bollinger Prize for poetry had only stirred up old arguments and done nothing to rescue him. His wife, Dorothy, she said was "incapable of taking direct action" and "refused to take responsibility of any kind." Hemingway had recently agreed to let his "Homage to Ezra" (1925) be republished in a collection of essays honoring the aging and erratic poet on his sixty-fifth birthday. But adulation would not free the iconoclast who edited Eliot's *Waste Land* into shape, championed James Joyce, and gave Ernest an early boost up the literary ladder. Olga said,

> Of course the easy way is for E.'s friends to leave him where he is and salve their consciences with tributes to his literary worth—he is simply crawling with literary parasites—none of whom, in the States at least, compromise themselves by touching on the subject of treason . . . it is surely time for his friends, if he has any, to see what can be done.

She closed the letter asking Hemingway to forgive her bluntness, but other than republish an old essay, "What else have you done for E.?"[11] The unspoken answer was: Nothing. Hemingway realized, however, that were Ezra to be let out of St. Elizabeth's, he would be a man without a passport, vulnerable to a trial for treason, and with no place to go unless Italy would take him back.

During the Hemingways' last week in Paris, Charley and Vera Scribner, on vacation, rendezvoused with Ernest, who declared the much revised novel now ready for book publication. Earlier in the winter, Adriana at Hemingway's request had submitted drawings to Scribner's for the dust jacket of the novel, which Charley, apparently not knowing her relationship with Ernest, selected to be used. Ernest was so delighted that he hosted a luncheon for "his partner," as he referred to Adriana, after which he and she walked through St. Germain stopping at a Deux Magots sidewalk table. Watching the young men on the boulevard, Hemingway said that any of them, who were not stupid, would wish to marry a woman as lovely as she. "Since I am not stupid," he continued, "I would feel the same way." When Adriana reminded him he was married, he agreed, but added that two people need not remain married. He might have added that not three blocks away was the apartment on rue Férou where he and Pauline had lived, and that they once sat deeply in love at a Deux Magots table. "I love you in my heart," he told Adriana, "and I cannot do anything about it." The young woman sat there paralyzed, as if waiting for an avalanche to fall. "All I could think of at that moment was that everything was ending, our beautiful friendship was over, finished." Unable to touch her gin and tonic, she waited immobilized. Finally, Ernest said, "I would ask you to marry me if I did not know you would say no." The moment passed. Ernest left a few francs on the table, and they rose to walk through rue Bonaparte, past the Beaux-Arts galleries, to the Seine.[12]

On March 21, the spring equinox, Ernest and Mary left Paris on the boat train to Le Havre, where the next day they boarded the *Ile de France* for New York. Adriana, who helped with the packing, accompanied them as far as the pier. At the Ritz they left behind a trunk, a box of china, and two boxes of books for the concierge to ship to Cuba.[13] Included in their personal baggage they took with them enmity, betrayal, and heartache. No sooner was the ship at sea than Ernest wrote Charles Scribner that his love for Mary and Adriana was like having his heart fed into a meat grinder.[14] To his London publisher, Jonathan Cape, he wrote, asking him to keep references to his war record off the British dust jacket of *Across the River and into the Trees*. Denigrating his most prized moments from the war, Hemingway insisted that he be featured as a writer only, not as a soldier. If the reviewers wanted to prove that he had never run the sub patrols, never flown with the RAF, never fought in the war, never been wounded, never killed anyone, that was fine with him.[15]

By the time the Hemingways reached New York, two installments of *Across the River* had appeared in *Cosmopolitan*, and the third was about to come out. Lillian Ross, who was still working on her *New Yorker* Profile of Ernest, spent more time with him, gathering more details. Marlene Dietrich visited again, saying how much she adored the early chapters of the novel, and Charles Sweeny and Evan Shipman, old friends from the early Paris days, dropped by the Sherry-Netherland to visit. At the Scribner Building, Ernest turned over his final revised draft of *Across the River* for publication in August. On April 5, there was a birthday lunch for Mary with journalist friends, and that night Buddy North, whose Ringling Brothers Circus was in town, invited Ernest, Mary, Hotchner, and Lillian Ross to be his guests at that extravaganza. Ernest fell in love with the big cats, the bears, and the elephants.

The following day, Ernest accidentally ran into Chink Dorman-O'Gowan, an old friend and survivor from the 1918 war not seen for over twenty years. A professional soldier, Chink, now retired from the British Army, had changed his given name of Smith to its original Gaelic form, O'Gowan. Reappearing in Hemingway's life, along with Charles Sweeny and Buck Lanham, Chink made it even more difficult for Ernest to leave the war behind. All three friends, professional military men to the core, felt badly used during the war, but Chink was the most vocal in his complaints. If Hemingway's Colonel was bitter about military politics, Dorman-O'Gowan was absolutely livid to the point of advocating armed rebellion. He was in the States lecturing for the Inter-Party

Government of Ireland, preaching the need to remove all British from Northern Ireland. Back in Ireland on his country estate, he was serving as a military adviser to the Irish Republican Army (IRA) while training IRA men in Dartry Woods and giving briefings to battalion-level officers.[16] Over the next several months his correspondence with Hemingway would continue to stoke Ernest's personal bitterness about the war, a bitterness over events whose significance inflated with his every telling of the tale.

On April 6, Ernest and Mary left New York, arriving in Cuba on April 8.[17] For thirteen of the last nineteen months they had lived at sea or on the road—Paris, Venice, Torcello, Cortina—during which time Ernest began, finished, and revised *Across the River and into the Trees* and returned heartsick to the Finca. Mary was returning to the Finca with an impoverished heart, despite her newly acquired Venetian gold trinkets.[18] What once seemed to be another of her husband's romantic but unrequited interludes had churned into a full-blown, embarrassing obsession for which she had no antidote, nor had he. The presence of Gianfranco Ivancich continually reminded Ernest of his now distant muse, Adriana. For Mary, the younger Gianfranco was a comfort as a listener to whom she could tell her woes, and also a potential but probably unrequited lover with whom to needle her husband. But nothing Mary did could distract Ernest from his deepening fantasies about the fields of love and war. In public, he was usually as charming as ever; but alone with her, he wore his melancholia like a shroud, spewing painful verbal abuse at her while interlarding his real war experiences with new inventions.

Having been an ambulance driver in Italy and a journalist in the Spanish Civil War, Hemingway began seriously rewriting his military service, making it appear as though he had been an armed combatant in both wars. He wrote Buck Lanham that World War I was his kindergarten, at which "If you go crazy from too many times up the same damned hill you can always look at fireing [sic] squad. It could look like two fireing squads if you had double vision from concussion. But you always saw the fireing squad, double vision or not, and sometimes you commanded it."[19] Spurred on by Dorman-O'Gowan's letters inviting him to be part of the IRA revolution, Hemingway's letters to Chink were so ambiguous that one was not sure if he was reporting what he observed or what he participated in. About the Spanish Civil War, he said: "We were beat when they took Irun but we ran it out for two and a half years into the longest holding attack in history. . . . I have it completely and accurate and straight now that have killed 122 (armeds not counting possible or necessary shootings)."[20] For two years during World War II, when submarines were thick in the Gulf, he commanded a Q-ship, the only civilian to do so. Seven of the eleven such ships were lost due to faulty security, which for his boat remained unbreached to this day. "We preyed on everything neutral that was doing any good for Germany and on Miss Submarine." Only four men from his nine-man crew were still alive. None of which was completely true: none of the *Pilar*'s crew was killed in action; they never attacked any submarines; the *Pilar* was not a ship of prey, nor were there eleven others like her in Cuba.

Hemingway claimed that he would probably have to fight in the Korean War as well. That's what they had done to him for thirty-two years, tossed him into the fray like a pit bull or a fighting cock with no one willing to take responsibility for him if the action screwed up. He could not remember all the times he had been "pitted." He might not be a professional like Chink, but Ernest implied that he had soldiered for six months in China; two years and three months at sea with his command; a fling with the RAF; and the rest of 1944 into 1945 with Lanham's 22nd Regiment. Three times he was recommended for the Distinguished Service Cross (DSC).[21] He had been in all those places, but not soldiering as he implied. The DSC was not an honor conferred on civilians.

Like many of his war stories, there was a substantial layer of fiction laid down over a foundation of fact until these fabrications devalued his very real and serious work during the war. It was as if he were reliving one of his own short stories. When Krebs of "Soldier's Home" (1925) returned from the war, he found he had to tell lies to be listened to, but "A distaste for everything that had happened to him in the war set in because of the lies he told. All of the times that had been able to make him feel cool and clear inside himself . . . now lost their cool, valuable quality and then were lost themselves."[22] Well Hemingway knew the feeling, having returned to Oak Park after his Italian wounding to spread outrageous stories about his foreign war. He told the *Oak Parker* that he had "received thirty-two 45 caliber bullets in his limbs and hands. Twenty-eight of the slugs, he said, were "extracted without taking an anesthetic."[23]

That was thirty years earlier, understandable exaggerations of a young man eager to prove himself in the world. But here at fifty, half a century old, as he liked to say, the boy was still inventing feats beyond belief for reasons that were not so clear. For those he admired, Ernest tailored the story to the strong suit of his listener. To Charles Scribner, an avid horseman in the British fox hunter mold, Ernest melded his tame experiences at a Wyoming dude ranch with observations of working cowboys to invent Hemingway the wild bronc rider: "I bucked out anything there was in the shoots [chutes] with a bear trap saddle when I need[ed] 100 dollars and did not give a what [you] call it if the back went or not. . . . In a bear trap saddle he can't throw you. You are with him for keeps. But it is 20/1 he breaks your back."[24] To academic Arthur Mizener, Ernest claimed to have been shot "twice through the scrotum" and through both knees, both hands, both feet, and his head.[25] By the end of August, he was telling a fellow writer, Robert Cantwell, that he had been wounded "on twenty-two different occasions . . . due to enemy action."[26] Mary, having no way of knowing where reality left off and fantasy took hold, could not question stories of his life before they met, but she was growing tired, if not concerned, with his constant retelling of them.

Martha Gellhorn, after reading the first installment of *Across the River and into the Trees*, was quick to conclude that her former husband doted only on himself. "I feel sick," she wrote Bill Walton, "shivering sick." She wept for the lost years she spent adoring him. Perhaps those who did not know him would find Colonel Cantwell plausible, but to her the story had "a long sound of madness and a terrible smell as of decay." When she read the second installment, she wrote Walton that this book was "God's vengeance; but Ernest will never know. He will go on . . . always feeling misunderstood . . . always feeling everything is someone else's fault and I think . . . he will end in the nut house."[27]

Mary was troubled and frightened by Ernest's behavior, disturbed by the letters arriving from Adriana, and unsure of the worth of the new novel. When coupled with his increasingly insulting behavior toward her, Mary was being pushed to her limits of tolerance. All his life he bent women to his will, either by romantic intensity in the courtship or by sullen and/or sarcastic treatment in the parting. All his life he fell in love with the emotional impact of a heart attack, undeniable and all-consuming. All his life he wanted a wife to whom he gave the responsibility for the order and discipline of his household. Once a wife, the woman quickly became a mother figure whom he began to resent just as he resented his own mother's control of the Oak Park home. Like his father, when he wished to punish, he demanded a detailed accounting of all expenditures, no matter how small. Unlike his father, he could, with his left hand, spend money as if it had no meaning.

His first three wives knew the game was over when he began purposely embarrassing them in public. In the presence of Adriana, Ernest frequently ignored Mary as if she were hired help; on their return to the Finca, his behavior grew worse. On May 5, barely a month after returning from Italy, Mary and her visiting cousin waited on board the *Pilar* for Ernest to meet them for lunch. When he arrived late, unapologetic, and with the young prostitute Xenophobia on his arm, Mary was hurt to the point of cold fury. The next morning she delivered to him a declaration of independence:

> As soon as it is possible for me to move out . . . I shall move. . . .
> in 1944 in bed at the Ritz Hotel in Paris . . . I thought you were
> a straight and honorable and brave man and magnetically
> endearing to me . . . although I was suspicious of your over-
> drinking . . . I believed you and in you. . . . I expected to con-
> tribute to the marriage . . . absolute loyalty to you and devotion
> to your projects . . . enterprising service to you and your family
> and house . . . alertness and tenderness towards you . . . [but] we
> have both been failures. . . . I have lost your interest in me, your
> devotion, and also your respect. Your principal failure . . . because
> of your accumulating ego and your increasing . . . over-drinking

. . . you have been . . . undisciplined in your daily living. Both privately and in public you have insulted me and my dignity as a human being and a woman devoted to you and have debased my pride in you in front of friends.[28]

The following day, Mary gave Ernest a detailed listing of how she spent the $1,000 he had deposited in her checking account twenty days earlier. Both an accounting and an indictment, the typed sheet showed that she ate out twice at lunch, bought some cheap costume jewelry, one dress, and some face creams, while spending the rest on household expenses. Only $79.35 went for her personal use. Until the end of June, Mary kept the daily record, including such items as thirty cents for gum and sixty-five cents for a zipper: punch and counterpunch.

While Mary was preparing her May 7 accounting, Ernest was writing Milton Wolf, a onetime friend and commander of the Abraham Lincoln Battalion in the Spanish Civil War. In response to Wolf's asking for a contribution to the Brigade's defense fund, Ernest replied that he helped individuals, not causes. If the Brigade had problems now with congressional investigations of loyalty, had they not brought that upon themselves? Had they not signed on to be tough?[29] He might as well have given Mary a copy of the letter. Had she not also signed on to be tough? The next day he wrote a disjointed letter to Senator Joe McCarthy, the man fomenting the Red scare and making "McCarthyism" a by-word for hysterical government investigations. In his harangue of the senator, Ernest offered to pay for his trip to the Finca where, depending on "Tail Gunner Joe's" weight, he could fight either Ernest or one of his sons. The reasons for the invective are not entirely clear, but the rhetoric was impressive:

> Senator you certainly bore the bejeesus out of some tax-payers and this is an invitation to get it all out of your system . . . with an old character like me who is fifty years old . . . and thinks you are a shit, Senator, and would knock you on your ass the best day you ever lived.[30]

There were no interhouse letters to Mary, but neither did she leave as threatened. Somehow a truce was reached, and his short, unhappy wife, for the first time in almost five years, began letters of inquiry to editors to see who was interested in her view of "life with Papa." By May 21, she had a contract with *Flair* magazine and once again there were two writers in the family.

All that summer Hemingway struggled with his wife, his writing, and his public image. First there were book galleys to correct for Scribner's followed by the page proofs. All the while new installments of the serial were appearing in *Cosmopolitan*, sanitized by nameless editors for their American readers. Faced with a much revised and altered typescript, Ernest was hard-pressed to get it right, making yet more changes in chapter endings, which he finished about June 3. Two days later he received the proof for the dust jacket that used Adriana's illustration with new lettering, but the publication date slipped from August to September. Now, with the book out of his hands and no longer emendable, came the reward of anxiety and second-guessing. Supportive words on the serial came in from various friends, whose enthusiasm was not always as strong as Ernest needed. His fishing and shooting friend, Mayito Menocal, Jr., said he was glad that Ernest had cut "the part about Eisenhower being complicated with Kay Summersby" because there would have been a libel suit, even if the general had been sleeping with his jeep driver.[31]

Meanwhile Lillian Ross, having completed her Hemingway Profile for *The New Yorker*, sent Ernest the page proofs for his suggestions or changes.[32] He immediately sent back his comments, which were minimal, saying that he sounded conceited. Ross said no one in the office agreed with him on the conceited part. "Of course," she said, "you talk your special kind of joke language. That's supposed to be . . . one of the points. It would be silly to make you sound like a Henry James character."[33] When the Profile appeared, subtitled "How Do You Like It Now, Gentlemen?" friends of Ernest were quick to respond. Marlene Dietrich was upset by her presence in the piece; Hotchner was cautiously positive, not knowing if Ernest would appreciate it or not. Slim Hayward thought it "lacked affection."[34] A number of readers took the Profile to be hostile on Ross's part, showing Hemingway as a badly dressed eccentric who liked to lecture to people while drinking champagne early in the morning. Ross later said,

> People who objected strongly to Hemingway's personality, assumed I did the same . . . they thought . . . I was ridiculing or attacking it. Other people did not like the way Hemingway talked . . . they didn't like his freedom; they didn't like his not taking himself seriously; they didn't like his wasting his time on going to boxing matches, going to the zoo, talking to friends, going fishing, enjoying people . . . they didn't like Hemingway to be Hemingway.[35]

Ernest himself was ambivalent about his portrait, reassuring when writing to Ross, "shocked" by it when he wrote Carlos Baker, who was working on the first critical book to cover all of Hemingway's fiction. To Dorman-O'Gowan, Hemingway said he was "sorry about that New Yorker thing." Some of the quotes were not actually his, but he thought the article was basically friendly. In another letter, Hemingway said he thought of Lillian Ross as "a good friend although you might not gather it from that Profile."[36]

On July 18, when overdue page proofs on *Across the River* arrived at the Finca, Ernest was in a horrible mood, furious with Jonathan Cape for misspelling Cantwell's name on the dust jacket proofs for the British edition, certain (as always) that Scribner's was not going to push the novel, and his ears still ringing from another concussion suffered on the *Pilar*. Climbing up on the flying bridge to relieve Gregorio at the helm, Ernest slipped on the wet deck as Gregorio turned sharply into the Rincón Channel. Falling into the gaffs, Hemingway's head smashed into a metal clamp, opening a deep, brightly bleeding cut on his skull. It took three stitches to close it, the odor of his own blood now as familiar as the pain—a force five concussion, he called it, measuring it in hurricane terms. His headaches returned, making him irritable as he sunk into a "black-ass" mood, due, he said, to his boredom, pride, and disgust. In August, he wrote Lillian Ross of being tempted, while diving deep into the Gulf Stream, not to come up. True or not, his account was in keeping with his anxiety over the novel and his marriage. "I love A[driana] to die of it," he told Charley Scribner, "and . . . I love

Mary as she should be loved; I hope."[37] It was an old dilemma, one he first experienced when married to Hadley and in love with Pauline; again when married to Pauline and in love with Martha.

With Cowley's biographical essay spread across *Life* magazine, a *Harper's Bazaar* photo essay in an earlier March issue, the Ross *New Yorker* Profile, and a sanitized serial version in *Cosmopolitan*, not to mention sidebars in several national magazines, Hemingway could not have been in a better or worse position vis-à-vis his hostile critics: better in the sense that no matter what the critics said, the reading public was fully alerted to the book; worse because there is nothing like a spotlight for bringing out predators. Released on September 7, *Across the River and into the Trees* was immediately reviewed by every major newspaper and magazine at home and in England, where it had appeared three days earlier. Avid admirers lined up on one side, rabid detractors on the other. John O'Hara prefaced his review by labeling Hemingway "the most important author living today, the outstanding author since the death of Shakespeare." Maxwell Geismar said, "It is not only Hemingway's worst novel; it is a synthesis of everything that is bad in his previous work and it throws a doubtful light on the future."[38] *Newsweek* said it was "his best and most carefully thought out book." *Time* called it a parody of Hemingway's style, giving his "admirers little to cheer about."[39]

East Coast intellectuals, who once put Hemingway at the forefront of American writers, were unusually harsh, as if the bad boy had betrayed them personally. Alfred Kazin felt "embarrassment, even pity, that so important a writer can make such a travesty of himself." Philip Rahv found the novel "so egregiously bad as to render all comment on it positively embarrassing to anyone who esteems Hemingway."[40] In the middle, the lukewarm group, who admired Hemingway but could not admire this novel, spoke of it in terms of texture and scene without passing judgments, hedging their bets. E. B. White paid left-handed homage to the novel with one of his parodies, "Across the Street and into the Grill," which began: "This is my last and best and true and only meal, thought Mr. Pirnie [not Ernie] as he descended at noon and swung east on the beat-up sidewalk of Forty-fifth Street. Just ahead of him was the girl from the reception desk. I am a little fleshed out around the crook of the elbow, thought Pirnie, but I commute good."[41]

Few and far between were those who understood the complexity of Hemingway's structure or his intent of rewriting the descent into the Inferno. Northrop Frye, who did not care for the book, at least saw that it was "intended to be a study in isolation, of how the standards of a decent soldier are betrayed by modern war." Phil Young, already at work on his groundbreaking psychoanalytic study of Hemingway's fiction, argued that while we may not enjoy the violent world of the novel, "we should be hard pressed to prove that it is not the one we inhabit." Old Paris friend and author Eliot Paul, taking a longer view, called Hemingway's "grasp of contemporary situations . . . profound and a decade ahead of his public's." Ben Redman's analysis of the reviews was quite accurate: "Perhaps we really do know too much about Hemingway, or at least his public poses, to judge his work impartially."[42] These mixed reviews had no apparent impact on sales, as the book quickly sold out the initial printing of 75,000; before the end of September Scribner's ordered a second printing of 25,000, with more printings to come. For twenty-one weeks *Across the River* registered on the *New York Times* best-seller list, running as number one for seven of those weeks. By the first accounting period, 125,000 copies had been sold. Between his forty-five-cent royalties for every copy and the healthy serial fee from *Cosmopolitan*, Hemingway paid off all his borrowings from Scribner's and would enter 1951 debt-free and ahead of the game.

Some good reviews, much public attention, and a best-seller did little to relieve his increasing angst as summer rolled into early fall. Soon Adriana Ivancich and her mother, Dora, were due to visit the Finca, filling him with expectations of the young girl's presence and fears of how Mary might behave. In August, when it looked as if they might not be able to afford the trip, Ernest sent a substantial check to cover the expenses. Adriana was overwhelmed; her mother was frightened, but wanted to make the trip to see her son Gianfranco, her only hope for restoring the family's fallen fortunes. Gianfranco, meanwhile, had managed to lose or be fired from his job (a matter of honor, Ernest called it) and was now, with Ernest's encouragement, writing a novel. By the end of August, a reporter from the European version of *Life* magazine was asking for a photograph of Adriana, for gossip was beginning to spread through Venetian society about the gondola scene in the *Cosmopolitan* serial. Claiming that Hemingway had melded two young women into the character of Renata, the September issue of *Europeo* published photos of Adriana and Afdera Franchetti, the younger sister of Hemingway's Italian friend, Barone Nanyuki Franchetti. Afdera was reported to have said that Ernest was "desperately in love with her . . . twice she had visited him in Cuba and they had recently spent a month together in Paris, winning millions of francs at Auteuil."[43]

To free his imagination, Dante needed his Beatrice; Petrarch, his Laura. So, too, did Hemingway need his unrequited and impassioned love for Adriana. Regularly, since leaving her behind on the dock at Le Havre, he had written her letters professing his love for her, his admiration of her artwork, and his concern for her future. When the bright blood streamed down his face on the *Pilar*, the heartsick lover professed that his first thought was taking better care of himself for her sake. On August 1, he longed for her looks, her presence, her walk, her talk, the quickness and beauty of her mind. The next day, like some medieval knight at the court of love, he pledged his utter devotion to her. No request of hers would be denied. A week later, she is his "reference point, his direction . . . the northern point on his compass."[44] Hemingway was ever a fond and forceful lover on paper, having wooed Hadley and Pauline at a distance with almost daily protestations of his devotion; but his letters to Adriana were different, filled with love without becoming suicidal in his loneliness. With the object of his affection geographically and decorously out of reach, Hemingway had the perfect romance—his love would ever be unrequited and thus never disappointed, not to mention its lack of consequences.

Unfortunately for Mary, her husband's hopeless love for the Venetian teenager did nothing to enliven their own marital bed. In August, while Mary was away from the Finca arranging housing for her aging and infirm parents, "Louella Parsons, the Hollywood columnist, reported on the radio that the Hemingway marriage was breaking up over an Italian countess with whom Ernest had fallen madly in love and that they were presently living together at the Finca."[45] A phone call from Ernest reassured Mary that the malicious gossip was unfounded, later discovering that in Venice, Afdera Franchetti claimed to be the model for Renata. When Mary returned home, she found Ernest no better for all his apologies. The two of them began a one-cushion billiard version of their conflict, playing shots off Charles Scribner through letters which they did not share with each other. On October 6, Scribner, disturbed by the correspondence, urged Ernest to be more understanding of Mary, who probably had good cause for her behavior. He cautioned that "a girl like A[driana] is really not for us."

The closer the Ivancichs were to arriving in Havana, the worse Ernest's behavior became. On October 12, Mary wrote a plaintive letter to Charles Scribner filled with disturbing details:

> He has been truculent, brutal, abusive, and extremely childish. . . . Last night with six at table, I declined to bet with one of our guests on a pigeon shooting match. . . . So Ernest denounced me several times as "cobarde" (coward). . . . At table his favorite and frequent means of protesting any word, glance, gesture or food he doesn't like is to put his full, freshly served plate on the floor. The other day he dumped the entire plate of bread and crackers on top of my plate . . . he has called me, and repeated the names . . . whore, bitch, liar, moron. On several occasions I have called him a shit . . . it looks like the disintegration of a personality to me.

She closed the letter asking if Charley knew of any jobs for her in New York, but cautioned him about answering her letter. Ernest tended, she said, to open her mail before she saw it.[46]

She might have added that her husband's head was still on fire from his latest concussion, that old shrapnel in his right leg was on the move, pressing against a nerve, bloating his leg like a balloon, that his blood pressure was once again out of control. She might have said that the New York reviews had hurt him to the quick, and that she knew how to hurt him more with the young and handsome Gianfranco. Ernest, of course, knew how to make Mary squirm: at table telling again and again about some nameless New York woman holding his penis through lunch and a matinee. In her journal, Mary continued to record his insults, embarrassments, and outrageous behavior. He called her "camp follower" and "scavenger." When she came home with a bruised arm where Gianfranco had gripped her too hard, Ernest exploded. "Displaying your badge of shame," he said, shooting out the lamp outside the front door, threatening to shoot off Gianfranco's arm.[47] At sunrise, the day before the Ivancichs arrived, Mary woke him with, "You defend your book publicly, but you don't defend your marriage. You don't write to Lolly Parsons or to anyone who will print it."[48] Ernest did not write the letter. Angry, hurt, and probably scared by her husband's increasingly irrational behavior, Mary did not give up. As complicated as foreign diplomacy, the unwritten rules for their game of love were always changing, never absolute, and difficult for an outsider to follow.

CHAPTER 15

Roadstead of the Heart

November 1950 to February 1952

All that fall Ernest was despondent, listless, tired, and without joy. His Cuban friends, including his doctors, saw the external signs without understanding that one of the causes was Adriana. After all, how could a man approaching fifty, married to his fourth wife, be lovesick? José Luis Herrera was puzzled enough by his friend's errant behavior that he finally became angry with him. "I have nothing in my head," Ernest complained. "You drink too much," José Luis told him. "I'm fed up with living," Ernest replied. "I can't write. I love only Adriana. I am going to commit suicide." José Luis, who had heard this threat before, was not impressed. "Fine," he told Ernest. "Fine, shoot yourself. Where is the gun? Tell me. I will load it myself and watch you pull the trigger." The next morning José Luis wrote Ernest a letter telling him that "his sickness was intangible and therefore incurable." There was nothing that his friends or doctors could do. He must cure himself. Now he was living in an unreal world, a fantasy world such as a child might construct. José Luis did not doubt that his old friend was indeed in pain, but he was not using it as a resource. Only Ernest could cure Ernest, and the remedy was at hand. He need only begin again to write, pouring his pain into his work. Therein lay the cure. Suicide was selfish when he had so many depending upon him—Mary, his children, his friends in Cuba and elsewhere. When José Luis was certain that Ernest had received his letter, he began to phone the Finca, but René would tell him that

Ernest did not wish to speak that day. On the third call, Ernest finally came to the phone, apologetic, saying, "Feo, I am a complete shit."[1] Then the crisis was over, and they did not speak of it again. José Luis then took all of Hemingway's guns from the Finca to his own house, telling Ernest that when he was drunk, he lost his human face. In August, José Luis said that Ernest tried to drown himself in the Gulf Stream "like Martin Eden," but after Adriana appeared at La Finca, Papa was a different man, changed and peaceful. He told José Luis that it was safe to return to him his weapons.

That fall when Adriana and her mother arrived, heads turned wherever the young girl passed, her white, white skin sending out electric signals that men old enough to be her father quite clearly appreciated. Juan Lopez, chauffeur at Finca Vigia, said that Ernest never went driving with the Italian beauty unless a third person were in the car, usually Roberto Herrera. Juan never forgot Adriana's long legs as he held the car door for her to climb in or out. At the Floridita Manuel Perez, the waiter, said that all of the staff were in wonder over this beauty that Papa brought with him like a prize for all to see. Roberto Herrera called her "majestic, elegant, gentle, and tender." Whenever the camera appeared to photograph Adriana and Papa, he always took off his glasses, for they made him look too old, he thought.

Late one night at the Finca, the Ivancichs gathered in the living room where Mary sang along with the music that she would always be true to Ernest, darling, in her fashion, urging him to dance a round with her, his face growing red with embarrassment, heavy as a bear, clumsy, finally throwing his glass of wine in her face. An ugly scene with Ernest's muse, Adriana the impossible, there watching, close enough to smell but never to touch. Shyly he gave her a copy of the book she inspired (albeit dedicated to Mary), eager for her response. "The girl is boring," Adriana told him. "How could your colonel love a girl who is so boring? A girl like that does not exist, if she is lovely and from a good family and goes to Mass every morning. Such a girl would not drink all day like a sponge and be in bed at the hotel." Hurt and saddened, he said he knew such a girl, more than one. Perhaps American girls were like that, she replied, but not a girl from Venice.[2]

For company Mary was polite and cheerful, ignoring Ernest's insults, turning them into jokes, keeping up appearances, ignoring whatever she could. While fishing on the *Pilar*, Adriana cut her finger on a dorsal fin. When Ernest began to suck the blood out of the young girl's wound, Mary turned her back on the spectacle. In private, René, the Finca's major domo, overheard her tell Adriana that she was not afraid of her. Adriana may have helped Ernest recover his ability to write, but nothing serious can happen between them. This little affair shall pass. Adriana and her mother lived in the guest cottage, leaving the Hemingways private time to keep the skirmish going off stage. By early December, Ernest was writing Hotchner that Mary was still giving him hell about visiting Jigee Viertel's hotel room in Paris a year earlier.[3] René remembered Mary telling Ernest that "when people mature they write better. On the other hand, you are writing worse." Ernest became furious, ripped a copy of *Across the River* into shreds, and threw it into the garden.[4]

Gradually, however, Hemingway's emotional life began to even out, following what was now a familiar cycle: a black-ass depression bottoming out in a wallow of irrational behavior that slowly ebbed as he moved back within the range of normal; his emotional temperature would continue to rise, reaching a manic peak, then gradually falling back into the normal range and from there deepen into black-ass behavior. Sometimes the cycle took several years to complete its course; at other times, it was compressed into months or days. At any point there could be a short cycle within a longer one. Frequently when the curve moved upward, he was writing well, followed by depression with a book's publication. Always when a book was completed he was faced with the immediately unanswerable question of what to write next. If the last book was as good as he could create, how then could he now create a better one? Each book used up experience he could not use again, making the answer more difficult to know and longer to find.

He had been cycling this way ever since 1919 when he returned from World War I: when euphoric, nothing could daunt him; when bottomed out, he was increasingly paranoid, moody, and implacable. All of his other wives had been through his entire range of responses, but this postwar trough that almost sucked Mary under was deeper than before and more vicious. He may have been reborn at Hürtgenwald, as he claimed, but it was a bloody rebirthing that embedded horrific images of burned bodies, severed limbs, and blood pumping from unstoppable wounds. That Mary weathered out his postwar depression was due only to her own mental toughness, her refusal to admit defeat, and her memory of their trysting in Paris. She did not yet understand the pattern of his behavior, but she realized that their life seemed to be evening out. Maybe after seeing his wife and Dora Ivancich behaving like chaperons to himself, older than both of them, he began to see how foolish he looked in love with Adriana. Whatever had happened, its effects were obvious: Ernest was writing again. When the *New York Herald Book Review* asked him which recently published books he would recommend to readers, he answered without malice that he enjoyed William Faulkner's *Collected Stories* and Irwin Shaw's *Mixed Company*.[5]

As soon as Adriana and her mother were in residence at the Finca, Ernest returned to what he called the "big book"—the sea, air, land book that was metamorphosing into something quite different than he first imagined. The novelist, Roger, disappeared after the Bimini section to reappear transformed in what would be *The Garden of Eden*.[6] In the sea story that remained, Hemingway took Thomas Hudson through a lonely and depressed period in Cuba while awaiting his next submarine patrol during World War II. His several former wives are all divorced from him or dead, his children killed in accidents, his painting suffering an hiatus. Back at sea, Hudson and his makeshift crew pursue escaping but well-armed Germans who have abandoned their disabled submarine, killed the natives on a small key in the Old Bahama Channel for their boats and food, and are fleeing through shallow passages between small islands. By Christmas Eve, 1950, Hemingway completed the draft of Hudson's dark patrol, ending with the German ambush that leaves the painter dying on the deck of his boat. The story's working title—*The Island and the Stream*—would change much later to *Islands in the Stream*. A week later he wrote Hotchner that Mary read the book in a one-night sitting, and was so moved by it, her arms prickled with goosebumps, that she forgave him all his sins. Adriana's response, he said, was the same, putting him back in the good graces of both women and all was right with the world.[7]

The period of grace was shortlived. Early in the new year, Dora received a French newspaper with Adriana's picture captioned: "Renata, Hemingway's new love." Mary said, "I told you so." Gianfranco tried to smooth it over. But very quickly Dora moved herself and her daughter into a Havana hotel.[8] Simultaneously, Ernest began writing what he thought to be the final section of the sea portion of the "big book"—the story of an old Cuban fisherman's losing battle with a giant marlin. The story, which was meant to counterpoint Hudson's pursuit of the German submariners, was one he had known since 1936 when he reported in *Esquire* about

> an old man fishing alone in a skiff . . . hooked a great marlin that . . . pulled the skiff far out to sea. . . . The old man had stayed with him a day, a night, a day and another night while the fish . . . pulled the boat. When he had come up the old man . . . harpooned him. Lashed along side the sharks had hit him and the old man had fought them out alone in the Gulf Stream in a skiff, clubbing them, stabbing at them, lunging at them with an oar until he was exhausted and the sharks had eaten all that they could hold.[9]

Like Hudson, the old fisherman was at the end of his career, fighting a losing battle against huge odds. Like *Across the River* and *For Whom the Bell Tolls*, it was a three-day story of inevitable loss, a central theme of Hemingway's fiction from his Paris days forward.

The night before Adriana left Cuba, Ernest hosted a formal party in her honor at the Finca for two hundred invited guests. A bar and buffet was set up by the pool, another inside the house; a small orchestra played on the patio. The Finca staff were delighted to see

Ernest looking so handsome in his tuxedo.[10] The next morning, February 7, Mary, Dora, and Adriana left by P&O ferry for Key West to pick up the waiting car and drive up the Florida coast to Jacksonville to catch the train to New York. On February 23, the Ivancichs, having been entertained in New York by Hotchner at Ernest's expense, boarded the *Liberté* to return to Italy. The one-sided passion of Ernest for Adriana was cooled by reality. They would remain friends; she would provide more illustrations for some of his work; and there would be continued correspondence; but his obsession was now a memory. Her presence in his life had inspired *Across the River* and inexplicably set him free to write about an old fisherman's epic conflict.

Begun in the new year, the first draft of the old man's battle with the marlin and the sharks was finished in six intense weeks.[11] In the evenings, Mary read each day's production, starting over from the beginning each time: "He was an old man who fished alone in a skiff in the Gulf Stream and he had gone eighty-four days now without taking a fish." Like Ernest, who had gone that many days and more without "taking" a submarine, a "tin fish," this old man's determination did not flag, nor did he ever lose faith in his ability to fish for the marlin. The old man was called Santiago—St. James—patron saint of Spain. By the time the story was finished, Mary told Ernest, "Lamb, I am prepared to pardon you for all the disagreeable things you have done to me."[12] When Hemingway finally put a title on the novella, it was on its surface as simple and direct as the text. He called it *The Old Man and the Sea*.

While Santiago was driving his harpoon into the marlin, whom he loved as his brother, other hunters were following the spore of Ernest Hemingway. For the next ten years, Hemingway would be fighting a rearguard action with biographers, trying to protect his flanks, keep his private life private, and at the same time control his life story to which there were already so many variants. Encouraged by the Cowley essay in *Life*, the Ross portrait in *The New Yorker*, and Sam Boal's two-part take on "Hemingway the man," in *Park East*,[13] academic scholars were beginning their determined pursuit of the writer. Charles Fenton at Yale, Philip Young at Penn State, and Carlos Baker at Princeton, each looking through different-colored glasses, were digging into Hemingway's past. After beginning his research with letters to Hemingway acquaintances, Carlos Baker tried to explain his motives to Hemingway:

> I would like to destroy the legend, puncture the windbags, clear the air a little, and show your achievement in something like its true dimensions. There has been enough malice and lying and misunderstanding . . . you can trust me. I don't want to invade what is private but only what the public have a right— and indeed a sort of obligation—to know.[14]

At the same time, Hemingway was writing Baker, objecting vehemently to any invasion of his life, public or otherwise, for it would destroy part of his stockpile of stories to write. If Baker had accepted a publisher's advance to write the book, Hemingway offered to pay the publisher to stop the project. He did not want to read in a stranger's book about his father's suicide, or about his affair with Pauline, or how coitus interruptus ruined his second marriage.[15] It was a strange letter, not unlike the ones he had written Cowley earlier. While seeming to say that there would be no biography, he was simultaneously revealing some of his life's most private parts.

In a long reply, Baker explained his research and his sources, protesting that Hemingway had misread his focus which was primarily literary, and his motives which were "entirely honorable."[16] Baker's letter crossed in the mails with Hemingway's reply to his previous letter. From his sickbed, recovering from bronchitis, Hemingway argued that his early life, his journalism, and, in fact, his act of writing were not open to the public. Having already laid down thirty years of inflations, contradictions, and inventions, he now vowed never to tell another person anything about his life, which was to him about as pleasant a subject as a fingertip torn to the quick when its nail was ripped off. A few days later, Ernest told Mary's Time/Life friend, Sam Boal, the same thing: no biography.[17] Yet in his third letter to Baker, Hemingway began feeding the professor harmless and sometimes false information about *Across the River* which Baker should know but could not quote. Thomas Mann's *Death in Venice*, Hemingway said, had little or nothing to do with his novel. Renata's name came from a girl he was once in love with, but the girl in his novel was invented. The Colonel was also invented, using places and situations Ernest knew about.[18]

After that, the gate was open. By April 1, Hemingway was giving Baker fairly detailed information about his early days in Paris, the lost manuscripts, the structure of *For Whom the Bell Tolls*, the writers from whom he learned (Twain, Conrad, Stephen Crane). Henry James and Herman Melville were useful when they were good, but they wrapped everything in miles of rhetoric. Ezra Pound was helpful about half the time. Gertrude Stein told him intelligent things, he said without elaborating. By the end of April, Hemingway was giving Baker details of his writing regime, memories of early days in Oak Park, how he taught himself French in Paris. This epistolary relationship ripened to the point that Hemingway trusted Baker with a typed draft of *The Old Man and the Sea* to read and return.

Viewed from a distance, the Hemingway-Baker correspondence can be read as Ernest's astute cultivation of an admiring college professor who once wrote Hemingway imitations as an undergraduate. That interpretation makes sense retrospectively knowing that Baker became Hemingway's official biographer. But if one reads the letters from the viewpoint of 1951, the story changes. Having lived so long in Cuba cut off from literary friends and with Mary never a particularly astute reader, Hemingway cultivated Baker from the same need that triggered similar letters to Malcolm Cowley and to Arthur Mizener when he was writing his book on Scott Fitzgerald. Baker admired Hemingway's work and told him so in literate analysis, much of which Hemingway confirmed. Having so far been denied the Pulitzer Prize and ignored for the Nobel, having had his last novel sorely misread by the critics, Hemingway, like many writers, needed positive reinforcement from respected sources. As he explained to Baker, he needed intelligent response but was always embarrassed by it, which made him seem surly. He assured Carlos that he did not want to influence the academic book by correcting it in draft. Trust was a self-fulfilling act: Carlos would be trustworthy because Ernest trusted him. Mostly by letter, Baker and others like him would provide the intellectual conversation that Hemingway so badly needed.[19]

At the same time he was encouraging Carlos Baker at Princeton, Ernest was also aiding and abetting Charles Fenton at Yale, who was working furiously on Hemingway's early years when he learned to write, first growing up in Oak Park, then on the *Kansas City Star* before the war, and after the war on the *Toronto Star*. Although Ernest insisted that it did a writer no good to have either his juvenilia or his early journalism reprinted, he was quite cooperative with Fenton, answering questions and directing him to useful sources. As for his later journalism in the 1930s, Ernest said he intended someday to collect and publish it himself.[20] Later that fall, when John Atkins, a British journalist, contacted him from London, Ernest reiterated that there would be no biography of him: too many people would be hurt by it; and he was sick of hearing about it. He would cooperate, however, if Atkins confined himself to Hemingway's published work. In a long, almost effusive letter, Ernest led Atkins through his novels and stories, how and when he wrote them, what he was trying to do in them, all the while getting in some body shots against those critics who refused to judge his work on its own merits.[21]

All that spring and summer, answering few letters and doing little fishing, Hemingway wrote feverishly on the sea book that started in 1936 Bimini and that now included a fourth section— Santiago's battle with the marlin and the sharks. Revising, eliminating, transposing, he worked steadily, trying to ignore letters of inquiry about his life. From Malcolm Cowley, Ernest learned that Philip Young, a professor seeking tenure at New York University, was digging into his past. Hemingway vowed to prevent Young or anyone else from writing about his life while he was still alive.[22] But no matter what threats he put on paper, his life intruded through the weak spots in his defense. From Memphis, Tennessee, his sister Madelaine kept him apprised of his mother's failing health. Having literally forced Grace Hemingway to come to Memphis, Madelaine soon put her into a nursing home, where her condition grew worse. Madelaine, affectionately known as "Sunny," held even less affection for her mother than did her older brother, Ernest. Grace Hall Hemingway was always a difficult woman to love and impossible to command. Approaching her seventy-ninth birthday, she was slipping into a state of hallucinations, no longer able to recognize her family. When the nursing home could no longer deal with her, Grace ended up in a Memphis county hospital mental ward for two weeks, unsure of her own identity. Madelaine wrote Ernest that their mother was "a pitiful old lady, lost, frightened, and at times frantic." It would be a blessing, the doctors assured her, if Grace could die. "They hold no hope for her improvement. This will be her last stop."[23] Eleven days after Sunny wrote that letter, their mother was dead.

Ernest remained at the Finca, but paid the burial expenses; his older sister Marcelline orchestrated the funeral; and Ursula, his younger sister, flew from Hawaii to Oak Park to bury the dominant mother from whom she and Ernest had escaped, both at an early age. Having spent most of his adult life blaming his mother for destroying their Oak Park home life, Ernest was not heart broken by her death, but the loss reopened old wounds and repressed memories. When Pauline read of Grace's death in the newspaper, she wrote to Ernest, quoting the line from Swinburne: "Life is not sweet in the end." Knowing of Ernest's professed hate for the mother he once called "an all-American bitch," Pauline also understood that the death of a mother is always painful, calling up memories of childhood when she was his love, and he her darling.[24] Pauline's letter arrived on June 30, the day of Grace's burial. Later that day, writing to Carlos Baker, Ernest said that her death reminded him of how happy their Oak Park home was when he was a child, "before everything went to hell." She did not, he thought, have a happy death.[25]

Three months later, at four in the morning, Pauline lay dying on the emergency operating table of Los Angeles' St. Vincent Hospital. The previous evening, speaking by phone with Ernest about the difficulties of their newly married younger son, Gregory, the two parents and onetime lovers' conversation degenerated into accusations, blame-laying, vituperation, and general misunderstanding. For whatever Gregory had done, including his marriage, Ernest was quick to blame Pauline. She hung up in tears, angry and hurt. During the night she woke with stomach pains; within hours she was dead. The autopsy revealed blocked arteries and hypertension, but the cause of death was

> a rare and unusual tumor of the adrenal medulla, which intermittently secretes abnormal amounts of adrenaline causing extremely high blood pressure. A variety of stimuli could cause the tumor to put out the adrenaline—a sudden stressful incident is often cited . . . her blood pressure skyrocketed . . . [and then] dropped. . . . She died of shock on the operating table.[26]

At the Finca, the October 2 phone call from Pauline's sister, Virginia, devastated Mary, who was quite close with Pauline following Patrick's illness. Ernest tried to cover his loss with an exterior hardness that infuriated Mary, who, stomping out of the living room, said he behaved like a vulture. How could Mary know about the Paris nights and Provence days, mountain flowers in the Wyoming high country, the beach at Hendaye, the hospital room in Billings, or any of the memories that flooded back into his head? Angry, he followed her into the bathroom and, unable to say it all, he spit into her face. "Next day," Mary noted in her journal, "[he] gave me $200 which I gravely accepted."[27] She did not read his letter to Charles Scribner, which said: "The wave of remembering has finally risen so that it has broken over the jetty that I built to protect the open roadstead of my heart and I have the full sorrow of Pauline's death with all the harbor scum of what caused it."[28] More than once that year, Ernest would mutter that people were dying who had never died before.

March through October, despite distractions and deaths, Ernest worked steadily, five days a week, on the "sea book," whose original plan was changing as he progressed on it. His one consistent correspondent on its progress was Charles Scribner, whom Ernest managed to confuse about exactly what it was he was writing. Ernest explained it to him at several points, each consistent if one knew the manuscript well. In March, Hemingway suggested that it could be published in the fall of 1952; meanwhile, he could live on the income produced by a television deal that Hotchner was creating for his short stories. By July, Scribner was worried that Hemingway had three novellas to sell to the magazines, stories which he would then hook together as a novel. On July 20, Ernest tried to explain that he had one very long book (2,000 pages of manuscript), which was broken down into four related sections—each of them a book that could be published separately. The first section (Bimini) he was cutting and revising in a major way; the last two sections (the sea chase and Santiago's marlin) needed nothing else done to them. By October 5, Hemingway was able to report to Scribner that the four subsections were essentially finished, totaling 182,231 words. Parts one and two—Bimini and Cuba—he would further revise after he had some distance from the manuscript. Parts three and four were ready to publish.[29]

Throughout his eight-month correspondence with Scribner, Hemingway belittled and railed against Scribner's newest best-selling author James Jones, whose media image and novel, *From Here to Eternity*, sent Hemingway into paroxysms of anger. Somehow forgetting that his own novel of World War I—*A Farewell to Arms*—was about a soldier who deserted from the Italian Army, Hemingway was furious that a novel about a deserter written by a self-proclaimed deserter overshadowed *Across the River*. Jones, he repeated several times, would eventually kill himself. It was not easy to admit that Mailer, Shaw, and Jones—young writers who grew up reading Hemingway—were passing him by. Nor was it pleasant to know that his early supporters and his own generation were passing from the surface of the earth: Max Perkins, Scott Fitzgerald, Hart Crane, Katy Dos Passos, Robert Benchley, Gertrude Stein, James Joyce, Sherwood Anderson, Josie Russell, Pauline, and his mother were all dead. Evan Shipman who once taught Ernest about the Paris race track was dying from cancer; and with a heart about to fail Charley Scribner's health was marginal. Archie MacLeish and John Dos Passos, once Ernest's boon companions, he now never saw or heard from. Ezra Pound was in the insane asylum. In October, Hemingway wrote Dorothy Pound, asking questions about Ezra's incarceration.[30] Ernest could not raise the dead, but he might be able to help the old poet who was his literary father in those long-ago Paris years.

As the Cuban season moved through the early fall hurricane months, Hemingway put away the all but finished "sea book" to answer pressing letters. The *New York Herald Book Review* wanted to know the three books that Hemingway recommended from the year's crop. He gave them three fairly obscure choices, adding as a joke that there were several other books he would like to have read if only they were available:

Longevity Pays: The Life of Arthur Mizener, by F. Scott
  Fitzgerald
The Critics: An Harpooner's Story, by Herman Melville
He and Lillian: The Story of a Profile, by Mary Hemingway
It Went Thataway: The Story of Existentialism, by Jean-Paul
  Sartre[31]

Having gotten wind of another academic critic on his trail, Ernest told his publisher to refuse Philip Young permission to quote from any of his work, for Ernest heard that the work was psychoanalytical. He wanted no one dissecting his psyche in public or anywhere else for that matter. At the same time he gave permission for Carlos Baker, whom he trusted, to quote as necessary. Better for Baker to quote whole passages, he told Charles Scribner, than to mutilate Hemingway's prose with ellipses.[32] He also suggested corrections to Baker's typescript for *Hemingway: The Writer as Artist*. About his participation in World War I, Ernest asked Baker to remove all references to his having been a soldier with the Italian Arditi (which happened only in his imagination), and suggested that instead of using the word "fought," Baker should say that Ernest "served" in that war.[33] For the first time, Hemingway's own fabrications were coming back to haunt him. A good after-dinner story made more interesting with invented details was one thing, but to have it made flesh in a scholarly book was quite another.

The new year began in the same key as the year gone by. In January 1952, Mary's maid, Clara, recently given three months wages and fired by Ernest, was found outside the Finca grounds, comatose, clutching an empty bottle of Seconal tablets. Apparently using Ernest's prescription at a local pharmacy, she purchased two bottles of the barbiturate. Lingering for three days in the hospital, she never recovered consciousness before dying. Ernest, having made several promises to do the same, wrote Charles Scribner that the threat of suicide had been Clara's defense against the world.[34] Charlie probably never got to read Ernest's long letter. In the early afternoon of February 11, Hemingway's publisher, banker, confidant, and friend died suddenly from a heart attack. Now there was no one left, Ernest said, with whom to share a rough joke.[35]

PART THREE

End Game

1952 TO 1961

The end is where we start from.

T. S. Eliot

Consume my heart away; sick with desire
And fastened to a dying animal
It knows not what it is; and gather me
Into the artifice of eternity.

W. B. Yeats, "Sailing to Byzantium"

CHAPTER 16

The Artist's Rewards

March 1952 to June 1953

All the signs were positive; all the readers agreed. *The Old Man and the Sea* was a stunning book, a story told as simply as a fable, and as tenderly as a love letter. When Broadway and Hollywood producer Leland Hayward read the typescript at the Finca, he insisted that it should be published as soon as possible in a national magazine, *Life* or *Look*. Ernest, chagrined as always with effusive praise, thought Scribner's might not like the idea. Hayward said he would take care of it, taking the typescript with him to New York. For the first time in many years, Ernest was allowing someone else to act as his agent. Simultaneously, he sent a typescript to Wallace Meyer at Scribner's, explaining at some length why what seemed a novella was actually a book that would stand by itself, a book probably better than anything else he had written.[1]

No sooner had Hayward and his attractive wife, Slim (Ernest's flirtatious friend and former Mrs. Howard Hawks), left Havana than the elected government of Carlos Prio was overthrown in an almost bloodless coup led by the kingmaker, General Fulgencio Batista, who quickly resumed business as usual in Havana. "The only blood that will be spilled," he promised, "will be that of those who oppose us." One dictator replaced another, which surprised no one. From exile, Prio predicted that "the Cuban people will throw Bastista out sooner or later." When accused of having amassed a fortune from his office, Prio said simply, "I think being poor is a sin."[2] On March 11, Ernest and Mary took the *Pilar* out to sea for a fishing vacation while the political dust settled in the capital. Ninety miles down the coast, from the isolated lee side of Paraíso Island, they fished and sunned, ate and slept, counted stars and watched a new moon rising. Safe inside the low island's coral reef, the *Pilar* was home, but the island, with its six palm trees and six pines, was their Eden.

On March 23, a storm rose up, holding them at the island until March 29, when they returned to the Finca to find that another of Ernest's old friends, Dick Cooper, was dead in Africa, Cooper who fished with Ernest in Bimini and fêted him during his 1933–34 safari.[3] There were also excited responses from Scribner's about the book, which they would publish in September and were submitting to the Book-of-the-Month Club. On May 19, the memorandum of agreement between Ernest and his publisher was signed for *The Old Man and the Sea*, with royalties jumping to an unusual 20 percent after the sale of the first 25,000 copies. At the same time *Life*, with Scribner's blessing, agreed to publish the novel in a single issue of the magazine with Ernest on the cover. By the end of May, Adriana Ivancich's dust jacket design, to Ernest's delight, was accepted by Scribner's in lieu of the three covers he rejected.[4] Once to be Mary's book, the dedication was changed, with Mary's approval, to Charles Scribner and Max Perkins—the two men who never lost faith in Ernest and never refused him a loan when he asked.

In all of his correspondence with his publisher, friends, columnists, and critics, Hemingway insisted he had no intention of commenting on the novel, nor would he come to New York for the novel's release. When the *New York Times* and the *Saturday Review of Literature* asked him for written comments to run in their book section, he was so noncommittal in his responses that they were hardly worth printing. Asked if he wished to talk about his writing process, he said: "If I have to talk about a book that I have written, it destroys the pleasure I have from writing it. If the writing is any good everything there is to say has been conveyed to the reader." How long is the big book? they wanted to know. "Very long," he replied. And when would they see it? "As and when it seems best to publish it." After the surfeit of Hemingway interviews and commentaries—Cowley, Ross, Boal—too much had been said about his private life. As he told Charles Scribner, Jr., who had taken over the firm from his late father, Ernest wanted to run only as a writer, not as a controversial public figure. This time out, critics and reviewers would have to deal with his text, for he was giving them no posturing for a target.[5] In *Green Hills of Africa* (1935) he had baited them without mercy—angleworms in a bottle, he called them. If they wanted to read *The Old Man* as allegory or myth, then they could make what they wanted of it. It would be the reviewers who found a resemblance between the shark attack on Santiago's marlin and the critics' attack on Ernest Hemingway.

If he went to New York, some son of a bitch would pick a fight which the columnists would lap up, encouraging everyone to think that Ernest was a bar-room brawler. Which is exactly what happened one Havana night in the Floridita bar. Ernest and Mary were drinking in his favored corner when a woman never seen before begins to tell him what a good time they both had in her bed back in 1944. Getting rid of her, he turns to find a huge man whispering in his ear, singing a dirty song that he has made up about Ernest, who hates to be touched and cannot abide dirty songs. Two left hooks and a right-hand chop as the man goes down ends the session. Fortunately, it happened in Cuba and not in the States, where such a story would confirm what a violent character he was. No one gave literary prizes to a bar fighter. Yet he told the story to Harvey Breit at the *New York Times*, saying it was an example of the person he no longer wanted to be. The new Hemingway would be "a good boy."[6]

Among the several guests in and out of the Finca that May were old friends from Ketchum: Taylor "Beartracks" Williams, Don Anderson, Elaine Perry, and newcomer Forrest "Duke" MacMullen. They put up at the Ambos Mundos, spending their days either at the Finca or out on the *Pilar* fishing. Throughout their visit Hemingway was his Ketchum self, but kept his mornings free to write. In the evening, Mary would meet their guests for daiquiris and cold stone crab at the Floridita, then take them to the jai alai matches or to a nightclub for the evening. One night it was the San Souci; another, the Tropicana. Juan, the Hemingway chauffeur, provided transportation, taking Mary back to the Finca when the evening was over.[7]

Increasingly disengaged from the mainland news—the Korean War, the fall elections—Hemingway, as he turned fifty-three, was intensely aware that he was approaching the end of his writing career. He had plenty of stories left in his head, but he knew the chances of pulling out another one as right as *The Old Man and the Sea* were slim. Ever since William Faulkner received the Nobel Prize for literature in 1949, Hemingway, for whom writing was a competitive sport, wanted the same recognition. In 1947, the prize went to André Gide for his "fearless love of truth and keen psychological insight," wording guaranteed to irritate Hemingway. The next year, T. S. Eliot was the Nobel laureate while Ezra Pound collected dust in the confines of St. Elizabeth's. But Faulkner's award was the one that goaded Ernest the hardest. It may have been only coincidence, but he started to write *The Old Man and the Sea* hard on the heels of Faulkner's much publicized Nobel Prize acceptance speech.[8]

Thus, when Harvey Breit approached Faulkner to review Hemingway's new book, Ernest was fully prepared to misread anything the man from Mississippi had to say. Breit, not understanding the situation, enthusiastically sent Hemingway the statement Faulkner made before he had even read the book:

> . . . A few years ago . . . Hemingway said that writers should stick together just as doctors and lawyers and wolves do. I think there is more wit in that than truth or necessity either, at least in Hemingway's case, since the sort of writers who need to band together willy nilly, or perish, resemble the wolves who are wolves only in pack, and, singly, are just another dog.
>
> Because the man who wrote the *Men Without Women* pieces and *The Sun Also Rises* and *A Farewell to Arms* and *For Whom the Bell Tolls* and most of the African stuff and most of all the rest of it, is not one of these, and needs no protection.
>
> So he does not need even this from another writer. Maybe he doesn't even want it. So he gets this for free from one who, regardless of how he rated what remained, has never doubted the integrity of it, and who has always affirmed that no man will

be quicker and harsher to judge what remained than [Hemingway] . . . and that if even what remained had not been as honest and true as he could make it, then he himself would have burned the manuscript before the publisher ever saw it.[9]

Hemingway's response to Breit bristled with resentment:

> So he writes to you as though I was asking him a favor to pro-
> tect me. Me, the dog. I'll be a sad son of a bitch. He made a
> speech, very good. I knew he could never, now, or ever again
> write up to his speech. I also knew I could write a book better and
> straighter than his speech and without tricks or rhetoric . . . as
> long as I am alive he has to drink to feel good about having the
> Nobel prize. He does not realize that I have no respect for that
> institution . . . I wish him luck and he needs it because . . . you
> can't re-read him.[10]

There the story ended. Breit buried Faulkner's statement, and apologized to Ernest for the contretemps.

The closer the publication date for *The Old Man* came, the more anxious Hemingway became. When not writing or fishing, he continued to argue with scholars hot on his trail. Every time Charles Fenton sent him a piece of his doctoral dissertation in progress, Hemingway pointed out mistakes and misunderstandings, complaining that Fenton talked to the wrong people. Survivors never remember right. Each of Hemingway's responses confused Fenton, revealing some new story that usually had little or nothing to do with Ernest's writing apprenticeship and was certainly not printable in the book. Going back, Hemingway insisted (having learned it for himself), going back was doomed. Everything was changed— the land, the people, the places. Fenton's every reply assured Ernest that his book was not a biography, that Ernest's private life would remain private, and, by the way, here are a few more questions, which Hemingway then would try to answer. Railing against the detective school of literary criticism and laundry-list biographers, Hemingway would, in every other letter, tell Fenton to give up the book. Biographers were the scavengers of literature, the eaters of carrion. He, by God, was going to plant enough booby traps on his corpse to fix them all. Fenton came right back, confident and cocky:

this book was going to be written whether Ernest helped or not, and Ernest continued to help, coolly retreating while setting up roadblocks and small ambushes.[11]

However, nothing Phil Young or his publisher Thomas Bledsoe at Rinehart said made Hemingway feel any better about the book that Young was writing. When Ernest received a copy of Young's paper presented at a professional meeting, it confirmed his worst fears. Young and others were practicing psychoanalysis without a license. As Ernest read Young's work, he had suffered a traumatic neurosis in 1918 from being wounded in Italy out of which came all of his writing. To say such a thing was, Ernest felt, as damaging as saying that he suffered from terminal syphilis. Despite his serious misgivings, six pages of them, Hemingway eventually gave in to Young's plea that his tenure and his family's well-being depended on the book. When Ernest learned that Young was a wounded veteran from World War II, he reluctantly told Charles Scribner, Jr., to give him permission to quote. Whatever Bledsoe had to pay Scribner's for the permissions, Ernest instructed his publisher to give his half back to Young.[12]

The three scholars—Baker, Fenton, and Young—were laying down for the postwar generation what would become the academic gospel on Ernest's fiction. Baker's book, *Hemingway: The Writer as Artist*, gave sympathetic, analytic readings of Hemingway's work up to *The Old Man and the Sea*, delineating themes, motifs, and symbolic effects that were frequently just below the surface of the fiction. Fenton's book, *The Apprenticeship of Ernest Hemingway*, gave readers the formative literary experience that Hemingway took to Paris with him in 1921—Oak Park roots, *Kansas City Star* cub reporter before the war, and *Toronto Daily Star* feature writer after the war. Phil Young's book, called simply *Ernest Hemingway*, linked Hemingway to the Twain tradition established with Huck Finn and argued that the wounded man appearing in various guises throughout the fiction was a result of Hemingway's own wounding in World War I. Just as Hemingway's most popular book since *For Whom the Bell Tolls* (1940) was set to sweep the nation, a new generation of academic scholars was about to discover there was more to his fiction than previously imagined.

These scholars would teach their findings to college students, many of whom became the high school teachers of the next generation of Hemingway's readers.

While this was happening, Ernest began to write a fiction which fit no one's theory. Had any of the new scholars read the new story about Nick Adams's escape into the Michigan woods pursued by game wardens, they would have been puzzled. Had they seen the beginnings of what would later be called *The Garden of Eden*, they would have torn up their manuscripts and begun again. On May 4, he told Malcolm Cowley that he was beginning a story placed up in Michigan, a story he had put off writing for a long time.[13] Set free by his mother's death, Hemingway was able for the first time since his early Paris fiction to return to the experiences of his youth. The summer of 1915, while transporting two tourists up Walloon Lake in the family motorboat, Ernest impulsively shot and killed a blue heron. When the game warden's son reported Ernest to his father, the warden went to the Hemingway cottage to arrest Ernest. Grace Hemingway faced him down, and later sent Ernest running cross-country to his uncle George's summer place at Ironton. After a few days, Ernest followed the advice of his father, went before the local judge, and paid his fine. The experience—a fugitive on the run from the law—loomed large for a boy barely turned sixteen, and it continued to haunt Hemingway, becoming in his imagination more serious than it was, more threatening. This incident became the first of several encounters with law enforcement that always produced in Hemingway a visceral response more intense than the event might warrant.

As Mary noted in her journal almost four years earlier, the heron story was ready-made for fiction. When Hemingway retrieved the incident, he changed the heron to an out-of-season deer and gave the adventure to his dark double, Nick Adams, about whom he had not written in many years. He found the lake, the woods, and the trout exactly as he had left them, directions still running true. It was like being there once more, only better, because he got to be Nick as a youth, not himself in his fifties. With the help of his younger sister, Littless, Nick escapes into the deep woods to his secret place, another Eden. There he provides fresh trout for supper,

and Littless cuts her hair short as a boy's, determined to stay with
her brother. Their relationship, bordering on incest, is a different
kind of couple in the garden. Littless already has lost her inno-
cence, knowing of good and evil; Nick has already sinned against
the local laws. The owner of the lakeside store, Mr. John, likes Nick
because "he had original sin."

> "You're going to have things to repent, boy," Mr. John had told
> Nick. "That's one of the best things there is. You can always
> decide whether to repent them or not. But the thing is to have
> them."[14]

Surely Hemingway was poaching a bit on Mr. Faulkner's territory, but Ernest didn't see any No Trespassing signs. And the brother-
sister relationship also owed something to J. D. Salinger's equally
precocious siblings in *The Catcher in the Rye*, a book Ernest read
when it came out in 1951.[15] Begun as a short story, "The Last Good
Country" began to swell, as had several earlier stories, into what
might become a novel, but, like his "Jimmy Breen" story in 1928,
Nick and Littless were left in the woods, and their story unfinished.
Perhaps Hemingway saw that it was moving from a relatively innocent incident into a tale of murder; perhaps he backed off from the
potentially incestuous relationship as being a taboo which no publisher would break. Or it may have been that the story's direction
reminded him of a more adult version of a lost Eden that had been
on his mind since his 1948 drive through Provence. There on the
coast at Grau du Roi where the fishing boat channel came right
through the middle of town, he and Pauline once honeymooned
while the Gypsy pilgrimage gathered at nearby Les Saintes Maries.
Those days too were a bit of Eden remembered. Not that either of
them was innocent of either knowledge or deed, but Grau du Roi
was their idyllic escape from the small gossips of Paris. It was the
new life.

Drawing on several marriages, his own and others, inventing
freely out of desire and experience, he began a story that completely changed whatever residual plans he might have had for the
"big book" about the sea, air, and land war.[16] The first volume of
that vaguely planned trilogy was now a four-part study of the sea

before, during, and after the war: the first part told of Thomas Hudson's idyllic life on Bimini and its loss; the second section showed Hudson outcast from Eden, lonely ashore in Cuba between submarine patrols; section three was the sea chase, Hudson's crew pursuing Germans, ending with Hudson bleeding to death on the boat's deck; the fourth section was Santiago's epic conflict with the marlin and the sharks, a different tale of duty, honor, and loss meant to counterpoint Hudson's experience. The air war was long ago abandoned, leaving only a handful of fragments. The ground war in France was related obliquely in *Across the River* as explanation for Cantwell's postwar bitterness. There remained stories to write about the war, but there would be no novel. The sea-air-land trilogy had fallen apart, largely due to the combined effect of Hudson's reminiscences on early life in Paris, the Mizener biography of Scott Fitzgerald, and Hemingway's own memories recharged by the nagging investigations by scholars.

What was developing, without a master plan, was a different sort of trilogy, whose cohesion was not dependent on recurring characters or a coherent chronology. Three separate stories were taking vague form, guided, if guided at all, by Marcel Proust's *Remembrance of Things Past*, a work to which Ernest referred repeatedly in the postwar period. The first story of Hemingway's sequence was completed: Thomas Hudson's painterly life, his fall from grace, and his redemption by duty performed, which Hemingway called *The Island and the Stream*. The second would become *The Garden of Eden*, the story of young artists whose art and life are compromised by destructive relationships. The third volume would become the partially fictive memoir of Ernest's own early days in Paris, *A Moveable Feast*. Paris in the Twenties was the lynchpin upon which all three stories in some way revolved. Having seen it all, having watched destructive forces interfere with the talents of artists, himself included, Hemingway was writing a complex, multilayered portrait of the artist in the twentieth century. His protagonists—painters and writers—begin their careers in Paris; all find momentary Edens; all, in various ways, largely due to the women in their lives, fall from grace into exile, either dead or dumbfounded.[17] The last voice Thomas Hudson hears tells him,

"You never understand anyone who loves you," words that might serve as an epigraph for all three books.

On Labor Day, more than five million copies of *Life* magazine went on sale all across America. From the cover a black and white visage of jowly, mustached Hemingway looked one dead in the eye. His hair thinned and graying, scars visible, mouth set, neither a smile nor a scowl, it was a face familiar if older, staring at the reader not exactly belligerently, but neither was it friendly. Slashed across the upper right-hand corner of the cover against a burnt orange background, it said:

AN EXTRA DIVIDEND IN THIS ISSUE
'THE OLD MAN
AND THE SEA'
BY HEMINGWAY
A COMPLETE NEW BOOK
FIRST PUBLICATION

Inside, beginning on page 35, the novella opened with Santiago preparing for his eighty-fifth day in search of marlin. Twenty pages later, it ended with the old man returned to his shack, sleeping, "dreaming about the lions." It was a precedent for *Life*, publishing a major writer's entire book without interruptive advertisements. It was also the largest run in the magazine's history, a run that quickly sold out. Never before had any author instantaneously reached so large an audience. Six days later, Scribner's published a first edition of 50,000 copies which sold out in ten days; simultaneously, the Book-of-the-Month Club published 153,000 copies, and Jonathan Cape brought out the British edition. Despite the serial and book club versions, for twenty-six weeks *The Old Man* listed on the *New York Times* best-seller list. Before the year was out, translations appeared in nine European languages. Within five years, readers in twenty-six languages as dissimilar as Persian and Latvian had access to translations.[18]

Reviewers' responses to the novella varied in direct proportion to the time lapse between the publication and their review. The first-week reviews were largely positive bordering on adulation. Hemingway was back, had found himself, had recovered his talent.

Conrad's and Melville's names were frequently used for comparative purposes. Carlos Baker called Hemingway "one of the few genuine tragic writers of modern times," curiously linking Santiago's struggle with that of King Lear. Harvey Breit gushed over the style, the power, and the beauty of the story. In Nashville, it was called "the old undiluted Hemingway magic." In Chicago, it was billed as "Hemingway at his incomparable best." *Time* magazine thought *The Old Man and the Sea* might be a masterpiece. After the first wave of such statements in prominent places, the New York intellectuals stepped in with counterattacks in all the usual places— *Commonweal, Commentary*, the *Partisan Review*. They had to remind their readers how awful *Across the River* was, and how vulgar Hemingway was in his public life: "As a man he has often made an embarrassing spectacle of himself with his posturings, his mooning over adolescent things . . . his antics at the Stork Club." Thus Seymour Krim was able to conclude that this novella was "only more of the same." John Aldridge, the following spring, was "unable to share in the prevailing wild enthusiasm" for *The Old Man and the Sea*, even though it was "a remarkable advance over his last novel."[19]

Hemingway read all the reviews his clipping service sent him, commented to friends on some of them, but generally remained aloof, determined to let the book rise or fall on its own. No whining or complaining. He turned down opportunities to appear on national television, still in its awkward infancy; declined a prestigious speaking opportunity at Princeton; and ignored letters to the editor at *Life*. The only response that apparently thrilled him was a private letter from the art historian Bernard Berenson, who preferred Hemingway's style to Melville's "inflationary magniloquence," and liked his old fisherman "far better than Ahab."[20] As important as the book's reception was the wonderful run of marlin in the Gulf Stream. Not only had Ernest caught his best-selling book, but he had also by September 13 pulled twenty-nine marlin, large and small, across the *Pilar*'s transom.[21] On September 23, Mary flew to New York for a recreational visit, shopping, and a little basking in the afterglow of Ernest's triumph. He preferred to remain close to the Gulf Stream, saying he would only get into trouble in New

York. There was also the problem of leaving the Finca when local burglars were raiding it and other homes in the area. Before Mary left, two men broke into the Finca, rifling cabinets and stealing whatever looked valuable while Ernest and Mary slept. Thereafter Ernest began setting perimeter defenses and traps inside the house. Ernest called the intruders the local mau-maus—referring to the quasi-guerrilla war being waged by the East African Mau Mau movement. By October, the Finca was twice robbed without alerting Ernest's "hopeless" night watchman, and Hemingway, with a loaded shotgun beside his bed, slept lightly, waking at the least sound to patrol the house.[22]

Back at Scribner's, Wallace Meyer was planning a *Hemingway Reader* to catch the wave of heightened interest in Ernest's work. In a letter to Charles Poore, editor of the collection, Ernest cautioned that his Italian war experience was largely devoted to convalescing and listening to the talk of those who actually fought in the war. From that secondhand knowledge and what he had acquired on his own, he was able with the help of large-scale maps to invent battles that he had never witnessed. "Then some son of a bitch will come along and prove you were not at that particular fight."[23] Meanwhile, Ernest's own interests were returning to East Africa where his son, Patrick, using part of his inheritance from his mother to buy a farm, was urging his father to visit. Darryl Zanuck's film version of "The Snows of Kilimanjaro" may have added to Ernest's desire to see the Serengeti again, although he noted sardonically the "minor change" Zanuck made by allowing Harry, the gangrenous writer, to live at the end instead of dying.[24] Ernest called it "The Snows of Zanuck." Stung time and again by Hollywood's treatment of his works, Hemingway continued to sell them for the best price he could get. Usually, he avoided the resultant movie. But when Leland Hayward took an option on the film rights to *The Old Man and the Sea*, Ernest, for the first and only time in his career, wanted to be involved in the filming, insisting that the marlin and the sharks be authentic, not backlot Hollywood rubber fish.

At the same time, he and Mary were doing background reading on Africa, planning to spend the summer in Spain, the fall and winter on safari with Patrick. Hemingway was looking forward to an elephant photo hunt, the only large animal he had not seen on his first safari in 1933–34. He had no intention of shooting an elephant, having gotten his fill of killing during the war. Through his reading, moreover, he was already identifying with the elephant. When thanking John Atkins for his straightforward book on Ernest's fiction, he said he would have been more cooperative had not other scholars been hunting him so hard. He felt as "spooked" as any fifty-three-year-old elephant carrying 100 pounds of ivory would feel.[25]

Life at the Finca was quickly becoming a three-ring circus, overrun with visitors, deluged with mail from strangers excited about *The Old Man and the Sea*, and attacked by night prowlers. How the thieves were able to avoid cats, dogs, fighting cocks, and numerous guests bedded in odd corners of the Finca is not clear, but the third break-in on January 17, 1953, ended when Ernest opened fire with his .22 rifle, drawing blood from one of the housebreakers.[26] The thieves were easier to discourage than were the guests. Gianfranco, Adriana's brother, still a permanent lodger upon whom Mary relied for moral support and errands, was returning to Venice, but his replacements arrived in numbers. Christopher La Farge, novelist and hunting companion from 1939, spent six weeks in residence in the guesthouse. Taylor Williams, friend and guide from Sun Valley, came to fish. Don Andrés, the Black Priest, could no longer make the trek up the hill because of his heart condition, but Hemingway's driver brought him back and forth. Evan Shipman, old friend from early Paris days, came to the Finca, as did Jack Hemingway, his wife Puck, and their two-year-old daughter Muffet (Joan), while Jack was on leave from the Army. While one group said hello, another said good-bye. With no prior warning, a lunch for four not uncommonly became a lunch for eight; a carefully planned supper might be abandoned at the last minute to dine out. Through all the chaos, Mary kept the staff organized and functioning, planned meals, paid bills, housed guests, and kept Ernest's life as uncluttered as possible.

Leland and Slim Hayward were in and out as movie plans developed, crashed, and flew again. Accustomed but not inured to

Ernest's effect on attractive women and theirs on him, Mary bit her tongue when Slim had the floor, for there was no way she could compete without angering Ernest. After the Hayward visit, Slim sent Ernest a letter, asking him to tell Mary that she, Slim, played a straight game, "being a woman, I know the women's rules and I try always to play from the ladies' tee, as I think you will attest." Decoded, Slim was telling Mary that she was not making a play for Ernest, whose heart all too often was a target of opportunity, as he was the first to admit.[27]

For months the trip to Europe and Africa was put on hold waiting for the movie plans to solidify, which did not happen until early April. In between visitors, Ernest and Mary spent as much time on the *Pilar* as possible, for it was the only place where they could find something like peace. With no ship-to-shore radio, to be out of sight of land was to be out of reach. The last week before Easter, they dropped anchor at their secret place, Mégano de Casigua, an uninhabited islet they called Paraíso Key. There, protected by a barrier reef and with Gregorio, their mate, for cook and company, they were free to swim and beachcomb naked, Ernest to write, Mary to fish for marlin bait in the lagoon. With the radio playing waltzes, the pre-lunch martinis cold and dry, Gregorio cooking fish and rice, Ernest and Mary sat in the shade of the side canvas, taking in the sea breeze. But no paradise is invulnerable. Roberto Herrera arrived on a sailboat to tell them that the Haywards and Spencer Tracy were arriving to discuss the filming of *The Old Man and the Sea*.[28]

On Good Friday, the Hemingways, the Haywards, assorted friends, and Spencer Tracy, once a drinking man but now a teetotaler, suppered at the Floridita. The week following Easter was spent visiting the fishing village of Cojimar, where Tracy saw prototypes for Santiago at work, hauling nets, carrying masts, more often than not a cigar stub clenched in their teeth. Tracy, who was co-producer on the pending film, initially was going to do the voice-over to the narrative while an authentic Cuban fisherman played the role of Santiago. But soon it was apparent that Tracy wanted to play the role himself, and that his film commitments would not allow him to begin for another two years. After much talk, the actor hosted a going-away supper at the Three Aces in Havana, and Mary recorded in her journal, "it has been the best year in harmony and good friendship between Papa and me." As quickly as possible, she and Ernest were back under the palm fronds of Paraíso Key, where, on May 4, while listening to the evening news, they heard that Ernest had won the Pulitzer Prize for literature. Having been disappointed when the Pulitzer Committee refused the prize to him for *For Whom the Bell Tolls*, Ernest was not particularly thrilled with the announcement, but Mary was delighted. He informed Scribner's that he would not reject the award as Sinclair Lewis once did, but he hoped he did not have to do anything more than say thank you.[29]

Despite island escapes, the tension produced by constant visitors was beginning to erode Ernest and Mary's better selves. The Haywards returned to interrupt once more the isolation on Paraíso, and Ernest was again fuming over Charles Fenton's investigations into his early life. He claimed that he was unable to continue with Nick and Littless in "The Last Good Country" because of Fenton's intrusions. Using registered letters from his lawyer, Alfred Rice, Hemingway was doing everything short of taking the young man to court to stop him. But he could not stop the arguments with Mary, which by June 1 had once more gotten out of hand. Mary's patience was worn thin with the previous five months of chaos; Ernest was testy from dealing with everything but his writing. For two years since finishing *The Old Man and the Sea*, his writing regime had been continually interrupted by death and business. On May 15, Ernest signed a contract with *Look* magazine for a photojournalism piece on their African safari for $15,000 in expenses (nontaxable) and $10,000 for the 3,500-word article.[30] When Mary found out, she exploded. Why had she not been told! She had been told. Had not! Her agent was trying to sell the same story based on the journals she would keep. Now that was a dead deal. On into the night the harangue, Mary the scolding wife, Ernest tight-lipped, unwilling to argue.[31] But like all their tiffs, this one, once aired, eventually blew itself out. By June 24, they were packed and on board the *Flandre* as the vessel sailed out of New York bound for Europe.

CHAPTER 17

The Phoenix

June 1953 to March 1954

On June 24, Ernest and Mary, fortified with 593 pounds of necessities stuffed into twenty-four pieces of luggage, settled down in their double suite on the SS *Flandre* bound for Le Havre, where Gianfranco met them at the customshouse. Awaiting their arrival was a rented Lancia and an Italian undertaker-cum-chauffeur, Adamo, who somehow tied down excess luggage on top of the car. First stop was the Ritz Hotel in Paris to store what they did not need for Spain or Africa; after Paris, they drove through Rambouillet to Chartres, to remember the last time Ernest prayed there in 1944. On down the Loire Valley they drove, Ernest in the front seat; Mary and Gianfranco in the back with the coats, cameras, maps, guidebooks, radio, bottled water, wine, and local papers. Turning south under gray clouds, they eventually arrived at Hotel Eskualduna in Hendaye, bringing back memories of long-ago summers on this same beach with Hadley and then with Pauline, staying in modest oceanfront hotels when a dollar was worth twenty-five francs, which almost paid for the room.[1]

On cold, cloudy July 6, they crossed into Spain, where Ernest had not been since 1939 when Franco's Republican forces finally defeated the Loyalists whom he had supported. All the way down from Paris, Ernest worried about Spanish reprisals, worried that they would not forgive him for *For Whom the Bell Tolls*. In the customshouse, a border guard, framed against a wall bearing the slogan—Franco–Franco–Franco—carefully inspected Hemingway's passport, glancing back and forth from the photograph to his face with an uncertain look. Then a smile of total recognition, a grasping of hands, Hemingway was back in the country where he once felt most at home. As they motored on through the mountains, down into San Sebastián, and over the pass to Pamplona, Ernest sat silently, pleased to see pines and rivers as he had left them, stone houses with brown tiled roofs, oxcarts, women in black dresses bowed down over vegetable gardens, sheep grazing near the pass. Seeing Spain for the first time, Mary was delighted, asking questions, listening to explanations, and making notes.

All that summer in Spain, everywhere that Mary went, she was sure to have her new Hasselblad with its telephoto lens and the Rolleiflex, taking photographs to illustrate potential travel writing. At Sumbilla, she talked her way into a woman's house in order to lean out her window for a shot of a vine-covered bridge. In Pamplona, she photographed bootblacks at the café, a religious procession in the street, Gypsy women cooking stews at the horse fair. At the morning *encierro*, she borrowed a woman's balcony for the best shot of the bulls coming down the cobblestone street, runners barely ahead of the horns. All across Spain, her camera was clicking—storks nesting in a church tower, Basque girls dancing, tavern faces out of Goya, oxcarts, Burgos Cathedral, peasant girls with scythes. At the country home of Dominguín, retired matador and now bull rancher, she photographed the house; at Valencia, the beach and the fish market; at Paterna, the underground homes dug into the hillside. When not photographing, Mary was asking questions, making judgments, and cataloguing discomforts for journalistic use. All the while, she was suffering from a nagging case of colitis which did not respond to treatment.

During the feria of San Fermín, the Hemingway party stayed at Lecumberri outside Pamplona, drove in early some days for the *encierro* in the streets, later on other days to watch the afternoon *corrida* from *barrera* seats. Hemingway could only have been more pleased if in the ring the picadors had not butchered the bulls so badly. Antonio Ordóñez, son of Niño de la Palma (hero of the 1925 San Fermín), was the brilliant attraction, performing beautifully and winning Hemingway's complete admiration. Mary, like Duff

Twysden in 1925, was also taken with "the handsome boy, slim, supple, the young smooth face grave but not tense . . . so deft . . . so controlled."[2] The Pamplona gathering that summer was like old home week. After warning those with him to beware of the pickpockets working the crowds, Hemingway immediately had his pocket picked. Peter Viertel, who joined the entourage at St. Jean-de-Luz, was largely bored with bulls and *botas*, but hung in for the entire spectacle. On the Pamplona plaza, they encountered Mary's old co-worker from Time/Life Charles Wertenbaker, and Bob Lowe from *Look* magazine. Bulls were dedicated to Hemingway by matadors not yet born when he saw his first *corrida*. *Botas* were filled and refilled with blood red wine; lobster and codfish stew simmered at breakfast; and always street bands, singing, the *raiu raiu* dancers hopping high, and at night a firework display raining embers down on uncaring roisterers. It was the old Pamplona with new faces, and private ghosts at every corner.[3]

By the end of July, the Hemingways had made the circuit—San Sebastián to Pamplona to Madrid to Valencia back to Madrid, from there to Burgos and back to San Sebastián. They had seen enough *corridas* to start Ernest thinking seriously about an updated version of *Death in the Afternoon*. Mary, who was half sick most of the trip, was weary but pleased. Gianfranco was still talking about running with the bulls in the morning *encierro*, and Adamo, their patient chauffeur, was ready to return home to Udine. Among the luggage were Ernest and Mary's new, handmade safari boots of Spanish leather. Back in Paris, they repacked at the Ritz for the boat trip to Africa. Driving south on August 4, they boarded the *Dunnottar Castle* in Marseilles two days later for the voyage up the Mediterranean, through the Suez Canal, and around the Horn of Africa to Mombasa.

Their safari guide Philip Percival, lured out of retirement, was there at the dock to greet them and their mountain of luggage. Twenty years earlier, Percival led Ernest and Pauline into the East African terrain where as a young man in 1909 he had accompanied the Theodore Roosevelt safari. Now sixty-nine years old and gaunt from tick typhus, Percival agreed to lead the Hemingway safari out of loyalty to Ernest, who had immortalized him as Pop in *Green*

Hills of Africa (1935), and out of loyalty to the Kenyan government that was desperate to regenerate the lucrative tourist hunters scared away by the Mau Mau bloodshed in northern Kenya. This native uprising over loss of tribal lands was less threatening to the white Kenyans than the ruling British reaction led the world to believe. By 1956, when the emergency was declared over, only 100 whites but over 13,000 black Africans were dead; 80,000 Kikuyu were penned up in detention camps; and Jomo Kenyatta, future president of independent Kenya, was serving a seven-year jail sentence.

At Percival's comfortable Kitanga Farm, Ernest was delighted to show Mary the changes wrought by twenty years since he had last stood on those grounds. Mayito Menocal, their wealthy Cuban friend, joined the Hemingways, along with Earl Theisen, the photographer hired by *Look* magazine to accompany the safari. Laden with weapons, ammunition, tents, kitchen gear, canned food, whiskey, and water, the caravan moved south, away from Mau Mau territory, to a game reserve opened only to the Hemingway safari, for the government was determined to keep them supplied with abundant animals and ample photo opportunities. After a two-year drought, East Africa was a place of dust, dry leaves, and bleached bones, which was disappointing to Mary. But Ernest knew that anywhere creeks ran or water pooled, they would find game. He also remembered the 1933–34 safari becoming an uneven competition between himself and Key Wester Charles Thompson: Ernest was the better shot, but Thompson got all the best trophies. Now, twenty years older, Ernest found himself in a different situation. His aim was not as steady. At fifty-four, with his genetically weak eyes grown worse, he wore reading glasses and wing-shooting glasses; his wing-shooting abilities were still sharp, but he had never been an accurate shot on standing game.[4] If the animal moved, he was deadly; if it did not, he could be embarrassing to himself.[5] Moreover, he was out of practice with large-bore weapons, having shot nothing larger than an antelope since his last African trip. Menocal, who hunted regularly, was much the better rifle shot, and his kills were often made after a Hemingway miss. That was not the story Theisen had come to photograph.

Close to their Salengai River camp, animal life was rampant:

four hundred elephants, twenty rhinos, and at least ten lions lived in the area.[6] Denis Zaphiro, a twenty-seven-year-old game ranger, saw to it that there were ample photo opportunities for Theisen. On the first day into the new country, Zaphiro met them on the dirt road, asking if Ernest was ready to kill a wounded rhino Denis had tracked down. Loading up his heavy .577-caliber weapon used as backup on dangerous game, Ernest walked up to within fifteen paces of the nearsighted rhino before pulling the trigger. Spinning completely about, the rhino raised an enveloping cloud of dust, into which Ernest fired again; the thrice-wounded rhino bolted into the brush. Denis and Ernest followed the blood spoor until light began to fail, but did not find the dead beast until the following morning.[7] A month later, Ernest and Mayito almost simultaneously fired on a leopard made to order for Theisen, who photographed Ernest seated beside the dead cat. Mary argued that Ernest did not know whose bullet killed the animal, but the photo was taken anyway. Privately Ernest promised Mary he would kill another leopard before the *Look* photo-essay ran, which he did, but only after pumping six shots into thick brush where his wounded leopard sought refuge. When Hemingway killed his lion, it was another messy affair. At two hundred yards, he pulled the trigger, heard the slug hit, and saw the lion disappear into the brush without even howling. A half hour later, with the wounded animal cornered, Ernest and Denis both shot twice before the lion died. Two days later, Menocal killed a magnificent black-maned lion with a single shot.

On the hunting part of the safari, Hemingway made few of the clean kills that marked his first safari. Theisen got his pictures, but Ernest's heart was no longer in the hunt. The Finca's walls were heavy with noble, preserved heads, and he had already begun to identify metaphorically with old trophy animals. Except for the lion, Zaphiro thought that Ernest was not greatly interested in hunting. "He did not, for instance, shoot or even want to shoot an elephant," Zaphiro said later. "He preferred to drive around and look at the animals."[8] In fact, as soon as Menocal and Theisen left the safari at Fig Tree Camp, Ernest and Mary spent more time and effort observing wildlife than killing it. Left for a period of time on their own when Percival returned to Kitanga, they explored the terrain, counted animals, learned their habits, watched the birdlife, and were as free in Eden as it was possible to be in a fallen world. Mary handfed an abandoned newborn Grant's gazelle who attached to her as his mother. At the Kimana Swamp camp, everywhere they looked, something unexpected waited to be seen. A pride of lionesses springing up with their cubs out of the tall grass, moving so smoothly, quickly into deep cover, delighted them. At regular times of day, an elephant herd came to the river, mothers and children, the matriarch standing guard, the yearlings deferential. Each morning was a wonder to see what animals left their traces in the camp at night. Coming back from the toilet tent in the dark, Mary surprised several zebras. One night Denis Zaphiro woke to find a leopard inside the tent with him. Upon discovering a young female, an old lioness, and her cubs close to camp, Ernest and Mary began leaving gifts of wildebeest haunch for them. Although Mary eventually killed a lion who refused to charge, it was the beauty and serenity of Africa, not the hunting, that was most important to both Hemingways.[9]

A year later Denis Zaphiro would fondly recall the craziness that Ernest and Mary brought with them to the safari:

> Papa and I driving at night recklessly through the flowers with the smell of dew on them. . . . The taste of neat gin in my mouth and the young giraffe wheeling away from the headlights as Papa leant out of the car and smacked its rump. The feat when he fell out and I backed into the darkness to find the broken form and there he was sitting up searching for his glasses, the pistol still clutched in his hand and his great shoulders shaking with silent laughter.[10]

Intrusions were few and far between, for Roy Marsh's single-engine Cessna brought mail from Nairobi on an irregular basis. In October, when there was talk that Hemingway was due for the Nobel Prize for literature, his hopes rose, only to be deflated when it went to Winston Churchill. A month later the unstoppable Charles Fenton broke through Ernest's defenses with a letter asking for permission for several quotes for the book version of his dissertation, which he promised "leaves completely undamaged all the material and situations you would write about yourself creatively." Ernest, in the middle of his Masai spear training, gave Fenton the necessary permissions, offering to bring him back a blooded spear from what he called his "fucking never-ending apprenticeship."[11] Letters from Hotchner recounted his ongoing negotiations with the television moguls. Ernest's short story, "The Capital of the World," was being performed in two mediums on the Ford Omnibus series. The dramatic adaptation by Hotchner would appear as a stage play, followed by a ballet interpretation of the story, music provided by Ernest's Paris acquaintance, George Antheil. If all went well, Hotchner had rosy plans for more television adaptations of Hemingway. Columbia Broadcasting System was interested in *Across the River and into the Trees*, and several of Ernest's short stories were natural fits for the medium.[12]

Left to their own devices, Ernest and Mary invented games, named the animals, feasted on local bounty, and observed the forbidden fruit of native girls, some already the third or fourth wives of cow-wealthy Masai men. On November 3, Ernest was made an honorary game warden, a title that carried no specific duties but to which Ernest gave the same weight as a battlefield commission.[13] When Mary made a Christmas shopping trip into Nairobi, she returned to find Ernest's head shaved, his clothes dyed the rusty ochre favored by Masai, and armed with a native spear with which he was practicing to kill a lion. With an imagination that operated quite beyond Mary's limits, her husband was creating an elaborate fantasy of becoming a Masai warrior, one with multiple wives, an erotic fantasy that had intrigued him since his first marriage. Shrewder, tougher, more tolerant, and perhaps more foolish than his earlier wives, Mary, realizing that his fantasies added to their sexual adventures, suggested that Debba, his native girl of choice, first might need a bath before joining the family. When Denis Zaphiro returned to the camp before Christmas, he found Debba "hanging around the staff encampment. . . . She was a slovenly-looking brat with a primitive greedy face. She was also none too clean." But he gave little credence to the suggestion that Ernest did more than talk about her as his "fiancée."[14]

On December 20, at the Kimana Swamp camp, Ernest wrote in Mary's journal that he was eager for Mary to turn her hair, as promised, a platinum blonde the way it was in Torcello when they were so happy. He said that

> Mary is an espece [species](sort of) prince of devils . . . and almost any place you touch her it can kill both you and her. She has always wanted to be a boy and thinks as a boy without ever losing any femininity. If you should become confused on this you should retire. She loves me to be her girls, which I love to be, not being absolutely stupid. . . . In return she makes me awards and at night we do every sort of thing which pleases her and which pleases me. . . . Mary has never had one lesbian impulse but has always wanted to be a boy. Since I have never cared for any man and dislike any tactile contact between men . . . I loved feeling the embrace of Mary which came to me as something quite new and outside all tribal law. On the night of December 19th we worked out these things and I have never been happier.[15]

Mary, happy to be complicit in her husband's sexual adventures, reproduced his statement, which he had signed and dated, in her own memoir years later.

From December into January 1954, with the rains having turned the dusty plains billiard table green, Ernest and Mary camped on the north slope of Mount Kilimanjaro. In his new role of honorary game warden, Ernest was quick to recreate an African version of Rambouillet. If elephants grazed through a shamba's cornfield, he was there to make sure they kept moving on. If a lion was killing Masai cattle, Ernest and his rifle were on the case. When natives appeared in the middle of the night with some emergency, it was never too inconvenient for him to attend to it. As honorary game warden and acting game ranger, Hemingway was in command of native game scouts and numerous informers reporting on poachers, a marauding leopard, and potential intrusions of Mau Mau. Here was an experience so rare that it seemed a dream to him, the stuff from which a book might come. Mary kept one set of notes, he another:

Old man on the road
Conversation about the house on the hill
We came to kill the lion. Lion ran off.
The old man killed his servants, reporting as a Mau Mau attack
Becomes a local hero
Policeman finally notes all were killed on 29th of the month, pay
    day.[16]

When he was not on patrol, leaving Mary with their safari natives,
he and she were walking their local area, checking on the buffalo
herd, on the elephants, on the old lioness—Adam and Eve after the
fall returned to an Eden less friendly but no less interesting.
Waking early before first light, Ernest would sometimes be out on
the trails, armed only with his spear, listening to the morning music
of birds and beasts.[17]

Mary, at first dubious about his game rangering, began to reap its
rewards when Ernest praised her excessively as "the bravest, loveli-
est, most understanding and best kitten in and out of bed, and more
fun to talk with on any subject and with sounder opinions . . . of
anyone . . . the best companion in the field when things are difficult that I have ever known bar none." When Mary told him that
Lady Churchill in middle age held many hearts, Ernest asked, "In
the palm of her hand?" Mary said, "Yes." Ernest, with a grin,
replied, "No better than you holding Mr. Scrooby."[18] With Ernest as
her armed backup, Mary photographed furiously—bat-eared foxes,
gazelles, kudu, rhino.

During this same period, Roy Marsh, their bush pilot, began taking Ernest and Mary on low-level flights along the river and the
plains, the excitement of which thrilled Mary and worried Ernest,
who understood the dangers of "flying on the deck." But soon in his
letters he was saying the "deck" was his home, while promising
Mary a low-level tour of Africa right up to the Congo River basin.
On January 21, they took off from Nairobi in Marsh's Cessna, making overnight stops along the string of northern lakes, until on
January 23 they were admiring the grandeur of Murchinson Falls
at low level when a flight of black and white ibis rose in front of
them. To avoid a collision, Marsh went beneath the large birds.

Then with a twang and a shudder the single-engine plane ripped through an abandoned telegraph line, ruining the prop and damaging the rudder. Banking sharply to the left, Marsh told his passengers, "Sorry, we're coming down now. Get ready. Get ready." As softly as a light plane can come to rest in heavy brush, Marsh cut the engine, dropping the Cessna into an opening—a successful landing, everyone walking away from it apparently unhurt. But it was soon obvious that Mary, riding in the co-pilot's seat, was in shock—weak pulse, rapid heartbeat—and later a doctor discovered two cracked ribs.[19] Ernest's back, right arm, and shoulder were badly bruised to the point of steady pain, but he and Roy made a camp, gathered firewood, hauled their meager supplies up from the crash site, and avoided the elephant herd into whose home they had descended. It was one o'clock in the afternoon. Roy Marsh's distress calls on the plane's weak radio went unanswered, but a high-flying commercial liner spotted the wreck, reporting that no survivors were visible. By sunset, newspapers around the world were setting banner headlines announcing the death of Papa. That night on the hillside, sleeping on grass bedding, Mary was awakened by Ernest, who asked her not to snore because the noise was making the elephants curious.

The next day a chartered boat, with no knowledge of their circumstance, appeared almost miraculously on the river below them. After negotiating with the elephant herd on the hillside and the boat captain, who overcharged them, Ernest, Mary, and Roy found themselves drinking a cold Tusker beer, watching the riverbank flow past on their way to Butiaba. There they were met by Reggie Cartright, who had been searching for them in his twin-engine, twelve-seat de Havilland. Assuring the rescued party he could take off from the rough dirt landing strip, Cartright got them aboard and started bouncing down the uneven field. No sooner were they airborne than they nosed down, smashing into the ground. The right engine caught fire, igniting a ruptured fuel tank, quickly turning the plane into a death trap. With the port door jammed, Marsh hurried Mary forward where he and she squeezed through a broken window too small for Ernest to follow. Trapped in a plane that was filling with smoke, Ernest tried to force the jammed door open, but his previously bruised shoulder, leg, and arm made his effort too painful to be effective. Left with no alternative, he butted his bare head against the door, finally wedging it open. By this time the entire plane was in flames, beer bottles exploding like pistol shots. Consumed in the fire were the Hemingways' passports, Mary's expensive cameras, thirty rolls of exposed film, three pairs of Ernest's bifocals, all of their money, and their $15,000 letter of credit.[20]

That evening at Masandi, celebrating their double escape at the bar with pilots and newfound friends, Ernest was groggy and disoriented. Discounting his exaggerations, this was at least his fourth serious concussion in the last ten years. Alcohol, his sovereign cure for head wounds, was guaranteed to make the concussion worse. Behind his left ear, the scalp was torn and clear fluid was leaking from the wound; one of his kidneys was badly hurt, his overworked liver damaged, his shoulder dislocated, his lower intestine collapsed, and he suffered temporary loss of hearing in his left ear and vision in his left eye. In the midnight toilet bowl he could all too clearly see the bloody urine. Later, X rays would reveal two crushed lumbar vertebrae. In steady pain, he tried as best he could to keep a pleasant face forward; like a wounded animal, he did not want to let anyone know how serious the damage was.[21] At fifty-four, he was in worse physical shape than when he was blown up at eighteen; his aging body was much slower to heal, never again regaining its full power.

On Monday, January 25, Ernest and Mary, both in considerable pain, were driven to Entebbe where journalists and airline representatives were waiting to interview them. On that same day, international newspapers and radio stations were reporting his probable death on the basis of the earliest news release. On Tuesday, the United Press news service reported and almost every newspaper's front page carried the full story, which began:

HEMINGWAY OUT OF THE JUNGLE;
ARM HURT, HE SAYS LUCK HOLDS

Entebbe, Uganda, Jan. 25—Ernest Hemingway arrived in Entebbe today having survived two plane crashes in the elephant country of Uganda.

His head was swathed in bandages and his arm was injured, but the novelist, who is 55 [sic] years old, quipped: "My luck, she is running very good."

He was carrying a bunch of bananas and a bottle of gin. With him was his wife, the former Mary Welsh. She had two cracked ribs. . . . He waved a swollen arm, wrapped in a torn shirt, and appeared to be in high spirits as he shrugged off the crashes . . . he apparently was not badly hurt.[22]

But Ernest was hurt even worse than he let Mary know. For three days, he rested in the privacy of their hotel room, and on January 28 flew to Nairobi, where the press reported that "he seemed tired and disinclined to talk."[23] At the New Stanley Hotel, Hemingway remained in his room as much as possible, drinking too much, the doctor told him, but paying no attention to the doctor, refusing X rays, determined to be as invulnerable as his obituaries and their next-day retractions would have him be. To reporters, he insisted he was in good shape, but Mary noted: "The urine samples he keeps in glasses in the bathroom are bright, dark red with an inch of sediment, the wound on the leg not good, hearing bad in the burned ear, eyes bad."[24]

Although Ernest was obviously in poor physical shape, he insisted that they complete the safari with deep-sea fishing just as his first safari had done. Still ailing from her mending ribs and bandaged knee, Mary left him in the Nairobi hotel while she went to Mombasa, where they were renting a fishing boat for a month. With their safari porters, the Percivals, Patrick and his wife Henny all arriving, Mary established their camp at Shimoni. From there she wrote to Ernest:

> It really is a fine place, this—a little like Parajiso, with the big narrow island straight in front and the open sea to the SW and blue high hills against the sunset to the W, Boabab trees . . . NO MOSQUITOES AT ALL. . . . I bought a case of gin and some Riesling and Chianti and whiskey. . . . The sea is silver now and a dugout with one of those Arab shaped sails floating across it against a golden sky.

Urging him to join them as soon as he felt well enough to travel,

Mary signed the letter: "Much love from half a woman or half a boy."[25]

Back in his hotel room, Ernest lived in his pajamas, doctored himself, took meals in the room, and spent part of each day dictating his comic version of the double crash for *Look* magazine, which offered him $20,000 for the exclusive. Illustrated with Earl Theisen photographs, the story ran for twenty magazine pages spread out over two issues. Called "The Christmas Gift," it was a rambling, loosely organized, comic, but remarkably written account of the experience, with asides on Senator Joseph McCarthy, the habits of elephants, the efficacy of Gordon's gin, memories of New York celebrities, strange dreams involving lions, his game ranger adventures, and the night sounds of Africa. In his dreams, he confessed that he was "always between 25 or 30 years old, I am irresistible to women, dogs, and on one recent occasion, to a very beautiful lioness." Nothing in the travel story gave any clue to how badly damaged Hemingway actually was, but he did comment on his obituaries that claimed he had "sought death all his life."

> Can one imagine that if a man sought death all of his life he could not have found her before the age of 54? . . . She is the most easy thing to find that I know of. . . . [I have spent my] life avoiding death as cagily as possible, but on the other hand taking no backchat from her and studying her as you would a beautiful harlot who could put you soundly to sleep forever.[26]

On February 22, Roy Marsh flew Ernest down to Mombasa, where he joined the seagoing safari party on the island. But his jammed vertebrae and other ills kept him largely housebound while the others fished. Then, compounding his problems, he tried to help extinguish a brush fire, but his damaged ear had so affected his balance that he tumbled into the blaze. By the time the natives pulled him out, he was burned on the arms, head, and lips, requiring more bandaging. On March 9, when it was time to call the safari done, Mary dealt with all the details, for Ernest was still recovering from his injuries.[27] Two days later, she supervised the move of forty pieces of luggage, including a leopard skin, several rugs, three hundred books, and African masks, on board the SS

Africa bound for Venice. Their great escape into the garden of Africa, begun so gaily and finished in pain, was over. As the roofs and palms of Mombasa dropped from sight, Ernest at the railing, his back in serious pain, was a shrunken man. His weight was down to 185; his face puffy with bruises and burns, his eyes unfocused. Plenty of times before he had been badly hurt. Each time he had trained himself back into physical shape. In 1918, when his right kneecap was largely missing, his head concussed, and his legs full of shrapnel, it took him more than a year to recover. In 1930–31, when his right arm was so badly fractured in an auto wreck that it seemed the damaged nerves would never regenerate, he slowly willed them back into action. This time, however, his head was dangerously muddled, and Gordon's gin was no cure. Given enough solitude, most of his injuries would mend, if not perfectly at least to the point that he was not in constant pain; but residual damage to the left side of his brain put him one step closer to that closely studied harlot of whom he spoke.

CHAPTER 18

Fortune and Men's Eyes

March 1954 to January 1956

From Mombasa, the Hemingways returned to Venice on March 23, checking in, once more, at the Gritti Palace, where Ernest finally submitted to X rays that revealed jammed vertebrae. In steady pain, he went back to bed, his thinking erratic with barbiturates and his vision still fuzzy. One of the first visitors allowed into his room was Adriana Ivancich, who was shocked to see him white-haired and twenty pounds lighter. Without Mary in the room, they had a tear-filled reunion, with Ernest apologizing for the scandal he had caused her with his novel. "Probably it would have been better," he said, "if I had never met you that day in the rain."[1] No longer jealous of the young woman, Mary was ready to hand her husband over to Adriana, to doctors, or to anyone else who would take him, for she had reached her limits as nurse and valet. Ernest, from his side of the court, complained that being trapped in a small room with her was no fun for a wounded man, for she woke surly and never kind.[2] But soon after arriving in Venice, Mary wrote her parents that Ernest was buying her jewels: "the most beautiful, delicate bracelet, very Venetian—a couple of hundred years old . . . and the next day came home with a pin representing part of a gondola and one of the mooring posts."[3] This expensive gesture was, by now, a familiar stage in their complex marriage game: whenever Ernest felt remorse for errant behavior, he usually resorted to gifts of money, clothing, or jewelry to make amends.

Their daily lives in Venice were made increasingly unpleasant by media pressures: reporters, magazines, newsreels, radio interviewers were all at the door. From America came startling offers for exclusives on their African adventures, which were already under contract with *Look*. No private life was left to them as the public fed vicariously on the Hemingway saga. They escaped briefly to the country, but the country could not cure the problem, nor could it mend Ernest's internal ills. He accepted the Award of Merit Medal from the American Academy of Arts and Letters, but begged off attending the New York ceremony, explaining to Archie MacLeish how badly beat up he actually was.[4] In April, his temper frayed from pain, Ernest arranged for Mary to visit London over Easter, pick up old friends of the *corrida*, and motor down to Madrid. Ed Hotchner would drive him down to join her in mid-May. Meanwhile, he checked into a Genoa clinic for further tests, then returned to the Gritti where he occasionally saw Adriana, who was now twenty-four and still unmarried, which for an Italian woman of her station was a cause for more gossip. When he and Hotchner departed Venice on May 6, Ernest's first letters were to Adriana, telling her that leaving her was like an amputation and that he would love her much and always.[5]

Driving along the French Riviera and through Provence with Adamo once more at the Lancia's wheel and Hotchner for travel companion, Ernest tried to be as jolly as possible, given his condition. They stopped at Monte Carlo for a brief evening at the gaming tables, visited the heart of Cézanne and Van Gogh country once more, and stopped long enough in St. Jean-de-Luz to lure Pete Viertel to Madrid, regaling him with fanciful stories of Debba, Ernest's "Wakamba bride." When Ernest arrived in Madrid, his paranoia popped up like an old friend when the newspaper *ABC* ran a brief paragraph about "an enemy of Spain" arriving in the city. After the San Isidro *corridas* (May 15–17), which Hemingway insisted they all attend, their party joined Viertel and the beautiful film star, Ava Gardner, at the country home of Luis Miguel Dominguín. Mary, keeping a perfect public face, was worried in private about Ernest, who looked as weary and ill as she had left him in Venice.[6]

At the Dominguín bull ring, Ernest watched the now retired

matador test the courage and stamina of heifers for breeding purposes. Afterward Ernest and Ava posed for photos with Luis Miguel, but when the Hemingway party returned to Madrid, Dominguín told Viertel that he did not trust Hemingway. Apparently, while evaluating Viertel's ability, Ernest judged that Pete would never write anything significant, which to the Spaniard was no way to speak of a friend. Viertel himself made little of it, but afterward wrote:

> The thing that disturbed me most was Papa's duplicity, a trait I had first become aware of in Paris when Hemingway had denigrated so many of his old friends. In this instance I sensed that his backbiting had been caused by his proprietary attitude toward bullfighting. . . . He was finding it difficult to accept growing old.[7]

Almost everyone who remembered the Hemingway of the previous summer found him incredibly changed by the African plane crashes, his beard whiter, his eyes frequently vacant, his moods mercurial. In Madrid he went to yet another doctor, who advised "continued rest, a careful diet, and a greatly reduced intake of alcohol."[8] On June 6, having driven back to Genoa, Ernest and Mary boarded the *Francesco Morosini* in order to reach Havana without passing through New York City. The Ivancichs, mother and daughter, came to the dock to see them off, a decorous parting and a final one. Ernest and Adriana would never see each other again.

Fifteen days later at sea, Ernest wrote that he had taken only four whiskeys since leaving Italy, which was boring the bejesus out of him and making life for Mary miserable. At lunch in the small ship's dining room, Ernest began harassing Mary about one of his numerous pocketknives she was supposed to have had repaired in Paris. Where was it now? Packed somewhere in the eighty-seven pieces of luggage stowed in the hold, but Mary could not remember in which piece. Ernest became furious, shouting, "You thief!" The other diners were stunned silent as Mary calmly finished her coffee. Returning to their cabin, she wrote Ernest a note: "You used to understand justice and that other people also had feelings and truthfulness. . . . I hope for your sake especially, and for all us friends and lovers of yours that you have not completely lost those qualities."[9]

Finally, thirteen months after leaving Cuba, they returned to the Havana pier, tired, overloaded with luggage, and ready to sit quietly at the Finca to recover from the trip. Instead, Mary almost immediately was forced to go to her father's side in Gulfport, Mississippi, where as a convert to Christian Science he was refusing to take drugs for his uremia and prostate cancer. In the sweltering July heat, Mary tried to bring reason back into her parents' house, while Ernest did his best to put the Finca back in order. On July 20, having gotten both parents into a nursing home, Mary returned to Havana. The next day, Ernest was being honored on his fifty-fifth birthday by the Batista government with Cuba's highest civilian award, the Order of Carlos Manuel de Céspedes. Ernest, who refused to do anything that might indicate he supported the Batista government, insisted the medal be presented at an informal ceremony, not at the presidential palace.[10]

August at the Finca was a continual circus of luncheons with old friends, all wanting to touch the man who had risen from the dead. Bob Lowe, former editor at *Look*, was there for five days, pushing a deal for an African documentary film, for which Ernest agreed to be consultant. Then Hemingway's Havana doctor, José Luis Herrera, was fed and fêted; three days later it was wealthy Lee Samuels, Hemingway's local supporter, who managed the collection of Ernest's manuscripts. Then Ava Gardner arrived, preceded by her much quoted statement that there were only two men she would want with herself on a desert island: Adlai Stevenson, the cerebral Democrat defeated by Eisenhower for the presidency, and Ernest Hemingway. Winston Guest showed up on his way to someplace else, followed by Luis Miguel Dominguín for nine days. In between Alfred Vanderbilt passed through the Finca wanting Ernest's help with some association of war veterans.[11]

Despite these steady intrusions, Ernest wrote almost every morning, standing at his typewriter to protect his back. He finished one short story and was twenty-one pages into another by mid-August.[12] His concentration was broken temporarily on September 2 when the *New York Times* reported that "Ernest Hemingway is going to write and appear in a motion picture about big-game hunting in Africa," which Darryl Zanuck would produce. That took two days of letters and phone calls to the coast and to Alfred Rice before everyone understood that Ernest Hemingway was never going to be an actor in or a writer of any Hollywood film. That was with his left hand. With his right hand, Ernest was responding to a local journalist's demand for a duel to assuage his honor offended by some remark of Mary's at a cocktail party. No dueling with journalists.[13] No filming with Zanuck. Be polite at Finca lunches, and write every morning on the story that was rapidly becoming "the African book."[14] Then came the annual Nobel Prize lottery to raise distractions to an entirely new level. On October 5, the *New York Times* reported that "Halldør Laxness, 52-year-old Icelandic writer, and Ernest Hemingway are the only candidates seriously considered for this year's Nobel Prize for literature, according to circles close to the Swedish Academy." Three weeks later, the *Times* said the Nobel was a sure thing for Hemingway because after his near-death experience, "some Swedish academicians expressed regret that they had not previously honored him."[15] None of which Hemingway found particularly flattering. If the "academy" that had passed him by so often had to choose only between some Icelandic bard and himself, it was not a field to be proud about, and if they were giving him the medal because he came close to dying, well, to hell with that.

But when the announcement came on October 28 from Sweden, there wasn't any way to say no to the Nobel Prize, not with the world's press corps at your front door and the Swedish ambassador at your dining-room table. So, leaving out his misgivings, Ernest said simply, "I am very pleased and very proud to receive the Nobel Prize for literature."[16] To the crowd gathered at the front door, he joked about the prize money, saying he would like to share it with his friends, the panhandlers outside the Floridita, but first his own debts must be paid.[17] When Harvey Breit called from New York, Ernest gave him as many pithy quotes as possible, saying he could not "but regret that the award was never given to Mark Twain, nor to Henry James, speaking only of my own countrymen."[18] When *Time* magazine told him they were running his face on their cover whether he helped with the story or not, he invited their reporter, Robert Manning, down for two days of *Pilar* fishing and Hemingway homilies: "Fattening of the body can lead to fattening of the mind. I would be tempted to say that it can lead to fattening of the soul, but I don't know anything about the soul." Hemingway also used the *Time* interview to make a strong public plea for the release of his old friend and mentor, Ezra Pound, from St. Elizabeth's Hospital. "Ezra Pound is a great poet," he said, "and whatever he did he has been punished greatly and I believe he should be freed to go and write poems in Italy where he is loved and understood."[19]

Hemingway excused himself from attending the Nobel award ceremony, saying that he was not yet fully recovered from his African injuries, but he nonetheless needed an acceptance speech for the American ambassador to Sweden to read at the event. Ernest's first impulse was satirical, asking rhetorically what it might profit a man to win such a prize if by doing so he destroyed his present writing through "small politenesses."[20] Finally he prepared a short statement that offended no one, but with barbs beneath its seemingly simple surface:

> Writing, at its best, is a lonely life. Organizations for writers palliate the writer's loneliness but I doubt if they improve his writing. He grows in public stature as he sheds his loneliness and often his work deteriorates. For he does his work alone and if he is a good enough writer he must face eternity, or the lack of it, each day.
>
> For a true writer each book should be a new beginning where he tries again for something that is beyond attainment. He should always try for something that has never been done or that others have tried and failed. Then sometimes, with great luck, he will succeed. . . . It is because we have had such great writers in the past that a writer is driven far out past where he can go, out to where no one can help him.[21]

In answer to Faulkner's earlier complaint that Ernest never took chances by attempting the impossible, Hemingway was asking his readers to look again at his work, for its very simplicity did not mean that it was easy to do, or that he did not try to push the limits of his talent. Because they read for immediate gratification, urban reviewers all too often had seen each work as a rerun of earlier themes, and nothing new. What few noticed was that he never repeated himself in the structure of his novels, that he pushed the short story genre beyond its previous limits, and that his style continued to evolve. If his themes were constant, so were those of Picasso.

By December 7, Ernest was in the *Pilar* anchored on the lee side of a small island, riding out a norther and hiding from his pursuers. He complained that he would have to move to Africa or stay permanently at sea in order to get his writing done. The Floridita was now impossible, as was the Finca and Cojimar. It was partially his own fault letting Cowley, Baker, Fenton, Young, Ross, and now Manning get inside his defenses. He worried that the publicity could actually destroy that internal well from which his writing was drawn.[22] He remained at sea through the Nobel award ceremonies, which he and Mary heard fade in and out on their shortwave radio. Returning to the Finca, his desk was covered with inquiries, offers, and announcements of arriving guests—more "brutal" interruptions. Time/Life wanted to give him a $10,000 check for the privilege of having the "first look" at his next book. *Argosy* magazine for men would pay $1,000 if Hemingway would let their photographer into the Finca to take pictures. And Hotchner had a $6,000 commitment from *True* magazine for a feature on Hemingway that required photographs and yet another interview.[23] His life, no longer his own, had become a public sideshow open to anyone. Always the hunter, he was now the hunted, the trophy head to be brought back on film. His broken body was healing more slowly than it ever had before; his mind was full of ants. His black-ass mood was descending like a caul as the year closed out with a National Broadcasting Company hour-long, unauthorized radio documentary, "Meet Ernest Hemingway—the man who lived it up to write it down." Ernest was characterized as "master of the four letter word" and "a two fisted drinker who could down a quart of gin a day if the conversation were good." Max Eastman got to refight his chest-hair battle with Ernest that took place in Max Perkins's office. Leonard Lyons told anecdotes; Al Capp, who never met Hemingway, said that the writer's one and only creation was Ernest Hemingway. Ed Scott, the *Havana Post* journalist who challenged Hemingway to a duel, read from Hemingway's letters to him. Cornelia Otis Skinner read her Hemingway parody, "For Whom the Gong Sounds," and young Marlon Brando read excerpts from *The Old Man and the Sea*.[24]

Into the new year, Ernest, sick of such publicity, kept as much to himself as possible, writing every day and seldom leaving the Finca. The second African story was now moving along nicely as a full-blown novel, unplanned as his novels frequently evolved, with him living in it each day, back at the good camp and the elephants moving, their dung piles smoking in the morning light. The first week in February 1955, he wrote 4,587 words, when previously a good week would have been half that many. His back and kidneys, not yet recovered enough for strenuous exercise, still bothered him, and he avoided anything likely to strain them, turning down invitations to return to Madrid for the San Isidro *corrida*.[25] On February 17, the death of Mary's eighty-five-year-old father took her to Gulfport for his funeral and its aftermath. While she was gone, Ernest did not slide into his customary funk when left alone; rather, he immersed himself in the novel. By the time Mary returned, he had 75,000 words on paper, words which he said were too rough to be printed while he was alive, words, he joked, never to be serialized in the *Sunday Visitor*, the Catholic newspaper for children.[26]

Written in more than one voice but with the character Ernest Hemingway as its focal point, the manuscript was an ironic, self-deprecating, and humorous account of the contemplative life of the writer juxtaposed against the active life of a temporary game ranger protecting the village of the Wakamba natives, one of whom, Debba, is promised to him as his second wife. Mary, his older wife, is barren, and the writer/hunter yearns for the child Debba will give him. Critics, biographers, and fellow writers all come in for comic kidding, but the Africanization of Ernest Hemingway is serious in the sense that he was looking for some way to escape from his too public life into a simpler world. With

Patrick now living in Tanganyika and Gregory there visiting, Ernest was ready to give up his no longer defensible Cuban hilltop in favor of Africa. He had retreated from Key West in 1939 and Ketchum in 1948, for the same reasons that were now making Cuba less the garden spot it once was.[27] Thirty-three years earlier in Paris, he set out to become the best writer of his generation, choosing great writers as his masters and immortality as his goal. He became the writer he set out to be only to find that the cost was high, and rewards sometimes tasted like ashes. In Africa, he explained,

> You do not have to be a literary character. . . . And I can pray to the Mountain, we have an illegal *shamba* at its foot, and to the trees, the special trees, and keep the customs and laws and break them as the young men do and pay fines and Miss Mary who can't have children can have Debba to help her as a second wife. Debba can have the children.[28]

At the end of his life, Tolstoy tried for religious reasons to dress and live as a peasant; Hemingway, for secular reasons, was moving in the same direction. He clearly understood the pure loneliness of a writer's life, and the burden of being the personage he had become. All his yesterdays with their wonderful stories and novels were just that, yesterdays. A writer is never free from the necessity of writing something better, different, more interesting than his last book, and each book comes with its own anxieties and difficulties. There is no decorous retirement plan except failure for a writer.

Mary, who understood his need to write the African fantasy, remained his supportive wife and faithful reader. She was, after all, a character in the book, with a larger role than Pauline's in *Green Hills of Africa*. If she did not object to sharing Ernest with the fictive version of Debba, perhaps it was more exciting to indulge his fantasy. In a letter to Harvey Breit which Ernest let Mary read, he said, "It doesn't seem so stupid to me to have five wives if you can afford them . . . instead of having one wife at a time and paying them alimony when you need another wife. . . . I am very faithful. But I can be faithful easier to four good wives than to one."[29] Despite a continued parade of Finca guests, despite her father's death in February, and her mother's move back to Minnesota in July, the burdens of which all fell on her shoulders, Mary was always supportive of Ernest's African fantasies until that October. When he announced that he wanted his ears pierced for gold earrings as a sign of his kinship with the Wakamba natives, Mary did her best to convince him that it was a bad idea. Finally she wrote an interhouse note, asking him to reconsider his decision, which would flout "the mores of western civilization," not to speak of the "deleterious effect" earrings would have on his reputation "as a writer and as a man." She continued,

> The fiction that having your ears pierced will make you a Kamba is an evasion of the reality which is that you are not and never can be anything but an honorary Kamba . . . I know that you are impassioned about Africa and the Africans, writing about them, and allured by the mystery and excitement of becoming one of them. And you know that I love the fun of make-believe as much as you do. But . . . there are other ways of proving brotherhood between you and the Kamba.[30]

That was the end of the earring crisis.

Despite his best efforts to keep visitors at bay that spring of 1955, Hemingway and the Finca were never without intrusions. First it was an undergraduate from Rutgers bearing a sheaf of short stories which he insisted Ernest must read. Then on the Wednesday of Easter week, four of Carlos Baker's students from Princeton were knocking at the front door, having first ignored the gate sign telling them no visits without an appointment. Once inside, Ernest was as grandfatherly as possible, soft-spoken, almost shy. The four sophomores, feeling quite adult drinking late morning martinis with the Man himself, listened to his stories about the early days in Paris and how he taught himself to write, stories that by this time were well rehearsed. When asked if he would ever run out of ideas for fiction, he said, "I don't see how I can quit."[31] On the morning of Good Friday, Professor Fraser Drew from Buffalo arrived by appointment to find Hemingway gray-bearded and overweight, dressed in working shorts and an old shirt. "Slow moving and slow speaking," Drew wrote in his notes. "His voice is quiet and low and his laugh

. . . is genuine and quiet, also. He is very kind and modest and unassuming." Noting that it was Good Friday, Ernest said, "I like to think I'm a Catholic, as far as I can be. I can still go to Mass, although many things have happened—the divorces, the marriages." He spoke of Father Andrés who lived in the village below the Finca. "He prays for me every day," Hemingway told Drew, "as I do for him. I can't pray for myself any more. Perhaps it's because in some way I have become hardened. Or perhaps it's because the self becomes less important and others become more important."[32] High on Ernest's prayer list were Mary's parents, fallen-away Catholics, Tom Welsh dead, but his soul perhaps still salvageable. Hemingway would send money to his favorite order, the Jesuits, or simply have Don Andrés pray for them at his morning Mass. "The prayers can't hurt them," he said, "and if not entitled to them they will be paid for anyway and the money can't hurt the church."[33]

Ernest might have included himself on his prayer list, for his body was recovering so slowly from the African crashes that now, a year later, he was still in pain. On April 19, with Mary's twenty-foot *Tin Kid* in tow and their locker well stocked with provisions, Ernest, Mary, and Gregorio took the *Pilar* ninety miles down the coast to Paraíso Key for a two-week escape. Each morning Mary fished the reefs, sometimes with Gregorio, but just as often on her own. Having become an excellent sailor as well as fisherwoman, Mary was perfectly capable of taking her open boat out beyond the reefs looking for marlin on her own. For most of the sojourn, Ernest did not fish at all. In the mornings, he would do his exercises and run on the beach, each day feeling stronger, and living part of each day writing in the Africa of his head. Eating well—Gregorio's red snapper in garlic and peppery tomato sauce—drinking little alcohol, reading during the midday heat, sleeping under a sea breeze, Ernest and Mary were at peace with themselves and the world elsewhere. By day, the water turned several shades of blue and green in the bay and along the reefs. At night, the constellations made their steady circle, great and small bear, lion, and dogs, the twins in their slow dance, and if late enough awake, Cassiopeia rising.[34]

On May 3, Ernest and Mary returned to the Finca, which continued to be overrun with guests. Juan Dunabeitia, the Polish sea captain known as "Sinsky," was in drunken residence for a week between sober voyages; Roberto Herrera was there every day working as a private secretary. Alfred Rice, Ernest's New York lawyer, came in to discuss the contract for the filming of *The Old Man and the Sea*, and Taylor Williams from Sun Valley visited on crutches with his foot in a cast. Outside the house, an unusual spring drought continued, turning green growth brown, ruining the flower and vegetable gardens. Then the Finca's aqueduct developed problems, forcing them to haul water in pails from the cistern.[35] Despite intrusions and emergencies, Ernest kept to his morning schedule, writing first and then exercising in the now tepid swimming pool. He was twelve pounds lighter and beginning to feel more like his old self, the old self that ignored doctor's orders, drinking too much too often.

By May 11, he had 404 typed pages of manuscript to which he added each day until June 1, when Pete Viertel and Leland Hayward arrived for the first serious talks about filming *The Old Man and the Sea*.[36] Worried that 98 percent of Hemingway's story took place in an open boat, Viertel suggested that after eighty-four days without a fish, Santiago might look for other work in old Havana before returning to his trade as a fisherman. Ernest listened but killed the idea. Santiago knew only one trade: fishing. It would never enter his mind to seek other employment. Insisting they stick to the story as he wrote it, Hemingway told his guests that this was the only movie of his work he had ever been involved in, and he wanted it right. Trying to joke about it, Viertel suggested that on the eighty-fifth day Santiago might "still not make a catch."

"The Jews have always had a superior attitude toward fishing," Ernest snapped, "probably because fish has never been part of their diet."

"I thought you'd gotten over your anti-Semitism with *The Sun Also Rises*," Pete snapped right back.

Ernest huffed while Pete glared. Hayward calmed both down. Ernest apologized, claiming that the anti-Semitism in *The Sun Also Rises* belonged to his characters, not to him. He was too old now to become anti-Semitic.[37] The evening went on, but it was going to be that kind of a working relationship among the three of them.

When the Cuban location filming began in September, Hayward sent Slim down as his emissary, joining Pete Viertel at the Finca. Putting a woman as attractive as Slim in close proximity to Ernest was a serious mistake. Pete moved into town; Slim moved into the Finca's small guesthouse. That evening before supper, Slim confided to Pete that Mary "had threatened quite calmly to shoot her if she made a play for Papa." When they joined Ernest in the Finca's living room, he was naked to the waist, dressed only in khaki trousers. Sucking in his stomach to prove to Slim how thin he was, Ernest smiled as his trousers dropped to the floor, leaving him stark naked.

"All right for the camera, Pete?" he asked.

"Perfect, Papa," Viertel replied. "Cut and print."

"Please, Papa," Slim pleaded, "put your pants back on!"

He and Pete were laughing, Slim looking away, Ernest pulling up his pants just before Mary walked into the room, curious about the laughter.[38] To her mother, Mary wrote that Slim Hayward was "pretty, quite tall, very slim, and she always has the most wonderful clothes and jewels." Before departing Havana, Slim made Mary a present of her belt and a gold bracelet. On the day of Slim's departure, Pete was shocked when Mary appeared with her once platinum-blond hair now dyed darker to the color of Slim's so admired by Ernest.[39]

Despite Hemingway's organization of the great marlin hunt, complete with hot catered lunches delivered at sea by Mary in the *Tin Kid*, the *Pilar* as camera boat, and native fishermen with hand lines in small, open boats, the film crew was unable to capture Santiago's huge jumping marlin. All of September was spent in this pursuit, which produced 400- and 500-pound marlin, but nothing like the 1,200-pound monster the script required. Already there was talk of moving to a rubber marlin in a Hollywood backlot tank. Hemingway refused, categorically and absolutely. In October and early November, he returned to his African novel, which grew to 694 typed pages by Thanksgiving. That fall Luis Miguel Dominguín came out of retirement to fight a series of South American *corridas* with his now brother-in-law, Antonio Ordóñez. In mid-November, *Sports Illustrated* offered Hemingway $1,000 expenses and a $3,500 fee for his impression of their performances in Caracas, but he and Mary never got to the airport.[40] November 17, after sweating under television lights waiting to receive the Order of San Cristóbal, yet another award from the Batista government, Ernest caught a cold. Then his right foot began to swell, followed by an infection first in his damaged right kidney, then in his left kidney, and finally his liver: acute nephritis and hepatitis was the diagnosis. Put to bed on November 20 under medication, a strict diet, and a limit of one whiskey and water per day, he would not rise again until January in the new year.

Each day the family doctor came to the Finca to check on his patient, making careful notes on his progress. Weak and woozy, Hemingway stuck to the doctor's regimen, fighting off boredom with books, the radio, and his African novel once his head cleared. And of course there were letters to read if not answer. Among them was an envelope bearing the distinctive handwriting of an old Paris friend, Sylvia Beach, who hoped they would meet again soon. "I must ask whether you approve of the way I have handled you in my memoirs," she said, "and whether you authorize my quoting from [your] letters?"[41] Twenty years earlier, when Gertrude Stein published her belittling portrait of Hemingway in *The Autobiography of Alice B. Toklas*, Ernest promised himself that when he had nothing else to write, he would produce his memoirs to even up the score. For several years now, he had been trying out his early Paris days in conversations, letters, and in the unpublished Bimini book. Whether it was Sylvia's letter that pushed him closer to keeping his promise, or the growing legend of Scott Fitzgerald as the madcap writer of the Twenties, is impossible to say, but by the time Ernest was back on his feet in January 1956, he was thinking seriously about the true book of his Paris apprenticeship.

CHAPTER 19

Intimations of Mortality

January 1956 to March 1957

After sixty days in bed, reading and writing, taking his medicine, not drinking, gradually recovering strength, Hemingway rose again at the end of January 1956 only to be sickened by "Who the Hell Is Hemingway?" in *True* magazine. Filled with tall tales, half truths, anecdotal stories from friends, and long quotes from Ernest's own letters and essays (all without permission), it was exactly the sort of story Hemingway now abhorred. Some critic named Pearson called Hemingway "the bronze god . . . who took obscene words off the backhouse wall and put them in print . . . here was the swash-buckling pirate in his own right, living it up to write it down. . . . He is notorious as master of the four-letter words. He drinks liquor by the quart . . . absinthe used to be his favorite drink."[1] Having spent two months without liquor and longer than that without having published a single four-letter word, Ernest had reason to resent such statements. Having tried without success to force Scribner's into publishing even longer obscene words, Hemingway's twenty-year total was exactly one "fucking" in *To Have and Have Not*.

Further into the paste-and-cut story, Hemingway discovered that among his friends were "convicts lately escaped from Devil's Island," and that Jed Kiley, whom he despised, was his "fishing companion." Edward Scott, the *Havana Post* journalist who challenged Hemingway to a duel, recounted the silly incident at great length, quoting Hemingway's last letter on the matter: "For good and sufficient reasons I do not choose to meet Mr. Edward Scott on the so-called field of honor nor anywhere else. I will answer no challenges from him. . . . If any tribunal interprets this as being motivated by cowardice I believe they would be in error. . . . At the present time I am fighting no duels with anyone."[2] Scott forgot to mention that Hemingway was, at that time, freshly back from his disastrous African plane crashes.

On February 6, Earl Wilson's gossip column in the *New York Post* carried an interview with Hemingway saying, among other things, that he was completely cured of hepatitis, that he still had the liver of a twenty-six-year-old, and that his doctors had ordered him to drink six ounces of whiskey a day for his health. "I figure I can do it if I put my mind to it," he was reported to have said with a drink in his hand. Affirming his recuperative powers did not make his liver any better, nor did his doctor's daily notes say anything about drinking that much alcohol. In fact, Hemingway was taking daily doses of several different drugs to keep his rapidly aging body functioning properly: Seconal to sleep; vitamin A for his weakening eyes; vitamin B complex to counteract the effects of alcohol; and methyltestosterone for sexual vigor. Much of this medication was self-prescribed on the basis of Hemingway's wide reading of medical research. When the hepatitis struck, his blood pressure jumped to 178/75; with bed rest and drugs, it gradually came down to 140/68 by the end of February. But by then his red blood cell count was 20 percent below normal. Worried about this anemia, Dr. Herrera immediately ran parasite checks which proved negative on both Ernest and Mary, who also tested anemic.[3]

On January 30, Fred Zinnemann, the director for *The Old Man and the Sea*, flew into Havana to discuss location filming with Ernest, who had scouted out several isolated fishing villages. For the next two months, Hemingway, when not sick, was working in some way on cinematic problems which he found a lot like organizing a safari. It was, in fact, becoming a Hemingway year in Hollywood. Pete Viertel's film script for *The Sun Also Rises* was soon moving into production with the money going to Hadley, as had all earnings from that novel. At the same time, Rock Hudson and Jennifer Jones were starring in a remake of *A Farewell to Arms*, the film rights to which Hemingway had foolishly sold outright before he learned to read the fine print. Having avoided any participation in the several film versions of his work, he was immersing himself completely in the filming of *The Old Man*, determined to have real sharks attacking an actual marlin in an authentic ocean. That was the Hollywood promise written down on paper; but as he was to learn, words written on the West Coast somehow had different meanings from standard English. Moreover, anything scheduled, promised, or planned meant absolutely nothing in the movie business.[4]

On February 10, Hemingway packed up the 856-page typescript of his African novel to devote himself totally to the film project, but he was worried how it would affect him to be away that long from his writing.[5] He might also have wondered how the movie business would affect his marriage. Two weeks later, Mary brought that question to his attention with her in-house state of the union message. Starting slowly, she explained in some detail how women enjoyed going out at night, particularly to the homes of others to see how they lived, decorated, dressed, and ate. Perhaps one night a year, she suggested, they might go out somewhere, anywhere, understanding, of course, that it would be an enormous sacrifice on his part. Pointing out that she had learned to play his games of hunting, sailing, and fishing, was it too much to expect him to humor her a little? Yet when she asked, he became defensive, calling her a liar, and Mary accused him of

> counter-attacking . . . as though I were your long-time enemy.
> . . . Has it ever occurred to you how lonely a woman of yours can get. Wake up alone, breakfast alone, garden alone, swim alone, sup alone. . . . It may be too much to expect that any of this will cause you to change your mind in thinking of YOU versus The Other.

She signed the note: "M. who feels her life slipping away in a welter of chaos."[6]

Ernest could not have been more in agreement about the "welter of chaos" that ruled their lives. Trying to coordinate the weather, film crew, blood bait, and sharks was proving almost impossible. When the camera crew was ready, the weather was too rough to film. When twenty gallons of slaughterhouse blood and four tubs of fish heads were standing by, the film crew was somewhere else. One part or another never quite got to the right place at the right time. Days were wasted. Money was spent and spent again. If not the sharks, then the marlin would not cooperate—too small, too far away, not jumping enough. When not wasting time at the dock, they wasted time in conferences or waiting for Spencer Tracy to show up. When he did arrive, he spent the first evening falling spectacularly off the wagon at the Floridita. The next day Ernest noted on his calendar: "Tracy *not* drinking." On the back of the page, he wrote a note to himself with reference to his conference with Tracy: "You must not humiliate a man in front of others if you expect to continue to work with him."[7] In March, a letter from Gary Cooper invited Ernest to go partners on producing a film of Stewart Edward White's *The Leopard Woman*, set in Africa. Even as much as White was once one of Hemingway's early literary models, Ernest said if he ever got finished with filming *The Old Man and the Sea*, he would never again get involved with movie making. It was not his metier. He joked that if he helped with *The Leopard Woman*, he could picture "that one necessary little bit they would want me to do without a double when I crash the Leopard Woman herself into the snow covered crater of Mt. Kilimanjaro (Kibo) and then carry her (personally) into Abyssinia. . . . Can hear myself being conned, 'Ernie, boy, you owe this to The Picture.'"[8]

In April, the film crew gave up on large, leaping marlin in the Gulf Stream, and Leland Hayward agreed to pay for a month's fishing off the coast of Peru where giant marlin were said to be commonplace. At Capo Blanco—wind blowing sand steadily over barren rocks with oil derricks rising out of the wasteland—they lived at the fishing club's preserve, rising early to spend all day in rough heavy seas trying to find Santiago's fish. Cameras careened, handlers held tight, but no fish floundered. Then Ernest boated a jumping 750-pounder, the largest he had ever taken, but only half the size needed. Larger still, a 950-pounder refused to jump. Other than working Hemingway's weight down to 209 pounds, strengthening his back, and improving his health, the month in Peru was time wasted from the movie's point of view. For backup, Hayward had already purchased film rights to color film of a 1,500-pound world-record marlin splashing in blue seas, and rubber marlins were in the making.[9]

Ernest and Mary were still in Peru when the May issue of *McCall's* magazine ran its "visit" at La Finca Vigia, describing Ernest, not yet recovered from his recent illness, as having "no bounce to his gait, no he-mannish bravado. This is a tired man with a sizable paunch." Handing out his homilies by rote on writing and husbanding, Ernest was on his best behavior, impressing the interviewer with "very dry martinis" and his enormous library piled up throughout the house. When asked his opinion about the Nobel Prize, he could not resist taking another crack at Faulkner whose novel, *A Fable*, Ernest found unreadable. He said, "One shouldn't win the Nobel Prize, then rewrite the Bible and become a bore—I accepted the Bible in its original version."[10] Considering that Ernest was working on his own version of the Garden of Eden, it was an ironic comment.

Upon returning to Finca Vigia in late May, Mary was soon stretched out upon a table with needles in her arm as fresh blood dripped into her veins: an attempt to cure her persistent anemia. Archie and Ada MacLeish were there on a rare visit, seeing Ernest for the first time in many years. Once close friends, they were now but graying shadows of the young men who rambled the Paris boulevards of the Twenties. Archie was there to plot a way to release the incarcerated, irascible Ezra Pound, who never had a good word to say about MacLeish's poetry. Strained as the Hemingway-MacLeish friendship had become during the 1930s, they united in their support for Pound, although it was Archie's persistence that eventually carried the day.[11] On his birthday, Ernest sent Ezra the last of the Nobel money, a $1,000 check, and promised to send him the Nobel medal as well.[12] By the end of the year, Archie was able to report on a workable plan for freeing Ezra. If Attorney General Brownell would agree not to prosecute on the charges of treason, then the question of release could be made on a medical basis, not a political one. Promising there would be no publicity, MacLeish drafted a letter to Brownell for Robert Frost, T. S. Eliot, and Ernest to sign.[13] It would take another year and half before the "midwife" to *The Waste Land* would be set free from his fifteen-year confinement.

After the long and exhausting distraction of movie making, Hemingway did not immediately return to the African novel; instead, to resharpen his blunted pen, he wrote six short stories, mostly about World War II experiences. Based on the ambush at the Rambouillet crossroads ("Black Ass at the Cross Roads") and his judicial hearing ("A Room on the Garden Side"), these stories used material that would have been in the "land" part of the "big book" had Hemingway ever completed that project.[14] With sarcastic references to the war novels of Shaw, Mailer, and James Jones, he insisted that his new stories were about real soldiers speaking in battlefield language about situations in which death was a constant. Scribner's could, he said, publish them after he was dead.[15] After being assured by doctors of his impending death first by high blood pressure and then by internal injuries, his death references, which were becoming more frequent, were understandable. It was the only ending to his story, an ending of which he had been certain since he was eighteen, but now, with friends dying all too regularly, it was not only a certainty but was close enough to smell. This awareness had an adverse impact on his writing, for the only ending that he could now imagine was the death of the protagonist. Even earlier, his novels had ended this way since *To Have and Have Not* (1937). Safe in the bank vault, his Bimini novel ended with Thomas Hudson's life leaking out of his wounds. Only Mary's pleading kept Santiago alive after returning with the shark-stripped skeleton of his marlin. With 200,000 words written on the African novel, Hemingway did not have an ending, although there were plenty of possible death's available—lions, leopards, and Mau Mau revolutionists.

That summer in Cuba, Ernest's red blood cell count rose close to normal; Mary's, however, remained dangerously low. After several blood transfusions, their Cuban doctors suggested a change of climate, which for Ernest was a good excuse to return to Spain where young Ordóñez was fighting brilliantly, and then continue on to Africa for a safari with Patrick. Hemingway booked passage on the *Ile de France* in what Mary referred to as their customary suite, which, with over 100,000 French francs in his Paris bank account, Ernest could well afford. In late August, Ernest took Mary to New York City, where they stayed in the borrowed quarters of Harvey Breit to avoid the press. There they went about last-minute shopping, seeing no one but hearing by phone from Sylvia Beach, who was in the city negotiating with her publisher on her memoirs. She still wanted him to read the "Hemingway passages" for changes he wished, but he assured her to go ahead with publication. It was not until he reached Paris that he read her typescript filled with inaccuracies of too long standing to be corrected.[16]

On September 1, Ernest and Mary boarded the *Ile de France* for a quick five-day trip across the Atlantic. Landing in France, they were met by their new Italian chauffeur with a rented Lancia, which took them first to Paris to reorient and to pick up funds. Pete Viertel found them at the Ritz "petit bar" sitting with Gary Cooper and a young lovely Ernest introduced as "La Comtesse." To Viertel, it was obvious that Hemingway "had once again embarked on one of his imaginary romances." That the relationship was not serious was made obvious by Mary, sitting at the far end of the table, who was massively unconcerned, "having become accustomed to Papa's flirtations." A few days later, Pete arranged a luncheon for Hollywood friends Mel Ferrer, Audrey Hepburn, and Rita Hayworth to meet Hemingway. Seated at a sidewalk café, the group was convivial, Ernest behaving modestly, apparently enjoying the adulation. But when an elderly man approached their table to ask for autographs for his daughter, Ernest turned cold. The movie stars signed, but when it was Ernest's turn, he said, "Sir, you look to me to be a cocksucker." The man departed, hurt; the table went cold. Admitting that he was losing tolerance in his old age, Ernest apologized for what Viertel called his "mercurial changes of mood."[17]

On September 17, the Hemingways traveled by car to St. Jean-de-Luz and crossed into Spain, where they settled into the privacy of the four-star Gran Hotel Felipe II in El Escorial, thirty miles outside Madrid. On the pine-shaded slopes of the Guadarrama Mountains, the hotel was a picturesque refuge perched above the imposing blue-gray granite monastery of San Lorenzo, with its maze of courtyards and rich treasury of Spain's past. In keeping with his idea of updating *Death in the Afternoon,* Hemingway followed the early fall *corridas* that were within easy driving distance. En route to El Escorial, he and Mary enjoyed two days of the Logroño feria where Antonio Ordóñez was brilliant in the ring. Afterward, Ernest made serious plans for the Zaragoza feria in October where Ordóñez promised to dedicate his best bull to Hemingway. The excitement that Ordóñez created in the bull ring was like old times, real and contagious.[18] But the *corridas,* while important to Hemingway, were not as important as the health of himself and Mary. The reason they were staying in El Escorial was its elevation (3,700 feet), which their Cuban doctors hoped would cure their persistent anemia. Their October 22 blood tests showed some improvement: Ernest's red cell count was near normal; Mary's remained 20 percent too low. Their Madrid doctor said that X rays showed nothing seriously wrong with Ernest's heart, that his cholesterol level was too high, and that Mary was much better. He advised that neither of them was fit for a return to Africa that winter, a trip Ernest was counting on to rekindle his African novel.[19] Ernest refused to accept that decision, saying he was going to Africa with or without the doctor's approval. He did agree to follow the prescribed regimen of diet and exercise, but ignored the doctor's request that he stop drinking all alcohol. As Mary and others noted during the trip, Ernest was once again drinking far too much far too often.[20]

An international crisis, however, conspired to keep the Hemingways out of East Africa. First, Egypt nationalized the Suez Canal; then on October 29, Israel invaded Egypt, trying to keep the canal open, but the Egyptians immediately sank forty ships, blocking the canal to all traffic. Not wanting to take trains through Egypt during the crisis, the Hemingways were faced with a long sea voyage around Africa to reach Mombasa, which neither wanted to make. Calling off the African trip, they returned in November to the Ritz Hotel in Paris, where they underwent another battery of medical tests. Mary was suffering once more from colitis, and nagging anemia was still with both Hemingways, Mary more so than Ernest. Moreover, his cholesterol count was twice normal, indicating possible liver problems. Soon he was referring to his "near fatal" liver condition. None of which stopped them from playing the horses at the Auteuil track, or from having dinner with the Duke and Duchess of Windsor at their country home outside Paris. Ernest found time to spend a day showing Leonard Lyons old Left Bank haunts, explaining fallaciously that he learned the city by driving a taxi after World War I.[21]

When a second test on January 8, 1957, confirmed an elevated cholesterol, Ernest put himself under the care of the *Ile de France* ship's doctor, Jean Monnier, who treated him for liver problems, an enlarged aorta perhaps due to his erratic blood pressure, and facial eczema. Between January 23, when the *Ile de France* sailed for New York, and February 14, when it docked in Cuba, Dr. Monnier injected Ernest with large doses of vitamin B complex, gave him drugs to lower his blood pressure, and treated his eczema with cortisone creme. Nevertheless, on March 2, Hemingway's cholesterol count was 408, driving him into a depressed state, certain that he was fatally ill. Dr. Monnier, responding to Ernest's worried letter, assured him that the laboratory analysis was always inexact, that most of his numbers were within a normal range, and that he should stop worrying and follow the prescribed lifestyle without fail. Then Dr. Monnier repeated what he told his patient on board the ship: "You must *stop drinking alcohol*. . . . I understand that it might be harsh, even painful in the beginning, but you must gradually reduce your drinking to nothing." Simultaneously, his new Havana specialist, Dr. Rafael Ballestero, told him much the same thing: rest, mild exercise, restricted diet, altered medication, and no alcohol.[22]

One of the new drugs, Serpasil, was made recently available to treat psychiatric problems ranging from schizophrenia to depression, anxiety, and nervousness. For Hemingway's anxiety and nervousness during alcohol withdrawal, Dr. Ballestero prescribed the recommended dosage of a .25 mg tablet taken twice a day. Possible side effects included lethargy and sometimes nausea until the patient adapted to the drug, but it could either lower or elevate blood pressure, which should be monitored throughout treatment. Always suspicious of drugs and their side effects, Ernest read and filed away detailed information on this trademarked version of reserpine. Ballestero also prescribed a once-a-month injection of a testosterone drug similar to what Hemingway had been taking orally since 1953. In September, Dr. Herrera continued the Serpasil, renewed Whychol for Hemingway's liver condition, and put him on Oreton, a steroid, to maintain male sex characteristics; Doriden, for a short time, to calm him down; and Ritalin, a mild central nervous system stimulant, to control impulsivity and hyperactivity.[23] He was now taking one drug to sleep, another to control his overactive mind, another to treat his damaged liver, and male hormones to leaven the results. There was no information available on how this pharmacological stew might interact. Some of these drugs, like Seconal, were not to be taken if drinking alcohol—a warning Ernest had ignored for years, but was now forced to obey.[24]

Returning to Finca Vigia with its attendant responsibilities did nothing to lessen Ernest's post-European depression. That his swollen liver which so alarmed Dr. Monnier was a bit less noticeable, and that his blood pressure was much lower did nothing to mitigate the loss of alcohol, upon which he had become dependent without ever admitting it. First he cut back on hard liquor, stopping completely on March 5; then he began limiting himself to "light wines," two glasses at supper. It was a painful and boring experience, facing the day completely sober. When Winston Guest stopped drinking, Ernest said he grew suspicious of his old friend. Now he could say the same about himself. He thought he had become a boring person to live with, and the only sovereign cure for being around a bore was the alcohol forbidden him. It was similar, he said, to driving a racing car without oil for lubrication.[25]

Along with his enlarged liver, Hemingway brought back from Paris a set of new luggage stuffed full of memories. In the storage room of the Ritz, management found old, forgotten trunks left there when Ernest and Pauline were moving out of the city in 1930. Four days before sailing on the *Ile de France*, Hemingway wrote Lee Samuels of finding his early manuscripts, many of the stories in holograph, some still in the blue copy books he used in the earliest Paris days. Some of it, he said, "was pretty exciting to see."[26] Samuels, a prosperous tobacco broker in Havana, was Ernest's longtime friend and admirer, his sometime banker always good for a loan, and the silent partner in the sale of Hemingway manuscripts when ready cash was needed. These selective sales, which do not appear to have been declared as taxable income by Hemingway, were always a possibility if financial times got really tough. When Ernest told Samuels that the discovery made the trip worth while, he meant financially, but those manuscripts and fragments would soon contribute to the memoirs Hemingway promised to write.[27] Back at the Finca in March, he spent several days sorting his treasure into coherent piles, remembering smells and sounds of a Paris long disappeared, seeing faces of all the old friends, hearing voices now dead. Jim Joyce, Scott and Zelda Fitzgerald, Gertrude Stein, Harry Crosby, Ernest Walsh, Jules Pascin, Ford Madox Ford, and most importantly, Pauline—the dancers all departed, the dancehalls closed down.

CHAPTER 20

Cuba Libre

April 1957 to December 1958

Ernest and Mary remained at the Finca through an extraordinarily hot, humid summer that dulled the appetite, ruined the fishing, and sharpened their tempers. Working steadily on his novel about the loss of Eden, Ernest's attention to his writing was consistently broken by a series of crises and emotional disruptions. His oldest son, Jack, now working as a stockbroker in Havana, became ill, forcing him to bed for two months. In June, Ernest learned that his old Paris days friend, Evan Shipman, was dead.[1] There were continuing problems with rental and upkeep of the Key West property, held jointly by Ernest, Patrick, and Gregory. With Pat in Africa, Greg constantly moving or not answering mail, and Ernest in Cuba, the simplest decision took weeks to reach. Meanwhile in Hollywood, where *A Farewell to Arms* was being remade, David Selznick was rewriting the love story in a more believable fashion which infuriated Hemingway, who had no control over the script.[2]

Hemingway's mail and phone conversations with Alfred Rice were equally frustrating. No matter what directions Ernest gave to Rice, he frequently managed to ignore or misinterpret them, sometimes acting as a literary agent without portfolio and without Ernest's consent. In August, Rice submitted a distribution of income from the Key West property showing that there was little or no profit, but giving no details on how the income was spent. Ernest was furious.[3] Inexplicably maladroit, Rice, each year, turned the Hemingway income tax return into a marathon event. Because of

303

Ernest's high earnings, he was forced to make quarterly tax payments against expected income. For this purpose, Hemingway set up a special account at the Morgan Guaranty, which for some reason bore no interest even though it usually had $50,000–$70,000 in it. Because Rice arranged for most of the foreign royalties to flow through his office rather than remain in foreign accounts, Ernest's income was always far higher than it might have been, pushing him into the highest tax bracket: for every taxable dollar he earned, eighty-one cents went to the government. Throughout the 1950s, Hemingway's tax bill ranged from $60,000 to $80,000 a year on gross incomes of less than $200,000.

Each morning began early, Ernest standing in front of his typewriter, pecking away at the story of David Bourne and his two women, Catherine and Marita, falling deeper into the abyss of sexual confusion. David wants to write stories about Africa; Catherine wants him to write the story of their marriage. There in the isolated village of Grau du Roi, where the fishing boats were docked literally at the fisherman's door, David was, bit by bit, giving up control of his life to the two women. It was all very exciting at first, and then more complicated and more exciting, with haircuts and blond bleaches, naked romps on far beaches, and nights with no rules. By midmorning, sweat was running down the seams of Ernest's face. On a good day he wrote until late morning, then went to the pool to swim his laps. On a not so good day, he worked on the tax statement for Rice or the list of questions from *The Paris Review*. Against his better judgment, Ernest agreed to participate in the *Review*'s author interview series, not realizing it would be thirty-two pages of questions. On March 4, he spent three and a half prime morning hours answering only three of editor George Plimpton's questions, which he found "profoundly uninteresting."[4]

When it wasn't Plimpton or Rice, it was the problem of how to get Ezra Pound out of the crazy house. Despite Ezra's difficult, insulting letters to MacLeish, Archie never stopped working the political scene, gathering White House support. Robert Frost, who personally disliked Ezra, supported MacLiesh's effort, albeit with misgivings. Tom Eliot in London added his name to the support group, and Hemingway signed every letter that Archie drafted and pledged $1,500 to be given to Pound to relocate when released. Unfortunately, because Pound was permitted visitors at St. Elizabeth's, he attracted among others, John Kasper, who started an "Ez for Prez" campaign. With Kasper's help, Pound continued to publish tracts on economic reform and political maleficence, which did nothing to help MacLeish's appeal.[5] In June 1957, Archie updated Ernest on the state of their mission, asking him to write one more letter stating his argument

> that Ezra has been in there for eleven years; that you under-stand the psychos say he can never be brought to trial; that his continued incarceration under those circumstances has already done us considerable damage abroad . . . that he is a very great poet . . . which raises considerations which . . . should be kept in mind since one of the great pastimes abroad is nailing our asses to the barn door as bloody materialists who care nothing for art or artists.[6]

Ernest was more than willing to write the letter, but feared that Ezra would not refrain from making political statements, nor from associating with men like Kasper. He could see the media all too easily needling Pound into racist statements.[7] In the letter MacLeish requested be written to Frost, Hemingway emphasized that he could not abide Pound's politics, his support of fascism, or his anti-Semitic and racist views. Nevertheless, Ezra was a great poet, a rare person, for whom a bit of mercy was not out of the question. If he were to die in St. Elizabeth's, the rest of the world would never understand. Citing the political problems of other great poets—Dante, Byron, Verlaine—Hemingway said their poetry outlasted the memory of their offenses. Let it be that way with Ezra.[8] Finally, on April 18, 1958, the indictment of treason against Pound was dismissed because he was and would always be incompetent to stand trial. On May 7 of that year he walked out of St. Elizabeth's free to return to Italy, where he told reporters, "All America is an insane asylum."[9] In his pocket was Hemingway's check for $1,500.

In August 1957, mired in one of his periodic funks about expenditures, Hemingway wrote up a "situation report" for Mary, listing his anticipated expenses that were growing out of control:

Cost of keeping Mary's mother in a rest home	$5,170
Jack Hemingway, various bills	$4,376
Gregory Hemingway	$7,860
Finca Vigia $3,000/month	$36,000
Income Tax (six months)	$40,000

He complained that no one (read, Mary) was making any attempt to hold down expenses. Due to his own unpopularity (read, irritable as hell), he was afraid to make suggestions, but he did note that despite his not drinking, the monthly liquor bill had gone up. His health, he reported, was improving: weight at 203 down from 220; cholesterol reduced from 428 to 208 due to diet and Mary's fine care. He noted that he was in the last half of the sixth month of not drinking, limited to two glasses of wine with dinner. He could not eat out in Havana because it was impossible to do on so little alcohol. He became very "nervous," which made him "unpopular."[10] Whenever Hemingway displayed such concern about money, its lack or its expenditure, he was frequently on the down slope of a depressed period. His detailed and frequent references to the effects of not drinking indicate that the drugs to control his "nervousness" were not working. That he called his condition "nervous" was even more disturbing, for that was the very word Ernest and his sisters once used in Oak Park to describe their father's deteriorating mental state. In 1904, Clarence Hemingway took his first self-prescribed rest cure for his "nerves." He suffered similar despondency and irritability in 1907–09 and 1917–19. Each time he moved further into isolation from his family. By 1928, when he put a pistol to his temple and ended his life, he was suffering from diabetes, angina, hypertension, and severe depression—a condition similar to Ernest's own that summer of 1957.[11]

Despite his physical ills, Hemingway was incredibly productive from late spring all through the summer and into the fall. Visitors came and went, meals were served, fishing provided, but he wrote no matter who arrived. Denis Zaphiro, the game ranger from Kenya, came by invitation and stayed four months, providing Mary the male attention so lacking from Ernest. While Zaphiro was at the Finca, the whole house was awakened at four one morning by a squad of nine Cuban soldiers "looking for a certain oppositionist. No search was carried out and the patrol left. . . . However, the next morning Machakosa [one of the Hemingway dogs] was found dead near the kitchen steps. The dog had been struck on the side of the head with the butt of a rifle or some blunt instrument."[12] Somewhere in the hills of Cuba, two young revolutionaries—Fidel Castro and Che Guevara—were beginning to worry the oppressive Batista government. In the few letters Hemingway wrote that year, he never mentioned anything political, knowing that his American citizenship would be no protection if the night patrol came for him. His lifelong study of revolutions told him that his class would be the first to go. It was not long before bombs were exploding in Havana. By the time one went off in San Francisco de Paula near the Finca, Ernest was already looking for a safe haven to wait out the fall of Batista and its aftermath.

Before Zaphiro returned to Africa, Ernest took a ten-day break to fly with Mary and Denis to New York for the Sugar Ray Robinson–Carmen Basilio boxing match. They put up at the Hotel Westbury on the east side of Central Park, with Ernest paying all the bills.[13] Toots Shor, the restaurateur, picked them up in his Cadillac on fight night. With almost ringside seats, they had a clear view of Sugar Ray's footwork so rare it might have been choreographed and Basilio's battered face puffing up between rounds. Blood and sweat popped off faces with each blow. Other evenings were less visceral, more cultural. One night Ernest dined with Marlene Dietrich while Mary and Denis supped on the in-port *Ile de France* with Dr. Monnier. There were nights at Broadway plays and fall afternoons at the ball park watching the Yankees.[14] Returning to Cuba via a short stop in Washington, D.C., Ernest quickly settled back into his writing routine, alternating between the loss of Eden novel and a new book he started almost accidentally in July when *Atlantic Monthly* asked him to contribute to its hundredth anniversary issue.

His first impulse was to write an essay for the magazine about his relationship with Scott Fitzgerald, but he soon put that sketch away, sending the *Atlantic* two new short stories: "A Man of the World" about a grotesquely blinded bar-room brawler, and "Get a Seeing-Eyed Dog" about a recently blinded writer coming to terms with his condition.[15] Between 1940 and 1957, he had published only two books, but locked away he now had the three-part Bimini book largely completed; in his work room there were 200,000 words written on the African novel; and a large portion of what later was published as *The Garden of Eden* in draft. With two long novels in various stages, he was now starting yet another book, which would become *A Moveable Feast*.

His drafts and revisions of *The Sun Also Rises*, one of the several manuscripts stored at the Ritz, had two unpublished scenes concerning Ford Madox Ford which needed little revision. Soon he was thinking of the memoir as a collection of "short novels"—each chapter a self-contained story. This structure was similar to that of *In Our Time*, his first collection of short stories, which he joined with one-page vignettes that he called "unwritten stories." Quickly he roughed out possibilities for chapters: first meetings with Pound, Stein, and Joyce; Ford Madox Ford and the *transatlantic review*; skiing at Schruns; the Paris apartments; the cafés; meeting Fitzgerald; trips to Pamplona.[16] By Thanksgiving, when Ernest and Mary, both flu-ridden, were bedded down at opposite ends of the Finca, Hemingway was well into his memoirs, averaging a thousand words a day. As he moved back and forth between the Eden novel and early Paris, he was well aware that he was writing about the same period from different perspectives, and that both books tied back to the memories of Thomas Hudson in the Bimini novel. As the year was running out, Leonard Lyons showed up for a Finca lunch, reporting later that Hemingway had put aside his "big novel" to work on an "exciting new project" unlocked by the recovery of his early manuscripts. Lyons said that Hemingway read to him "pieces he's just finished on F. Scott Fitzgerald, Ford Madox Ford and Gertrude Stein."[17]

On New Year's Eve, the phone call from Minnesota told Mary that her mother was dead. She was on a flight out of Havana on the first day of 1958, leaving Ernest with a relatively quiet Finca, which lasted only a few days before a winter storm tore a tree limb off the giant ceiba tree, smashing a hole in the roof above Mary's bed. She returned late that evening to find her bed soaked but the roof repaired. The rest of the winter was one storm after another, bringing unnaturally cold temperatures and effectively ruining the winter fishing. In the village of San Francisco de Paula, Hemingway reported there was unemployment and hunger;[18] in Havana, violence continued—bombs by Castro's rebels and savagery by Batista's national forces. Dead bodies were being dropped off in rural ditches just as they had in the bad old days with Machado. The revolution that Hemingway anticipated was arriving at his doorstep.

Late winter through spring into summer, visitors came to the Finca to be fed and entertained. In January, it was Ernest's old fishing and hunting friend Tommy Shevlin, Hollywood people, and New York columnists; in February, journalists and Hollywood executives; in March, more columnists and sports writers; in May, the Canadian ambassador. When visitors were not interrupting, Alfred Rice and the annual income tax misunderstandings could ruin a morning or sometimes a week. Simply keeping track of his savings accounts, checking accounts, and his seven safety deposit boxes in five different banks in four different towns was a major accounting problem. Having gone almost a year without drinking hard liquor, in March 1958, Hemingway began not only taking his two glasses of Spanish *rioja* with supper but also allowing himself whiskeys.

By that March, "Papa's Liquor" bill for the month was $94 for wine and $45 for whiskey; Mary's was $95.69 for vodka and gin. Throughout the summer, the liquor bill varied, but Hemingway's personal consumption was averaging four to six bottles of whiskey a month and two or three cases of wine. To visitors he claimed he was drinking only light wines and one or two whiskeys, but the numbers say that his need for alcohol was regaining control of his life.[19] Combined with his continued daily intake of tranquilizers, antidepressants, heart medicine, testosterone steroids, and large doses of vitamins, Hemingway's drinking, which was forbidden with several of the drugs, contributed to his steadily deteriorating health. His immune system was noticeably deteriorating: he was sick more often than in previous years, and it took him longer to recover. His condition was also having its effect on Mary. By March, she was taking one pill and Ernest two of Doriden, a sedative to calm the nerves. When used with alcohol, Doriden was potentially addictive and its effects multiplied.[20] It is little wonder that house guests found Ernest nodding off at night in his large living-room chair.

Despite the accumulative effect of drugs and alcohol, Hemingway rose up every morning to write the Paris sketches: Scott worrying about the size of his penis; Cheever Dunning out of his mind on drugs; Zelda Fitzgerald's need to destroy Scott; the pomposity of Ford; Sylvia's bookshop; the loss of his manuscripts. Connecting the pieces was the youthful Hemingway learning his trade: a portrait of the artist as a young man on his way up. In six months the draft was finished, but lacked a conclusion and a title. Titles were always tough, but since finishing *A Farewell to Arms* (1929), he usually had no trouble with conclusions. Yet now, turning fifty-nine in July, he was unable to end either the Paris book or the African novel. He would have the same problem with the Eden novel.

While Ernest was living largely in seclusion during the day, retreating into himself when he was not writing about the Paris days, Mary was assessing her own condition. In notes to herself, she wrote:

> You try all your life to merge. Falling in love is building the beautiful deception of two in one. But it is a dream. You are always alone. There are thousands of contented [people] who are never bothered by this. Who knows it and . . . can live with it . . . is strong. . . . "Togetherness" is not a cup of Lipton tea. It is wordless desperation.[21]

It was a good summer for taking stock, for the Cuba around them was crumbling into uncontrolled violence. From their village, young men had been arrested, tortured, and imprisoned on suspicion of aiding the Castro rebels. In April, the police sergeant who led the night sortie on the Finca was killed along with several others. Stories circulated about bodies found in wells, women beaten and tortured, informers on both sides found dead with their tongues cut out. A threat of a general strike hung in the air like a whiff of gas, and those who remembered the general strike bringing down the Machado regime in the 1930s held their collective breath.

At the Finca in July, Ernest and Mary lived cautiously but without any political intrusions. When Ernest stopped work on his Paris memoir, Mary began typing it for his revisions while he turned his full attention to the Eden book, which he did not share with Mary as he had with *The Old Man and the Sea* and the Paris book. In August, Hemingway's concentration was broken when he learned that *Esquire* magazine intended to reprint three of his Spanish Civil War stories in an anthology. Stating emphatically that *Esquire* had purchased only first serial rights to his stories, Hemingway directed Alfred Rice to forbid their republication, for he planned to revise and publish them himself in his next collection of short stories. As a peace offering, he said they could publish one story, "The Butterfly and the Tank."[22] Three days later, the story broke in the *New York Times*:

> Ernest Hemingway, stating that the passage of time could affect the public's reaction to a writer's work, instituted court action yesterday to prevent *Esquire* magazine from reprinting three short stories he wrote in the Thirties . . . in papers filed in Supreme Court yesterday by Alfred Rice, his attorney, Hemingway charged that to reprint the stories would do more than violate his property rights. Reprinting, he said, would also result in "great injury and irreparable damage" for reasons other than the commercial value of the stories.[23]

Hemingway was furious with the statements written by Rice and attributed to him. The *Times* story the next day was headlined:

HEMINGWAY SAYS HE WILL DROP SUIT.
"Those statements were made by my lawyer, Alfred Rice, and I have just called him up and given him hell for it," Mr. Hemingway said on the telephone . . . "two of the stories were not as good as I wanted them and I wanted to revise them before letting them go into book form."

In claiming that changing times also changed the way people might read the stories, Rice cited as an example "the writings of men during the time Russia was our ally to the present attitude of people to such men and their writings now that Russia is perhaps our greatest enemy." Ernest said pointedly that Rice may have meant well by such a statement, but that "it does not represent my view." It was not to change the political tone of the stories that he wished to revise them: "I only wanted to remove some of the clichés."[24]

Hemingway might have added that any publicity calling attention to his political position in the Thirties would also raise questions about his present political position in regard to the Batista government. Quickly, Ernest, Mary, and Gregorio took the *Pilar* far out into the Gulf Stream, where the men tore open bunks to take out "heavy rifles, sawed-off shot guns, hand grenades and canisters and belts of ammunition for automatic rifles" and threw the arsenal overboard.[25] Had the government discovered the cache, Heming-way would have been hard-pressed to explain their presence. Immediately after the *Times* stories, Ernest contacted old Ketchum friends, Lloyd and Tillie Arnold, asking them to find a suitable place to rent for the winter. On August 25, they told him the large and well-appointed Heiss house could be rented for $175 a month, to which Hemingway immediately agreed.[26] What may have appeared an overreaction to someone on the mainland, Hemingway's concern for the safety of himself and Mary was well grounded in a lifetime of observing how personal grudges had a way of killing old enemies once revolution set everyone free from the law. He may have been a great friend of the Cuban people, but in the dark of night he was just another rich Americano who was exploiting the Cuban poor. As he explained to Patrick, he was not being unduly frightened, not when one saw the kinds of murder going on all around him. It was not going to get any better soon. Batista would fall, and the new rulers would do some more killing to even things out. He was ready to move out of Cuba, for the rebel government that seemed inevitable would shut down the freedom of the coast to boats like the *Pilar*.[27]

Ernest and Mary spent most of September, when not in bed with bad colds, arranging matters at the Finca so that it would function smoothly while they were in Idaho. First, Mary flew to Chicago to visit friends; then, Ernest picked up Toby Bruce in Key West to be his driver, and on October 6 began the long cross-country drive, meeting Mary and continuing north and westward across the plains to Yellowstone and over to Ketchum by October 15. There they would winter while Ernest hoped to finish both the Paris book and the Eden book, which was already at 160,000 words. Then they would go to Spain in May for the San Isidro *corrida*, remaining there all summer. In the fall they might go on to Africa now that the Suez Canal was reopened. That was the plan as the fall hunting season opened with birds plentiful and flying strong in the dry wind.[28]

In Ketchum, Alfred Rice's latest bad news on income taxes caught up with the Hemingways. With $170,000 income from his published writing and another $15,000 from stock market investments, minus $31,200 for business expenses and personal deductions, Hemingway was left with $153,800 taxable in the 81 percent bracket. The bottom line was a 1958 tax bill of $95,000. After his quarterly installment in January 1959, Ernest would still owe $25,000 on April 15.[29] With almost $90,000 in his New York checking account, Ernest was able to pay his taxes without much pain, and he always insisted that Rice never cut corners when it came to the government. His attitude was partially patriotic, but it was also his residual antipathy for any situation that would take him before the law. But in the Idaho sunshine, Ernest seemed unfazed by his tax bill or anything else. Soon Mary was reporting to Hotchner that Ernest was back into his regular routine, his weight "down to 205, pressure okay, drinking with caution," and back to writing in the mornings and shooting in the afternoons. She urged Hotchner to join them, saying there was plenty of room in the huge house.[30] The Heiss log cabin, located within a stone's throw of Christiania's Bar and Restaurant, became their command post for the fall hunting season.

Those who knew Ernest from his earlier years in Ketchum were disturbed to find him appearing more aged than he actually was, his beard white, his speech slower. "When he came back after [those accidents]," Bud Purdy found him changed. "He was really whacked on the head on that one airplane wreck. I think that's pretty much what did it. He wasn't as sharp after that, I don't think."[31] Locals like Taylor Williams, the Purdys, Don Anderson, Forrest "Duke" MacMullen, Dr. George Saviers, and Don Atkinson formed a Ketchum version of the "summer people" Ernest once gathered around himself at Walloon Lake after the first war, or at Pamplona for the bullfights or skiing at Schruns in the 1920s, or fishing in Key West in the 1930s. Hunters all, they enjoyed the bird season in the pheasant fields around Dietrich and Gooding, along Silver Creek and the irrigation canals where the ducks gathered.

In the Heiss garage, Ernest hung ducks, snipe, and pheasant to age, checking them each day, sniffing for the ripeness he favored. Don Anderson preferred his fresh from the fields, but Hemingway kept his hung by their heads until they were almost ready to pull loose on their own. There he also kept and fed Mr. Owl. Forrest MacMullen explained how the predator came to be there:

> we were hunting, and we'd spooked some birds, and had knocked one down, and the owl went for the bird, and Papa winged it. And he felt bad right after that, he says "I shouldn't have shot that owl." And that's when we picked the owl up, and took it back up to Ketchum, put it in the garage you know, with the firewood. And we used to maybe get a road-killed rabbit that was fairly fresh and we'd take them up, and we even on occasions would sit under a tree down in Silver Creek area and shoot blackbirds out of the trees. So it was the case that there were times when we were just out shooting blackbirds for Mr. Owl.[32]

On Fridays the Ketchum "family" would gather in the Hemingways' front room to watch the Friday-night fights on television. There was always food, wine, and plenty of analysis. One evening, Bud Purdy remembered,

> We were having a party up at his place for Friday Night Fights—God, he just loved to see those, hear 'em or see 'em on television. And I was, you know, throwing my arms around, he had his granny glasses sitting on the mantle, God I'm knocking 'em on the floor—bam! and broke 'em. Now you'd think that'd

make a guy unhappy—"Oh! Never mind, that won't hurt a damn thing," he says. He must have had another pair, I don't know, but anyway I broke his glasses, and that didn't get him excited at all. He was very—I know with us he was always—God he just treated us like royalty.

In public places that winter season, it was not like the old days in Ketchum when Ernest could go about his life unimpeded by strangers seeking his handshake, autograph, or a photo standing beside him. Mary protected him as much as she was able. Ruth Purdy remembered that those nights when they would eat lamb shanks together at the Christiania,

> Mary would have him in the back, away from the general public, and then she would sit on the edge. They usually put us in that round corner over there in the Christiania, and Bud and I would sit here, and then Papa next to me, and then Mary on the outside so that when people came up, they—she could fend them off. But he was always so generous with his autographs and having pictures taken with him. So if it was possible, Mary would try to protect him, because people, you know, they don't think, and they would take so much of his time when he wanted to be enjoying his lunch or his dinner.[33]

No longer were Ernest and Mary habitués of the Sun Valley Lodge, for now they were more reclusive, sticking with those hunters with whom Ernest felt secure. Mornings he was writing either on his Paris memoir or on David Bourne's fictive life at Grau du Roi. Until the late January snows closed out the bird hunting, there were afternoons in the fields and along the watercourses. With a picnic lunch set out on the tailgate of the station wagon, a fire built to cook and warm, jokes to be told, the air clean, and the sky a brilliant blue, it was the old life recovered. In the field, Ernest seldom took the first shot, preferring to shoot backup, but when he shot, he seldom missed. Before, during, or after shooting, he was always careful, enforcing if necessary the unwritten rules of the shotgun: never approach the car with the breech closed; never point the barrel at anyone; cross a fence with great care, first placing the shotgun against the fence post. And never go into the fields twice with the same fool. As Forrest MacMullen recalled, "One time we were in the stock rack on this pickup at Bud Purdy's place, and this fellow was standing next to Papa, and Papa wasn't looking at him, and the fellow pulled the gun up and fired right next to Papa's ear, and Papa went 'woof,' and I saw the look in Papa's eyes, and that old boy never went out with us again after that incident."

There in Ketchum, where the winter snow did not fall until the new year, Ernest's life became quite simplified: early morning writing, lunches of cold duck or hot soup, bird-hunting afternoons once or twice a week, quiet evenings sometimes with friends, sometimes alone with Mary, and occasional suppers out with his doctor George Saviers and his wife, or with Bud and Ruth Purdy. There was almost no literary talk, for most of his hunting friends were not bent that way, saying right out that they had never read any of Ernest's work. He liked them the better for it, for it was not his notoriety but his outdoors skills that drew them to him. Only Dr. Saviers admitted to being a Hemingway fan from his college days.

When asked whom Ernest admired, Forrest MacMullen quickly said "the mountain men."

> He envied those fellas coming down when the traders would come up and trade with the trappers for their furs and for the furs they'd exchange whiskey, lead shot, powder, and a few items, maybe pots or pans or whatever, and they used to have foot races and shooting contests. I guess they used to get drunk and chase the Indian women up there. Papa mentioned that several, several times, as far as envying the mountain men the enjoyment they got out of life.[34]

A close Cuban friend once said that Ernest was "a man for another era," born either too late or before his time, a man unwilling to conform to midcentury expectations.[35]

CHAPTER 21

Exiles from Eden

January 1959 to January 1960

From Ketchum, Ernest and Mary stayed up to date on the Cuban revolution's progress. At the very moment that wire services mistakenly reported the Castro rebels' defeat, Batista and his close associates were leaving the country by plane for the safety of the Dominican Republic, taking with them as much of the Cuban treasury as possible. In Havana nightclubs and casinos, tourists celebrating New Year's Eve were hustled back to their cruise ships in the harbor. The next morning in Ketchum, with newspapers hounding Ernest for a statement, he told them: "I believe in the historical necessity for the Cuban revolution, and I believe in its long range aims. I do not wish to discuss personalities or day to day problems." That afternoon, he enlarged his statement for the *New York Times*, adding that he was "delighted" with the revolution's progress. As soon as he hung up, Mary urged him to modify his statement, reminding him that he had no idea what was happening in Havana. Firing squads might be already at bloody work. Reluctantly, he called the *Times* back to change "delighted" to "hopeful." More privately, Ernest admitted that Castro's problem was not the departed Batista regime but the deeply entrenched American interests whose money bought them sweet deals in the past and would be difficult to displace. Castro, he said, was facing enormous problems.[1]

On January 3, snow finally came to Ketchum, piling up two feet over the next four days and marking the end of the long hunting season. Toward the end of January, Bud Purdy invited the seasoned hunters out to his ranch on Silver Creek for the annual magpie shoot, marking the absolute end of field activity until the following autumn. In the Whicher house where they had moved before Christmas, Hemingway settled in to write steadily on *The Garden of Eden*. Cut off from his research library at the Finca, he ordered through the Scribner Book Store an expensive copy of *Records of Big Game Hunting, 1892* to go along with his second copy of *The Wanderings of an Elephant Hunter*. In Hemingway's novel, David Bourne's recollection of his father's elephant hunt was grounded in the accurate details that were Hemingway's trademark.

In February, his semiannual royalty report from Scribner's showed an income of $21,295 on sales of 39,071 copies of his work. The only book apparently out of print was *Across the River and into the Trees*; his best seller continued to be *The Old Man and the Sea*— 15,585 copies. Although these figures did not reflect the considerable income from foreign translations and television adaptations, Hemingway's six-month income from Scribner's alone was slightly more than the $20,000 annual median family income of the top 5 percent of the nation. Hemingway usually had more money in his special tax account than 99 percent of the nation made in a year. Had he left his foreign income in the country of origin, paying local taxes on it, his income after all taxes would have exceeded $100,000 a year. In a nation where only 29,000 tax returns listed "author" as profession and probably only 5 percent of those were able to live on their income, Hemingway's financial position was substantial, not even counting his almost $100,000 worth of blue chip stocks, his property in Key West, Cuba, a lot in Bimini, and four newly purchased lots in Ketchum. For the young, experimental writer of those early Paris days who made a fashion statement out of his relative poverty, Ernest Hemingway had come a long way from the cold-water flat above the lumber yard on rue Notre-Dame-des-Champs. Now all but finished was his wry, nostalgic Paris memoir, remembering himself even poorer than he ever was.[2]

That winter in Ketchum, Ernest worked steadily on the complex relationships between artists and women in *The Garden of Eden*. His fictional writer David Bourne was involved in sexual experi-

ments with his wife Catherine and her newfound friend, Marita—
a story Ernest did not think publishable in his lifetime. However, on
his night table lay a newly minted copy of Vladimir Nabokov's
Lolita, in which Humbert Humbert's fascination with his prepu-
bescent stepdaughter was more sexually outrageous than anything
Ernest's triad did in the dark.[3] Working as he did in bursts, the
manuscript of *Garden* was now close to ten years in its making.
Approaching its final length—over two thousand pages—the draft
needed to be revised for consistency just as his African novel did.[4]
When younger, it was one book at a time: write, revise, and publish.
These later books were being written under far different circumstances. Afterward, many would say that because he left them
unfinished, he was no longer able to make the revisions they needed. But to make that judgment one must ignore the talent and
diversity at work in *The Old Man and the Sea, Across the River,* and
the posthumous *A Moveable Feast.* One must also ignore the massive revisions he made to the Bimini novel, and completely disregard the possibility that these "unfinished" novels were linked in
ways that made their endings interdependent. Under no financial
pressure to bring any of these books to completion, he always imagined there would be time to finish them. They were to be his legacy, his most complex undertaking. It was like working a crossword
puzzle in three dimensions. All he needed was time, which, unfortunately, was no longer on his side. It did not take a medical degree
for him to see the truth in the mirror as he carefully combed his
hair forward to cover his balding head.

On February 18, when Hemingway thought he had the conclusion of *Garden* in sight, his concentration was shattered by the
death of Taylor Williams, his oldest Ketchum friend from the early
days of Sun Valley. Having recuperated from a cerebral hemorrhage suffered the previous spring, the Colonel, as Ernest fondly
called Williams, died suddenly when the wall of his stomach
opened, flooding his lungs. Taking Taylor's death particularly hard,
Ernest was one of the pall bearers at the funeral. Mary, equally dis-
tressed, wrote to Charley Sweeny, himself recovering from a recent
stroke, that she was depressed "with this fucking business of growing old." It was so easy when they were young to be courageous, but

with age "the exercise of courage narrows down, becomes less fun, and so it's harder . . . what a bloody bore . . . when you begin to wear out. . . . Papa once said to me that he had never given his body any quarter, and I think that's the way to do it."[5] At fifty, with all of Ernest's friends going under, Mary was painfully aware that her husband and his old world were rapidly aging.

By the end of February, Ernest and Mary were packing up to return to Cuba, but with every intention of establishing a place of their own in Ketchum. Despite tourist traffic, there was easy access to diverse bird hunting, and Ernest found it a good place to write. Mary was less enthusiastic about the isolation of Ketchum, where interesting friends were few and cultural activities minimal, but what Ernest wanted she wanted. While she was making floor plans to build a house on their four-lot block, Ernest became interested in Dan Topping's hilltop home, which was on the market for $50,000. On seventeen acres with Big Wood River running below it, the gray, concrete exterior executed in the fashion of the Sun Valley Lodge resembled a fortress. On March 16, without having reached a decision, they left Ketchum with Ed Hotchner, driving south to Las Vegas and the next day to Phoenix. There in a motel room, they watched the second half of Hotchner's television adaptation of *For Whom the Bell Tolls*. It was a short drive the following day to Tucson, Arizona, to visit the seventy-four-year-old painter and old friend, Waldo Peirce. Then east past the O/bar/O ranch in southern New Mexico to follow the Rio Grande down to the Gulf, before bearing east to New Orleans. There Hotchner left them to complete the 4,000-mile drive on their own to Key West. On March 29, they flew into Havana to find the revolution a true socialist uprising, the kind Ernest once hoped for during the Spanish Civil War.[6]

But he also knew that revolutions had a way of turning out badly in the long run. It still might be best to have a safe haven in which to wait things out. Almost as soon as he got back to Cuba, Ernest put a $50,000 check in the mail to buy Topping's Ketchum house outright.[7] Home at the Finca for less than a month, Ernest and Mary labored over unanswered mail, outstanding bills, necessary repairs, and contingency plans for their household while they went to Spain for the summer *corridas*. One of the first new letters to arrive came from Charlie Scribner, Jr., who wanted to tap into the college trade market with a new collection of Hemingway short stories. He was confident that such an anthology would be quite profitable, even more so if Ernest would do short introductions to each story: "a short summary of the circumstances under which it was written . . . [or] a word or two about a character, or how you feel about the story." Ernest responded immediately asking about length and due dates. Scribner suggested 2,500 words minimum, maximum as many words as Ernest cared to write.[8] Feeling that he was in époque mode, Ernest agreed to write the essay. During two manic periods of writing—1947 to 1950, and 1955 to 1958—he published two novels and laid aside four other books all but finished. In his Cuban safety deposit box he had stored the three-part book which would become *Islands in the Stream* and the 200,000 words written on the African novel, *True at First Light*. With him at the Finca he had forty-two chapters of *The Garden of Eden* ready to photostat for safekeeping, and the all but finished Paris memoir, *A Moveable Feast*. The plan was to publish the Paris memoir in 1960; the following year, Scribner would publish a new edition of *Death in the Afternoon* with a lengthy appendix of material Hemingway would gather the coming summer of 1959.[9]

What was less apparent to him and those around him was the emotional pattern of the last twenty years: periods of intensive writing followed by fallow, emotionally depressed periods during which his behavior became erratic and increasingly paranoid. Each trip down his emotional roller coaster took him deeper into his private demons. Each time down, it was more difficult to climb back up. But each time he recovered, his writing exploded. In January 1959, he was peaking from such a productive period. The next thirty months was the dark trip down, this time into newfound depths. The various daily medications that he took for his blood pressure, nerves, liver, insomnia, eyesight, and fatigue were already working against each other, particularly when he was drinking. For ten years he had been taking weekly doses of Oreton-M, a synthetic testosterone that "stimulates the development of male sexual characteristics . . . both the physical and mental status are improved."[10] Usually prescribed for late-developing children, impotence, and aging males during their climacteric, the effects of long-term Oreton usage were not established. Nor was it known what effects Oreton might have when taken with drugs like Serpasil (to relieve anxiety, tension, and insomnia), Doriden (to tranquilize), Ritalin (to stimulate the central nervous system), Eucanil, Seconal (to get to sleep), massive doses of vitamins A and B, and other drugs for an alcohol-damaged liver. Nor was it known what effect alcohol might have on this pharmacological stew, but when Hemingway returned to Spain for the summer his daily wine consumption would be an acid test.

While Ernest kept as invisible as possible at the Finca, the Castro revolution was rapidly transforming the political face of Cuba. Batista officials were under arrest; trials of Batista soldiers ended with public executions, which enflamed the American press, the same press that had largely ignored the violence that characterized the Batista years. In early April, Castro announced that he would visit the United States as a "truth operation," an attempt to quell rumors, answer questions, and refute false claims about his government. As soon as Hemingway heard of Castro's plan, he asked José Luis Herrera, a strong Castro supporter, to set up a meeting between the writer and the revolutionary. As Herrera remembered it,

> Ernest insisted that a meeting with Castro be set up when he learned that Castro was going to New York at the head of the Cuban delegation to the United Nations. He wanted Castro to be briefed on American politicians and the idiosyncrasies of the American people. Castro assigned Vazquez Candela, assistant editor of the newspaper *Revolution*, to go to Hemingway's house. Late at night at Vigia, Ernest opened the door with a pistol in his pocket.[11]

Unarmed, Vazquez arrived with serious misgivings that the trip was worth making, but after two hours conversation with Ernest, he changed his mind. Sitting in the living room, sipping an Italian white wine, with Bach and Ravel playing softly on the Capehart, Ernest put Vazquez at his ease. The journalist was amazed that Hemingway was concerned that Fidel be warned of the traps he would face with the press and others. Hemingway spoke from his briefing notes, which included information of the biases of various journalists and their publications. He warned that Fidel would be heckled viciously by some organizations, heckled by college students to see how he would react. At all costs, he must not become angry, lose his temper, or make threats. He must expect trick questions from his enemies on *Time* magazine and the *Miami Herald*. He must have direct answers on the influence of communism in the new Cuba. If he could promise to oppose communism, he could have anything he wanted from America. But the ongoing executions must be explained, and the general calmness in Havana and across the country should be emphasized. When Vazquez parted, Hemingway asked that he tell his comrades that Ernest strongly supported the actions of the revolution. In July, when Castro appeared on *This Is Your Life* on TV, he was asked to explain the executions taking place in Cuba. He said, "Let me tell you what Hemingway thinks about that: 'The executions in Cuba are a necessary phenomena. The military criminals who were executed by the revolutionary government received what they deserved.'"[12]

On April 22, Ernest and Mary stowed their considerable luggage on board the *Constitution* bound for Algeciras, Spain, settled into their stateroom, and located the first-class bar. A quick, uneventful passage set them down on the Spanish dock, where their host, Bill Davis, with the practiced eye of a man who collected celebrities, met them. Their considerable luggage was piled on top of a rented pink Ford for the drive to Málaga, just beyond which lay the Davis domain, the doubly gated property called La Consula. Four years later, when the photographer Ben Sonnenberg visited with Bill and Annie Davis, he felt that he was living in a more expensive version of Sara and Gerald Murphy's Villa America at Antibes during the Twenties. At La Consula, the great, the wealthy, the talented, and the famous gathered under its arcades and around its glittering, sixty-foot swimming pool to be entertained, fêted, and flattered by Bill Davis, who "wore blue deck shoes and white duck trousers and that kind of short-sleeved [polo] shirt. . . . He was bald and tall and built like an athlete . . . his mother's family had been the model for the Ambersons in Booth Tarkington's novel. . . . Bill had an obsessive interest in the very rich and their 'arrangements.'"[13] Exactly why the Hemingways were staying as houseguests at Consula was never completely clear to Mary—something about Bill being an old friend with great *afficion* for the *corrida*. Although Ernest would find plenty of ways to spend money that summer, Bill Davis was providing more largesse than either Ernest or Mary had experienced from previous hosts.

As soon as Ernest was moved into his second-floor room, he began working on the introduction to his short stories promised to Scribner's by June 1. As with so much that Hemingway wrote, this essay revealed more about his state of mind than it did about its purported subject: the art of his short story. Written in a voice hardened and condescending, the commentary, whose audience was to be high school and college students, was filled with failed humor, bewildering slang, and gratuitous comments on fellow writers. Belittling the goal of a long life, he advised his reader, "I cannot say fie upon it, since I have never fie-ed on anything yet. Shuck it off, Jack. Don't fie on it. . . . Do I hear a request for ballroom bananas? I do? Gentlemen, we have them for you in bunches." As for the well-made short story in which a gun hung on the wall early in the story must reappear later in some important way, he advised, "With a good enough writer, the chances are some jerk just hung it there to look at it. Gentlemen, you can't be sure. Maybe he was queer for guns, or maybe an interior decorator put it there. Or both."[14] That Hemingway actually thought such offhand comments were appropriate for his audience seems to indicate that either his head or his heart was not in the project. But there is a disturbing tone to his slangy language that harkens back to letters and drafts written in his black-ass period after returning from the European war.

When Mary typed the first draft of the essay, she was "dismayed" by what seemed to her to be "tendentious, truculent and smug . . . [containing] brutal, irrelevant references to a friend of ours." In a note to Ernest, she pointed out passages that needed to be cut, advising him that "This is not like you." Ernest bristled. He cut out the part about their "friend," but left in a long aside on Faulkner's small talent, which was another ominous sign.[15] Whenever he dug up his old grievance with Faulkner, he was usually on the dark side of his emotional curve. Faulkner, he claimed, was always making disparaging remarks about him but maybe that was just the "sauce" talking. That was Faulkner's problem: he drank too much and wrote when he was drunk. That and he talked too much. A writer, said Ernest while doing the same, should never talk too much.

On May 12, Ernest put aside the draft essay to pack up for the trip to Madrid, where Antonio Ordóñez was on the cartel for the San Isidro feria, the beginning of a long and bloody summer. Before leaving Consula, Ernest wrote George Saviers in Ketchum, insisting that he and his wife join Ernest's band of *corrida* gypsies at the Pamplona feria in July.[16] A similar invitation would be sent to Hotchner as a familiar pattern emerged: Ernest assembling a cadre of "summer people" to witness, carouse, and be instructed. The season's focus was the developing competition between Luis Miguel Dominguín, who was returning to the *corrida* from his early retirement, and his brother-in-law, Antonio Ordóñez, reputed to be the best matador in many years and also the son of Cayetano Ordóñez, who in 1925 fought as Niño de la Palma and became the fictional Pedro Romero in *The Sun Also Rises*. Not only was Antonio married to Carmen Dominguín, but both he and Luis were managed by Luis's two brothers. As Hemingway would note, "It looked very hard on family life and very good for bullfighting. It also looked very dangerous."[17] What Ernest did not anticipate was how hard the summer would be on him, his wife, and their marriage.

In the Twenties and early Thirties when Ernest and his wife (first Hadley, then Pauline) followed the *corridas* across Spain, they were not compelled to attend them all. After Pamplona and Valencia there was time to rest up for Madrid. This summer they were beginning on May 30 and continuing to late August, following Antonio back and forth across the wide expanse of Spain. With every *corrida* Hemingway became more involved with Antonio, whom he would watch from front-row seats or down in the narrow *callejon* between the *barrera* and the seats. He had no need for tickets for he came and went as part of Antonio's *cuadrilla*—his picadors, banderillos, personal surgeon, and assorted handlers—"our outfit," Ernest called it, as if he were back in the military. From

Cordoba to Seville in time to eat before watching the pics mutilate the bulls, Mary sick with fever, Ernest anxious. The next morning on the road to Madrid for a late lunch and the next afternoon, May 30, out to Aranjuez.

Sitting with Bill Davis and Ernest, their wives having returned to La Consula, was John Crosby for the *New York Herald Tribune*. On his second bull, Antonio performed at a level seldom seen. Crosby wrote:

> The lines of the passes became very simple, very slow. Just as a good painter eliminates and eliminates and eliminates, so a classic matador scorns the rococo trimmings. . . . Cape, man and bull blend into a single composition that hangs there in the air and imprints itself on the retina. . . . This was one of the moments that the true aficionado lives for, suffering through countless bad fights.

Then, suddenly, backing up on rough ground, making a back-to-the-bull pass, Antonio slipped, the cape moved aside, the bull caught him quickly with his horn, deep into his left buttock. Just as quickly the other matadors were in the ring, taking the bull away from the bleeding Ordóñez, now arguing with his handlers who wanted him to leave the ring. Refusing to do so, Antonio picked up his cape and painfully returned to his work.

> The crowd was hushed, respectful. To square his bull, Ordóñez made a slow pass, agonizingly slow. The bull charged, wheeled, and was still . . . Ordóñez sighted down his sword and with his ebbing strength went in over the horn. It was a marvelously clean and beautiful kill and, as his banderilleros carried him from the ring to the waiting ambulance . . . he was awarded both ears and the tail of the brave bull.[18]

In the Madrid hospital Antonio was repaired by skilled surgeons, and there he got the only kind of rest he would find that dangerous summer. Ernest and Bill Davis returned to La Consula to restore their own depleted energies.

In his writing room, Ernest finished and mailed his preface for the short stories, finished a short story "Black Ass at the

Crossroads," began writing up his notes on the bullfights, and answered mail. Hotchner was working out a four-story deal with CBS and their Buick sponsors which came together as Hemingway had specified. There would be four live shows bringing the H&H Corporation set up by Hotchner and Hemingway a total of $240,000 for basic rights and Hotchner's adaptations.[19] In New York, Charles Scribner, Jr., was trying his diplomatic best to draft his response to Ernest's preface, which was clearly inappropriate for almost any audience. He agreed with Ernest's list of stories to be included, but wanted to do some judicious editing of the preface. "You did not want to sound pompous," Scribner wrote, "and hit upon a kind of jocular informality. But I am afraid that, insofar as readers will not be expecting this, they may misinterpret it as condescension."[20] After digesting Scribner's response and weighing it in the same basket with Mary's less than enthusiastic critique, Ernest sent Scribner a brusque telegram to stop not only the preface but the entire short story project. It was, he said, a mistake to try to do three things at once. He would keep his attention totally focused on the *corrida*.[21] It was the first time that anyone at Scribner's had told him a piece of his writing was unpublishable.

On June 27, four weeks after his wounding, Antonio was back in his "suit of lights," entering the bull ring at Zaragoza with Luis Miguel Dominguín beside him, their first meeting in the summerlong, *mano-a-mano* competition, in which the two matadors would each face three bulls apiece in the same afternoon. The pattern would become so ingrained that Ernest could and did follow it in his sleep: drive, eat, dress, watch, eat again if nothing went wrong, sleep briefly to drive on the next morning. Some days there would be no time for sleep, and they would drive through the night: Zaragoza, Alicante, Barcelona, Burgos. By the time they reached Pamplona for the San Fermín feria, the *mano a mano* had caught the attention of American periodicals. *Sports Illustrated* wanted to publish Ernest's take on Antonio and Luis Miguel in the August feria at Málaga. Ernest wired back that he could not because the material would become part of his new edition of *Death in the Afternoon*.[22]

The San Fermín feria brought together in Pamplona Ernest's entire entourage: Mary, Bill and Annie Davis, George and Pat Saviers from Ketchum, Antonio who was not on the feria cartel, and Ed Hotchner. It was the turning point in Mary's summer, which to that moment had been relatively unruffled except for her nagging colds. "Pamplona," Ernest wrote afterward, "is no place to bring your wife."

> It is a man's fiesta and women at it make trouble, never intentionally, of course, but they nearly always make or have trouble . . . if she can drink wine all day and all night and dance with any groups of strangers who invite her, if she does not mind things being spilled on her, if she adores continual noise and music and loves fireworks, especially those that fall close to her or burn her clothes . . . if she doesn't catch cold when she is rained on and appreciates dust, likes disorder and irregular meals and never needs to sleep and still keeps neat and clean without running water; then bring her. You'll probably lose her to a better man than you.[23]

He could have added that an inattentive husband might well contribute to his wife's discomfort, for in Pamplona, Ernest's attention was once more distracted by an attractive young woman, Valerie Danby-Smith, who soon was hired on as his secretary. As Mary could not fail to note, her husband and the eighteen-year-old Irish girl with the dark hair and lovely smile became inseparable. In almost any photograph of Ernest taken during Pamplona, Valerie is within reach. She was his ideal student, eager to learn about Spain, *corridas, toreros*, wine, and of course writing. Soon Ernest was dictating his business letters for her to type, while largely ignoring Mary, who was limping about on a painfully broken toe. To Mary this was now familiar behavior, reminding her of Ernest's infatuation with Adriana ten years earlier.

When the Hemingway *cuadrilla* returned to La Consula, Ernest opened Alfred Rice's letter, which began, "I have shockingly bad news for you." Because Rice neglected to report $45,000 on Hemingway's 1957 tax return, he now explained that his mistake, for which he was dreadfully sorry, was going to cost Ernest perhaps as much as $28,000 in back taxes. A month later he recalculated his error to the tune of another $20,000, for a total of $48,000 due on his $45,000 error. "Because it is entirely my neglect," Rice wrote, "I will pay the interest instead of you on the additional tax."[24] Coming as it did when Ernest was emotionally and physically stressed, this new incompetence left him furious. When Rice insisted that he was due 10 percent of all movie and television income because he read the contracts for Hemingway, Ernest redressed him, making it clear to his attorney that he was becoming an unaffordable liability who should not push his luck. Yet, as always to Rice, he signed the letter "Ernie," a form of his name he detested, permitting no one else to use it but his father, dead these thirty years.[25]

For July 21 at La Consula, Mary arranged an elaborate sixtieth birthday party for Ernest, a fête richer than any of his previous birthdays. It began at 10:00 p.m. and continued on through the night, into the following morning, and through part of the day. Invitees included Antonio and Carmen, the Saviers, Hotchner, Valerie, Buck Lanham, David and Evangeline Bruce, Gianfranco Ivancich and his wife, the Maharajah of Cooch-Behar, assorted Spaniards, roving guitars, and a small orchestra. The forty invited guests were supplemented by numerous gate-crashers. Six cases of rosé wine, four cases of champagne, and vast amounts of whiskey and gin washed down the several baked hams, casseroles of codfish and shrimp, and fifty pounds of Chinese sweet-and-sour turkey. The three-tiered cake had ninety candles: sixty for Ernest and thirty for Carmen Ordóñez, whose birthday was also on the twenty-first. After presents and cake came thirty minutes of fireworks, which set a palm tree aflame, bringing out the local fire brigade. At six-thirty the next morning the orchestra was still playing, and guests were drinking Bloody Marys around the pool.[26]

What should have been a triumph for Mary became another intolerable performance by Ernest, who either ignored her completely while keeping arm-in-arm with Valerie, or spoke to her in an abusive, sarcastic manner. He had done this before during depressed periods: treating Mary as if he wished her out of his life. Buck Lanham could not understand why Mary put up with it, or why Ernest did it. Buck took his old friend to task over his cruel behavior, but Hemingway ignored him, later insulting Lanham to the point that their relationship was never the same. Too many late nights, too much wine for too many days, too much adulation and not enough solitude—whatever the cause, Ernest was going down into his depressed persona, a man Mary knew from past experience, but a man very like a stranger.

The summer *corridas* now seemed endless to Mary. After Luis Miguel's goring at Valencia at the end of July, she stayed more and more at La Consula with Annie Davis, leaving the men to their own devices. The two matadors were alternately wounded, hurt, or gored time and again during the bloodiest *corrida* season in many years. No one could remember when there had been so much wind blowing the capes, exposing the bodies of the matadors to the horns. When *Sports Illustrated* made Ernest a new offer for a personal essay on the *mano a mano*, he said the price was $30,000 for four to five thousand words, but only if one of the matadors was killed in the ring or permanently disabled, which by August he fully expected to happen.[27] With Luis Miguel and Antonio taking more and more risks, there was excitement and tension every time they entered the ring. Something tragic or magnificent or both might happen that day.

At Málaga on August 14, when the wind calmed and the bulls were each a dream of a bull, the magic became almost unbearable. Eric Sevareid was there, sitting close to Bill Davis and Ernest, who said, "It was the greatest bullfight I have ever seen." It was as if the two matadors were writing a picture-perfect textbook on their art form. Each pass was poetry, each bull was brave, each matador at the height of his powers. Every sword thrust was perfect. Sevareid wrote:

> Luis Miguel Dominguín is the world's second-greatest bull fighter . . . when he was lifted like a willow wand on the horns of the fifth bull for what seemed an eternity, classic Greek tragedy seemed to have reached its climax. . . . A great bullfighter like Dominguín is in command of the bull because he knows the bull. Ordóñez, the master, is in command of the bull because

he is in command of himself. He knows himself. It is the difference between talent and genius, between what a great man can do for himself and [what] the gods can do for him with their touch.[28]

Leaving Mary behind at La Consula, Ernest, Antonio, and his crew flew the length of Spain in an aging DC-3 for the next day's *corrida* in Bayonne.

They were joined there by Slim Hayward and Lauren Bacall, who complained that Ernest did not understand how great Luis Miguel truly was in the bull ring.[29] By this time it was more than obvious that Hemingway was deeply committed to Antonio in the competition, a commitment that rankled Luis Miguel. Ernest's blatant favoritism toward the younger matador was not an ill-formed judgment. Time and again, Antonio was outperforming Luis Miguel in ways so obvious that most of the knowledgeable critics would eventually agree with Hemingway that Ordóñez had triumphed in the *mano a mano*. However, Hemingway could have told a different story, a tale of loss, the sort of story that he often wrote when he was young: the aging professional choosing to go out on his feet, selecting his own terrain upon which to lose. But now that he was old enough to have fathered both men, his story was on the side of youth. Once he told Martha Gellhorn that no one he knew had ever recaptured lost youth, but that summer in Spain he forgot his own advice.

Back at La Consula, Mary festered, angry with Ernest's neglect, furious with his belittling the pain of her broken toe, and tired of his bragging and his camp followers. Earlier, when Ernest spent a long supper ignoring her for conversation with Lauren Bacall and Slim, Mary had interrupted the conversation to offer Bacall her two closed hands, asking her to choose one. Bacall pointed to Mary's left hand, which when she opened it revealed a bullet. "That is for anyone who moves in on my man," she said.[30] Throughout August and into September, Mary and Ernest saw little of each other, and when they did he always managed to say the wrong thing, followed by the usual epistolary apologies.

With a younger brother's flair for bad timing, Leicester

Hemingway's letter caught up with Ernest in mid-September, announcing that for three years he had been working on a biography of Ernest. Now that he had a publisher, he needed Ernest's permission to reprint several letters used in the text. "You once told me you weren't going to do it [an autobiography]," Leicester wrote, "but that you hoped somebody who really knew you would do a book about you some day and maybe it would be me." Hemingway's response was quick: this book violated the agreement between them that neither would write about the other. Not until he read the entire manuscript would Ernest decide what he thought about its publication. Until then, he refused permission to publish any of his letters.[31]

With his own flair for equally bad timing, Ernest told Mary in mid-September that he had invited Antonio and Carmen to meet them in Cuba on November 1 and drive west with them to Ketchum. Mary was less than thrilled: guests coming into Finca Vigia where they had not been in residence for almost a year. They had no idea what shape the house was in, or to what degree the new Castro government was restricting travel. Ernest seemed unconcerned with whatever problems there might be. Mary, the realist, immediately made plans to return in advance of the royal party, leaving Ernest to his own ill temper, infected kidneys, and smart mouth. On September 20, she flew from Madrid to Paris, stopping briefly at the Ritz. Annie and Bill Davis were worried about her coolness, but Ernest made light of it. Besides each other, no one knew that Mary was once again threatening to leave him, despite the rather large ring Ernest gave her in Madrid, making her "feel like an extortionist." She made it clear to her husband that she was playing the housewife's role in Cuba and Ketchum only long enough to make the two houses presentable. Beyond that she was not certain, but her own welfare would dictate what she did. It was impossible, she told him, to write the letter about their personal relations. "Too clogged up with emotion and loneliness and heartbreak . . . all evidence, as I see it, shows that you have no further use for me in your life. I am therefore beginning to arrange my removal from it, and hope to establish a new life for myself."[32] She signed the letter with "love and devotion," adding a note hoping that there were good pictures in heaven for Bernard Berenson, recently dead.

Hemingway's immediate answer reminded her of his support when she was in trouble, reminded her of the pleasures they had enjoyed. Her letter had broken his heart, but she had written such letters before. Maybe there was some hope. As for himself, the letter could not have come at a worse time. His head was in bad shape. He was trying to write and her "Dear John" had ruined that for him, but he would write somehow because he was a professional. His neck was hurting him, and Rice now needed $51,000 to pay their back taxes. So she could see that she was not the only one in the family with difficulties. He did not want to hold her against her will, but she was going to have to tell him that she was leaving face to face, not in a letter. No middle-of-the-night surprises that she was leaving him.[33] Three days later, he wrote Mary another letter filled with news about Antonio and about problems with his own body, spirit, bankbook, and writing. He was, he said, deep in a "black ass," implying that his condition was a result of her previous letter. On October 27, Ernest received a telegram from Hotchner, to whom Mary had related her decision to leave Ernest. After listening to her side, Hotchner told Ernest not to worry, for Papa was still calling the shots.[34]

From Havana, Mary wrote a long letter detailing the situation in the country and at the Finca. Their friends were surviving in reduced circumstances. Some were optimistic that Americans could still operate in Cuba; others were not. There was very little American currency in circulation, she said, so Ernest should bring enough with him to ensure getting back out of the country. All their Finca staff were fine, but the house itself was in sad shape: almost every machine was either broken or malfunctioning. Their cars needed overhauls; the pool pump was broken (family of dead rats inside); pool filter tanks a mess; record player not working properly; kitchen stove barely cooking; and the *Pilar* needed extensive repairs and cleaning. Mary was replacing windowpanes in the *casita* broken by an explosion during the revolution, and she was attacking the insects eating up the library table. Her bedroom roof and the living-room ceiling were leaking once more. Despite these massive problems, she was not daunted: "I find it lovely being here at home again. . . . Fascinating and happy too, the atmosphere of Cuba . . . everybody so proud of the government's honesty, so proud . . . of their new home-building program, so proud of Fidel's tree-planting which is everywhere visible . . . I hope so very much they will not be disappointed."[35] In the same envelope Mary included a three-and-a-half-page, single-spaced typed letter headed "THIS IS THE PERSONAL LETTER," in which she enumerated with examples the several ways Ernest had mistreated her over the course of the summer, all of which reaffirmed her decision to leave him. She was no longer able to withstand his neglect, "disparagement, cruel and unjust abuse and criticism." When she was sick in Spain, he was never sympathetic; when she broke her toe at Pamplona, he did not take care of her.

> Most hurtful of all . . . your compliments and attentions and interest and kisses for many girls and women, nothing for me. Nothing spontaneous towards me on your part, not even on the night of your birthday party . . . if I went to ask you a simple question . . . your face took on a look of irritation and impatience and you would say, "I haven't got time. I have to go shit now. I have to go swim now."

In Pamplona, he "excoriated" her for days after she was unable to ease a night cramp in his leg. In Valencia, over a minor issue, he called her "the biggest liar I have ever known." No longer did he ask her politely to do anything; he always gave a direct order. "I will not submit," she said, "for the rest of my life to being ordered about." She yearned for "friendship, solidarity, and affection," none of which was he likely again to provide. Therefore, as soon as she repaired the Finca and stocked the new Ketchum house for the visit of Antonio and Carmen, Mary intended to move into a small New York apartment to restart her life as a journalist.[36] Ernest's response was a telegram thanking her for the work she was doing and disagreeing with her complaints and conclusions while respecting her right to hold them.[37] So long accustomed to waiting wives and adoring women, with Martha the one anomaly, Hemingway still did not get the message.

On October 27, Hemingway piled three gun cases, sixteen bags, one suitcase, and six cartridge bags on board the *Liberté* bound for New York. In the pigskin suitcase was packed a small box holding a $4,000 platinum and diamond pin for Mary. On his third day at sea, during which time he remained almost exclusively in his cabin, he wrote Annie Davis a black-ass letter filled with loneliness. He dreaded what awaited him at the Finca, where he would be lectured day and night about his numerous shortcomings, be told by Mary that he could no longer write, that his Paris memoir was worthless, that he was an egotistical, stupid son of a bitch. And he would take it all from her without saying a word, never complaining, trying to make everyone happy while paying the bills. It was as if Mary were trying to drive him to suicide, but her attempts, while well timed, had failed.[38] Whenever he wanted to emphasize his loneliness or trump an irritated wife, Hemingway was apt to threaten suicide, but this letter was different. In the same way that he blamed his mother for driving his father to suicide, he was now blaming Mary. The game was changing rapidly, moving on to dangerous ground. He had invoked the word "suicide" too often, embarrassing friends with detailed directions of how he would do it, taking satisfaction in their discomfort of his scenario. Now that his body was clearly failing, the specter of killing himself loomed larger.

Arriving in New York on November 1, Hemingway avoided most of his friends there, delivered the Paris memoir to Scribner's, and approved of Mary's newfound apartment before boarding the flight south with Antonio and Carmen Ordóñez. They landed at the Havana airport to a twelve-foot Saint's Day banner, music, flags, and photographers welcoming Ernest back to the new Cuba. Surrounded by reporters, Ernest said, "I am very happy to be here again because I consider myself a Cuban. I have not believed any of the reports against Cuba. I sympathize with the Cuban government and with all *our* difficulties [Hemingway's emphasis]." He told reporters, badgering him for a statement about U.S.-Cuban relations, that he considered himself a true Cuban. Then he kissed the hem of the Cuban flag too quickly for the photographers to capture the moment. When asked to repeat it, he refused, saying, "I kissed it with all my heart, not as an actor." Everyone applauded.[39]

In public, Ernest was his jovial self, glad to be home; in private, he and Mary continued their marital and martial games, this time more seriously than ever before. He was sicker than she knew; she was more scared than he knew. On November 8, Mary wrote Annie Davis a lighthearted letter, apparently glad to have Ernest home, but complaining of having to go to Ketchum in advance to prepare the house for visitors. On the same day, Ernest wrote Bill Davis that his relationship with Mary was as difficult as ever. While agreeing to play hostess until Antonio and Carmen left Ketchum, she was still planning to return to her New York apartment in January 1960. She was, Ernest wrote, determined not to let his writing interfere with her own plans to write. He was suffering her demands as cheerfully as possible, hoping to work himself into shape to finish the books in progress. He apologized for the black-ass letter written on board the *Liberté*, but, he claimed, it had been worse than the winter in Hürtgen, his usual absolute zero for black ass. If only Valerie were at the Finca, he might get his life and his letters under control.[40] But Valerie was not there, nor would she ever be the muse he sought. The muse, it seemed, had left no for-warding address.

As soon as she could, Mary with her Jamaican maid, Lola Richards, flew to Chicago en route to Ketchum, leaving Ernest to drive west with their visitors. Ernest, Antonio, Carmen, and Roberto Herrera crossed to Key West, where a new Buick station wagon was waiting for them, courtesy of his television sponsor and in return for a statement they might use in their advertising. The 4,000-mile drive ended at midnight, November 19, when the Buick pulled into Ketchum. The next morning Ernest was on the phone to Bud Purdy, setting up a duck hunt on Purdy's ranch. No sooner had Ernest talked to Bud than a phone call from Antonio's sister in Mexico cut the visit off before it began. Antonio explained that he and Carmen must leave immediately to help his sister.[41] Ernest was despondent. Realizing that he was behaving erratically, slipping in and out of moods too quickly, Lloyd and Tillie Arnold did their best to cheer him up. Don Anderson, Duke MacMullen, Lloyd, and Ernest began a friendly series of trap shoots off the backyard of the Hemingway house. On Thanksgiving Day, the men were throwing clay targets with a handtrap and Ernest was powdering them consistently over the barelimbed cottonwoods. On Friday nights, the same group would gather around Hemingway's television set to watch the boxing matches with Ernest making book on each fight. It was almost like old times.

Had it not been for Mary's intention to leave him, Ernest had much to be happy about. Everyone at Scribner's was excited about his Paris book: Harry Brague said that "the Paris stuff is the Hemingway that no one can ever imitate. It is superb throughout . . . there are some passages I like better than anything Hemingway ever wrote before."[42] Two days after Thanksgiving, Mary's plans were postponed. Crossing frozen terrain while hunting ducks with Ernest and George Saviers, she tripped and fell. Making sure that her loaded shotgun did not accidentally go off, Mary protected it but landed heavily on her left elbow, shattering it on the ice. As soon as they could drive her to the hospital, Saviers and a colleague began the complicated restoration of her seriously damaged elbow. After being released from the hospital, Mary remained in pain to which Ernest was unsympathetic, acting as if she had somehow done this on purpose to interfere with his writing.

By mid-December, Hemingway was moody and depressed, given to emotional outbursts. He objected to doing the grocery shopping even though he was the only one in the house who could drive. As the snow outside the house deepened, arguments and accusations flared up inside. Ernest kept notes; Mary wrote him letters. He said. She said. At two minutes after midnight, December 15, Mary wrote an in-house letter about Ernest's objection to helping her undress, his calling it "maid's work." Mary promised, with an edge to her voice, that she would never ask him to do that again.

> Then you begged me not to make a fight before going to bed. I begged you please to go to bed. . . . Then you came back from your room and made three accusations. I had done this, you said, "to all your husbands."—It is false and you have No proof. Then you came and said, "You think, now I can get rid of him." False, and wholly false. Then you came and said, "You can only go to bed happy if you have made the fight and made somebody so

miserable so they can't sleep all night." . . . Look, Lamb—if you
want to get rid of me, please *just say so* calmly and without all
the insinuations and assaults and cruelties. Just say so. But please,
let us NOT go on with the Nightly false accusations and hurts. I
love you. Yes I do.[43]

By the time Christmas had come and gone, Mary was becoming
less defensive and more concerned about her husband's increasingly disturbed moods and fantasies, which could surface with the
abruptness of turning on a light switch. Driving through Ketchum
one cold, snow-blown night, Ernest became upset when he saw
lights on in their local bank. "They" were in there checking on his
accounts, he said. Tillie Arnold thought it was probably the cleaning women. "They're trying to catch us," Ernest replied. "They
want to get something on us." Mary asked who "they" were. "The
F.B.I.," he replied.[44]

CHAPTER 22

The Body Electric

January 17, 1960, to July 2, 1961

At two in the morning in Shoshone, their breaths blowing steam in the subfreezing air, Ernest, Mary, and their maid Lola boarded the Union Pacific's "City of Portland" on the first leg of their return to Cuba. They arrived in Havana by plane from Miami to find Finca Vigía like a refrigerator; without heat, usually unnecessary in Cuba, it was ill fortified against the norther that chilled the island. Ernest immediately returned to his ever-lengthening account of the previous summer's *mano a mano*, and Mary soon agreed that they should bring Val in from New York City to handle his mail and the piles of unfiled paper. By February 8, the young Irish girl was in residence at the Finca, her presence acting as a stimulus to Ernest's writing which was soon progressing at an almost alarming rate. In less than four weeks he wrote 17,000 words on what was growing inexorably into a book, not the 30,000 essay contracted with *Life*.[1]

In New York, Scribner's was eager to publish the untitled Paris sketches, either in the fall of 1960 or the following spring. Charles Scribner, Jr., said, "The pieces are magically effective and it will make the year for us, whatever year they appear." He also urged Ernest to consider publishing one or more of the chapters in periodicals that were begging for them, sight unseen. Hemingway hedged: the book needed another month's work, which he could not afford to give it until the bullfight story was finished. However, the Ordóñez-Dominguín story, he told Scribner, would either be a long appendix for a new edition of *Death in the Afternoon*, or a separate volume.[2] There were those, Ernest wrote, who probably thought he had no book, that he was borrowing money like Scott Fitzgerald against empty paper, but Charlie knew the Paris book was real and ready to publish should anything happen to him. If Scribner was reading the letter carefully, he must have wondered at the outdated reference to Fitzgerald who surfaced whenever Ernest felt unappreciated. Had he been closer to the Finca, the Scribner owner might also have worried that Ernest was making references to the possibility of overwork killing a man, and that he was not sleeping more than four hours a night. These signs went unheeded at the time, but in retrospect would loom larger.

Money, time, deadlines, endings, movies, television—pressures were building. Functioning as the H&H Corporation, Hemingway and Hotchner were embarked on a lucrative venture that had no immediate end in sight. Although he worried about the deals Hotchner was making for television shows, movies, and the theater, Ernest had to do little but approve them. Hotch was already at work on their next Buick-sponsored production, an hour-long version of "The Snows of Kilimanjaro" with Robert Ryan cast as Harry the dying writer. "Snows" would be followed by "The Gambler, the Nun, and the Radio," fulfilling their four-show contract. Buick was so pleased with the impact of the Hemingway dramas that they immediately gave him another new car and asked for a second series for 1961–62 if Hotchner could guarantee happy endings to adaptations of *A Farewell to Arms*, *The Sun Also Rises*, *To Have and Have Not*, and "The Short Happy Life of Francis Macomber," ludicrous conditions that Hotchner rejected out of hand.[3] The H&H enterprise had an option on Frederick Burnham's *Scouting on Two Continents* as a source for a television series in which Gary Cooper expressed interest. Cooper also wanted to make a movie of Hemingway's short story "After the Storm," with Hotchner doing the film treatment. Ernest warned Hotchner not to get excited about the idea until someone put up hard money. He himself wanted no part in financing any movies or Hotchner's reader's theater collection of Hemingway material entitled *Scenes of Love and Death*. Ernest could easily afford his low-risk profile, for he was literally being swamped with offers of money. German television had recently bought the TV version of "The Killers" for $2,000. In all of these ventures, Ernest risked nothing, and Hotchner did the work: writing the film script adaptations, arguing with the sponsors over their desire to censor productions, and casting the scripts.[4]

With Mary writing an article on Carmen Ordóñez and Valerie tending to tedious correspondence, Ernest buried himself in the story of the two bullfighters, which by the end of February was over 30,000 words. Trapped in a chronological narrative, he found it difficult to leave out any of the *corridas*, many of which began to sound quite similar. He was also faced with the problem of how to end a story over which he had no control. Unless one of the *toreros* was killed or conceded the contest, there was no satisfactory conclusion, particularly when the *mano a mano* was now scheduled to continue into the 1960 season. On February 26, he asked Time/Life for another extension on his deadline, saying he had two thirds of the piece written. The *Life* editor, Ed Thompson, found no problem with the extension, which in turn Ernest could not meet. Thompson wired Hemingway to stop worrying about when the piece was finished, for they wanted it whenever it came. If it ran longer than 30,000 words, there would be extra money for Ernest.[5]

Life was a trade-off. In his early Paris years, Ernest saw clearly, drank hard, lived cheap, stayed up late, worked the next day, but could not sell a story. Then there were no pills to take, no worries about blood pressure, no failing liver or sick kidneys, no doctors poking and prodding. Now with every hand asking for his words, his name, or his presence, the money could not buy him sleep or provide a new liver. He was "in the money," all right, but the money could not save him or his friends. Neither fame nor fortune was going to cure Gary Cooper's prostate cancer. At Massachusetts General, Ernest's friend was recuperating from radical prostectomy, tubes running into his body at his arm and out of his body below, "looking like some sort of still," Coop wrote, "making a low grade grape juice."[6]

All Ernest could do was write and not think about friends, or about Cuban politics growing steadily more threatening. At his writing platform, standing and typing, he was pounding out a prodigious number of words each day. Blood flowed, bulls died, matadors were rushed to emergency surgeons, wounds healed, the dangerous summer went on and on. Preoccupied in the Ciudad Real bull ring, Luis Miguel was losing the contest, but refused to admit it. What preoccupied Luis Miguel so?

"Death," I said. It was all right to say it in English if you said it low. "Antonio carries it around for him in his pocket."[7]

That was, he knew, the way all true stories ended, and he had carried that knowledge with him for a long time now.

All that late winter and into the spring of 1960, the Finca was devoid of intrusions, except for a week's visit from George Saviers. By the first week in May the grounds became an explosion of color. Around the pool and house, verbena, bougainvillea, and cola de cameron were in bloom. Jacaranda blossoms floated in the pool, and the air was sweet with the scent of frangipani. In three and a half months Hemingway wrote 84,000 words describing one *corrida* after another.[8] When the weather warmed, he swam a half mile each day in the Finca pool, and fished infrequently. His weight fell to 198, the first time it was below 200 in many years. On Sunday afternoons, he, Val, René, Juan the chauffeur, and Pichilo the gardener attended the cockfights, sometimes fighting Hemingway cocks, sometimes not, but always betting on the bloody fray.[9]

In the Cuban capital and across the country, life was less idyllic. In Oriente province, the Movement of Revolutionary Recovery demanded free elections to turn the country away from communism. These rebels against the Castro government were being tracked down by Fidel himself. On May Day, Castro stirred a crowd of 250,000 to a frenzy, charging that the United States was fomenting counterplots against him. He warned that Cuba must find a successor for him, for he might be "disappeared" by the northern aggressor. He had good cause for such suspicions. The U.S. Senate was funding a Voice of America radio station to broadcast into Cuba as if it were a nation occupied by the enemy, while the Congress gave President Eisenhower power to withhold $350 million in Cuban technical aid. There was talk of using the U.S. sugar quota money to reimburse displaced Cubans whose property was confiscated by the Castro government. On May 6, former President Harry Truman charged that Castro was a dictator, sowing the seeds for his own destruction. On May 7, Cuba resumed formal relations with Soviet Russia. It did not take a political scientist to see which way the winds were blowing.[10]

At the end of May, Ernest declared that the 100,000-word preliminary draft of the bullfight book was done. However, he was planning to return to Spain for more material on the *mano a mano*, which would extend the story to 150,000 words.[11] With anti-American slogans appearing on familiar walls, Mary urged Ernest to think first of moving as many of their valued possessions as possible off the island, but he refused to consider the idea. This was their home. In her biography, Mary said later, "For seven months I had been considering some manner by which, with the least trauma for each of us, I could retire from what seemed to me his new style of living. But I shelved the idea. He seemed to have so many grave problems confronting him that I could not increase them."[12] Not the least of these problems, which Mary never quite specified, was Hemingway's intake of alcohol, which had once again risen dramatically from the prescribed two glasses with supper. Their January to June liquor bill from Licores Manzarbeitia in Havana was $1,550.49 for eighteen bottles of liquor and fifty-five cases of wine during a period with almost no Finca visitors.[13] Hemingway was fighting with imaginary demons by night and sometimes by day, increasingly worried about money when there was no worry, increasingly questioning the loyalty of old friends. His old concerns about libel suits resurfaced; he warned Hotchner not to call the town Billings in the TV production of "The Gambler, the Nun, and the Radio," for there were people still alive from 1930 who might be offended.[14] He could, when necessary, put on a straight face for the world, keeping whatever was raging inside him under control, but when alone with Mary, he was becoming a stranger. Firmly believing that in his work was his deliverance, he pushed himself harder and harder, adding another 10,000 words to the bullfight book before turning back to the Paris book.[15] His pre-1946 depressions usually followed the completion of a book when he did not know what to write next. His post-1946 depressions were different. Because he was leaving work largely completed but not quite finished, one or more books were always begging for attention. As a result, he would move back and forth among them, even during his depressed periods, and unfinished work was always lurking at the back of his mind. As summer approached in Cuba, Ernest Hemingway was a man pursued, a writer unable to outrun his demons.

At the end of June, Ernest flew Hotchner in from New York to help edit the *mano-a-mano* story for the *Life* essay that was now promised at 40,000 words.[16] But whatever Hotchner suggested to eliminate, Ernest called vital to the narrative. Only with difficult discussion was Hotchner able to reduce the essay version to 70,000 words, or twice the length of *The Old Man and the Sea.* On July 6, after Hotchner left, Ernest reported to Charlie Scribner, Jr., that the book text now reached 120,000 words. Time/Life might not accept the essay, but the book version was a solid piece. First, he said, they should publish the Paris book, then the bullfight book. He had revised and arranged the order of the Paris sketches, but was too stale to add any more. He would try again later, but they already had enough for a book. His weight was down to 194; his eyes were better now with new glasses. The morning news, he said without specifics, was disturbing. Certain that his outgoing mail was being read by postal officials, Hemingway never mentioned Castro or what was happening in the country. But that morning, the Havana news and broadcasts from Florida announced that Castro was threatening to appropriate the property of American foreign nationals in retaliation for Eisenhower cutting off the Cuban sugar quota. Unnamed U.S. officials said they were worried about the safety of Americans in Cuba.[17]

By July 7, Valerie had typed up the bullfight book and Ernest had corrected it; Hotchner had come and gone. Hemingway was making plans to leave for Spain toward the end of the month, but Mary refused to go with him. She was not about to suffer through a summer like the last one. She and Val would wait in New York for Ernest to return. Valerie, on the other hand, wanted to go to Spain with Ernest, but Mary made it clear that was not an option. In fact,

Mary was determined to place some limits on her husband's subsidizing the young Irish girl. Her in-house letter began:

> Honey—in the midst of all our other preoccupations, I feel we must think a bit about Valerie and what would be good for her . . . I re-suggested to her the idea of taking some courses at Columbia this fall, to augment her education. . . . She was not interested. . . . In consideration of taking Val out to Ketchum this fall, perhaps you should include an estimate of how much use you will make of her as secretary, and the costs of equipping her for life out there and paying her room in town. . . . We must remember that . . . the people of her age are away at college in the fall and she would have little chance of companionship among her own age group.[18]

They certainly could not use Val as a cook and housekeeper, for it "was not at all her cup of tea." Val well understood the conflicted triangle in which she held down one precarious corner. As she wrote to Bill Davis, Mary, who ruled the roost, was intent on keeping her far away from Ernest, who was no longer making the crucial decisions. Resenting Mary's plan, Val wanted to be under no obligation to her, and said she would strike out on her own as soon as life with Mary became too uncomfortable.[19]

On July 25, Hemingway, Mary, and Val took the P&O ferry to Key West, where the immigration officer remarked that Val's visitor's visa needed to be renewed. Mary said that this information "sent Ernest into a disproportionately large tizzy. He muttered about the dire consequences of law-breaking."[20] Ernest flew on to New York, leaving Mary, Val, and their considerable luggage to follow by train from Miami. After conferences with Alfred Rice, Scribner's, and Hotchner, Hemingway boarded the TWA night flight to Madrid, arriving there the next morning, August 5. Two days after landing, he was cabling and writing Hotchner that the *mano-a-mano* essay should say nothing about the shaving of the bulls' horns, for Dominguín was suing people on that issue. He felt terrible from lack of rest, and had not written Mary because he was dead tired.[21] The next day in New York, Mary received a panicky phone call from Hotchner, telling her that the radio news reported

Ernest seriously ill at Málaga. The false report sent Mary scurrying: she booked a flight to Spain, contacted CBS News, sent cables, and sweated the emergency out while feeling helpless to do anything. Finally the news dispatch came through that Ernest was alive, followed by his telegram: REPORTS FALSE ENROUTE MADRID LOVE PAPA.[22] A second reassuring telegram came from Annie Davis: ERNEST OK.[23]

For the second time, he was not dying or dead as reported in the news, but neither was Hemingway "OK." A week later, tired and lonely, he complained that La Consula was full of strangers making him "nervous" and unable to sleep. His head was not right, and he worried that he was having a complete nervous breakdown. It had happened this way before, he assured Mary, and he had recovered to write wonderfully. He asked her to send Val to him if it could be done without creating a scandal, for there was so much mail that he was too tired to answer. The overwork was "deadly"; he could not sleep. Drinking only wine in small amounts was "bad" for him, but without it he became more "nervous." He, who often claimed that he always woke cheerful in the morning, was now waking in terrible shape.[24] In Mary's breezy and detailed letters to Ernest about her life in New York—plays, luncheons, friends to see—she showed little concern about her husband's complaints. But on August 20, Mary sent Val to Europe as Ernest requested, hoping her presence might calm him down.[25] All through September Mary received long, rambling, repetitive letters from Ernest filled with complaints, worries, and other clues that he was deeply mired in the slough of despondency. His weight dropped to 187. Worried that he was overdosing himself with his medicines, he decided to cut them to the bare minimum, despite his "nervousness." When Ernest saw his face on the cover of the September *Life* magazine, he was horrified. He confessed that his mind was in the worst shape ever, and he understood why Mary refused to come with him.[26]

Unnaturally worried about libel suits over the bullfight book, now titled *The Dangerous Summer*, he wired Scribner's to delay setting type until he had a chance to make more revisions.[27] As his several letters to Mary indicate, he was completely disillusioned with the bullfight business and all its components except Antonio. Having worked his head stupid getting the right photos for *Life*'s first installment of his essay, Hemingway was mortified by the magazine's final choices, which he felt were terrible. How could he ever apologize to Antonio and Luis Miguel? After his trying so hard to balance the photos so that each man looked his best, *Life* had ruined his reputation for honesty. He could only imagine how awful the Spanish version of *Life* would be, making him not only look stupid but also appear as a betrayer. If shooting himself would make things right with the two matadors, he would do so, but right now he could not afford that "luxury." On September 23, Ernest wrote a plaintive letter to Mary, saying how he wished she were with him to keep him from "cracking up."[28]

On October 8, Ernest landed back in New York, where he did his best to project his confident public persona; but inside he was a shaken, worried man, his self-confidence badly eroded, his memory playing tricks on him, and his nervous system clearly in trouble. Once in Mary's 62nd Street apartment, he refused to go outside, claiming that someone sinister was waiting out there for him. As quickly as possible Mary got him to Ketchum, where they both hoped that rest and quiet would restore his equilibrium. As they arrived at the Shoshone train station, two men in top coats came out of the Manhattan Cafe across the street. "They're tailing me out here already," Ernest told George Saviers, who met them at the platform. On the short drive to Ketchum, Ernest complained about his kidneys and his blood pressure, which he thought was rising again. When back in his Ketchum writing room, he seemed to be making progress on the Paris book, but his mind would not rest. A call to Morgan Guaranty in New York confirmed bountiful amounts in his various accounts, but the information did not relieve his mind. "He's confusing us," he told Mary. "He's covering up something." When she demanded to know what possible reason the bank might have for doing so, Ernest replied, "I don't know. But I know." He worried that a cottonwood tree blown across the Big Wood River formed a natural bridge across which "anybody" could infiltrate his defenses.[29] On either side of the front door, he had crude glass portals built so that he could see whoever was at the door.

Wherever he looked he found fears. Morose, losing weight rapidly, silent, brooding, and paranoid, Ernest was being sucked into a black hole from which he would not emerge. He worried about his income taxes, his property taxes, and his bills, worried there would not be enough money to pay them. At this time he owned almost $400,000 in Morgan Guaranty bank shares. He worried, quite rightly, that he would not be able to return to Cuba, where his manuscripts and his reference library representing his literary capital was at risk. He worried about the FBI finding out that he brought Valerie into the country illegally, her visa expired. On October 25, he sent Hotchner a $1,500 check to pay Val's tuition at Columbia (a charade) and to apply to her New York living expenses.[30] Thereafter, to keep Mary from finding out how much money he was giving to Val, he arranged to communicate with her through George Saviers, who would be her postal station and banker. Then Hemingway began to worry that he had put Saviers at risk, so he wrote an alibi note for George stating that Saviers never knew what the letters contained or why they were being mailed.[31]

When two college professors from Montana State University showed up at Hemingway's door, they were shocked to see the ghost of the man standing before them. One of them later wrote, "The only resemblance to the man we had imagined was in the fullness of the face. And even the face was pale and red-veined, not ruddy or weather-beaten. We were particularly struck by the thinness of his arms and legs. . . . He walked with the tentativeness of a man well over sixty-one. The dominant sense we had was of fragility."[32] And when Hotchner came out to Ketchum before Thanksgiving, he too was shocked to find Ernest in such bad shape. Hotchner wrote Bill Davis that the symptoms from the previous summer had grown worse. Mary, he reported, was on the verge of seeking psychiatric help for Ernest, whose grasp of reality was, in some crucial ways, completely missing.[33]

To say that Hemingway was opposed to being treated as mentally ill would be an understatement. Anyone growing up in the first half of this century was loath to be labeled "crazy," for mental illness marked that person as a liability. As Ernest's fictional character, the shell-shocked Nick Adams, said in 1932, "It's a hell of a nuisance once they've certified you as nutty. No one ever has any confidence in you again."[34] George Saviers gently suggested that Ernest should seek help at the Menninger Clinic, but Hemingway refused to go to a solely psychiatric hospital. Then Saviers suggested the Mayo Clinic in Rochester, Minnesota, where Ernest could go to treat his high blood pressure, which had suddenly zoomed to 250 over 125. On the last day of November, Hemingway and Saviers climbed into Larry Johnson's single-engine Piper Comanche to fly across the snow-covered midwest to Rochester, where that night Ernest stood at the check-in desk of St. Mary's Hospital. Fifty-one years earlier, Dr. Clarence Hemingway stood on that same spot, arriving for a clinical visit and refresher course. He wrote a postcard to his eleven-year-old son: "It will be only a few years before you and Papa will be visiting clinics together."[35]

At St. Mary's that night, Ernest was having difficulty answering simple questions: name, address, next of kin, names of parents. When asked the name of his mother, Ernest blanched, mumbled, and became nervously agitated. Saviers stepped in quickly, saying he would finish the form but first it was important to get Ernest into bed and sedated. As a result, Ernest was registered in Saviers's name.[36] By train and plane, Mary followed Ernest to Rochester, checking into the Kahler Hotel as Mrs. George Saviers. On December 4, Ernest in his hospital room wrote "To WHOM IT MAY CONCERN" that his wife Mary never knew of or participated in any of his illegal acts, knew nothing of his finances, used Saviers's name only to avoid the press, and "was never an accomplice nor in any sense a fugitive."[37] For reasons he was never able to articulate fully, Hemingway was certain that state and federal agencies were pursuing him for unnamed crimes.

During his initial physical exam with Dr. Hugh Butt, Hemingway gave his medical history of having hepatitis in 1918 and jaundice in 1956. Dr. Butt's summation said nothing about Hemingway's several serious concussions. The battery of diagnostic tests showed most of Ernest's numbers to be within normal range, except his blood pressure (160/98) and his blood sugar at 130 percent. More tests suggested that he had a mild case of diabetes mellitus. His enlarged liver in conjunction with his diabetes suggested that he might have hemachromatosis, but no follow-up tests were done to confirm that possibility.[38] Hemingway's chronic and severe depression was attributed to his prolonged use of Serpasil, the Ciba company's trade name for their reserpine medication, whose known side effects included depression.[39] Dr. Howard Rome, in charge of Hemingway's psychiatric evaluation, explained to Ernest that his Serpasil depressions "were accelerated by the use of Ritalin which apparently was prescribed to off-set the depression. Thus . . . the situation was compounded."[40] No mention in writing was made of Hemingway's paranoia and delusions, but shortly after his admission to St. Mary's, electroshock therapy began.

With his bowels and bladder completely empty, Ernest was strapped down on the gurney, a white gown his only cover, his muscles slowly relaxing as the injection took effect and the white room began to soften. The nurse applied a greasy jelly to his temples, placed a rubber gag between his teeth to prevent injury, and fixed the electrodes in place. Then the doctor in white pushed a button for electric current to jolt Hemingway's brain into an induced *grand mal* seizure, the equivalent of a concussion. It was some time before he woke from the comalike state, his mouth dry, his head fuzzy, unable to say where he was or why. Ten times Ernest was wheeled into the white room for more electricity to overload his neural connections. Ten times he was convulsed. Ten times he awoke wondering. As one neurologist would later write: "I have no doubt that ECT [electroconvulsive therapy] produces effects identical to those of a head injury. After multiple sessions of ECT, a patient has symptoms identical to those of a retired, punch-drunk boxer. After one session of ECT the symptoms are the same as those of concussion."[41] For a head like Hemingway's, already several times concussed, such a treatment could produce serious brain damage. Short-term memory loss was an expected side effect of ECT, but long-term loss was always a possibility. Later research found one woman's life was ruined after fifteen ECT treatments, at lower voltage than Hemingway sustained, that left her unable to remember the names of close associates, unable to recall if she had money or where it was, and completely erasing three years of her memory.[42]

Late on Christmas Eve, Mary Hemingway sat down on her hotel-room bed and wept as she wrote in her journal that Ernest seemed "almost as disturbed, disjointed mentally as he was when we came here. . . . He no longer insists that an FBI agent is hidden in the bathroom with a tape recorder. . . . He still says . . . that he feels terrible. He still mumbles about breaking the immigration law (he has some unspoken guilt about Val). He is convinced that the Ketchum house will be seized for non-payment of something. . . . Still feels penniless . . . still waits for the FBI to pick him up."[43] Six days later, on New Year's Eve, she wrote out her resolutions:

1. I will not worry or fret or brood about other women in love with Papa.
2. I will try to make each single day, the greatest, the most perceptive, pleasurable, carefree and happy.
3. I will not be sad or miserable at night. I will go to bed hopeful.
4. I will be disciplined only by my own tastes, not by phony customs.[44]

Mary Hemingway was standing with her back to the edge of her own limits, emotionally bankrupt, and in her own words, "I feel I too may begin to confuse illusion with reality."[45]

The charade of patient George Saviers was not discovered by the press until January 11, 1961, after which time the hospital was hardpressed to keep reporters, freelance writers, and the curious away from their celebrity. Finally, Mayo Clinic issued a statement that Hemingway was being treated for hypertension, and "his condition is regarded as satisfactory. . . . It is necessary, however, that his right to privacy be respected and that he have the benefit of rest and quiet." On his hospital-room door, Hemingway placed a hand-lettered sign which should have disturbed his doctors, who were about to send him home cured:

FORMER WRITER Engaged
in PREPARATION OF SCHEDULED
FULL SCALE NEWS CONFERENCE
AS PROMISED in THE
P-D by OUR SPOKESMAN.
PLEASE DO NOT

DISTURB UNLESS Absolutely
NECESSARY TO OBTAIN photographs
OR CONFIRMATION OF TREATMENT
given EXCLUSIVELY TO THE P-D.[46]

On January 22, Hemingway was discharged from St. Mary's well enough, he was told, to return to Ketchum, where he arrived that evening in Larry Johnson's airplane. There he began keeping a meticulous daily record of his morning weight and bowel movements. January 23, his body, which once weighed as much as 260 pounds, now weighed 171. By March 12, he was down to 166 1/2. On April 5, he scaled out at 164, 36 pounds lighter than a year earlier. When first back in Ketchum, Mary was relieved that Ernest seemed so much better. He remained somewhat silent but not visibly morose. Not ready to deal with visitors, even old friends, Ernest canceled the Friday-night parties watching the televised fights. He and Mary took daily two- to four-mile walks on the iron-hard road running north out of Ketchum, Ernest in front, Mary several paces in the rear. In the evenings, they read from the more than thirty new volumes ordered from the Scribner Book Store, titles diverse as Lawrence Durrell's *The Black Book*, Hershey's *The Child Buyer*, Styron's *Set This House on Fire*, a biography of Ezra Pound, and Shirer's *The Rise and Fall of the Third Reich*.[47] Ernest and Mary had become a country of two with fragile borders, each needy in different ways. Outside their gray, concrete house on the hilltop, the snow piled deep, and in the early mornings when he woke, Ernest could see deer watering on Big Wood River at the foot of the hill.

Each morning Hemingway woke before Mary, made his breakfast, and went to his writing room, where the Paris book with nineteen sketches completed and the bullfight book at 150,000 words were waiting to be finished. But through all of February he apparently wrote nothing but a few letters in which he usually said out of habit that he was "working hard." In New York, Hotchner mounted his reader's theater tour of Hemingway's work, while in Los Angeles, film producer Jerry Wald was bringing together a final contract for *Adventures of a Young Man* based on several of Ernest's short stories. Hemingway's six-month royalty report from

Scribner's was for $28,977.33, an increase over the previous six months.[48] None of this information gave Ernest ease of mind, for he was now living in a constricted world that was growing more hopeless each day he could not write. If the problem had been what to write next, he might have been able to face it as he had so many times before. But the problem was how to finish work waiting for an ending, always the most difficult task for him.

Draft after draft was begun on the introduction to the Paris sketches, but each attempt was put aside as inadequate. He told Harry Brague at Scribner's that he had eighteen chapters arranged in their proper order, and was working on the nineteenth chapter, but still had no title. It was, he said, difficult to find a good title with his reference library in Cuba. He asked Brague to send copies of the *Oxford Book of English Verse* and the King James *Bible* with clear print—his old standbys for good titles. In closing, he gave the condition of his health, adding, "You, Max, and Charlie Scribner are accustomed to the lies of Scott—but this is the true gen."[49] Harry Brague must have wondered about that curious sentence, for Scott Fitzgerald was twenty-one years in the grave, Max Perkins and Charles Scribner were both dead, and Charles Scribner, Jr., was a young boy in the 1930s.

By March 1, Hemingway was exhibiting more disturbing symptoms of his returning depression. Deeply worried that he would never return to Finca Vigía, he continued to follow Lee Samuels's directions for funneling money to his Cuban staff through Canadian banks. Samuels assured him by letter that it was both legal and ethical, as far as he knew.[50] The very chance that this ploy was illegal was enough to resurrect Hemingway's paranoia about the FBI. The day he received Samuels's letter, Hemingway warned Hotchner to be careful what he wrote because mail coming into Ketchum might be read by anyone. Nor were the phones safe, for everyone tended to listen in.[51] Around the solstice, March 21, what began as a simple question—had Mary paid Social Security tax on their maid, Mary Williams—evolved into a full-scale emotional explosion. Mary assured Ernest that it was not a problem. He wanted to see her checkbook. She refused to show it to him. He said that when the FBI came in to investigate, they would certainly look at her checkbook. She said, not in America, they could not do that. They were both furious. Ernest wrote two letters to Alfred Rice detailing the three-day war. Mary would not listen to him, he said, and she blamed his concern on his mental illness and his imagination.[52]

On April 15, Hemingway awoke to a newscast claiming that an army of anti-Castro revolutionaries had invaded Cuba. Before the day was done, the Bay of Pigs disaster would be a dark failed piece of American foreign diplomacy. The Central Intelligence Agency, working with the anti-Castro movement centered in Miami, had armed, trained, and arranged transportation for a small army whose appearance on the Cuban shore they hoped would trigger a general uprising against the communist-leaning Castro government. It was possibly the worst intelligence fiasco of the cold war period. The dissident Cubans were in Miami. Castro was generally popular in Cuba, his reforms approved. A well-armed and well-trained Cuban militia quickly decimated the invaders, for whom there was no escape route. For Hemingway, the Bay of Pigs disaster marked the end of any hope that he might one day return to Cuba. From the darkness into which he was again descending, he was certain he would never again see the Finca, his library, the *Pilar*, or his paintings. The manuscripts for what would become *Islands in the Stream* and *True at First Light*, the African novel, were, he thought, lost to him.[53]

Three days after the Bay of Pigs, Hemingway wrote Charles Scribner, Jr., that the Paris sketches could not be published in their present condition. For a month he had worked on the ending without success. If published, there would be several libel suits, and the book was unfair to Hadley, Pauline, and Scott Fitzgerald. If he had good health, enough time, sources to check, and impeccable taste, he might be able to make the magic work, but worries and his stay at Rochester had broken him down. Since returning from Rochester, everything he had done to the book, he said, made it worse, and there was nothing to do but admit his failure. The only way the book could be published would be to call it fiction, and for Scribner's to bear the burden of all libel suits.[54] The letter was written but not mailed on Tuesday. On Thursday, Mary told Ernest that he was clearly getting worse, and she thought he should return to Rochester for more treatments.

On Friday morning, Mary went downstairs to breakfast and found Ernest

> in the front vestibule of the house with his shotgun, two shells and a note he had written me. For an hour I talked to him— courage, his bravery, faith, love—and managed to delay any decisive action until George [Saviers] arrived, perceived the situation and managed to take Papa to the Sun Valley hospital where they put him to bed and gave him sedatives.[55]

Poor flying weather kept Hemingway in the local hospital under careful watch. On Monday, April 24, he convinced George Saviers to allow him to return home to complete some unspecified chores. Don Anderson, his boon hunting companion, and nurse Joanie Higgons went along to make sure there were no problems. Ernest was quickly out of the car and into the house. By the time Don reached the living room, Ernest was ramming a shell into his shotgun, but Anderson was able to overpower him, get the gun away, and return Ernest to the hospital. The following day, Larry Johnson, with both Don and George Saviers along, flew Hemingway against his will to Rochester. Mary remained in Ketchum, too emotionally torn apart to go through the clinic routine again.[56] When the plane landed to refuel in Rapid City, South Dakota, Ernest with Don at his heels began going through the hangar and parked cars looking for a gun. At one point he walked toward the whirling prop of an airplane, stopping only when the plane cut its engine.[57]

Hemingway's first Rochester letter to Mary was difficult to read and barely coherent, repeating over and over again that she must keep him informed of her expenditures so that he would know if there was enough money to cover their bills. During his first three days at the clinic, Hemingway went through three sessions in the white room with the electroshock, making his handwriting wobbly and strange. The four-page letter rambled, asking for checks, worrying about taxes, professing loneliness, repeating himself as if he had not said the same thing twice earlier. In closing he said that he was taking the letter to the authorities to get it past censorship, as if it were a wartime situation. His last line apologized for taking three days to write her, and he signed it "Big Kitten."[58] His letters thereafter repeatedly asked about amounts in various bank accounts, never knowing if he could write a check, and all the information that Mary supplied could not put that worry to rest. He was, for example, certain that he had not put aside enough money in his special tax account to cover his 1960 IRS bill. When Morgan Guaranty sent him a letter giving the balance at $136,211.57, he continued to fret, insisting that Mary tell him the worst possible scenario so they could be prepared for it. Nothing she or Rice could say assuaged his fear.[59] On May 5, he reported having a session in the white room the day before which had left him unable to write, and there would be more treatments at the rate of one every two days. Kept in the locked wing of the hospital where a light burned all night long, Ernest was under close surveillance, but was able to leave his room. When he got through by phone to Gary Cooper dying from cancer, Coop told him, "I bet I make it to the barn before you do."[60] On May 13, the actor was dead, and Hemingway, named an honorary pall bearer, was said to be too ill to attend the funeral.

Dr. Howard Rome assessed Hemingway as having the "classical" symptoms of depression: "loss of self-esteem, ideas of worthlessness, a searing sense of guilt, of not having done better by you [Mary], by his family, by his friends." Ernest had reentered the Mayo convinced that he would never be able to write again, which filled him with "humiliation and chagrin" and "all but overwhelmed him with agitation, restlessness, and . . . money matters." As he seemed to improve with the shock treatments, Hemingway and Rome frequently discussed suicide. Ernest pointed out that Rome needed to trust him for there were numerous ways he could kill himself. He did not need a gun when there was glass to break or his belt to form a noose. On his honor he promised Rome he would not kill himself at the clinic. They shook hands, confirming their pact, and thereafter Ernest "went out almost daily for walks, for swims, for target shooting, for meals." The shock treatments continued until Rome was convinced that Ernest was truly better.[61]

But at the end of May, when Mary finally went to Rochester to visit her husband, she was discouraged by what she observed. As she explained to Jack and Patrick,

> My first day there [May 23], Papa showed only intense hostility to me—I'd railroaded him there, making them destroy his memory, would be happy only keeping him as a fixture in a madhouse, would steal his money, etc. . . . The second day was calm and harmonious. . . . The third day—7 hours—he made plans for getting out of there, grew angry because I demurred at the idea of going to the fiesta of Pamplona.

After three days, Mary was appalled that the doctors thought Ernest was improving. He told her that he could not go back to Ketchum because he would be put in jail for nonpayment of state taxes, a situation she had connived. Rice, he said, was lying to them about the federal tax bill; it had to be more. The Morgan Guaranty bank statements were mistaken.[62]

Deeply worried that the Mayo treatments were not helping Ernest, Mary could not face another round of suicide attempts in Ketchum. Their game was no longer a game, and she had exhausted her emotional resources. In New York, she sought advice from a psychiatrist who recommended the Hartford Institute of Living. On June 7, she flew to Hartford, Connecticut, where Dr. Gordon Edgren assured her the Institute, complete with ample grounds, library, swimming pool, and gymnasium, was ready to help in Ernest's long-term recovery. That night, back in her New York City apartment, Mary wrote a carefully phrased letter to Dr. Rome at Mayo, asking for his advice on the Institute of Living. Without saying so directly, she desperately wanted Rome to recommend that Ernest be transferred to Hartford, for she knew he would not go voluntarily, particularly if she urged him. She told Rome, "I would much prefer that Papa does not now know anything of all this, remembering his convictions about how I was railroading him into a madhouse."[63]

By phone on June 15, Mary assured Ernest that she had "great confidence" in Howard Rome's judgment.[64] However, for reasons Rome must have personally given Mary, he did not recommend the transfer to Hartford. Having watched Ernest in the presence of Rome, Mary was certain that her husband had gulled the doctor about the state of his mind. When Rome asked her to come to his office, she was "dumfounded to see Ernest there, dressed in his street clothes, grinning like a Cheshire cat." Rome said that Hemingway was ready to go home. In Ernest's presence, Mary could not bring herself to argue with the doctor's decision. Two days later, in a rented Buick with George Brown, Ernest's sometime trainer and old friend, driving, Ernest and Mary began their last cross-country trip west, arriving in Ketchum on June 30. The next day, Ernest seemed happier than he had been in a long time. After a long country walk, he visited George Saviers, and stopped by the Sun Valley Lodge to see Don Anderson, who was out of his office. That night Mary, George Brown, and Ernest were sitting in a corner table of the Christiania Restaurant. When Ernest asked their waitress about two men at another table, he was told they were salesmen. Salesmen would not be out on a Saturday night. "They're FBI," Ernest said. Mary redirected his attention to the bottle of wine on the table, and the meal ended pleasantly enough. Later that evening, Ernest and Mary harmonized on a favorite Italian tune as they went to their separate bedrooms.[65]

Sunday morning, July 2, Ernest was awake before the sun rising over the mountains east of Ketchum lit his bedroom window. There would be no more white rooms with electrodes stuck to his head. He could not go back to Cuba, but neither could he go back to a locked ward. If he could not write, then he could not write, but there was one thing left he could do well, a thing for which he had practiced all his adult life. In bathrobe and slippers, he padded softly past Mary's room where she was sleeping soundly. Down the stairs and into the kitchen, he found the ring of keys on the windowsill, and moved toward the basement stairs. In the locked storeroom where Mary had his shotguns for safekeeping, the odor of gun oil and leather was an old friend. From the box of 12-gauge shells, he pulled out two and dropped them in his pocket. Picking up his favorite Boss shotgun, he turned out the light and climbed slowly back up the stairs to the first floor.

Born in July, blown up in Italy in July, Pamplona in July, it was, of all the months, his most memorable. On the first of July each summer of his youth, the family boarded the steamer that carried them up Lake Michigan for their two months at Windemere. July was the cottage, the lake, and the woods. It was trout fishing and camaraderie with the summer people, baseball games in the village, campfires in the night. July was faces and places no longer within reach. July was the big wound in Italy when he died for the first time only to come back out of the explosion to find his kneecap somewhere in his boot and his head ringing like a bell. Now, so many Julys later, he stood in the foyer beside the empty gun rack, broke open the breech of his shotgun, slipped in two shells, and snapped the breech shut. The taste of gun oil and powder solvent filled his mouth as cold steel made contact against his hard palate. The clock on Mary's bedside table clicked as the minute hand moved to 7:30. Then two, almost simultaneous explosions woke her to her widowhood, her world, changed, utterly changed.

Coda

October 26, 1998

Ernest Hemingway was the embodiment of America's promise: the young boy from Oak Park who set out to become the best writer of his time. With pluck and luck, talent and wit, hard work and hard living, he did just that. In the process he told us that pursuit was happiness, that man alone was no fucking good, and that any story followed far enough would end badly. Before he burned out, he lived constantly out on the edge of the American experience. In the process he fathered sons, wrote books, influenced friends, and won every prize available to a writer. He remodeled American short fiction, changed the way characters speak, confronted the moral strictures confining the writer, and left behind a shelf of books telling us how we were in the first half of this century. His is a classic American story: the young man who transforms himself following his ambition, succeeds beyond his dreams, and finally burns out trying to be true to the person he has become. His imagination, which created "Big Two-Hearted River," also created his paranoia. His ambition, intensity, creative drive, sense of duty, belief in hard work, and faith in the strenuous life carried him to the pinnacle of his profession, provided him wide recognition and considerable wealth, before destroying him when he could no longer meet their demands. It is an old story, older than written words, a story the ancient Greeks would have recognized.

Chronology

1940

Mar. 7 *The Fifth Column* opens in New York.

c. July 25 Hemingway delivers *For Whom the Bell Tolls* typescript to Scribner's.

Sept. Martha Gellhorn, Hemingway, and his three sons are at Sun Valley Lodge.

Oct. 21 *For Whom the Bell Tolls* is published.

Nov. 21 Ernest and Martha are married in Cheyenne, Wyoming.

Dec. 21 Scott Fitzgerald dies.

1941

Jan. 31 Hemingways depart San Francisco en route to China war zone.

Feb.–April Hawaii, Hong Kong, Namyung, Canton Front, Chungking, Rangoon.

April 29 Ernest is back in Hong Kong.

May 6–17 Ernest flies to Manila, Guam, Wake Island, Hawaii, San Francisco.

June 1–15 Ernest and Martha are in New York City and return to Cuba.

mid-Sept. Hemingways are at the Sun Valley Lodge.

Oct. 27 Martha's book, *The Heart of Another*, is published.

Dec. 3 Leave Sun Valley to return to Cuba.

Dec. 7 Japanese attack Pearl Harbor.

1942

Mar.–Aug. Ernest edits *Men at War*, writes preface.

May German submarines begin raiding in the Gulf of Mexico. Hemingway proposes using the *Pilar* for armed patrols. He also initiates a counterintelligence operation in Cuba.

July 16 Martha leaves for two-month Caribbean assignment for *Collier's*.

July 28 *Pilar*'s first short patrol in Cuban waters.

Aug. More short patrols along northwest coast.

Nov. Counterintelligence operation taken over by Gustavo Durán.

Nov. 20 *Pilar* begins first fully armed cruise.

1943

Jan.–Mar. *Pilar* on short patrols along northwest coast of Cuba.

May 20–
July 20 *Pilar* on first extended patrol in Old Bahama Channel.

June 27 Martha finishes *Liana*.

Aug.–Sept. *Pilar* in port awaiting next assignment and having repairs.

Sept. 20 Martha leaves for England on *Collier's* assignment.

Oct.–Dec. Hemingway alone at the Finca. No sub patrols assigned.

1944

Feb. 1 Hemingway closes down *Pilar* patrols.

Mar. 13 Martha returns to Cuba from England.

April 23 Ernest and Martha fly to New York, where he becomes *Collier's* front-line correspondent.

May 13 Martha leaves by freighter in convoy for England.

May 17 Ernest lands in England by military aircraft. Soon meets Mary Welsh.

May 23 Ernest is in car wreck, severe scalp lacerations and concussion.

May 31 Martha arrives in London.

June 6 D-Day: Normandy invasion. Ernest at Omaha Beach.

June 15–30 Hemingway flies missions with the RAF.

July 18 With Patton's army at Néhou, France.

July 28 He joins the 22nd Infantry Regiment.

Aug. 18–24 Hemingway at Rambouillet with David Bruce of OSS.

Aug. 25 Liberation of Paris. Hemingway at the Ritz Hotel.

Sept. 7 Hemingway leaves Paris to rejoin 22nd Regiment.

Sept. 26 Hemingway returns to Paris and Mary Welsh.

Oct. 6 Hemingway cleared of charges of being armed correspondent. Stays in Paris.

Nov. 9–   Hemingway returns to 22nd Regiment for the Battle of
Dec. 3   Hürtgen Forest.

1945

Mar. 6   Hemingway departs Paris for return to Cuba.

April 12   President Franklin D. Roosevelt dies in office.

May 8   Mary arrives to live at the Finca. Germany surrenders.

June 20   Auto accident with Ernest driving. Mary hospitalized.

Oct.–Dec.   Hemingway works on Bimini novel begun before the war.

1946

Feb.–June   Ernest in "black-ass" depressed mood, but writes Bimini novel steadily.

Mar. 13   Ernest and Mary are married. Mary becomes pregnant.

July 21   Ernest has 1,000 pages written on Bimini novel.

July 28   Gertrude Stein dies in Paris.

Aug. 19   En route to Ketchum, Idaho, Mary's fallopian tube bursts. Emergency surgery; she almost dies. No baby.

Sept. 12   Ernest and Mary arrive at Ketchum.

Nov. 18   Hemingways depart Ketchum for New Orleans.

Dec. 1   Hemingways in New York City

1947

June 13   Hemingway awarded Bronze Star for World War II service.

June 17   Max Perkins dies.

July–Aug.   Hemingway's blood pressure becomes dangerously high.

Aug.–Sept.   Hemingway is involved in Dominican Republic coup attempt.

Oct. 3   Hemingway in Ketchum to avoid possible Cuban arrest.

Nov.–Dec.   Hemingway works on the Bimini novel in Ketchum.

Dec. 24   Hemingway meets Lillian Ross.

1948

Feb. 1–20   Ernest and Mary leave Ketchum and return to Cuba.

Mar. 7   Malcolm Cowley arrives in Havana to write Hemingway essay for *Life*.

Mar.	Peter Viertel and John Huston arrive in Havana.
June	Aaron Hotchner arrives in Havana.
Sept. 7	Hemingways sail from Havana for Italy.
Sept. 25	Hemingways leave Genoa to drive through northern Italy.
Oct. 22	Hemingways arrive at Gritti Palace in Venice.
Nov. 1	Hemingways move to Locando Cipriani on Torcello.
Nov.	Ernest writes "The Great Blue River" for *Holiday* magazine.
mid-Dec.	Back in Venice, Ernest meets Adriana Ivancich. He and Mary move to Cortina.

1949

Jan. 21	Mary breaks her right ankle skiing.
early Mar.	Hemingways return to Venice. Meet Sinclair Lewis.
mid-Mar.	They return to Cortina. Ernest begins a short story that will grow into *Across the River and into the Trees*.
Mar. 28	Ernest's eyes become infected with erysipelas. He spends ten days in a Padua hospital.
April 30	Hemingways sail from Genoa to return to Cuba.
May 27	Arrive at Finca Vigia.
July–Oct.	Hemingway writes steadily on *Across the River*.
Sept.	Hemingway contracts with *Cosmopolitan* to serialize *Across the River*.
Nov. 16	Ernest and Mary fly to New York en route to Europe on *Ile de France*.
Nov.–Dec.	Hemingways, Viertels, and Hotchner in Paris together.
Dec. 24	Hemingway and entourage leave Paris by car for Provence.

1950

Jan.	Hemingways back in Venice at the Gritti Palace.
Feb.	Ernest alternates between Venice and Cortina, where Mary breaks her left ankle skiing. First installments of *Across the River* run in *Cosmopolitan*.
Mar. 7	Hemingways depart Venice by car for Paris.
Mar. 21	Hemingways leave Ritz Hotel to meet *Ile de France* for trip home.
Mar. 27– April 6	Hemingways in New York City.

April 8   Hemingways arrive in Cuba.

May 13   Lillian Ross "Profile" of Hemingway appears in *The New Yorker*.

June 3   Hemingway finishes revisions to book galleys for *Across the River*.

July   Ernest suffers another concussion on board the *Pilar*.

Sept. 7   *Across the River and into the Trees* is published in New York.

Oct. 28   Adriana and her mother Dora Ivancich arrive at the Finca.

Nov.–Dec.   Hemingway completes his Bimini novel, calling it *The Island and the Stream*.

1951

Jan.   Hemingway begins writing *The Old Man and the Sea*.

Feb. 7   Mary, Adriana, and her mother leave Cuba for trip to New York.

Feb. 17   Hemingway finishes first draft of *The Old Man and the Sea*.

April–Oct.   Hemingway works on revising and cutting the Bimini novel.

July 28   Grace Hemingway dies. Ernest does not attend the funeral.

Oct. 2   Pauline Pfeiffer Hemingway dies in Los Angeles.

1952

Feb. 11   Charles Scribner, Sr., dies in New York.

May 4   Hemingway begins "The Last Good Country."

Sept. 1   *Life* magazine prints *The Old Man and the Sea* in one issue.

Sept. 8   Scribner's publishes the novel in hardback.

1953

May 4   Hemingway wins the Pulitzer Prize for *The Old Man and the Sea*.

June 24   Ernest and Mary sail from New York bound for Europe on the *Flandre*.

June 30   They dock at Le Havre and drive to Paris.

July 3   Leave by car for Spain.

July 6–14   In Pamplona for *feria*, first time since 1931.

Aug. 6   Hemingways board the *Dunnottar Castle* in Marseilles for Mombasa.

Sept.–Dec.   Hemingways on safari in Kenya.

1954

Jan. 21   Safari ends.

Jan. 23–24   Ernest and Mary survive two plane crashes at Murchinson Falls.

Feb.   Recovering in Nairobi, Ernest writes "The Christmas Gift."

Feb. 22   Ernest joins Mary at Mombasa for fishing.

Mar. 11   Hemingways board the SS *Africa* at Mombasa bound for Venice.

Mar. 23   Hemingways arrive in Venice.

Mar.   Hemingway accepts the American Academy of Arts and Letters Award of Merit Medal.

May 6   Hotchner and Hemingway depart Venice by car for Spain.

May 15–17   Ernest attends the San Isidro *feria* in Madrid.

June 6   Hemingways board the *Francesco Morosini* at Genoa bound for Havana.

July 21   Ernest is awarded Cuba's highest civilian award, the Order of Carlos Manuel de Céspedes.

Oct. 28   Hemingway is awarded Nobel Prize for literature. He is working on the African novel, *True at First Light* (1999).

1955

Jan.–June   Hemingway works on the African novel.

July–Sept.   Hemingway assists with the script and filming of *The Old Man and the Sea*.

Oct.–Nov.   Hemingway returns to the African novel.

Nov. 20   Ernest sick with nephritis and hepatitis. Remains in bed into January.

1956

Feb. 10   Hemingway abandons the African novel to work on *The Old Man and the Sea* filming.

April–May   Ernest and Mary in Peru, fishing for a giant marlin for the film.

c. May 23   Hemingways return to the Finca. Ernest writes several World War II short stories.

Sept. 1   Hemingways board the *Ile de France* bound for Europe.

Sept. 17   Leave Paris for Spain by car.

Sept.–Oct.   Attending *corridas* in Spain.

Nov. 17   Leave Spain, return to Paris.

1957

Jan. 23   Ernest and Mary on board *Ile de France* returning to New York. They take with them two trunks full of Hemingway's 1920s writing found stored at the Ritz.

Feb.–June   Hemingway is at work at the Finca on what will become *The Garden of Eden* (1986).

c. July   Hemingway begins his memoir, published posthumously as *A Moveable Feast* (1964).

Sept. 22–28   Ernest, Mary, and Denis Zaphiro in New York City.

Oct.–Dec.   Hemingway alternates between the African novel and memoir.

Dec.   The Castro revolution to overthrow the Batista government in Cuba gathers head.

1958

Jan.–July   Hemingway writes steadily on his Paris memoir and *The Garden of Eden*.

May 7   Ezra Pound is released from St. Elizabeth's Hospital.

Aug.   Ernest rents a house in Ketchum for the winter.

Oct. 6–15   Ernest drives from Key West to Ketchum. Mary joins him there.

Nov.–Dec.   Ernest writes mornings, hunts in the afternoons.

Dec. 31   Batista flees Cuba. Castro revolution succeeds.

1959

Jan.–Feb.   Hemingway works on *The Garden of Eden* at Ketchum, reaching forty-five chapters.

Feb. 18   Taylor Williams dies.

Mar. 16–29   Ernest and Mary leave Ketchum and travel to Havana.

April   Hemingway buys the Topping house in Ketchum.

April 22   Hemingways board the *Constitution* bound for Algeciras, Spain.

May   Hemingway writes "The Art of the Short Story" at La Consula.

June–Sept.   Ernest follows the Ordóñez–Dominguín *corridas*.

July 7–14   At the Pamplona *feria*, Valerie Danby-Smith joins the Hemingway party.

July 21   Ernest's sixtieth birthday party at La Consula.

Sept. 20   Mary flies from Madrid to Paris and back to Havana. Threatens to leave Ernest.

Oct. 27   Hemingway boards the *Liberté* bound for New York.

Nov. 1   Arrives in New York. Leaves copy of Paris memoir with Scribner's.

c. Nov. 4   Ernest, Antonio, and Carmen Ordóñez arrive at Havana airport.

Nov. 19   Ernest and the Ordóñezes arrive at Ketchum.

Nov. 27   Mary shatters her elbow in a hunting accident.

Dec.   In Ketchum, Ernest becomes more paranoid and withdrawn.

1960

Jan.–May   Hemingway writes steadily on *The Dangerous Summer*.

Jan. 17   Ernest and Mary take train to Miami and fly to Havana.

Feb. 8   Valerie arrives to act as Ernest's secretary.

July 25   Ernest, Mary, and Val leave Havana by ferry for Key West.

Aug. 4   Ernest flies to Madrid. Mary and Val remain in New York.

Aug. 20   Mary sends Val to join Ernest in Spain.

Oct. 8   Ernest returns to New York. Soon after, he and Mary go to Ketchum.

Oct.–Nov.   Hemingway's erratic moods, paranoia, and despondency become worse.

Nov. 30   Dr. George Saviers flies with Ernest to the Mayo Clinic, where he undergoes electroshock treatments.

1961

Jan. 22   Ernest is released from Mayo Clinic and returns to Ketchum.

Feb.–Mar.   Ernest loses weight, cannot write. Becomes more morose.

April 15   Bay of Pigs fiasco in Cuba.

April 21   Ernest prevented from shooting himself. Sedated and hospitalized in Ketchum.

April 24   Second attempt to kill himself is thwarted.

April 25   Ernest is flown back to Mayo Clinic.

May 23   Mary visits Ernest at Mayo, finds him no better. Doctors disagree.

June 26–30   Ernest is released from Mayo and driven to Ketchum.

July 2   Ernest Hemingway commits suicide with his favorite shotgun.

Notes

The following abbreviations are used throughout the Notes.

Newspapers & Periodicals

NYT	*New York Times*
NYTBR	*New York Times Book Review*
SRL	*Saturday Review of Literature*

People

AI	Adriana Ivancich
Berenson	Bernard Berenson
Cowley	Malcolm Cowley
CS	Charles Scribner
CSjr	Charles Scribner, Jr.
EH	Ernest Hemingway
Fenton	Charles Fenton
GHH	Grace Hall Hemingway
Hotchner	A. E. Hotchner
Lanham	Charles "Buck" Lanham
MacLeish	Archibald MacLeish
MG	Martha Gellhorn
MP	Max Perkins
MW	Mary Welsh
MWH	Mary Welsh Hemingway
PPH	Pauline Pfeiffer Hemingway
VDS	Valerie Danby-Smith

Libraries

JFK	John F. Kennedy Library, Boston

LOC   Library of Congress
PUL   Princeton University Library
Stanford   Stanford University Library
UTex   Humanities Research Center, University of Texas
UVa   University of Virginia Library

Hemingway Books

AFTA   *A Farewell to Arms* (Scribner's, 1929)
AMF   *A Moveable Feast* (Scribner's, 1964) **
ARIT   *Across the River and into the Trees* (Scribner's, 1950)
By-Line *By-Line: Ernest Hemingway*, ed. William White
           (Scribner's, 1967) **
CSS   *The Complete Short Stories of Ernest Hemingway*
           (Scribner's, 1987) **
DS   *The Dangerous Summer* (Scribner's, 1985) **
           88 Poems, ed. Nicolas Gerogiannis (Harcourt Brace, 1979) **
FWBT   *For Whom the Bell Tolls* (Scribner's, 1940)
GOE   *The Garden of Eden* (Scribner's, 1986) **
Islands *Islands in the Stream* (Scribner's, 1970) **
           Men at War (Crown Publishers, 1942)
OMAS   *The Old Man and the Sea* (Scribner's, 1952)
SAR   *The Sun Also Rises* (Scribner's, 1926)
SL   *Ernest Hemingway: Selected Letters*, ed. Carlos Baker
           (Scribner's, 1981) **
           True at First Light (Scribner's, 1999) **

Other Books

Baker   Carlos Baker, *Ernest Hemingway: A Life Story*
               (Scribner's, 1969)
Bruccoli   *The Only Thing That Counts*, ed. Matthew Bruccoli
               (Scribner's, 1996)
Burwell   Rose Marie Burwell, *Hemingway: The Postwar Years
               and the Posthumous Novels* (Cambridge University
               Press, 1996)
Conversations   *Conversations with Ernest Hemingway*, ed. Matthew
               Bruccoli (University Press of Mississippi, 1986)

** Works published posthumously

Donaldson   Scott Donaldson, *Archibald MacLeish* (Houghton
             Mifflin, 1992)

Fuentes   Noberto Fuentes, *Hemingway in Cuba* (Lyle
             Stuart, 1984)

Hanneman   *Ernest Hemingway, A Comprehensive Bibliography,*
             Vol. 1, ed. Audre Hanneman (Princeton University Press,
             1967)

High on   Lloyd Arnold, *High on the Wild* (Grosset & Dunlap,
the Wild   1968)

HIW   Mary Hemingway, *How It Was* (Knopf, 1976)

HL   James Brasch and Joséph Sigmund, *Hemingway's Library*
             (Garland Publishing, 1981)

H:PY   Michael Reynolds, *Hemingway: The Paris Years* (Blackwell,
             1989; Norton, 1999)

HReading   Michael Reynolds, *Hemingway's Reading* (Princeton
             University Press, 1981)

HR   *The Hemingway Review* (University of Idaho Press)

Kert   Bernice Kert, *The Hemingway Women* (Norton, 1983)

LG   Linda Miller, *Letters from the Lost Generation* (Rutgers
             University Press, 1991)

Meyers   Jeffrey Meyers, *Hemingway* (Harper & Row, 1985)

Papa   Gregory Hemingway, *Papa* (Houghton Mifflin, 1976)

Paporov   Uri Paporov, *Hemingway en Cuba* (Moscow, 1979; siglo XXI
             editores: Mexico City, 1993), Spanish trans. Partida
             T. Armando

Rollyson   Carl E. Rollyson, *Nothing Ever Happens to the Brave* (St.
             Martin's Press, 1990)

Ross   Lillian Ross, *Portrait of Ernest Hemingway* (Simon &
             Schuster, 1961)

Slim   Slim Keith with Annette Tapert, *Slim* (Simon & Schuster,
             1990)

True Gen   Denis Brian, *The True Gen* (Grove Press, 1988)

TWMAA   Martha Gellhorn, *Travels with Myself and Another* (Allen
             Lane, 1978)

Viertel   Peter Viertel, *Dangerous Friends* (Doubleday, 1992)

YH   Michael Reynolds, *Young Hemingway* (Blackwell, 1986;
             Norton, 1998)

PART ONE

Chapter 1. Ringing the Changes

1. *FWBT*, p. 471.
2. *Havana Post*, March 15, April 25, 1940.
3. "Notes on the Next War," *Esquire* (Sept. 1935).
4. EH–Perkins, July 13, 1940, Scribner Collection, PUL.
5. Rollyson, pp. 153–4. Martha's story was not published.
6. "Ernest Hemingway Talks of Work and War," *NYT* (Aug. 11, 1940), reprinted in *Conversations*, pp. 17–20. *NYT*, July 26–Aug. 3, 1940.
7. EH–Gustavo Durán, March 5, 1940, Baker Collection, PUL.
8. "Post-war Writers and Pre-war Readers," speech before American Association of Adult Education printed in *New Republic* (June 10, 1940), 789–90. See Donaldson, pp. 334–6.
9. "War Writers on Democracy," *Life*, June 24, 1940, 8.
10. Gerald and Sara Murphy–EH, [fall 1926] and Sept. 6, 1926, *LG*, pp. 21–4.
11. [July 29, 1940], *LG*, p. 252.
12. [c. late December 1940], *LG*, pp. 260–1.
13. *NYT*, July 31, 1940.
14. Perkins–EH, July 31, Aug. 1, 1940, PUL; I am indebted to the meticulous research of Robert Trogdon's unpublished essay, "Making the Blockbuster."
15. Quoted in Kert, p. 343. See Kert throughout for the clearest view of the Hemingway-Gellhorn relationship. Edna Gellhorn's framed portrait remained in Finca Vigia long after Martha's disappeared. It is now at the JFK.
16. Harry M. Hagen, *This Is Our . . . St. Louis* (St. Louis: Knight Publ., c. 1970), p. 540.
17. Rollyson, p. 4. "Mrs. Gellhorn Still on the Firing Line," *St. Louis Post Dispatch*, Dec. 15, 1963.
18. Martha Gellhorn, "Cuba Revisited," *Time Out* (Jan. 7–14, 1987).
19. Quoted in Kert, p. 343; Kert was the last biographer to have access to the Gellhorn papers at Boston University before Gellhorn closed them into the next century.
20. c. Aug. 8, 1940, Bruccoli, p. 285.
21. See *Hemingway's First War* (Princeton U. Press, 1976) for revisions to *SAR* and *AFTA*. See Thomas Gould's "Authorial Revision and

Editorial Emasculation in . . . *For Whom the Bell Tolls*," in *Blowing the Bridge*, ed. Rena Sanderson (New York: Greenwood Press, 1992), pp. 67–82.

22. Scribner's, many years later and without fanfare, restored the bulls' appendages in the text.

23. MP–EH, Aug. 26, 1940; EH–MP, Aug. 26, 1940, Bruccoli, pp. 289–94.

24. EH–MG, [nd], two notes, JFK.

25. Paporov, pp. 42–4.

26. See *Reading;* it has been suggested that Toby Bruce selected the library shipped to Cuba in December 1940. A letter from Pauline to EH, November 1940, in Fuentes, p. 328, makes it clear that Bruce inventoried and packed books EH selected.

27. Kert, p. 344.

28. EH–Hadley, Dec. 26, 1940, *SL*, p. 520.

29. J. Donald Adams, "The New Novel by Hemingway," *NYTBR* (Oct. 20, 1940), 1; Margaret Marshall, "Notes by the Way," *The Nation* (Oct. 26, 1940), 395. Howard Mumford Jones, "The Soul of Spain," *SRL* (Oct. 26, 1940), 5; Clifton Fadiman, "Hemingway Crosses the Bridge," *New Yorker* (Oct. 26, 1940), 66; Edmund Wilson, "Return of Ernest Hemingway," *New Republic* (Oct. 28, 1940), 591–2.

30. Hanneman, Vol 1, pp. 51–2; the six previous Hemingway books' combined first printings totaled only 57,804 copies.

31. EH–Durán, [fall 1940], Baker Collection, PUL. Neither claim was even close to the truth.

32. Author interview with Bud and Ruth Purdy, 1995.

33. EH–MP, c. Oct. 12, 1940, *SL*, pp. 517–8.

34. Author interview with Purdys.

35. EH–CS, c. Oct. 21, 1940, *SL*, p. 519.

36. *NYT*, Nov. 21, 1940. Certificate of Marriage, JFK. Witnesses: Jean Wilson and William E. Mullen.

37. PPH–EH, [Nov. 22, 1940], in Fuentes, pp. 327–8.

38. "Back to His First Field," *Kansas City Times* (Nov. 26, 1940), in *Conversations*, pp. 21–4.

39. Matthew J. Bruccoli, *Fitzgerald and Hemingway: A Dangerous Friendship* (New York: Carroll & Graf, 1994), pp. 204–6, 229.

Chapter 2. To Mandalay and Back

1. *TWMAA*, pp. 19–33.

2. *Ta-Kung-Pao*, Chungking (Feb. 23, 1941), quoted in Warren K. J. Sung's M.A. thesis, Tamkang College of Arts and Sciences, June 1979. For Sung's thesis I am indebted to Marsha Goin and her late husband John.

3. Hollington K. Tong, *China and the World Press* (Nanking, 1948), p. 159.

4. *TWMAA*, pp. 40–1.

5. *Ibid.*, pp. 49–53.

6. Augustus Pfeiffer letter (July 21, 1941) relaying information from an EH letter of July 14, 1941. H. H. Kung was married to Madame Chiang Kai-shek's sister.

7. *TWMAA*, p. 55.

8. "ERNEST HEMINGWAY Tells How 100,000 Chinese Labored Night and Day to Build Huge Landing Field for Bombers," *PM* (June 18, 1941), pp. 16–17.

9. *Chungking Central Daily News* (April 15, 1941) in Warren K. J. Sung's M.A. thesis.

10. EH–MG, May 2, 1941, JFK.

11. EH–MG, May 12, 15, 17, and 19, 1941, JFK.

12. *NYT*, April 20, 1941: Gallup Poll reports 79% opposed to sending troops; 69% opposed to sending planes; 67% opposed to sending ships.

13. *NYT*, April 24, 1941, p. 6.

14. "ERNEST HEMINGWAY Says We Can't Let Japan Grab Our Rubber Supplies . . . ," *PM*, June 11, 1941, p. 6.

15. "After Four Years of War in China Japs Have Conquered Only Flat Lands," *PM*, June 16, 1941, p. 6; "ERNEST HEMINGWAY Says China Needs Pilots As Well as Planes to Beat Japanese in the Air," *PM*, June 17, 1941, p. 5.

16. Russell Whelan, *The Flying Tigers* (New York: Viking Press, 1942), pp. 34–5, 211.

17. "ERNEST HEMINGWAY Says Aid to China Gives U.S. Two-Ocean Navy Security," *PM*, June 15, 1941, p. 6.

18. EH–Henry Morgenthau, July 20, 1941, JFK.

19. "Ernest Hemingway, Noted Author, Visits Key West," *Key West Citizen*, June 7, 1941.

20. "Joe Russell, Local Saloon Operator, Dies in Havana," *Key West Citizen*, June 21, 1941.

21. EH–PPH (c. Aug. 1, 1941), misdated in *SL* as June 9, 1941, p. 524.

22. Registration certificate, Aug. 23, 1941, JFK.

23. MP–EH, April 4, 1941, PUL; EH–MP, April 29, 1941, PUL, in Bruccoli, pp. 307–8.

24. EH–PPH, July 19, 1941, *SL*, p. 525.

25. "Snoopers Find Ideal Nazi Base Off Mexico," *Baltimore Sun*, Aug. 22, 1940.

26. "Miskito Keys: Ideal Hideouts for Nazis," *Baltimore Sun*, Aug. 23, 1940.

27. "Nazi Found in Costa Rica, Too," *Baltimore Sun*, Aug. 27, 1940.

28. EH–Leicester Hemingway, June 28, 1941, in *My Brother, Ernest Hemingway* (1961; reissued 1996, Sarasota, FL: Pineapple Press) pp. 300–1.

29. MG–Jane Armstrong [July 25, 1941, and Aug. 22, 1941], private collection.

30. EH–MP, Aug. 26, 1941, in Bruccoli, pp. 309–10.

31. EH–Janet Flanner, April 8, 1933, *SL*, pp. 386–9.

32. MG–Jane Armstrong [Aug. 22, 1941], private collection.

33. EH–MG [nd], internal evidence places it in 1941, JFK.

34. Jonathan Utley, *Going to War with Japan* (U. of Tennessee Press, 1985), pp. 151–6.

35. EH interview in *St. Louis Star-Times* (May 23, 1941), p. 1, in Bruccoli, pp. 29–30. A *Saturday Review of Literature* poll of thirty-nine literary critics gave twenty-one votes to *FWBT* as the best novel of 1940—*NYT*, April 26, 1941.

36. EH–MP, Sept. 1, 1941, Bruccoli, pp. 312–3.

Chapter 3. Voyagers

1. EH–MP, Nov. 15, 1941, *SL*, pp. 528–9.

2. *Slim*, pp. 43–4.

3. *High on the Wild*, p. 67.

4. LOC, Copyright Division, renewed in 1968 as Martha Gellhorn.

5. *SRL* (Dec. 6, 1941), p. 10, in Berg, p. 405.

6. EH–MP, Nov. 15, 1941, Bruccoli, pp, 313–4.

7. Glenway Wescott, "The Moral of Scott Fitzgerald," *New Republic* (Feb. 17, 1941), pp. 213–4.

8. Hanneman, Vol. 1, pp. 217–9; EH–MP, Nov. 15, 1941, *SL*, p. 527.

9. EH–Sinclair Lewis, Nov. 15, 1941, Yale.

10. EH–MP, Dec. 11, 1941; EH–CS, Dec. 12, 1941, *SL*, pp. 531–3.

11. On earnings of $137,357, Hemingway paid $104,000 in 1941 taxes,

$4,000 of which he was forced to borrow from Scribner's to meet the bill.

12. MG–Evan Shipman, April 7 [1942], private collection.

13. EH–MP, May 30, 1942, Bruccoli, pp. 318–20; MP–EH, June 8, 1942, Bruccoli, pp. 320–2; MP–EH, July 8, 1942, *SL*, pp. 533–5.

14. See chap. 6 of my early book, *Hemingway's First War* (Princeton U. Press, 1976).

15. *Men at War*, p. xi.

16. *Ibid.*, pp. xiv–xv.

17. EH–Mr. G., May 3, 1942, JFK.

18. Cdr. C. Alphonso Smith, USNR, "Battle of the Caribbean," *United States Naval Institute Proceedings* (Sept. 1954), 976–82.

19. *U-Boat War*, pp. 567–78. War Diary, Commander, Gulf Sea Frontier on microfilm, National Archives.

20. War Diary, May 1, 1942.

21. War Diary, May 18, 1942, OPNAV update.

22. See *NYT*, Jan. 4, 1942, p. 4; Jan. 11, 1942, p. V, 7:1; Jan. 25, 1942, p. 20; April 19, 1942, p. III, 7.

23. *NYT*, June 28, 1942, p. 21.

24. *NYT*, July 26, 1942, p. 22.

25. See *Reading*, Item 1357, Felix Luckner, *The Last Privateer*, misidentified in *SL*.

26. Office of Naval Intelligence publications ONI 220-M and ONI 220-G. EH's copy of 220-M at JFK.

27. *Havana Post*, May 2, 1942.

28. Spruille Braden, *Diplomats and Demagogues* (New York: Arlington House, 1971), pp. 282–4.

29. National Archives, Confidential Letter File, American Embassy, Havana, 1942–3.

30. "The United States and Cuban-Spanish Relations," Oct. 28, 1942, copy in the Hemingway Papers at the JFK.

31. *NYT*, Jan. 4, 1942, p. 1; Jan. 2, 1942, p. 11; Feb. 1, 1942, p. 6.

32. "The Invaders," *Newsweek* (July 6, 1942), p. 304; *Newsweek* (Aug. 17, 1942), pp. 29–31.

33. *NYT*, July 2, 1942, pp.1, 8.

34. *Newsweek* (July 13, 1942), pp. 27–8.

35. *Havana Post*, April 14, 1942.

36. National Archives, RG-84: Foreign Service Posts, Havana Embassy Confidential File 1Comejen: a 942-43 Part 2: 711-815.6.

37. MG, "Cuba Revisited," *Time Out* (Jan. 7–14, 1987).

38. Olive G. Gibson, *Isle of a Hundred Harbors* (Boston: Bruce Humphries, 1940), pp. 55–60.

39. Jack Hemingway, *Misadventures of a Fly Fisherman* (Dallas: Taylor Publishing, 1986), p. 39; *Papa*, p. 47.

40. *TWMAA*, p. 64.

41. Rollyson, pp. 172–4.

42. Kert, p. 371.

43. For a full account, see MG, "Messing About in Boats," *TWMAA*, pp. 64–106. Her itinerary included Haiti, Puerto Rico, St. Thomas, Tortola, Virgin Gorda, Anguilla, St. Martin, St. Barthélemy, Saba, St. Kitts, Surinam, French and Dutch Guiana.

44. "A Little Worse Than Peace," *Collier's* (Nov. 14, 1942), pp. 18–9, 84–6; "Holland's Last Stand," *Collier's* (Dec. 26, 1942), 25–9.

45. EH–MG, July 31 [1942], JFK. For a very different version see Gregory's *Papa*, p. 80.

46. EH–MG, Aug. 10/16, 25, Sept. 1, 8, 19, 31, Oct. 14, 15, 1942, JFK.

47. *Havana Post*, Sept. 9, 1942. EH–Col. Hayne D. Boyden, Nov. 2, 1942, JFK.

48. Braden, *Diplomats*, pp. 284–5.

49. FBI File, Oct. 8, 1942. Hemingway's FBI File was obtained for the author under the Freedom of Information Act by Russell Judd Boone in 1982.

50. EH–Shipman, Aug. 25, 1942, *SL*, p. 538.

51. FBI File, Oct. 9, 1942.

52. Item 527, JFK.

53. FBI File, Oct. 9, 10, 1942.

54. War Diary, June–October 1942.

55. See http://www.uboat.net/boats.htm

56. *Havana Post*, Sept. 9–20, 1942.

57. Item 273, JFK; Consuelo Hermer and Marjorie May, *Havana Manana* (New York: Random House, 1942); *Clipper Guide to Cuba* (Havana, 1947); Fuentes, pp. 9, 10, 229–30.

58. EH–Hayne D. Boyden, Nov. 2, 1942, JFK. It has been commonly held that the *Pilar* patrols began in June 1942. Letters and documents at the JFK make it clear that the first armed cruise did not take place until mid-November.

59. *Pilar* papers, JFK; Typed report of the incident dated Dec. 10, 1942, Havana, also at JFK.

60. War Diary, Dec. 9, 1942.
61. C. H. Carson, "Memorandum for Mr. Ladd," June 13, 1943, FBI File.
62. D. M. Ladd, "Memorandum for the Director Re: Ernest Hemingway," Dec. 17, 1942, FBI File.
63. John Edgar Hoover–Agent Leddy, "Re: Ernest Hemingway," Dec. 17, 1942, FBI File. Hoover has mistaken Leicester Hemingway's news stories for those of Ernest.
64. Hoover memorandum, Dec. 19, 1942, FBI File. Several references to EH prior to 1942 suggest that the FBI followed his activities throughout the 1930s, particularly his pronouncements on avoiding the next war and his indictment of the government in *New Masses* for the death of veterans in the 1935 Matecumbe hurricane.
65. Kert, pp. 375–6.

Chapter 4. American Patrol

1. Quoted in Kert, p. 376.
2. EH–MG, Jan. 7, 1943, JFK.
3. "Communication with Pilar" (March 7–14, 1943) in *Pilar* Papers, JFK, listing code words and directive to track the *Comillas* from the time she rounded Cape San Antonio.
4. Nov. 9, 1942, letter to EH without signature, JFK.
5. *Pilar* Log (1942–3), JFK.
6. War Diary, Jan. 23, 1943.
7. "Confidential to the Ambassador," Feb. 10, 1943, JFK.
8. Hemingway FBI File, "Memorandum for Mr. Ladd," June 13, 1943.
9. War Diary, April 1–10, 1943. *Torpedoes in the Gulf,* pp. 235–8; Jurgen Rohwer, *Axis Submarine Successes: 1939–45* (Naval Institute Press, 1983).
10. Quoted in Donaldson, p. 358.
11. EH–MacLeish, April 4, 1943, *SL*, p. 544.
12. EH–MacLeish, c. May 5, 1943, *SL*, p. 544.
13. EH–Allen Tate, Aug. 31, 1943, *SL*, pp. 549–51.
14. War Diary, April 1–May 20, 1943.
15. War Diary, May 22, 1943.
16. *Pilar* Log, JFK. Although the 1941 calendar on which the log was kept would seem to indicate that these events took place in 1942 (see Baker), Hemingway letters from 1942 place him elsewhere, and the War Diary indicates 1943. See George Miller memorandum

to "Master, Yacht Pilar," June 2, 1943, from Liaison Office in *Pilar* Papers, JFK. EH–MG, June 3, 1943, JFK, and following confirms this point.

17. In Fuentes, Gregorio remembers Confites as a supply base, but as the *Pilar* Log makes clear, the supply base was Nuevitas.

18. *True Gen*, p. 144. See also EH–MG, Thursday, June 1943, JFK, response to her chap. 16.

19. *Pilar* Log, June 8–10, 1943, JFK.

20. *Pilar* Log, June 11–14, 1943, JFK; War Diary, June 6–14, 1943. Postwar accounts of U-boat losses do not mention a sub lost at this date in these waters, but at the time, the kill was taken to be true.

21. EH–MG, June 16 and 30, 1943, JFK.

22. *Liana* (Scribner's, 1944), p. 279.

23. EH–MG, undated in-house letter, clearly 1943, JFK.

24. EH–MG, June 22, 1943, JFK.

25. *Pilar* Papers, JFK. *Papa*, p. 78. EH–MG, June 17, and Wednesday, June, undated 1943, JFK. Martha did not have all the male cats castrated as has been suggested elsewhere.

26. EH–MG, June 7, 1943, JFK; six pages are typed, single-spaced, one is holograph.

27. *Pilar* Papers, along with July 9, 1943, letter from Miller at Nuevitas, JFK.

28. EH–Mr. [Roy] Hawkins, July 20, 1943, JFK.

29. War Diary, July 19, 1943.

30. Philip Wylie and Laurence Schwab, "The Battle of Florida," *Saturday Evening Post* (March 11, 1944), 14–5, 52–8. If Hemingway's patrols were as foolish and childish as some critics have expressed, then the same must be said of the efforts of hundreds of other private yachtsmen.

31. EH–Mr. [Roy] Hawkins, July 20, 1943, JFK.

32. Ellis O. Briggs, *Shots Heard Round the World* (New York: Viking Press, 1957), p. 68. Briggs has Winston Guest present at the shoot, but EH letters clearly put him in Colorado.

33. Briggs, *Shots Heard*, p. 73

Chapter 5. Intermezzo

1. MG–EH, June 28, 1943, quoted in Kert, pp. 379–80.

2. Author interview with Gregory Hemingway.

3. EH–MP, May 30, 1942, PUL, in Bruccoli, p. 318.

4. EH–Mr. G[rover], c. May 5, 1942, JFK.

5. EH–MacLeish, c. May 5, 1943, LOC, in *SL*, p. 545.

6. EH–MacLeish, Aug. 10, 1943, LOC, in *SL*, pp. 548–9.

7. EH–Allen May, Aug. 31, 1943, Fuentes, p. 340.

8. Lilian Beath–EH, Sept. 1 and 3, 1943, JFK; Marcelline Hemingway Sanford–EH, Sept. 9, 1943, JFK.

9. MG–EH, Oct. 21, 1943, Kert, p. 384.

10. War Diary, October 1943.

11. EH–Hadley Mowrer, Nov. 25, 1943, *SL*, p. 555; EH–MacLeish, Dec. 26, 1943, copy in Baker files, PUL.

12. Kert, pp. 388–90.

13. EH–MG, Jan.13, 1944, JFK.

14. EH–MG, Jan. 31, 1944, JFK.

15. EH–Ramon LaValle, Feb. 2, 1944, Baker Collection, PUL.

16. Charles Colebaugh–EH, March 10, 1944, JFK.

17. *Collier's* (March 4, 1944), quoted in Kert, p. 391.

18. EH–MP, March 12, 1944, PUL and JFK, in Bruccoli, p. 327.

19. Quoted in Kert, pp. 391–2.

20. Spruille Braden–EH, March 7, 1944, JFK. EH–Charles Colebaugh, March 30, 1944, JFK. In London he showed the letter, which he carried in his shirt pocket, to more than one person.

21. Earl Wilson, "It Happened Last Night," *NY Post*, May 2, 1944.

22. OSS, Shepherdson–Robert Joyce, May 1, 1944, JFK.

23. Quoted in Kert, p. 392.

24. Julia Edwards, *Women of the World: The Great Foreign Correspondents* (Boston: Houghton Mifflin, 1988), pp. 130, 149–57. Iris Carpenter, *No Woman's World* (Boston: Houghton Mifflin, 1946), pp. 32–5, 44–55.

25. EH–MP, March 12, 1944, Bruccoli, p. 332.

26. *The Diaries of Dawn Powell*, ed. Tim Page (South Royalton, VT: Steerforth Press, 1995), p. 231.

27. A signed one-dollar bill, a "short snorter," signed by Hemingway and other passengers, including John Ringlin North, on May 17, 1944, JFK.

28. Kert, p. 392.

29. *TWMAA*, p. 280. Martha remembered the voyage lasting eighteen days; she apparently arrived on May 31.

30. *HIW*, pp. 93–4.

31. *The Times* (London), "U.S. War Correspondent Injured," May 25, 1944, p. 2. Kert, p. 398.

Chapter 6. Putting on the Ritz

1. "Voyage to Victory," *By-Line*, p. 340.
2. "OMAHA BEACHHEAD (6 June–13 June 1944)," *American Forces in Action Series*, CMH Pub 100-11, Center of Military History (Washington, D.C., facsimile reprint, 1984), p. 41.
3. *By-Line*, pp. 344–55.
4. Group Capt. G. W. Houghton, RAF, to F/Lt. R. G. Teakle, July 28, 1944, JFK.
5. "London Fights the Robots," *Collier's* (Aug. 19, 1944), in *By-Line*, p. 361; Baker, pp. 395–7.
6. Quoted in Baker, p. 399.
7. *88 Poems*, "First Poem to Mary in London," p. 104.
8. *HIW*, pp. 102–6.
9. H. R. Stoneback, "Hemingway's Happiest Summer," *North Dakota Quarterly*, Vol. 64, no. 3, 1997, pp. 190–3. For more details than possible here, see the entire essay.
10. *ARIT*, p. 224.
11. Duke Shoop, "Dine on Chili and Wine," *Kansas City Star*, July 31, 1944, pp. 1–2.
12. EH–Mary Welsh, July 31, Aug. 1, 1944, *SL*, pp. 558–61.
13. "Hemingway 'Captures' Six," *NYT*, Aug. 4, 1944, p. 3.
14. Hemingway–Lanham Chronology, 1944–5, Baker Collection, PUL. Hereafter cited as Lanham.
15. Henry T. Gorrell, "A Close Hemingway Call," *Kansas City Star*, Aug. 6, 1944, p. 6.
16. Robert Capa, *Slightly Out of Focus* (New York: Henry Holt, 1947), pp. 166–8.
17. *Ibid.* Ten years later Capa would step on a Viet Minh landmine in Vietnam and die.
18. Stoneback, "Hemingway's Happiest Summer," p. 197. Hemingway signed in: "August 6, 1944 Ernest Hemingway Finca Vigia–San Francisco de Paula-Cuba Avec 4[iem] Division USA."
19. Quoted in Meyers, p. 404.
20. *True Gen*, pp. 150–9.
21. See Stoneback's "Hemingway's Happiest Summer," pp. 199–201, for the original research on this previously dark period of Hemingway's war.

22. Maj. R. L. Norling (G-4), Aug. 20, 1944, handwritten note, JFK.

23. World War II diary of Col. David K. E. Bruce, *OSS against the Reich*, ed. N. D. Lankford (Kent State U. Press, 1991), pp. 160–1. Hereafter cited as Bruce.

24. Robert Aron, *France Reborn*, trans. Humphrey Hare (New York: Scribner's, 1964), p. 287.

25. Bruce, pp. 165–6.

26. David Bruce–EH, June 12, 1955; attached to the note is a 1947/48 account of the four days at Rambouillet given to a reporter, JFK. Russians taken prisoner on the eastern front were often put into German uniforms to fight on the western front.

27. Bruce, pp. 168–9. For a more colorful description of this scene and those preceding, see Hemingway's "Battle for Paris," and "How We Came to Paris," reprinted in *By-Line*, pp. 364–83.

28. Bruce, p. 170.

29. Bruce–EH, Aug. 23, 1944, JFK.

30. Bruce, pp. 171–8.

31. *The Very Rich Hours of Adrienne Monnier*, trans. Richard McDougall (New York: Scribner's, 1976), pp. 416–7; Noel Riley Fitch, *Sylvia Beach and the Lost Generation* (New York: Norton, 1983), pp. 402–7.

32. Malcolm Cowley, "Hemingway at Midnight," *New Republic* (Aug. 14, 1944), pp. 190–5.

33. EH–MW, Aug. 27, 1944, unfinished and unmailed, *SL*, pp. 564–5. Mary says it was misdated, for she arrived at the Ritz on August 26, *HIW*, p. 113.

34. *HIW*, p. 114.

Chapter 7. Down among the Dead Men

1. War Diary, JFK; EH–MW, Sept. 8, 1944, *SL*, pp. 565–6.

2. Lanham, pp. 9–11; Hemingway's ETO Chronology, p. 13; War Diary, pp. 11–12. Today, near the postwar bridge, a bronze plaque quotes Lanham in French: "Avant l'arrivée des ingénieurs vos adroits artisans ont construit ici un pont en 45 minutes." [Before the arrival of engineers, your adroit artisans built a bridge here in 45 minutes.] Beneath the name Lanham is the date: 10.9.44.

3. EH notes on endpaper of *A Few Facts About France: Part I*, JFK.

4. *Collier's* (Nov. 18, 1944), reprinted in *By-Line*, pp. 392–400.

5. Lanham, pp. 15–16.

6. *88 Poems*, "Poem for Mary (Second Poem)," p. 107.

7. Lanham, p. 17.

8. EH–MW, Sept. 23–24, 1944, JFK.

9. Hemingway Collection, JFK.

10. MW–EH, Oct. 1, 1944, JFK.

11. Cdr. Harry C. Butcher (PRD, SHAEF)–EH, Oct. 2, 1944, JFK. It was the Third Army because Hemingway had never gone through formal channels for transferring to the 22nd Infantry.

12. Transcript of EH testimony on Oct. 6, 1944, Nancy, France, JFK.

13. EH–Paul Leahy, June 26, 1952, JFK.

14. EH–*Collier's*, Press Wireless, attention Lacossitt, undated, but postmarked Oct. 25, 1944, JFK.

15. *HIW*, pp. 127–36; AG 201–EH, Nov. 9, 1944, SHAEF orders to report to the First Army.

16. The details of the 22nd Infantry's battle in Hürtgenwald is largely based on Robert Rush's detailed history—"Paschendale [sic] with Treebursts"—which he posted on the Web and which is "the complete account of the 22d Infantry Regiment in the Hurtgen Forest, with the day by day Regimental Journal Files and After Action Reviews of the surviving soldiers." Also the Lanham-Hemingway Papers at PUL; Rose Marie Burwell's interview with Bill Walton at the JFK; Charles Whiting, *The Battle of Hürtgen Forest* (New York: Orion Books, 1989).

17. War Diary, Sept. 1944, and his "War in the Siegfried Line," *Collier's* (Nov. 18, 1944), reprinted in *By-Line*, pp. 392–400.

18. EH–Henry La Corsitt, Nov. 16, 1944, in Fuentes, p. 351.

19. Robert Rush, "Paschendale [sic] with Treebursts".

20. EH–MW, Nov. 16–18–19–20, 1944, in Fuentes, pp. 351–6. MW–EH, two letters both dated Nov. 14, 1944, JFK.

21. MW–EH, Nov. 15, 1944, JFK.

22. Lanham, p. 27.

23. EH–MW, Nov. 23, 1944, Fuentes, p. 361.

24. EH–MW, Nov. 25, 1944, Fuentes, p. 364.

25. EH–MW, Nov. 29, 1944, in Fuentes, p. 369.

26. Walton reading from unpublished memoir in Burwell interview, JFK.

27. Whiting, pp. 133–4; Rush; Garcia was the only Medal of Honor winner at Hürtgenwald to live to receive his award.

28. EH–MG, Dec. 5, 1944, JFK.

29. Burwell interview with William Walton, JFK.

PART TWO

Chapter 8. Starting Over

1. EH–MW, March 6, 7, 13, 16, 1945, JFK.
2. PPH–EH, March 17, 1945, JFK.
3. EH–MW, March 20, 1945, JFK. See also EH–Lanham, April 2, 1945, *SL*, p. 578; EH–MP, April 14, 1945, PUL.
4. See *Hemingway: The 1930s*; EH–Lanham, April 14, 1945, *SL*, p. 586.
5. EH–MW, April 9, 1945, *SL*, p. 581; EH–Lanham, April 14, 1945, *SL*, p. 585. Lanham book: *Infantry in Battle*.
6. EH–MW, April 14, 1945, *SL*, p. 584; Baker, p. 447.
7. EH–Carol Gardner, c. December 1945, Fuentes, pp. 386ff. See also EH–Lanham, April 14 and 20, 1945, *SL*, pp. 585–8.
8. EH–Lanham, June 9, 1945, Fuentes, p. 383.
9. *Papa*, pp. 95–6; Meyers, pp. 418–20; Baker, pp. 448–9.
10. MW–EH, October or November 1945, Mary Hemingway Papers, JFK.
11. Mary Welsh Journal, June–July 1945, JFK.
12. Kert, p. 421.
13. EH–MP, July 23, 1945, *SL*, p. 593; Mary's Journal, 1945, JFK.
14. MW–Pamela Churchill, July 4, 1945, JFK.
15. MW–EH, undated [1945], JFK.
16. Kert, p. 421.
17. Mary's Journal, Oct. 7, 1945, JFK.
18. MW–Eleanor Welch, undated answer to Oct. 1, 1945, telegram, JFK.
19. Mary's Journal, Oct. 13, 1945, JFK.
20. MW–Welch, Oct. 13, 1945, JFK.
21. Mary's Journal, Dec. 19, 1945, JFK.
22. See "Martha Gellhorn Hurt in Crash," *NYT*, Dec. 14, 1944, p. 6.
23. Martha Gellhorn, *Love Goes to Press*, ed. Sandra Spanier (U. of Nebraska Press, 1995).
24. MG–EH, May 28, 1945, and EH–MG, undated and perhaps unsent, Fuentes, pp. 376–81.
25. MSS Items 310, 310a, 525a, and 564c, Hemingway Collection, JFK.
26. EH–Childnics, Oct. 19, 1945; EH–Mouse, Oct. 24, 1945 (both letters to his sons), JFK; EH–MP, Oct. 31, 1945, Bruccoli, p. 336.

27. MWH–Parthy Vanderwicken, Dec. 20, 1945, JFK.

Chapter 9. Rules of the Game

1. The best study of this period is Rose Marie Burwell's *Hemingway: The Postwar Years and the Posthumous Novels* (Cambridge U. Press, 1996). See also Robert E. Fleming's equally perceptive *The Face in the Mirror: Hemingway's Writers* (U. of Alabama Press, 1994). Because different editors, including Mary Hemingway, apparently did not realize Hemingway's objective, they removed significant material from the posthumous publications. To speak of the published *Islands in the Stream, The Garden of Eden*, or *A Moveable Feast* as Hemingway's work is, therefore, only partially true.

2. MW–EH, October or November 1945, Mary Hemingway Papers, JFK.

3. MW–EH, Jan. 27, 1946, Sunday (misdated 28th), Mary Hemingway Papers, JFK.

4. "Dearest Kittener" letters in Mary Hemingway Papers, JFK.

5. EH–Lanham, Feb. 21, 1946, PUL.

6. EH–MW, Jan. 24, 1946, JFK.

7. MW–EH, Jan. 27, 1946 (misdated Jan. 28), JFK.

8. Mary's Journal, March 13, 1945, Mary Hemingway Papers, JFK. March 14 is usually thought to be the date of the wedding.

9. MWH–Connie Bessie, March 27, 1946, JFK.

10. MG–MWH, misdated April 29, [1946], by Mary as 1945 in her papers, JFK.

11. MG–MWH, July 25, [1946], also misdated as 1945.

12. *Slim*, pp. 74–5.

13. Hadley Richardson–EH, Jan. 8, 1921, JFK.

14. Dr. James Gough–MWH, May 6, 1946, Mary Hemingway Papers, JFK.

15. EH–Mouse [Patrick Hemingway], June 21/30, 1946, JFK. Grace Hemingway–EH, June 30, 1946, JFK.

16. Mary's Journal, June 23, 1946; Mary Hemingway Papers, JFK.

17. EH–Lanham, June 30, 1946, PUL.

18. *Ibid.*

19. Grace Hemingway–EH, July 21, 1946, UTex.

20. EH–Lanham, June 30, 1946, PUL.

21. EH–MG, Aug. 5, 1946, JFK, marked "unsent" in Hemingway's hand.

22. EH–Lanham, Aug. 25, 1946, JFK; *HIW*, p. 189.

23. EH–Lanham, Aug. 28, 1946, JFK. EH checks written to hospital and to RNs Hazel Miller and Edith Vance; paid bill from Casper Typewriter Exchange, Aug. 27, 1946; Nonresident Wyoming fishing license, Aug. 30, 1946; East Gate entry permit, Yellowstone, Sept. 12, 1946: all at the JFK and in private collections.

24. EH–Slim Hawks, Oct. 9, 1946, photo facsimile on wall at Ketchum Korral.

25. Baker, pp. 458-9.

26. Mary Harington, "They Call Him Papa," *New York Post Weekend Magazine* (Dec. 28, 1946), 3; Roger Linscott, "On the Books," *New York Herald Tribune Book Review* (Dec. 29, 1946), 13; *New Yorker* (Jan. 22, 1947), all three reprinted in *Conversations*, pp. 42–9.

27. Connie Bessie–MWH, Nov. 18, 1946, JFK.

Chapter 10. Year of the Dog

1. EH–MWH, May 5, 1947, JFK.

2. EH–MP, March 5, 1947, *SL*, pp. 615–8.

3. *True Gen*, p. 187.

4. EH–MWH, May 2, 3, 4, 1947, JFK; EH–Lillian Ross, July 2, 1948, *SL*, p. 645.

5. EH–MWH, May 2, 1947, JFK.

6. EH–MWH, May 5, 1947, JFK.

7. EH–MWH, May 14, 1947, JFK.

8. EH–Lanham, May 24, 1947, PUL.

9. EH–Lanham, June 5, 1947, PUL.

10. Mary Hemingway File, Misc. personal notes, dated June 4, [1947], but more likely June 14, JFK.

11. EH–MWH, June 26 and July 8, 1947, JFK.

12. Faulkner–EH, June 28, 1947, JFK.

13. Faulkner–EH, "Dear Brother H," July 19, 1947, JFK.

14. EH–Faulkner, July 23, 1947, *SL*, pp. 623–5.

15. EH–CS, Sept. 18, 1947, *SL*, p. 628. Townsend Ludington, *John Dos Passos: A Twentieth Century Odyssey* (New York: Dutton, 1980), pp. 432–3.

16. *NYT*, Aug. 7, 1947.

17. *NYT*, Aug. 21, 1947.

18. Paporov, pp. 93–6.

19. *NYT*, Sept. 30, 1947.

20. Paporov, pp. 100–4.
21. Thomas Leonard, *Day by Day: The 1940s* (New York: Facts on File, 1977), pp. 716–28. Dated license to operate a motor vehicle in the park, JFK. EH–MWH, October 2, 1947, JFK.
22. EH–MWH, October 1947, JFK. Mary sent the newspaper clippings to him.
23. *Diario de la Marina* (Oct. 17, 1947), in Fuentes, p. 252.
24. Fuentes, pp. 253–4; EH–MWH, Oct. 3, 1947, JFK. Herrera also said Hemingway returned a week later to dispose of his "arsenal," which could not have happened with Ernest in Sun Valley.
25. EH–Lanham, Oct. 24, 1947, PUL.
26. EH–Lanham, Oct. 24, Nov. 27, Dec. 28, 1947, PUL.
27. *High on the Wild*, p. 85; Baker, p. 463. *NYT* obituary, Dec. 22, 1947.
28. EH introduction to 1948 edition of *AFTA*.

Chapter 11. Enter Biographers, Stage Left

1. Constance Montgomery, *Hemingway in Michigan* (Vermont Crossroads Press, 1977), p. 199.
2. Ross, p. 12.
3. Viertel, pp. 14, 16.
4. *Ibid.*, pp. 10–14.
5. Mary's typed travel log, JFK, says they left on Feb. 15, but numerous letters and other dateable events (the Santa Fe snowstorm) insist they left Feb. 1. EH–Gregory, Feb. 21, 1948, JFK.
6. Earl Wilson, "It Happened Last Night," *NY Post*, Feb. 26, 1948.
7. Robert Joyce quoted in *True Gen*, pp. 195–8.
8. EH–Malcolm Cowley, April 9, 1948, private collection.
9. EH–Cowley, April 13, 1948, private collection.
10. EH–Cowley, June 9, 25, 28, July 5, 15, 1948; Cowley–EH, June 22, 1948, all in a private collection.
11. EH–Cowley, July 15, Aug. 19, 25, Sept. 3, 5, Nov. 15, 16, 29, Dec. 31, 1948, all in a private collection.
12. Malcolm Cowley, "A Portrait of Mister Papa," *Life* (Jan. 10, 1949), 86–101.
13. EH–Peter Viertel, March 10, 1948, private collection.
14. Viertel, pp. 30–41; the movie, staring John Garfield and Jennifer Jones, became *We Were Strangers*.
15. Viertel, p. 46.
16. EH–Viertel, June 10, 1948, private collection.

17. Viertel–EH, June 16, 1948, JFK.
18. EH–MacLeish, Aug. 27, 1948, LOC.
19. EH & MWH–Viertels, June 28, 1948, six pages, typed and hand-written, single-spaced, in private collection.
20. EH–W. G. Rogers, July 29, 1948, *SL*, pp. 649–50.
21. EH–Lillian Ross, July 28, 1948, *SL*, pp. 646–9. See *Young Hemingway*.
22. EH & MWH–Viertels, June 28, 1948, private collection.
23. EH–Viertels, July 9, 1948, UVa.
24. *Papa*, pp. 3–12; Hotchner–EH, June 11, 1948, JFK; contract between *Cosmopolitan* and Hemingway, June 11, 1948, JFK. The novel has been mistakenly identified as *Across the River and into the Trees*.
25. EH–Hotchner, June 27, 1948, UVa; Hotchner–EH, July 7, 1948, JFK; Hotchner–EH, July 21, 1948, JFK; EH–Hotchner, Sept. 7, 1948, UVa.
26. EH–Viertel, Aug. 8, 9, 1948, private collection; Royalty report, Aug. 30, 1948, JFK.

Chapter 12. Sentimental Journey

1. "A Veteran Visits the Old Front," *Toronto Daily Star*, July 22, 1922.
2. Mary Hemingway's Italian Journal, unpublished, Mary Hemingway Collection, JFK; hereafter cited as Italian Journal. See Baker and Meyers.
3. *AFTA*, p. 270.
4. Italian Journal, Sept. 26, 1948.
5. EH–Cowley, April 25, 1949, private collection.
6. Italian Journal, Nov. 14, 1948.
7. Italian Journal, Sept. 17, Nov. 12–14, 1948.
8. Italian Journal, Nov. 14, 1948.
9. See *YH* index for D'Annunzio.
10. See *H:PY*.
11. EH–Viertel, Nov. 12, 1948, private collection.
12. *Ibid.*
13. EH–Patrick and Gregory Hemingway, July 17, 1949, PUL.
14. See any of the picture guidebooks to Venice, and Sean O'Faolain, *A Summer in Italy* (New York: Devin-Adair, 1950), pp. 199–213.
15. Italian Journal; EH–David Bruce, Nov. 27, 1948, JFK.
16. Baker, p. 648.

17. "The Great Blue River," *Holiday* (July 1949), in *By-Line*, pp. 403–16.

18. EH–CS, November 1948, PUL.

19. EH–Viertel, Nov. 12, Dec. 13, 1948, private collection.

20. EH–CS, Dec. 9 and 31, 1948, PUL.

21. EH–Alfred Rice, Dec. 15, 1948, *SL*, pp. 654–7.

22. EH–Viertel, Dec. 13, 1948, private collection.

23. Baker, pp. 469–70; Kert, pp. 435–41.

24. *AFTA*, p. 118.

25. Quote in Kert, pp. 435–43.

26. EH–Viertel, Jan. 19, 1949, private collection. Letter begun on Jan. 19 and finished Feb. 9.

27. EH–Cowley, Jan. 24, 1949, private collection.

28. EH–Cowley, March 9, April 25, 1949; Cowley–EH, May 3, 1949, all in a private collection.

29. PPH–EH, undated [Christmas 1948], JFK; EH–PPH, Jan. 26, 1948 [sic], misdated. Should be 1949, JFK.

30. Hotchner–EH, Feb. 17, 1949, UVa; EH–Hotchner, March 9, 1949, UVa.

31. Italian Journal, March 1949, JFK.

32. *ARIT*, p. 7.

33. EH–Lanham, March 11, 1949, PUL.

34. Italian Journal, March 1949; Baker, p. 471; EH–Jack [?] April 11, 1949, from Cortina, JFK.

35. Kert, pp.442–3.

Chapter 13. Venice Preserved

1. Typescript *ARIT*, opening page, "Cortina d'Ampezzo, March, 1949," JFK.

2. See *HReading* and *HL*.

3. EH–Patrick Hemingway, May 29, 1949, PUL; *NYT*, May 23, 1949, reports EH in Cristobál, Canal Zone, on May 22.

4. The name Renata probably comes from the character in D'Annunzio's novel *Notturno*, a novel Cantwell likes (p. 52).

5. For explanations of hexanitrate and numerous other obscure references in *ARIT*, Miriam Mandell's superb *Reading Hemingway: The Facts in the Fiction* (Metuchen, NJ: Scarecrow Press, 1995) is indispensable.

6. EH–Kip Farrington, May 29, 1949, JFK.

7. Baker, p. 473.

8. GHH–EH, June 3, 1949, JFK.

9. EH's Scribner book bill for April–July 1949: *Human Destiny* by Pierre Lecomte du Noüy "to G. Hemingway," JFK. The "G." could have been Gregory, but Grace is more likely.

10. EH's Scribner book bill for April–July 1949, JFK.

11. Letter, Oct. 26, 1819, written from Venice (published in *Byron's Letters and Journals*, Vol. 6, ed. Leslie A. Marchand).

12. The World War II experience of Hemingway's friend and professional soldier from the 1918–24 period—E. E. Dorman-O'Gowan—has been suggested as a model for Cantwell. But Hemingway's accidental reacquaintance with Dorman-O'Gowan in March 1950 took place well after the typescript for *ARIT* was completed and book galleys corrected.

13. EH–Carlo Kechler, Aug. 11, 1949, JFK.

14. EH–CS, July 22, 1949, PUL.

15. EH–CS, Aug. 27, 1949, *SL*, p. 672.

16. EH–MacLeish, Aug. 27, 1948, LOC.

17. EH–William Seward, Aug. 11, 1949, JFK.

18. EH–Dos Passos, Sept. 17, 1949.

19. EH–Viertel, Sept. 29, 1949, private collection.

20. Eric Dorman–O'Gowan memoir, Carlos Baker files, PUL.

21. EH–Mouse and Gigi, July 17, 1949, PUL.

22. EH–Teresa, Sept. 24, 1949, JFK.

23. EH–AI, Oct. 3, 1949, JFK.

24. EH–CS, Aug. 24 and 25–26, 1949, PUL.

25. EH–Ross, Oct. 3, 1949, JFK.

26. EH–CS, Sept. 8, 1949, PUL; Hotchner–EH, Sept. 3, 1949, JFK.

27. EH–Al Horwits, Oct. 3, 1949, JFK.

28. EH–CS, Sept. 21, 1949, PUL; CS–EH, Sept. 21, 1949, JFK. $5,000 was for the coat; $5,000 for other expenses.

29. EH–CS, Sept. 14, 1949, PUL.

30. EH–Viertel, Sept. 29, 1949, private collection; EH–MWH, Sept. 29, 1949, JFK; EH–Hotchner, Sept. 29, 1949, UVa.

31. EH–CS, Oct. 1, 1949, PUL.

32. EH–CS, Oct. 4, 1949, PUL; EH–Hotchner, Oct. 11, 1949, UVa.

33. Kert, p. 444.

34. CS–EH, Oct. 13, 1949, PUL; Hotchner–EH, Oct. 24, 1949, and numerous other earlier letters, JFK.

35. Lanham–EH, Oct. 30, 1949, PUL.

36. *NY Post*, Nov. 18, 1949, p. 38.

37. Lillian Ross, "Profiles: How Do You Like It Now, Gentlemen?" *The New Yorker* (May 13, 1950), p. 36.

38. EH–Harvey Breit in a letter appearing in *NYTBR* (Sept. 17, 1950), 14. In *Conversations*, p. 62.

39. See Adeline Tintner, "The Significance of D'Annunzio in *ARIT*," *HR* (Fall 1985), 9–13; George Montiero, "Hemingway's Colonel," *HR* (Fall 1985), 40–45; Peter Lisca, "The Structure of Hemingway's *ARIT*," *Modern Fiction Studies* (1966), 232–50; Major James Meredith, "The Rapido River and Hurtgen Forest in *ARIT*," *HR* (Fall 1994), 60–6.

40. CS–EH, undated [Nov. 1949], JFK. Hotchner–EH, undated [Dec. 1949], JFK.

41. *HIW*, p. 249.

42. Viertel, pp. 80–6.

43. *88 Poems*: "The Road to Avallon," p. 122; "Poem to Miss Mary," p. 119; "Across the Board," p. 120; "Black-Ass Poem after Talking to Pamela Churchill," p. 121.

44. Mary's Journal, December 1949, JFK.

45. Viertel, p. 98.

Chapter 14. The Middle Parts of Fortune

1. "Profile," *The New Yorker* (May 13, 1950), pp. 42–3.

2. Kert, pp. 447–8.

3. Cited in *ibid.*, pp. 448–9.

4. EH–Cowley, Jan. 27, 1950, Gritti Palace, private collection.

5. Baker, p. 482.

6. *ARIT*, pp. 151–7.

7. *SRL* (July 9, 1966), p. 9.

8. EH–Hotchner, [late Jan. 1950], UVa.

9. Kert, p. 449.

10. Juanita Jensen–Papa and Mary, Nov. 29, 1949, JFK.

11. Olga Rudge–EH, March 13, 1950, JFK, marked "Rec. Mar. 16, 50."

12. Kert, pp. 450–1, citing *La Torre Bianca*, pp. 96–101, and correspondence from Adriana, October 1980.

13. R. Mourelet–EH, April 5, 1950, JFK.

14. EH–CS, March 22, 1950, PUL, cited in Baker, p. 482.

15. EH–Jonathan Cape, March 21, 1950, Cape Archives.

16. Interview with private source. See
    www//cavan.local.ie/history/people/soldiers

17. Turista Card #1095, stamped April 8, 1950, Havana, JFK.

18. See Mary Hemingway's last will and testament, dated Oct. 26, 1979,
    JFK.

19. EH–Lanham, April 15, 1950, PUL, *SL*, p. 687.

20. EH–Dorman-O'Gowan, May 2, 1950, *SL*, p. 691.

21. EH–Dorman-O'Gowan, May 21, July 10, July 15, Aug. 8, 1950,
    PUL.

22. *Collected Short Stories*, p. 111.

23. *YH*, p. 57.

24. EH–CS, July 19, 1950, PUL, *SL*, p. 706.

25. EH–Arthur Mizener, May 12, 1950, *SL* pp. 694–5.

26. EH–Robert Cantwell, Aug. 25, 1950, *SL*, p. 709.

27. MG–William Walton, Feb. 3, March 9, 1950, courtesy of Rose
    Marie Burwell.

28. MWH–EH, May 6, 1950, JFK.

29. EH–Milt[on Wolf], May 7, 1950, private collection.

30. EH–Joséph McCarthy, May 8, 1950, JFK, *SL*, p. 693; the letter may
    not have been sent.

31. Mayito Menocal, Jr.–EH, April 28, 1950, JFK.

32. Ross–EH, April 26, 1950, JFK.

33. Ross–EH, May 5, 1950, JFK.

34. Hotchner–EH, May 17, 1950, JFK; Nancy (Slim) Hayward–EH,
    May 21, 1950, JFK. "Profile" appeared in *The New Yorker* (May 13,
    1950), pp. 36–62, at that time the longest profile the magazine had
    printed.

35. Preface, *Portrait of Hemingway* (New York: Simon & Schuster,
    1961), pp. 14–15.

36. EH–Dorman-O'Gowan, May 21, 1950, JFK; EH–Harvey Breit, July
    9, 1950, *SL*, pp. 701.

37. EH–CS, July 19, 1950, *SL*, pp. 706–7; EH–Dorman-O'Gowan, c.
    July 27, 1950, *SL*, pp. 707–8; Baker, pp. 484–5; EH–CS, July 9–10,
    1950, *SL*, p. 704.

38. John O'Hara, "The Author's Name Is Hemingway," *NYTBR* (Sept.
    10, 1950), pp. 1, 30; Maxwell Geismar, "Across the River and into
    the Trees," SRL (Sept. 9, 1950), pp. 18, 19.

39. "The New Hemingway," *Newsweek* (Sept. 11, 1950), pp. 90–95; "On
    the Ropes," *Time* (Sept. 11, 1950), pp. 110, 113.

40. Alfred Kazin, "The Indignant Flesh," *The New Yorker* (Sept. 19, 1950), pp. 113–18; Philip Avrh, *Commentary* (Oct. 1950), pp. 400–2.

41. *The New Yorker* (Oct. 14, 1950), p. 28.

42. Northrop Frye, *Hudson Review* (Winter 1951), pp. 611–12; Philip Young, *Tomorrow* (Nov. 1950), pp. 55–6; Eliot Paul, *Providence Sunday Journal* (Sept. 10, 1950), p. VI-8; Ben Ray Redman, "The Champ and the Referees," *SRL* (Oct. 28, 1950), pp. 15, 16, 38.

43. AI–EH, Aug. 25, Sept. 4, 1950, JFK; Baker, p. 486.

44. EH–AI, July 3, Aug. 1, Aug. 2, Aug. 9, 1950, UTex. See N. Ann Doyle and Neal B. Houston, "Letters to Adriana Ivancich, *HR* (Fall 1985), pp. 14–29.

45. Kert, p. 455.

46. MWH–CS, Oct. 12, 1950, PUL.

47. Mary's Journal, misdated 1951, typed draft from rough notes, JFK. EH–Dorman-O'Gowan, Oct. 15, 1950, private collection.

48. EH holograph note dated "0600 27/10/50" in Box 6, Other Material, Folder: Notes Miscellaneous, JFK. EH–Harvey Breit, Oct. 26, 1950, PUL.

Chapter 15. Roadstead of the Heart

1. Paporov, pp. 177–9. Feo was Ernest's nickname for his friend.

2. Kert, pp. 456–7, based on *La Torre Bianca*, pp. 136–40, 162–6.

3. EH–Hotchner, [Dec. 7, 1950], UVa.

4. Quoted in Paporov, p. 196.

5. *New York Herald Book Review* (Dec. 3, 1950), p. 6.

6. The diligent reader will follow my oversimplifaction of this narrative's various drafts with Rose Marie Burwell's book-length study of Hemingway's postwar writing.

7. EH–Hotchner, Jan. 5, 1951, private collection.

8. Kert, pp. 459–60.

9. "On the Blue Water: A Gulf Stream Letter," *Esquire* (April 1936), reprinted in *By-Line*, pp. 239–40.

10. Anna Stark in Paporov, p. 193.

11. Item 190, *The Old Man and the Sea* typescript with holograph corrections, JFK. Because only a typescript remains, there has been speculation that the novella was written years earlier, but EH's daily word count seems to indicate that this typescript is the first draft.

12. Paporov, p. 197.

13. "I Tell You True," *Park East* (Dec. 1950), 18–9, 46–7; (Jan. 1951) 36, 48–9.

14. Carlos Baker–EH, Feb. 15, 1951, JFK.

15. EH–Baker, Feb. 17, 1951, Stanford.

16. Baker–EH, Feb. 21, 1951, JFK.

17. EH–Baker, Feb. 24, 1951, Stanford; Sam Boal–EH, Feb. 27, 1951, JFK; EH–Sam Boal, March 10, 1951, JFK.

18. EH–Baker, March 10, 1951, Stanford.

19. EH–Baker, April–Aug. 1951, Stanford. Baker held up his end of the trust, but was disappointed with Hemingway's evasiveness. "He lied to me," Baker said. "Why would a grown man tell lies?" See Bill Walton's comment in *True Gen*, p. 304.

20. Fenton–EH, Aug. 20, Sept. 9, Sept. 18, 1951, JFK; EH–Fenton, Aug. 31, Sept. 13, Sept. 23, 1951, private collection. Fenton's book, *The Apprenticeship of Ernest Hemingway*, was serialized in *Atlantic Monthly* (March–May 1954) and published that year by Farrar, Straus.

21. EH–John Atkins, Oct. 24, 1951, private collection. Atkins's book was *The Art of Ernest Hemingway* (London: P. Nevill, 1952).

22. EH–Cowley, May 13, 1951, private collection. .

23. Madeline Hemingway–EH, June 17, 1951, JFK.

24. PPH–EH, undated, marked "Rec. June 30, 1951," JFK.

25. EH–Baker, June 30, 1951, Stanford.

26. Kert, pp. 463–4. Certificate of Death, attached to Alfred Rice–EH, Oct. 22, 1951, JFK.

27. Mary's Journal, October 1951, JFK.

28. EH–CS, Oct. 2, 1951, PUL, in *SL*, p. 737.

29. EH–CS, March 5, April 11–12, May 18–19, July 20, Oct. 5, 1951, *SL*, pp. 720–39. CS–EH, March 20, July 6, July 30, 1951, Scribner Archives, PUL.

30. EH–Dorothy Pound, Oct. 22, 1951, PUL, in *SL*, pp. 741–2; EH–D. D. Paige, Oct. 22, 1951, PUL, in *SL*, pp. 739–41.

31. "On the Books," *New York Herald Book Review* (Dec. 9, 1951), p. 3.

32. EH–CS, Oct. 12, 1951, PUL.

33. EH–Baker, Oct. 7, 1951, PUL.

34. EH–CS, Feb. 1, 1952, Scribner Archives, PUL; *HIW*, pp. 291–2.

35. Wallace Meyer–EH, telegram, Feb. 11, 1952, JFK; EH–Vera Scribner, Feb. 18, 1952, PUL, in *SL*, pp.748–9.

PART THREE

Chapter 16. The Artist's Rewards

1. *HIW*, pp. 295–6. EH–Wallace Meyer, March 4, 7, 1952, *SL*, pp. 757–60.
2. *Newsweek* (March 24, 1952), pp. 60–1; *Time* (March 24, 1952), p. 38.
3. *HIW*, pp. 296–7. Marjorie Cooper–EH, March 23, 1952, JFK.
4. Signed copy, Hemingway Collection, JFK. EH–Adriana Ivancich, May 31, 1952, UTex, in *SL*, pp. 762–3.
5. *NYTBR* (Sept. 7, 1952) and *SRL* (Sept. 6, 1952), reprinted in *Conversations*, pp. 66–9. EH–CSjr, May 12, 1952, PUL. Also letters to Harvey Breit and others too numerous to cite.
6. EH–Breit, Aug. 4, 1951, JFK. Breit did not publish anything about the incident.
7. James Plath interview with Forrest MacMullen, 1998. MacMullen did not fish.
8. EH–Breit, June 23, 1952, JFK.
9. Faulkner quoted in Breit–EH, June 25, 1952, JFK.
10. EH–Breit, June 27, 1952, *SL*, pp. 768–70.
11. EH–Charles Fenton, June 12, 1952, private collection; EH–Fenton, June 22, 1952, PUL; EH–Fenton, June 18, July 29, 1952, *SL*, pp. 764–5, 774–8; Fenton–EH, June 7, June 14, July 24, July 31, 1952, JFK.
12. EH–Philip Young, March 6, May 27, 1952, *SL*, pp. 760–2; EH–Baker, June 4, 1952, Stanford.
13. EH–Cowley, May 4, 1952, private collection.
14. "The Last Good Country," *CSS*, p. 523. The published version has been sanitized. The manuscript is at the JFK.
15. *HL*, p. 323. Hemingway met Salinger during the liberation of Paris, and enjoyed reading the young soldier's copies of *The New Yorker*.
16. When *The Garden of Eden* began is difficult to pinpoint. Carlos Baker said 1946; Rose Marie Burwell thinks 1948. Because I do not think he could have begun the story before his mother and Pauline were both dead, I suggest 1952.
17. My analysis remains speculative because we have yet to read Hemingway's texts as he left them to us. See Burwell and those who follow for other views.
18. Hanneman, Vol. 1, pp. 63–4, 87, 175–205. In America, the book sold retail for $3.00.

19. See *Hemingway the Critical Reception*, ed. Robert O. Stephens ([n.p.]: Burt Franklin Co., 1977), pp. 339–71.

20. Berenson–EH, Sept. 6, 1952, quoted in Baker, p. 656.

21. Daniel Longwell–EH, Aug. 8, 1952, JFK; EH–Berenson, Sept. 13, 1952, *SL*, pp. 780–1; Baker–EH, Oct. 23 and Nov. 7, 1952, JFK.

22. EH–Patrick Hemingway, Sept. 22, 1952, PUL and JFK; EH–Alfred Rice, Oct. 8, 1952, JFK.

23. EH–Charles Poore, Jan. 23, 1953, *SL*, p. 800. See *Hemingway's First War* for the "son of a bitch" who fulfilled this prophecy.

24. EH–Hotchner, July 21, 1952, UVa.

25. EH–John Atkins, Dec. 28, 1952, private collection.

26. EH–Berenson, Jan. 24, 1953, *SL*, p. 802; Baker, p. 508.

27. Nancy (Slim) Hayward–EH, July 12, 1953, JFK.

28. Mary's Journal, March 1952, JFK.

29. EH–Wallace Meyer, May 6, 1953, *SL*, pp. 821–2.

30. EH–William Lowe, May 15, 1953, JFK.

31. EH–MWH, in-house letter, June 1, 1953, Fuentes, pp. 396–9.

Chapter 17. The Phoenix

1. MWH's Spanish Journal, private collection; *HIW*, pp. 322–5; Baker, p. 511.

2. MWH's Spanish Journal. Niño de la Palma was immortalized as Pedro Romero in *The Sun Also Rises*.

3. MWH's Spanish Journal; Viertel, pp. 182–9.

4. When wing-shooting with a shotgun, the hunter keeps both eyes open, tracking the bird. Hemingway apparently did the same with a rifle when the animal was moving.

5. See MWH's African Journal, 1953–54, JFK.

6. Baker, pp. 514–15.

7. *HIW*, p. 345. See this text for the most detailed account of the safari.

8. Quoted in Meyers, p. 502.

9. MWH's African Journal, JFK; *HIW*, pp. 342–66; Philip Percival–MWH, Dec. 3, 13, 1953, JFK. They did, however, fill their licensed quotas, taking back a number of heads: two lions, one leopard, nine antelope, one buffalo, warthog, and several leaping hares. EH–Percival, Feb. 27, 1954, JFK.

10. Denis Zaphiro–MWH, Jan, 6, 1955, JFK.

11. Fenton–EH, Nov. 26, 1953, JFK; EH–Fenton, Dec. 5, 1953, private collection.
12. Hotchner–EH, Dec. 1 and 14, 1953, JFK.
13. Honorary Game Warden form #128, dated Nov. 3, 1953, JFK.
14. Zaphiro is quoted in Baker, p. 659.
15. *HIW*, pp. 370–1.
16. Notes are similar to but not the same as document in JFK.
17. EH–Harvey Breit, Jan. 3, 1954, *SL*, pp. 825–7. EH–Alfred Rice, Jan. 11, 1954, EH–John Hemingway, Jan. 12, 1954 [misdated 1953], both at JFK.
18. MWH's African Journal, Jan. 3 and 4, 1954, JFK.
19. *HIW*, pp. 376–7; Hemingway, "The Christmas Gift," *Look* (April 20, May 4, 1954), reprinted in *By-Line*, pp. 432–3.
20. MWH'sAfrican Journal, JFK; EH–James Kidder, American Consulate, Feb. 10, 1954, listing losses for insurance purposes. The airline insurance reimbursed 15,500 shillings. The plane was not overloaded because the bulk of the Hemingway luggage was left behind at Entebbe and Nairobi.
21. Numerous Hemingway letters from the period at the JFK. MWH's African Journal, JFK; Baker, pp. 520–3.
22. *NYT*, Jan. 26, 1954, pp. 1:6. This story became the basis for a popular song "The Heming Way," lyrics by Ogden Nash, beginning, "A bunch a bananas and a bottle of gin."
23. *NYT*, Jan. 29, 1954.
24. MWH's African Journal, Feb. 7, 1954, JFK.
25. MWH–EH, Shimoni, Tuesday [1954], probably Feb. 9, JFK.
26. "The Christmas Gift," *Look* (April 20, May 4, 1954), reprinted in *By-Line*, p. 460. Dictated to Mrs. Kitty Figgis.
27. MWH–her parents, March 9, 1954, Nyali Beach Hotel, JFK.

Chapter 18. Fortune and Men's Eyes

1. Kert, pp. 478–9.
2. EH–Hotchner, March 14, 1954, private collection.
3. MWH–parents, April 4, 1954, JFK.
4. MacLeish–EH, May 5, 1954, JFK.
5. EH–Adriana Ivancich, May 9, 1954, *SL*, pp. 830–1.
6. Viertel, pp. 222–9; Kert, p. 480.
7. Viertel, pp. 228–9.
8. Baker, p. 525.
9. *HIW*, pp. 400–1.

10. *Ibid.*, pp. 402–5.

11. MWH, Aug.–Nov. 1954 account book; EH–Hotchner, Sept. 9, 1954, private collection; MWH–parents, Oct. 5, 1954, JFK.

12. EH–Jack Hemingway, Aug. 17, 1954, private collection.

13. See Pedro Sánchez Pessino–EH, Aug. 24, 1954, JFK.

14. Published as *True at First Light* (Scribner's, 1999).

15. *NYT*, Oct. 26, 1954.

16. *NYT*, Oct. 29, 1954.

17. *HIW*, p. 411.

18. "The Sun Also Rises in Stockholm," *NYTBR* (Nov. 7, 1954), p. 1.

19. "An American Storyteller," *Time* (Dec. 13, 1954), pp. 70–7. See also Robert Manning, "Hemingway in Cuba," *Atlantic Monthly* (Aug. 1965), pp. 101–8, reprinted in *Conversations*, pp. 172–89.

20. Item 713, JFK, paraphrased here for lack of permission to quote.

21. Reprinted in *Conversations*, p. 196.

22. EH–Hotchner, Dec. 7, 1954, private collection.

23. E. K. Thompson (*Time*)–EH, Dec. 20, 1954, JFK; EH–Hotchner, Dec. 31, 1954, private collection.

24. As described in Jack Gould's "Radio in Review," *NYT*, Dec. 22, 1954, p. 34.

25. EH–Bill Davis, Feb. 25, 1954, private collection.

26. EH–R. M. Brown, Sept. 14, 1954, UTex, in Burwell, p. 138.

27. The manuscript to what is now called *True at First Light* has been closed to most scholars. I am relying on Rose Marie Burwell's account of that MS, which she read at Princeton. See Burwell, chap. 5.

28. Letter to R. M. Brown, UTex, quoted in Burwell, p. 143.

29. Quoted in *HIW*, p. 422.

30. MWH–EH, Oct. 4, 1955, JFK. Given male decorum in 1999, EH was only forty-four years ahead of the curve.

31. "Hemingway Tells of Early Career," *Daily Princetonian* (April 14, 1955), reprinted in *Conversations*, pp. 99–102.

32. Fraser Drew, "April 8, 1955 with Hemingway," *Fitzgerald/Hemingway Annual*, 1970, pp. 108–16, reprinted in *Conversations*, pp. 89–98.

33. EH–Dorman-O'Gowan, March 14, 1955, private collection.

34. MWH Notebook, April 19–May 3, 1955, JFK.

35. *HIW*, pp. 422–3.

36. EH–Baker, May 2, 1955, Stanford; EH–Jack Hemingway, May 11, 1955, private collection.

37. Viertel, pp. 251–4.

38. *Ibid.*, pp. 267–8. For a slightly different account, see *Slim*, pp. 144–5. Mary in *HIW* does not mention the scene.

39. MWH–Mrs. Welsh, Sept. 25, 1955, JFK. Viertel, p. 269. *Slim*, pp. 146–7.

40. Richard Johnston (*Sports Illustrated*)–EH, Nov. 14, 1955, JFK; Sid James–EH, telegram, Nov. 22, 1955, JFK.

41. Sylvia Beach–EH, Nov. 6, 1955, JFK.

Chapter 19. Intimations of Mortality

1. *True* (Feb. 1956), p. 18. EH read the February issue by Jan. 22, 1956.

2. *True*, p. 30.

3. Hemingway medical files, JFK. EH–Alfred Rice, Jan, 24, 1956, JFK and *SL*, pp. 853–5.

4. EH–Jack Hemingway, Jan. 22, 1956, private collection.

5. EH–CSjr, Feb. 10, 1956, PUL.

6. MWH–EH, Feb. 27, 1956, JFK.

7. 1956 Calendar, Jan.–March, JFK.

8. Cooper–EH, March 5, 1956, JFK; EH–Cooper, March 9, 1956, JFK and *SL*, pp. 855–6.

9. MWH–parents, April 22, 29, May 7, 1956, JFK; EH–Wallace Meyer, April 2, 1956, *SL*, pp. 857–8; EH–Percival, May 25, 1956, *SL*, pp. 860–1.

10. Kurt Bernheim, "*McCall's* Visits Ernest Hemingway," *McCall's* (May 1956), reprinted in *Conversations*, pp. 105–8.

11. MacLeish–EH, June 23, 1956, JFK. Donaldson, pp. 441–2.

12. EH–Ezra Pound, July 19, 1956, *SL*, pp. 864–5. The medal was apparently given to a Catholic shrine in Cuba instead.

13. MacLeish–EH, Dec. 15, 1956, JFK.

14. MWH–Baker, Sept. 19, 1961, JFK: "About the novel, *Land, Sea and Air*, would you help me . . . to let fade away the idea that any such book existed in writing."

15. EH–CSjr., Aug. 14, 1956, in *SL*, pp. 868–9. Other stories were: "Get Yourself a Seeing-Eyed Dog," "Indian Country and the White Army," "The Monument," and "The Bubble Reputation."

16. Sylvia Beach–EH, Sept. 8, 1956, JFK; Margaret Marshall (Harcourt, Brace)–EH, Sept. 7, 1956.

17. Viertel, pp. 308–10.
18. EH–Hotchner, Sept. 30, 1956, UVa.
19. EH medical files, Oct. 22, 1956, JFK.
20. EH–Breit, Nov. 5, 1956, *SL*, pp. 872–73; Baker, p. 535.
21. Wally Windsor–MWH, Nov. 25, 1956, JFK. "The Lyons Den," *NY Post*, Jan. 21, 1957.
22. Jean Monnier–EH, March 18, 1957, and Rafael Ballestero–EH, March 20, 1957, EH medical files, JFK.
23. EH medical files, JFK.
24. His 1957 tax statement to his tax lawyer (JFK) lists the following drugs for Hemingway: Whychol (10/day all year); Ecuanil (1/day, 300 days); Seconal (80 tabs); B-complex (8/day, all year); Vi-Syneral (4/day all year); Oreton M (3 weekly, all year); Serpasyl (3/day for 8 months); Ritalin (1.5/day for nine months); Doriden (1/day for 2 months).
25. EH–Hotchner, May 20, 1957, UVa. See Tom Dardis, *The Thirsty Muse* (Boston: Ticknor & Fields, 1989), pp. 157–209, for the best analysis of Hemingway's alcoholism.
26. EH–Lee Samuels, Jan. 19, 1957, UTex. For a complete list of these MSS, see Lee Samuels–EH, Sept. 6, 1957, JFK.
27. Burwell, pp. 150–3.

Chapter 20. Cuba Libre

1. Ellen Shipman Angell–EH, June 25, 1957, Fuentes, pp, 413–14.
2. EH–Wallace Meyer, May 24, 1957, *SL*, p. 875.
3. EH–Rice, Aug. 28, 1957, JFK.
4. EH–George Plimpton, March 4, 1957, *SL*, p. 874.
5. C. David Heymann, *Ezra Pound: The Last Rower* (New York: Viking Press, 1976), pp. 210–37.
6. MacLeish–EH, June 19, 1957, JFK.
7. EH–MacLeish, June 28, 1957, *SL*, pp. 876–8.
8. EH–Robert Frost, June 28, 1957, enclosed in letter to MacLeish, *SL*, pp. 878–80.
9. Heymann, *Ezra Pound*, pp. 250–7.
10. "Situation Report," dated Aug. 18, 1957, JFK.
11. *YH*, pp. 64, 70–1, 77–87, 100–2.
12. *NYT*, Aug. 22, 1957, p. 8.
13. Hotel Westbury bill for Sept. 22–28, 1957, for all three, $582.47, JFK.

14. *HIW*, pp. 446–7.

15. EH–Breit, June 16, 1957, PUL. See Item 486 at JFK for likely draft of Fitzgerald story. *Atlantic Monthly* (Nov. 1957), pp. 64–8.

16. A synopsis of Item 692.5 at JFK.

17. "The Lyons Den," *NY Post*, Dec. 12, 1957.

18. EH–Gianfranco Ivancich, Jan. 31, 1958, *SL*, pp. 881–3.

19. Mary Hemingway account pages appended to tax information for 1958, JFK.

20. EH 1958 tax information, JFK; Duke Medical School library, medical historian, and current warnings on labels.

21. Recently opened Mary Hemingway Collection, Notes, Miscellaneous, JFK.

22. EH–Rice, Aug. 3, 1958, JFK. Draft and revisions.

23. Layhmond Robinson, "Hemingway Brings Suit to Stop Reprint of Spanish War Stories," *NYT*, Aug. 6, 1958, p. 1.

24. *NYT*, Aug. 7, 1958, p. 27.

25. *HIW*, pp. 449–50.

26. Arnolds–EH, Aug. 19 and 25, 1958, JFK.

27. EH–Patrick Hemingway, Nov. 24, 1958, *SL*, pp. 887–9.

28. *Ibid.*

29. Rice–EH, Oct. 8, 1958, JFK.

30. MWH–Hotchner, Nov. 5, 1958, JFK.

31. Author interview with Bud and Ruth Purdy, 1996.

32. John Unrue interview with Forrest MacMullen, 1995.

33. Author interview with Purdys, 1996.

34. John Unrue interview with Forrest MacMullen, 1995.

35. Paporov, p. 43.

Chapter 21 Exiles from Eden

1. EH–Gianfranco Ivancich, Jan. 7, 1959, *SL*, pp. 890–1. Note drafting statement undated in Hemingway Collection, JFK. *HIW*, pp. 457–8. EH–Harry Brague, Jan. 24, 1959, *SL*, pp. 891–2.

2. *Historical Statistics of the United States*, Vols. 1 and 2 (Washington, D.C.: U.S. Government Printing Office, 1975).

3. Scribner Book Store bill, Jan. 1959, JFK. Mailed *Lolita* to Ketchum on Oct. 24, 1958.

4. Again, see Rose Marie Burwell for the detailed examination of these manuscripts.

5. EH–Harry Brague, Feb. 22, 1959, *SL*, pp. 893–4: he was on chap. 45

of *Garden*. MWH–Charles Sweeny, March 3, 1959, JFK.

6. Waldo Peirce–EH, March 23, 1959, JFK; EH–Jack Hemingway, March 30, 1959, private collection.

7. *High on the Wild*, p. 128.

8. CSjr–EH, April 7 and 16, 1959, PUL; EH–CSjr, April 12, 1959, PUL.

9. EH–CSjr, April 12, 1959, PUL; EH–Alfred Rice, April 10, 1959, JFK.

10. See *Physician's Desk Reference to Pharmaceutical Specialties and Biologicals* (1947 edition) and *Professional Products Information*, (1947 and 1953 edns.).

11. Paporov, pp. 397–8.

12. *Ibid.*, pp. 398–9. Hemingway briefing notes, filed under Cuba, undated, JFK.

13. Ben Sonnenberg, "La Consula," *Paris Review* (Summer 1991), pp. 277–9.

14. "The Art of the Short Story," *Paris Review* (1981, 25th anniv. issue), 85–103.

15. *HIW*, p. 469.

16. EH–George Saviers, May 11, 1959, private collection.

17. *DS*, p. 65.

18. John Crosby, "Afternoon with the Bulls," *New York Herald Tribune* (June 1959).

19. Hotchner–EH, May 13, 1959, JFK; Hotchner–EH, telegram, May 26, 1959, JFK. After paying Hotchner's expenses plus 50% of the money, Rice's 1%, and taxes on the remainder, Hemingway took home less than $25,000 on the deal.

20. CSjr–EH, June 24, 1959, JFK.

21. EH–CSjr, undated draft in blue spiral notebook once part of the Bill Davis Collection and now in a private collection.

22. Two wires dated July 7, 1959. *Sports Illustrated*–EH and EH–Syd James, JFK.

23. *DS*, pp. 135–6.

24. Rice–EH, June 29 and July 27, 1959, JFK.

25. EH–Rice, Aug. 8, 1959, JFK. Dictated to VDS.

26. Baker, p. 547. MHW, July 22, 1959, addressee unknown, JFK.

27. EH–Thompson Time/Life, telegram, Aug. 8, 1959, JFK.

28. Eric Sevareid, "Mano a Mano," *Esquire* (Nov. 1959), pp. 40–4.

29. EH–MWH, Aug. 20, 1959, written from Bilbao, private collection, copy in JFK.

30. *Slim*, p. 187.
31. Leicester Hemingway–EH, Aug. 31, 1959, JFK; EH–Leicester, Sept. 14, 1959, copy in Fuentes, p. 307, and in private collection.
32. EH–MWH, Aug. 31, 1959, JFK; MWH–EH, Oct. 8, 1959, JFK.
33. EH–MWH, Oct. 13, 1959, JFK.
34. EH–MWH, Oct. 15, 1959, JFK; Hotchner–EH, Oct. 27, 1959, JFK.
35. MWH–EH, Oct. 19, 1959, private collection, copy in JFK.
36. MWH–EH, undated but appended to letter of Oct. 19, 1959, read in a private collection, possibly a copy in JFK.
37. EH–MWH, Oct. 26, 1959, private collection and JFK.
38. EH–Annie Davis, Oct. [sic] 3, 1959, "a bord Liberte" misdated, actually November, private collection.
39. Paporov, p. 400.
40. MWH–Annie Davis, Nov. 8. 1959; EH–Bill Davis, Nov. 8, 1959, both in a private collection.
41. Baker, p. 551. *HIW*, pp. 477–9.
42. Brague–EH, Nov. 5, 1959, JFK.
43. Hemingway notes in a private collection; MWH–EH, Dec. 15, 1959, JFK.
44. *HIW*, p. 481.

Chapter 22. The Body Electric

1. EH–Bill Lang (Time/Life), Jan. 11, 1960, JFK; Hotchner–EH, Jan. 31, Feb. 10, 1960, JFK; EH–Hotchner, Feb. 8 and 18, 1960, UVa.
2. CSjr–EH, March 23, 1960, JFK; EH–CSjr, March 31, 1960, JFK.
3. Hotchner–EH, April 5, 1960, JFK.
4. Hotchner–EH, Jan. 31, Feb. 10, 13, March 5, 1960, JFK; EH–Hotchner, Feb. 8, March 12, 1960, UVa.
5. Ed Thompson–EH, telegrams, April 6 and 14, 1960, JFK.
6. Hotchner–EH, April 20, 1960, JFK; Gary Cooper–EH, May 2, 1960, JFK, in response to EH telegram.
7. *DS*, p. 187.
8. EH–Hotchner, May 9, 1960, UVa.
9. EH–Gianfranco Ivancich, May 30, 1960, *SL*, p. 903; MWH–Annie Davis, May 13, 1960, private collection.
10. *NYT*, April and early May 1960.
11. EH–Rice, May 31, 1960, JFK.
12. *HIW*, p. 485.
13. Newly opened material (1998) in Hemingway Collection, JFK.

14. EH–Hotchner, June 27, 1960, JFK.
15. EH–George Saviers, June 20, 1960, *SL*, p. 904.
16. Hotchner–Bill and Annie Davis, June 29, 1960, private collection.
17. EH–CSjr. July 6, 1960, *SL*, pp. 905–6. *NYT*, July 6 and 7, 1960.
18. MWH–EH, July 13, 1960, in-house letter, JFK.
19. VDS–Bill Davis, July 7, 1960, private collection.
20. *HIW*, p. 485.
21. EH–Hotchner, Aug. 7, 1960, UVa.
22. *HIW*, p. 488.
23. Hotchner–Bill Davis, July 26, 1960, and telegram to Bill Davis undated, both in private collection. Annie Davis–MWH, telegram, Aug. 11, 1960, JFK.
24. EH–MWH, Aug. 15, 1960, JFK.
25. MWH–EH, Aug. 19, 1960, JFK; VDS–MWH, Aug. 27, 1960, JFK.
26. EH–MWH, Sept. 3, 1960, JFK. EH–MWH, Sept. 7, 1960, JFK. Similar statement to Hotchner in EH–Hotchner, Sept. 8, 1960, UVa.
27. CSjr–EH, telegram [Aug. 15, 1960], and letter, Aug. 15, 1960, JFK.
28. EH–Hotchner, Sept. 17, 1960, UVa; EH–MWH, Sept. 23, 1960, JFK.
29. *HIW*, pp. 492–3.
30. EH–Hotchner, Oct. 25, 1960, UVa.
31. EH–George Saviers, Nov. 12, 1960, private collection.
32. Seymour Betsky, "A Last Visit," *Saturday Review* (July 26, 1961), p. 22, quoted in Baker, p. 555.
33. Hotchner–Bill Davis, Nov. 19, 1960, on Christiania Motor Lodge letterhead, private collection.
34. "A Way You'll Never Be," *CSS*, p. 310.
35. Clarence Hemingway–EH, Oct. 1910, read in the Carlos Baker files at Princeton.
36. Baker, p. 556. Saviers interview on documentary film not yet made public.
37. Letter dated Dec. 4, 1960, *SL*, p. 909.
38. Dr. Howard Butt–EH, Jan. 19, 1961, in Hemingway's own medical files, JFK.
39. "Reserpine in the Treatment of Neuropsychiatric Disorders," *Annals of Internal Medicine* (Sept. 3, 1952).
40. Dr. Howard Rome–EH, Jan. 21, 1961, in Hemingway's own medical files, JFK.
41. S. Sament, "Letter," *Clinical Psychiatry News* (1983), 11.
42. L. Andre, "ECT: The Politics of Experience," given at Quality of

Care Conference, Albany, New York, May 13, 1988.

43. Mary Hemingway note, Christmas Eve, 1960, JFK.

44. Note written on Kahler Hotel letterhead and dated 01:45 hrs, 1961, JFK.

45. Christmas Eve note cited above.

46. Hemingway's own medical files, JFK.

47. Scribner Book Store order sheet July 1960–Jan 1961, JFK.

48. Jerry Wald–EH, Jan. 30, 1961, JFK; EH–Hotchner, Feb. 18, 1961, UVa; Harry Brague–EH, Feb. 13, 1961, JFK.

49. EH–Brague, Feb. 6, 1961, *SL*, pp. 916–18.

50. Lee W. Samuels–EH, March 3, 1961, JFK.

51. EH–Hotchner, March 6, 1961, UVa.

52. EH–Rice, March 22 and 23, 1961, JFK.

53. Susan Beegel, scholar and editor of the *Hemingway Review*, first saw the relationship between the Bay of Pigs and Hemingway's attempts at suicide.

54. EH–CSjr, April 18, 1961, PUL. This letter was not mailed. MWH sent it to Harry Brague on July 18, 1963.

55. MWH–Ursula Hemingway Jepson, April 25, 1961, JFK.

56. *Ibid.*

57. Baker, pp. 560–1.

58. EH–MWH, April 28, 1961, JFK.

59. Joséph Lord–EH, May 15, 1961, JFK. Telephone notes EH kept at St. Mary's, JFK.

60. Quoted in Meyers, p. 559. Hadley Mower–EH, May 20, 1961, JFK.

61. Dr. Howard Rome–MWH, Nov. 1, 1961. Hemingway's own medical files, JFK.

62. MWH–Jack and Patrick Hemingway, June 2, 1961, JFK.

63. MWH–Dr. Howard Rome, June 7, 1961, JFK.

64. EH notes from phone conversation dated June 15, 1961, JFK.

65. *HIW*, pp. 500–2.

Acknowledgments

Standing on the backs of scholars before me, I have, with help from many friends, brought this last volume of my Hemingway biography to term. Had it not been for Carlos Baker's work, his example and his encouragement, none of these volumes would have been written. Twenty-six years ago, Carlos called Charles Scribner, and said, "Charlie, there's a young man in my office who needs to see the Hemingway-Perkins correspondence." For several beats of my heart, I could not breathe. The same thing happened when Jo August first handed me the blue *cahiers* containing the first draft of *The Sun Also Rises* in which the ink seemed scarcely dry.

This last volume owes much to many. Quite literally it depended upon the help of Al DeFazio and Rose Marie Burwell. Al loaned me his files on the Hemingway-Hotchner relationship; Rose Marie loaned me all of her files and notes on Hemingway's posthumously published manuscripts and on the Scribner Archive materials at Princeton. Their combined help reduced by three years the research time I spent on this book. At the John F. Kennedy Library in Boston, curator Stephen Plotkin was vital to my research, always keeping me informed when new materials were opened. Interlibrary loan at North Carolina State University and at the Santa Fe Public Library brought me what I needed. Maurice and Marcia Neville provided generous access to crucial materials not available to the public. Dave Meeker gave the same sort of help with Martha Gellhorn materials. John and Marsha Goin opened to me their Hemingway collection before it was sold. Ann Adelman's copyediting eliminated enough errors to make an author blush. Bob Lewis's keen eye read proof to prevent my usual mistakes.

I am equally grateful to Bernice Kert for her book, *The Hemingway Women*, to Larry Martin for keeping me in mind, to John Unrue for interviewing Forrest MacMullen, to Ken Kinnamon for loaning me the Paporov book, and to Marty Peterson who opened doors, always remembered, set a great table, and put to rest the question of which onion sandwich was the better. At North Carolina State University, I depended on Amy Vondrak and Ed Hoffman for their research skills, and on Sarah Smith for keeping me focused. In Idaho, I was given assistance by Marsha Bellavance, Buck Levy, Pierre Saviers, Don Anderson, Duke MacMullen, Bud and Ruth Purdy, Clara Spiegel, and the historical section of the Ketchum Library. In New York, it was Miriam Altshuler, my agent, and Amy Cherry, my editor, whose great faith in this project was vital. In Santa Fe, I relied on my son-in-law, Ed Shipman, for moving us, lifting, hauling, wiring, and advising. Calico-Hickey was here for me when my back would not work. David Salazar provided creature comforts at El Farol's bar and restaurant. Samuel Adelo translated, on short notice, crucial sections of the Paporov book. Tom Riker's conversation and sense of humor kept my head straight. Shauna got us into the house, Tor and Murph fixed the roof, Ed built the drain, Dierdre and Elijah kept the house warm. Finally, I must thank the Hemingway Society, my friends here and abroad, and the numerous strangers who have written me over the years, urging me to finish this work.

Index